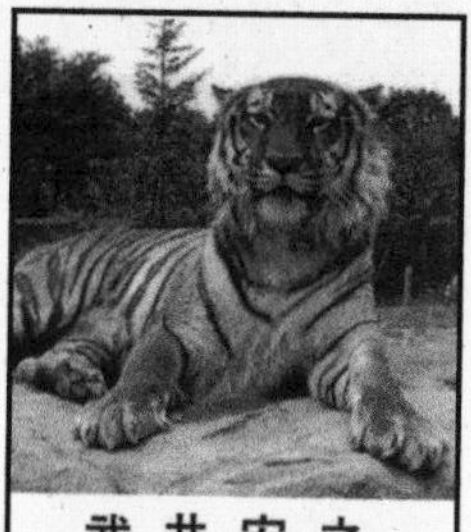

武井宏之

The fact that this series is running in *Shonen Jump* magazine is miraculous enough, but now we've made it all the way to volume 10! Thanks for all your wonderful support, everyone!

—*Hiroyuki Takei*

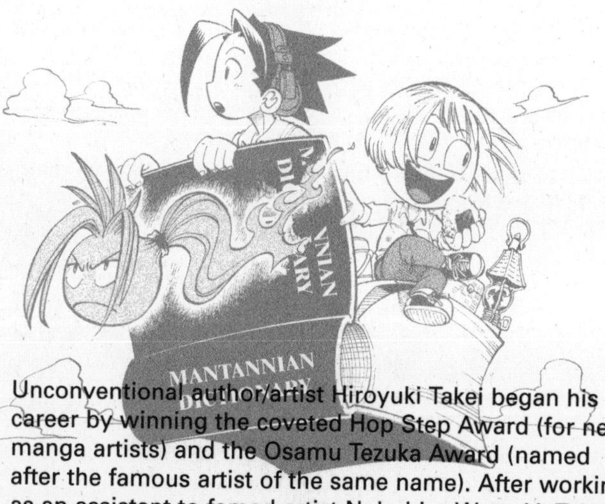
MANTANNIAN

Unconventional author/artist Hiroyuki Takei began his career by winning the coveted Hop Step Award (for new manga artists) and the Osamu Tezuka Award (named after the famous artist of the same name). After working as an assistant to famed artist Nobuhiro Watsuki, Takei debuted in **Weekly Shonen Jump** in 1997 with **Butsu Zone**, an action series based on Buddhist mythology. His multicultural adventure manga **Shaman King**, which debuted in 1998, became a hit and was adapted into an anime TV series. Takei lists Osamu Tezuka, American comics and robot anime among his many influences.

SHAMAN KING VOL.10
The SHONEN JUMP Manga Edition

This graphic novel contains material that was originally published in English in **SHONEN JUMP** #41-44.

STORY AND ART BY
HIROYUKI TAKEI

English Adaptation/Lance Caselman
Translation/Lillian Olsen
Touch-up Art & Lettering/Kathryn Renta
Additional Touch-up/Josh Simpson
Design/Sean Lee
Editor/Pancha Diaz

Editor in Chief, Books/Alvin Lu
Editor in Chief, Magazines/Marc Weidenbaum
VP, Publishing Licensing/Rika Inouye
VP, Sales & Product Marketing/Gonzalo Ferreyra
VP, Creative/Linda Espinosa
Publisher/Hyoe Narita

T 252341

Printed in the U.S.A.

Published by VIZ Media, LLC
P.O. Box 77010
San Francisco, CA 94107

SHONEN JUMP Manga Edition
10 9 8 7 6 5 4 3
First printing, September 2006
Third printing, November 2008

SHAMAN KING is rated T for Teen and is recommended for ages 13 and up. This volume contains suggestive situations and realistic and fantasy violence.
ratings.viz.com

www.viz.com

THE WORLD'S MOST POPULAR MANGA

www.shonenjump.com

SHONEN JUMP MANGA

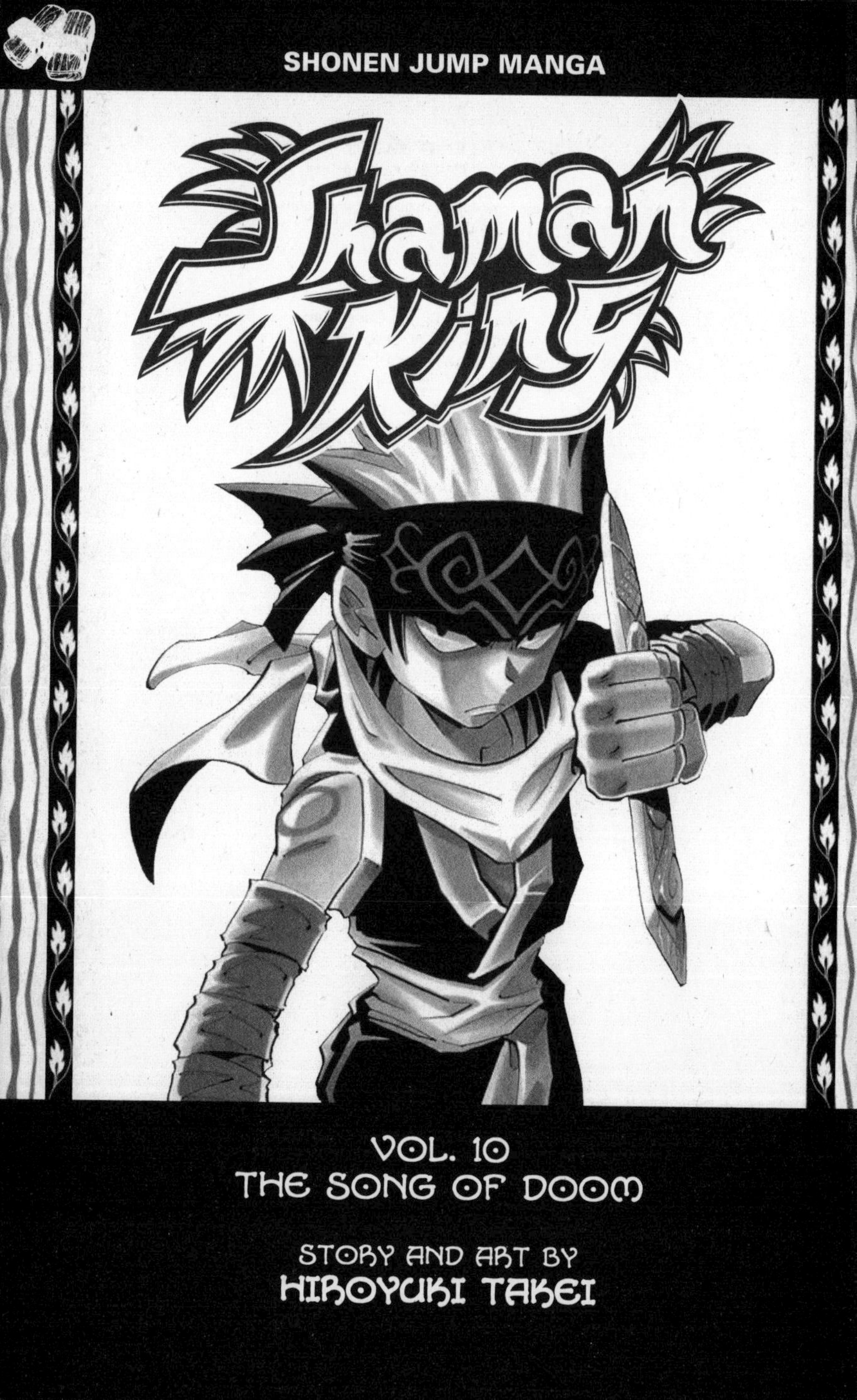
Shaman King

VOL. 10

THE SONG OF DOOM

STORY AND ART BY

HIROYUKI TAKEI

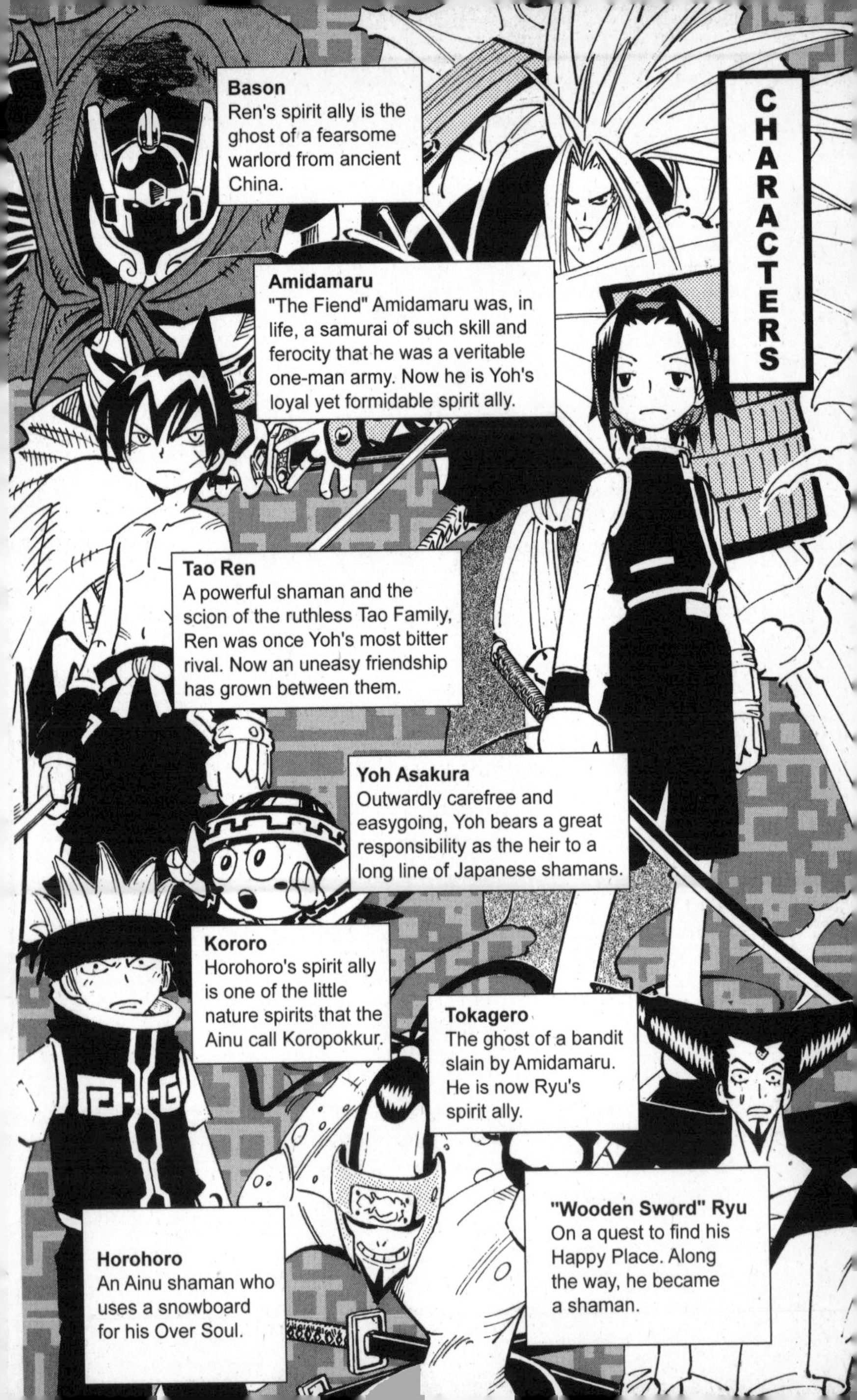
CHARACTERS
Bason
Ren's spirit ally is the ghost of a fearsome warlord from ancient China.
Amidamaru
"The Fiend" Amidamaru was, in life, a samurai of such skill and ferocity that he was a veritable one-man army. Now he is Yoh's loyal yet formidable spirit ally.
Tao Ren
A powerful shaman and the scion of the ruthless Tao Family, Ren was once Yoh's most bitter rival. Now an uneasy friendship has grown between them.
Yoh Asakura
Outwardly carefree and easygoing, Yoh bears a great responsibility as the heir to a long line of Japanese shamans.
Kororo
Horohoro's spirit ally is one of the little nature spirits that the Ainu call Koropokkur.
Tokagero
The ghost of a bandit slain by Amidamaru. He is now Ryu's spirit ally.
"Wooden Sword" Ryu
On a quest to find his Happy Place. Along the way, he became a shaman.
Horohoro
An Ainu shaman who uses a snowboard for his Over Soul.

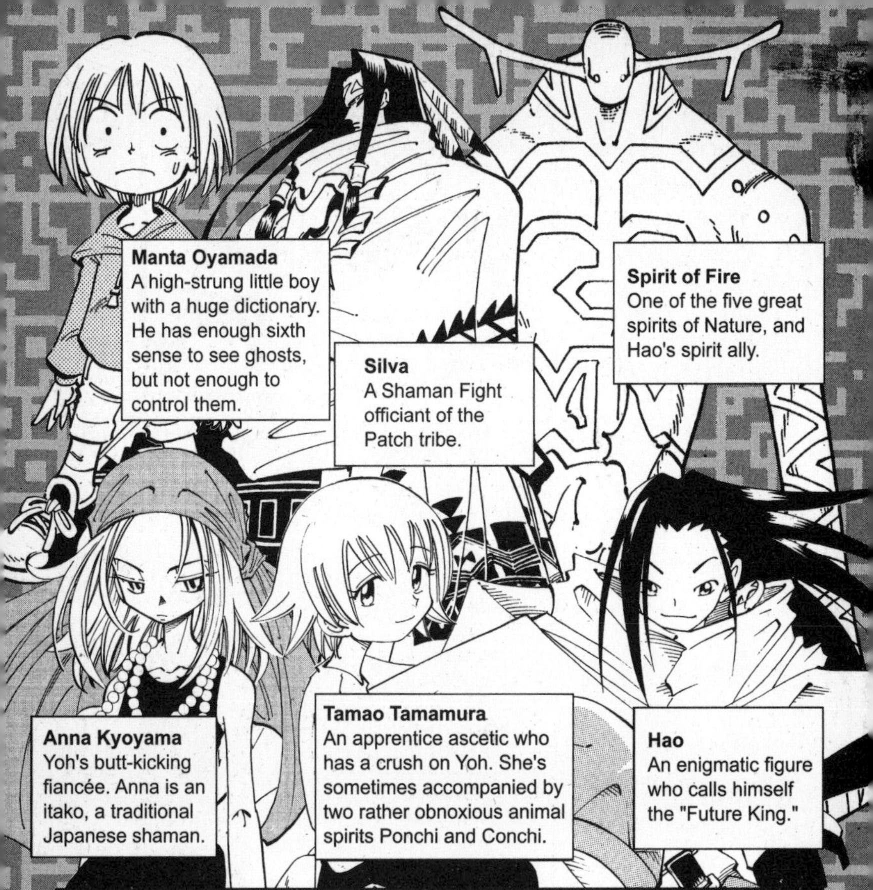

Manta Oyamada
A high-strung little boy with a huge dictionary. He has enough sixth sense to see ghosts, but not enough to control them.

Silva
A Shaman Fight officiant of the Patch tribe.

Spirit of Fire
One of the five great spirits of Nature, and Hao's spirit ally.

Anna Kyoyama
Yoh's butt-kicking fiancée. Anna is an itako, a traditional Japanese shaman.

Tamao Tamamura
An apprentice ascetic who has a crush on Yoh. She's sometimes accompanied by two rather obnoxious animal spirits Ponchi and Conchi.

Hao
An enigmatic figure who calls himself the "Future King."

THE STORY THUS FAR

Yoh Asakura not only sees dead people, he talks and fights with them, too. That's because Yoh is a shaman, a traditional holy man able to interact with the spirit world. Yoh is now a competitor in the "Shaman Fight," a tournament held every 500 years to decide who will become the Shaman King and shape humanity's future.

Having passed the fierce preliminaries, Yoh prepares for the main competition. After a brief detour to the wilds of China, Yoh and his friends arrive ready to fight, but end up on an airplane that suddenly disappears thousands of feet over North America! Now they must discover the location of the Patch Village and make their way there. But even as they do, steps are taken to ensure that they never reach their destination...

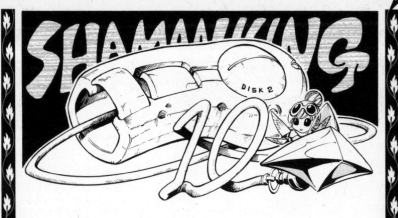

VOL. 10
THE SONG OF DOOM

CONTENTS

Reincarnation 81: Route 66 Turbo

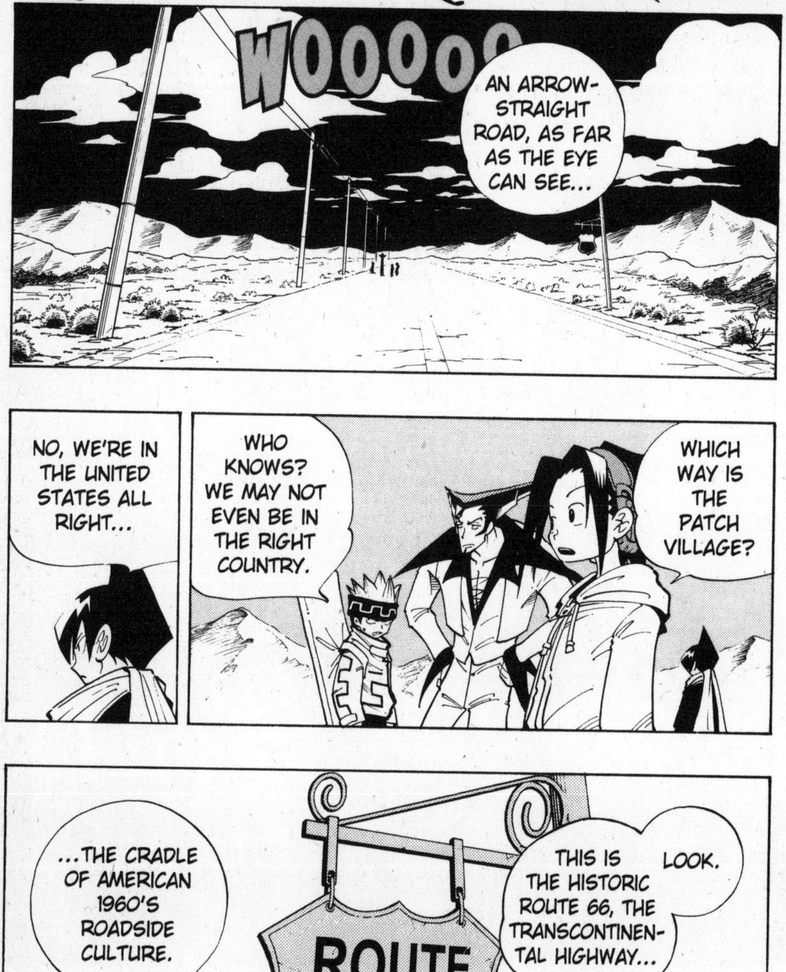
WOOOO
AN ARROW-STRAIGHT ROAD, AS FAR AS THE EYE CAN SEE...
WHICH WAY IS THE PATCH VILLAGE?
WHO KNOWS? WE MAY NOT EVEN BE IN THE RIGHT COUNTRY.
NO, WE'RE IN THE UNITED STATES ALL RIGHT...
LOOK.
THIS IS THE HISTORIC ROUTE 66, THE TRANSCONTINENTAL HIGHWAY...
...THE CRADLE OF AMERICAN 1960'S ROADSIDE CULTURE.
ROUTE 66
KREEK

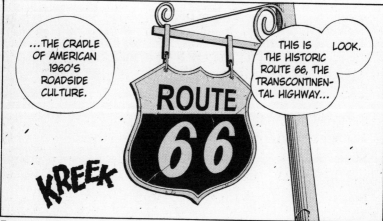

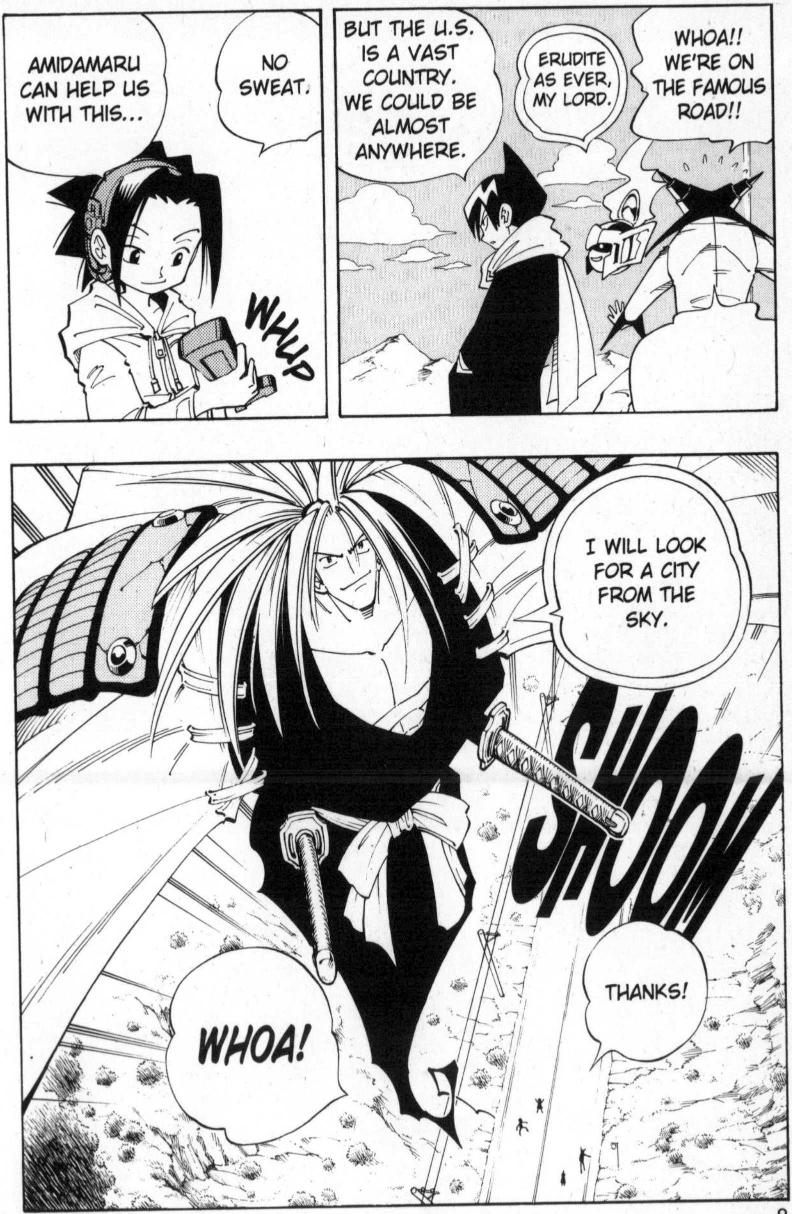
WHOA!! WE'RE ON THE FAMOUS ROAD!!
ERUDITE AS EVER, MY LORD.
BUT THE U.S. IS A VAST COUNTRY. WE COULD BE ALMOST ANYWHERE.
NO SWEAT.
AMIDAMARU CAN HELP US WITH THIS...
WHUP
I WILL LOOK FOR A CITY FROM THE SKY.
SHOOM
THANKS!
WHOA!

Reincarnation 81: Route 66 Turbo

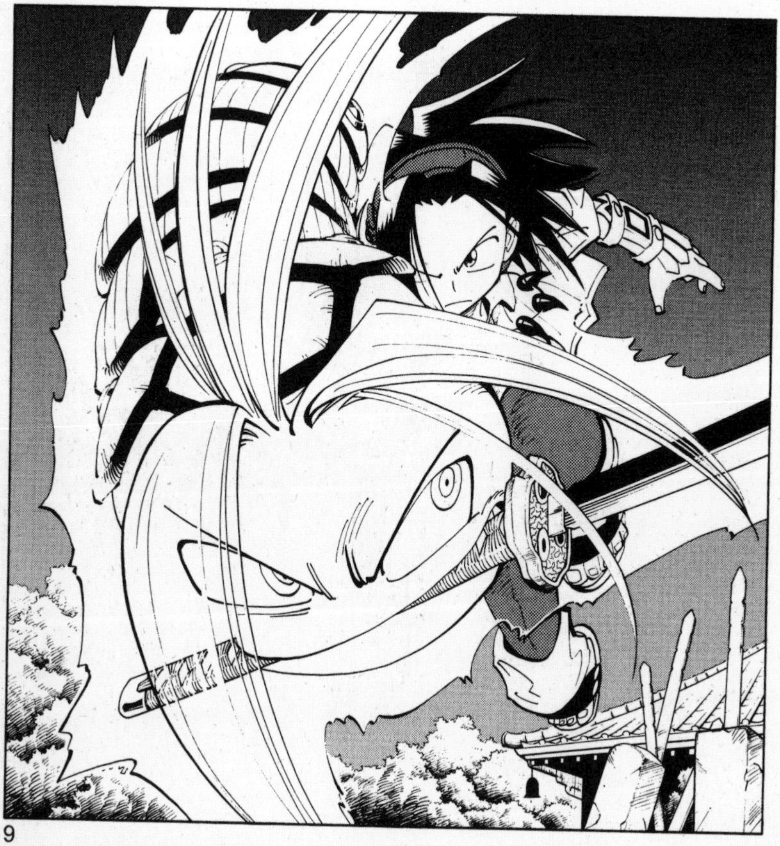

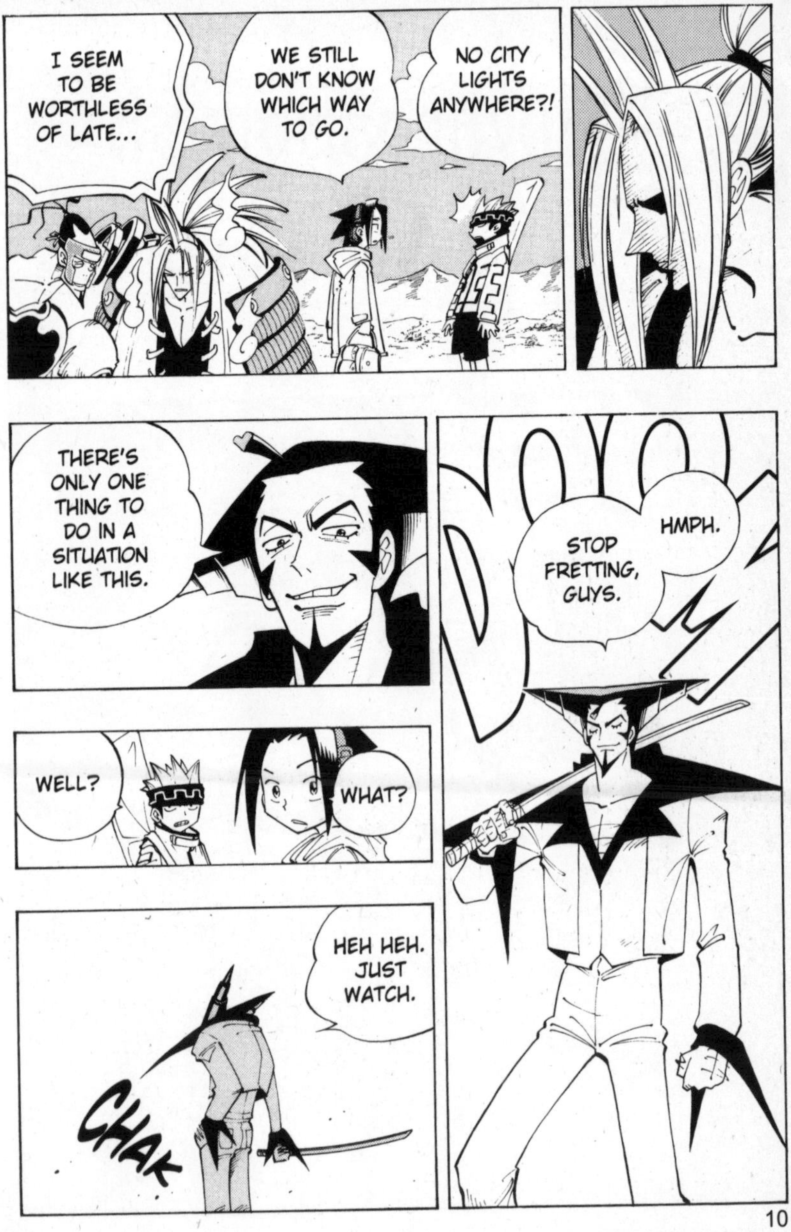
NO CITY LIGHTS ANYWHERE?!
WE STILL DON'T KNOW WHICH WAY TO GO.
I SEEM TO BE WORTHLESS OF LATE...
HMPH.
STOP FRETTING, GUYS.
THERE'S ONLY ONE THING TO DO IN A SITUATION LIKE THIS.
WHAT?
WELL?
HEH HEH. JUST WATCH.
CHAK

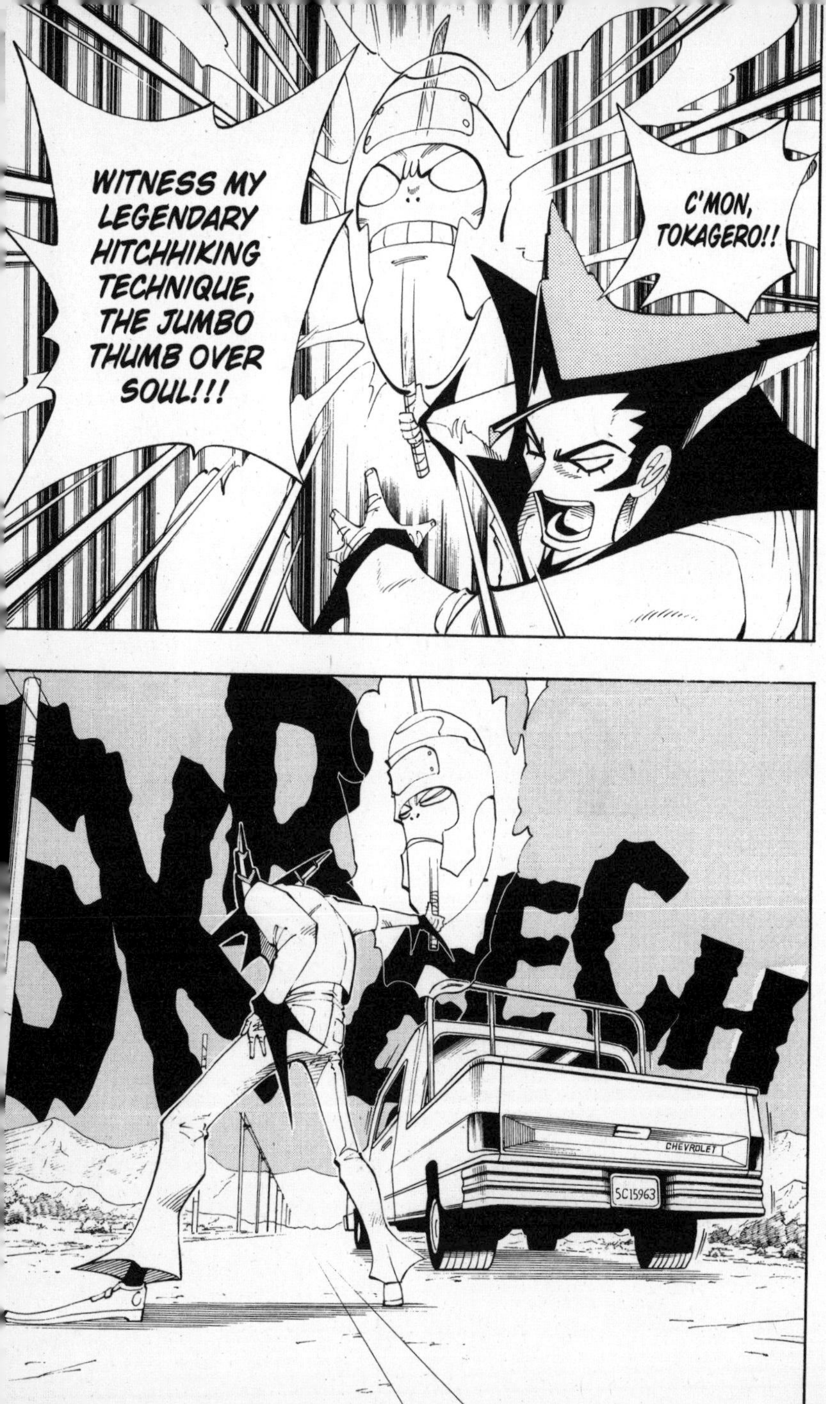
C'MON, TOKAGERO!!
WITNESS MY LEGENDARY HITCHHIKING TECHNIQUE, THE JUMBO THUMB OVER SOUL!!!
CHEVROLET
5C15963

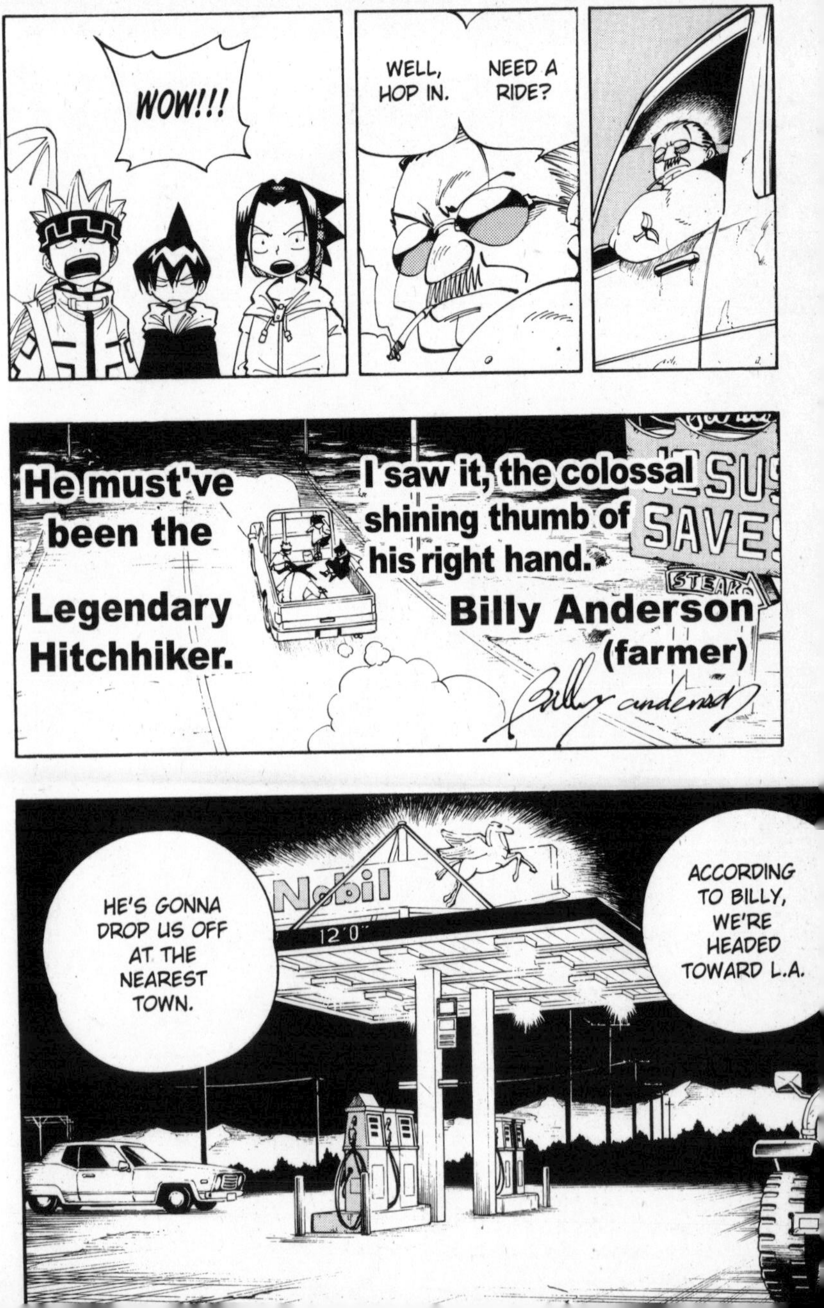

NEED A RIDE?
WELL, HOP IN.
WOW!!!
I saw it, the colossal shining thumb of his right hand.
Billy Anderson (farmer)
He must've been the Legendary Hitchhiker.
ACCORDING TO BILLY, WE'RE HEADED TOWARD L.A.
Nobil
HE'S GONNA DROP US OFF AT THE NEAREST TOWN.

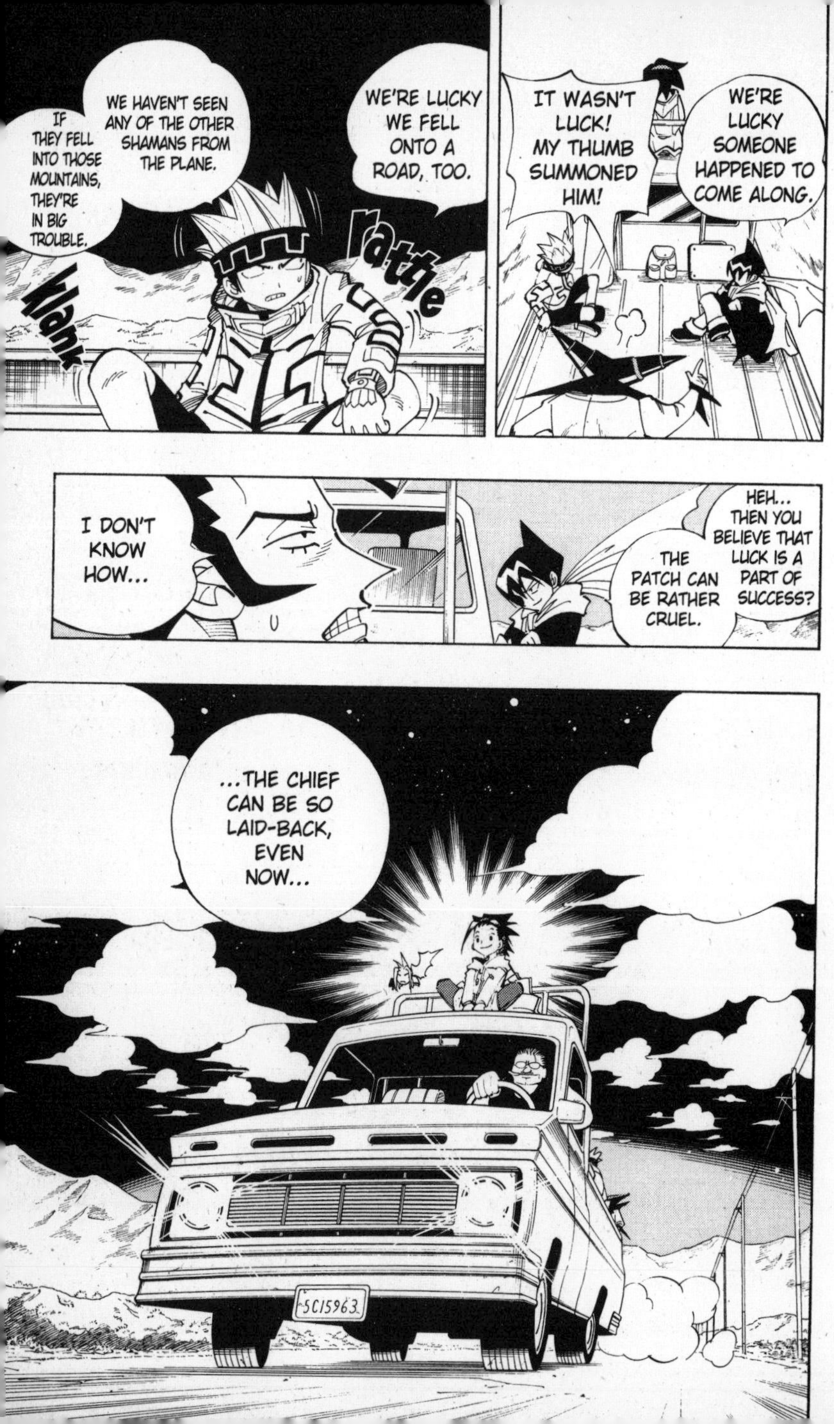
WE'RE LUCKY SOMEONE HAPPENED TO COME ALONG.
IT WASN'T LUCK! MY THUMB SUMMONED HIM!
WE'RE LUCKY WE FELL ONTO A ROAD, TOO.
rattle
WE HAVEN'T SEEN ANY OF THE OTHER SHAMANS FROM THE PLANE.
IF THEY FELL INTO THOSE MOUNTAINS, THEY'RE IN BIG TROUBLE.
klank
HEH... THEN YOU BELIEVE THAT LUCK IS A PART OF SUCCESS?
THE PATCH CAN BE RATHER CRUEL.
I DON'T KNOW HOW...
...THE CHIEF CAN BE SO LAID-BACK, EVEN NOW...
5C15963

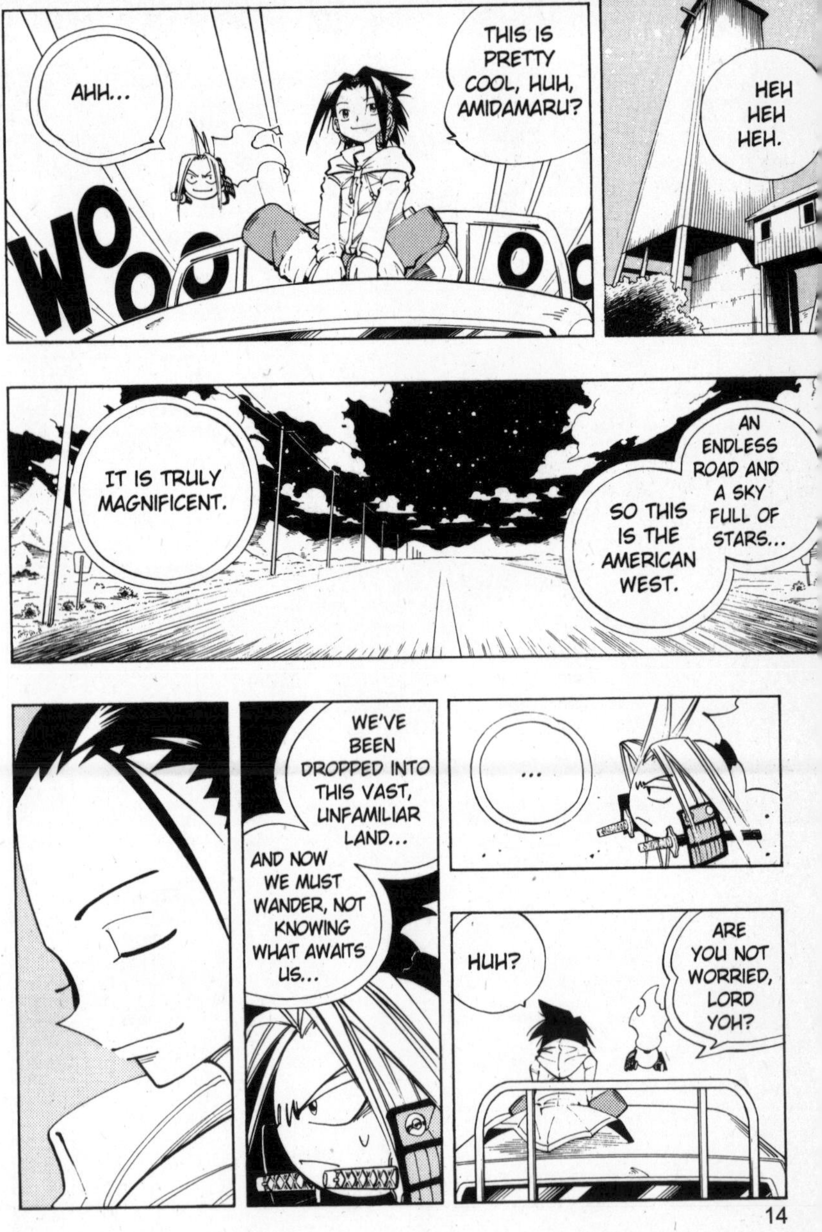
HEH HEH HEH.
THIS IS PRETTY COOL, HUH, AMIDAMARU?
AHH...
WOOOOO
AN ENDLESS ROAD AND A SKY FULL OF STARS...
SO THIS IS THE AMERICAN WEST.
IT IS TRULY MAGNIFICENT.
...
ARE YOU NOT WORRIED, LORD YOH?
HUH?
WE'VE BEEN DROPPED INTO THIS VAST, UNFAMILIAR LAND...
AND NOW WE MUST WANDER, NOT KNOWING WHAT AWAITS US...

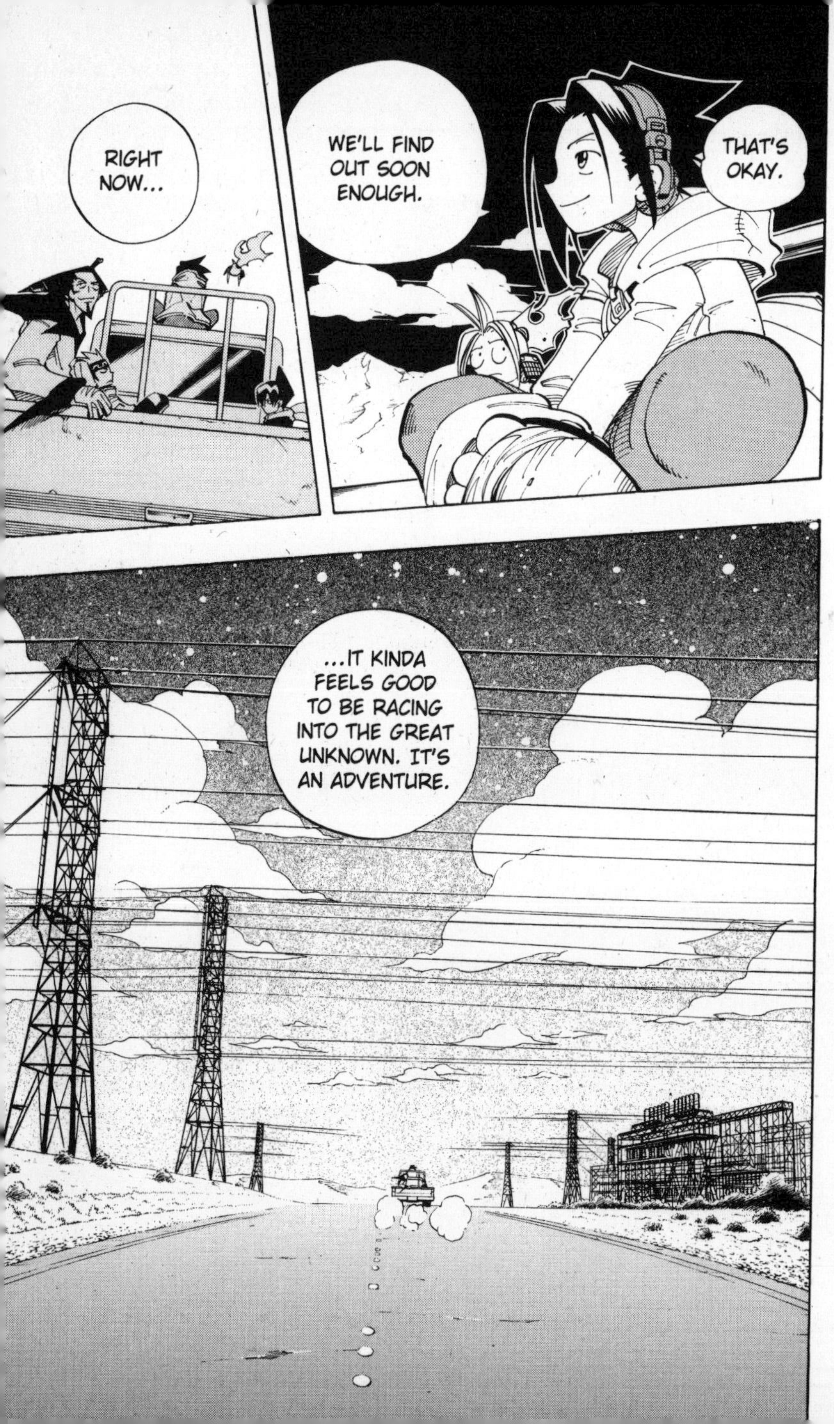
THAT'S OKAY.
WE'LL FIND OUT SOON ENOUGH.
RIGHT NOW...
...IT KINDA FEELS GOOD TO BE RACING INTO THE GREAT UNKNOWN. IT'S AN ADVENTURE.

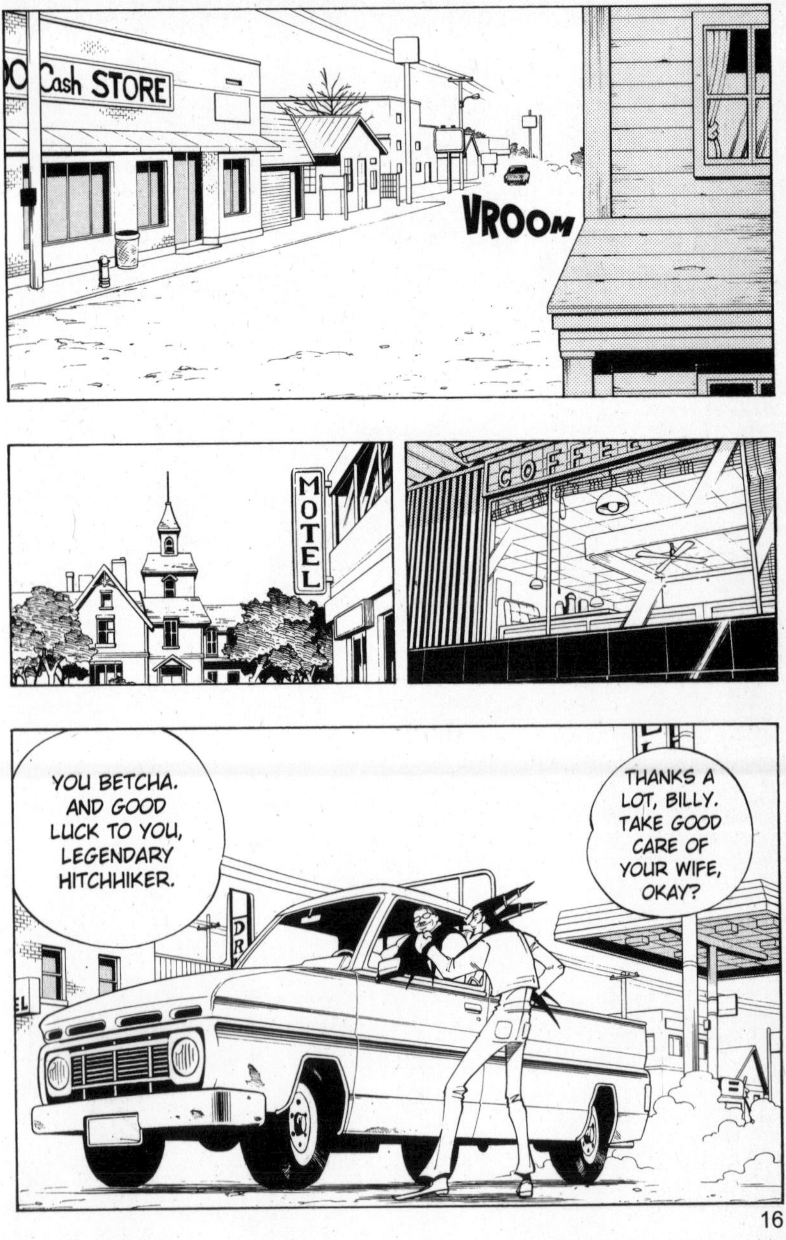
Cash STORE
VROOM
MOTEL
THANKS A LOT, BILLY. TAKE GOOD CARE OF YOUR WIFE, OKAY?
YOU BETCHA. AND GOOD LUCK TO YOU, LEGENDARY HITCHHIKER.

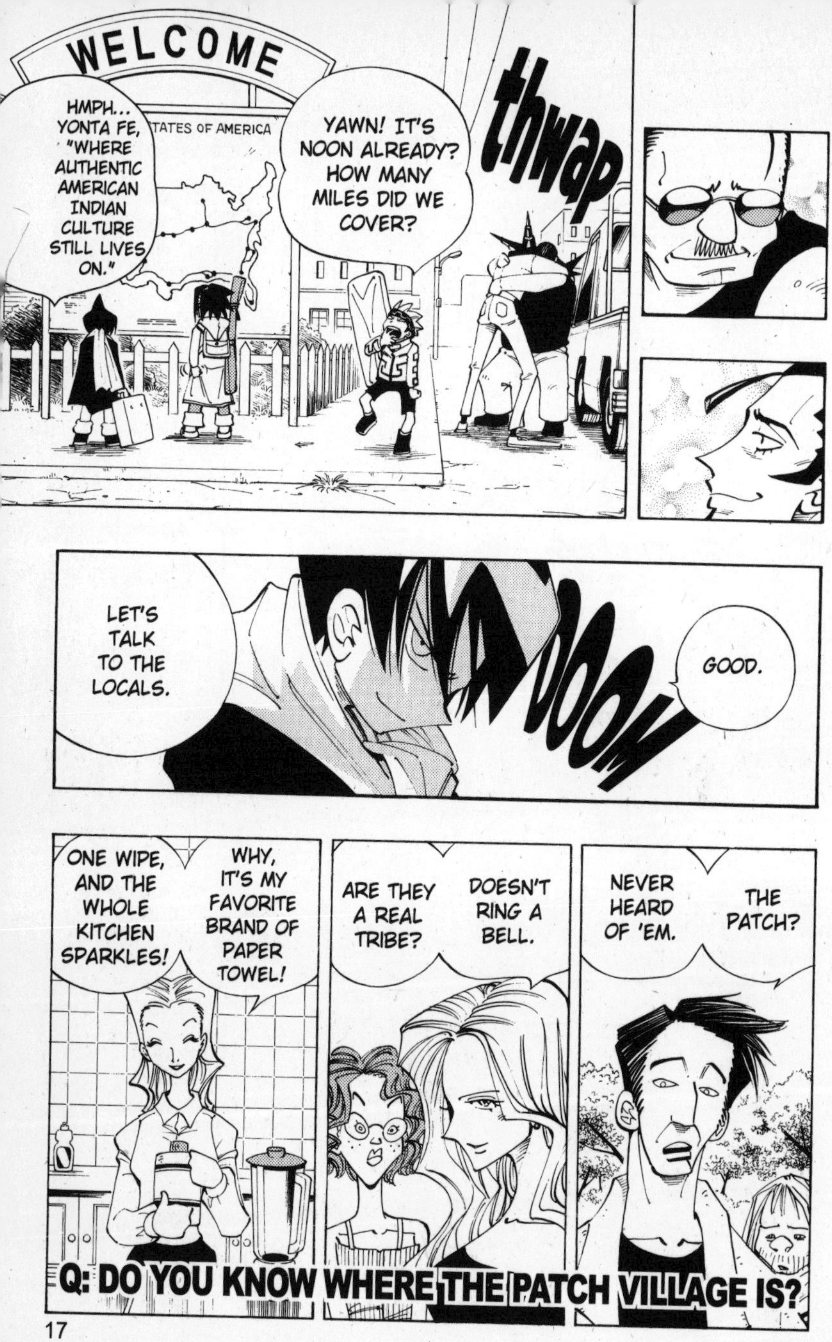
thwap
YAWN! IT'S NOON ALREADY? HOW MANY MILES DID WE COVER?
WELCOME
TATES OF AMERICA
HMPH... YONTA FE, "WHERE AUTHENTIC AMERICAN INDIAN CULTURE STILL LIVES ON."
GOOD.
DOOM
LET'S TALK TO THE LOCALS.
Q: DO YOU KNOW WHERE THE PATCH VILLAGE IS?
THE PATCH?
NEVER HEARD OF 'EM.
DOESN'T RING A BELL.
ARE THEY A REAL TRIBE?
WHY, IT'S MY FAVORITE BRAND OF PAPER TOWEL!
ONE WIPE, AND THE WHOLE KITCHEN SPARKLES!

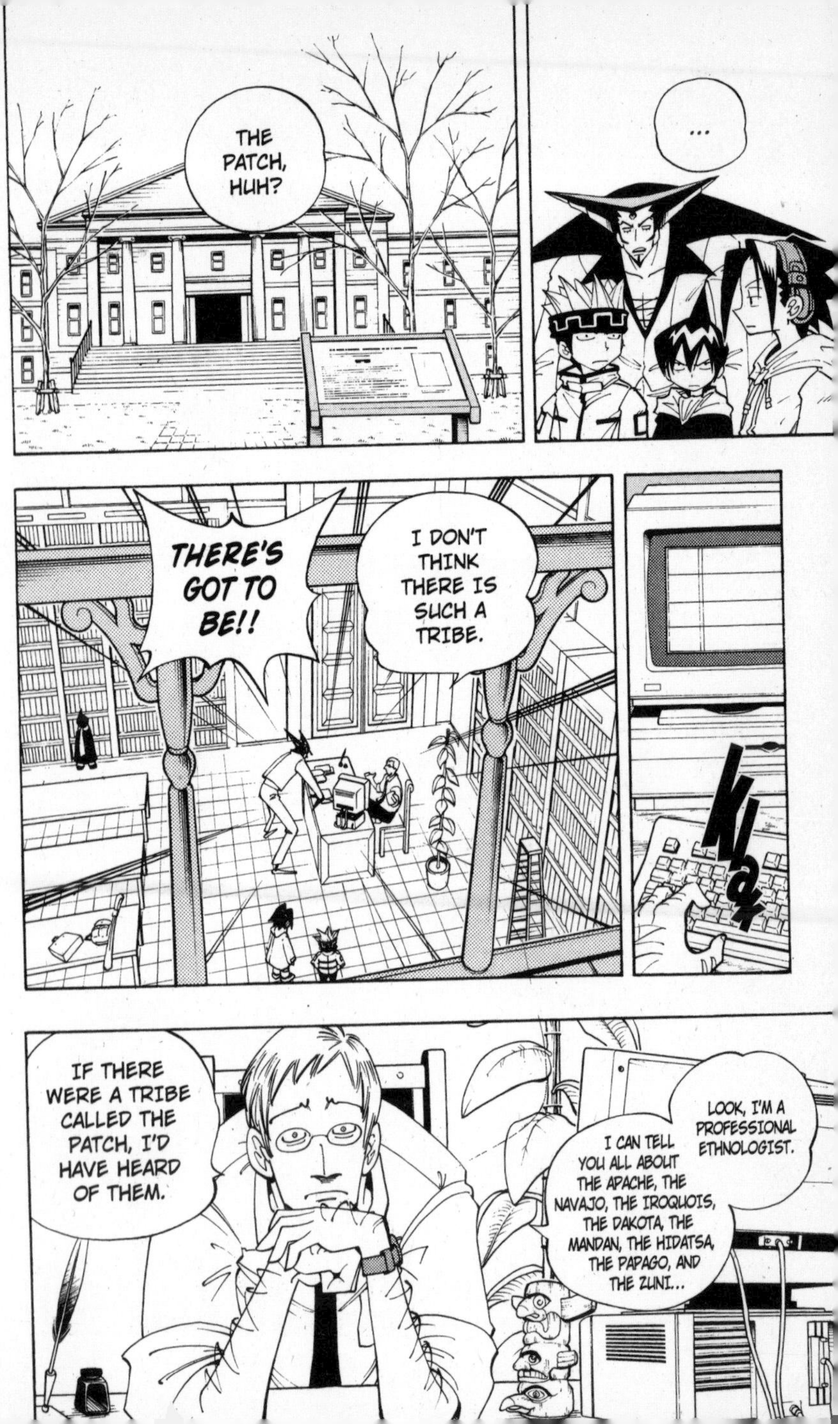
...
THE PATCH, HUH?
KLAK
I DON'T THINK THERE IS SUCH A TRIBE.
THERE'S GOT TO BE!!
LOOK, I'M A PROFESSIONAL ETHNOLOGIST.
I CAN TELL YOU ALL ABOUT THE APACHE, THE NAVAJO, THE IROQUOIS, THE DAKOTA, THE MANDAN, THE HIDATSA, THE PAPAGO, AND THE ZUNI...
IF THERE WERE A TRIBE CALLED THE PATCH, I'D HAVE HEARD OF THEM.

READ THIS WAY

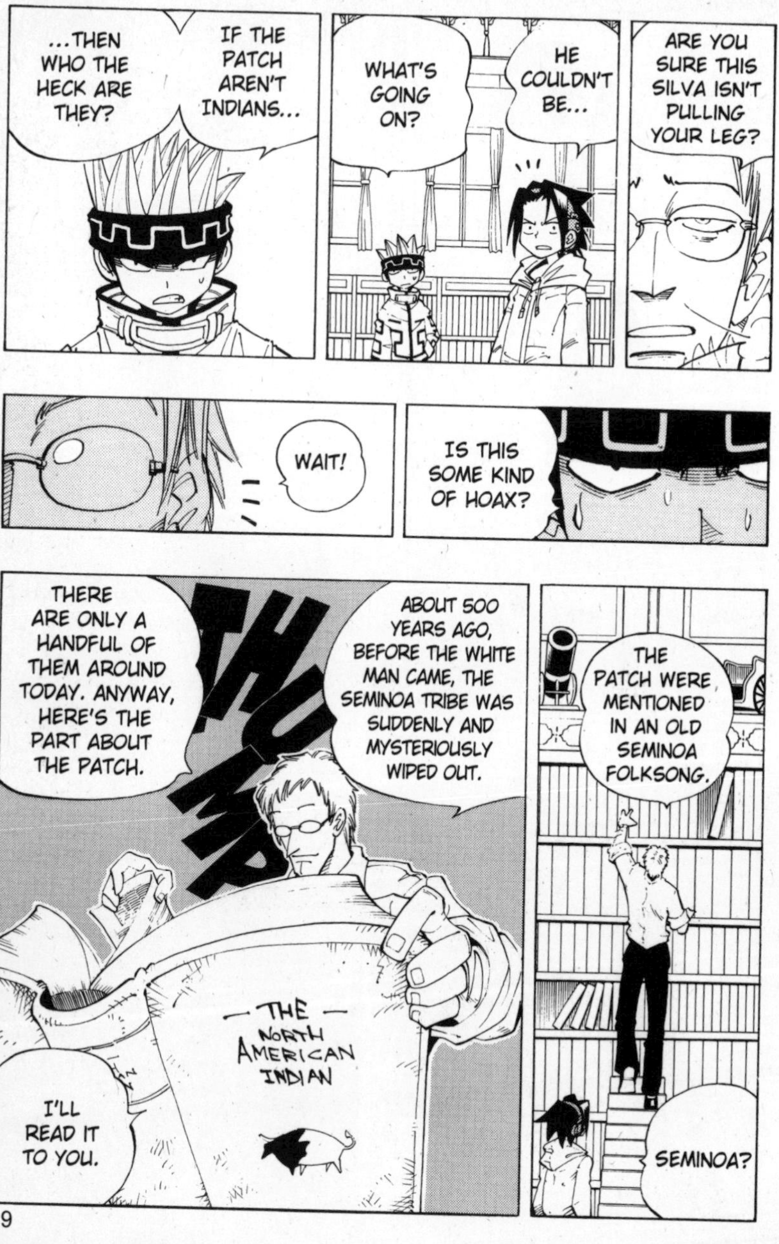

ARE YOU SURE THIS SILVA ISN'T PULLING YOUR LEG?
HE COULDN'T BE...
WHAT'S GOING ON?
IF THE PATCH AREN'T INDIANS...
...THEN WHO THE HECK ARE THEY?
IS THIS SOME KIND OF HOAX?
WAIT!
THE PATCH WERE MENTIONED IN AN OLD SEMINOA FOLKSONG.
SEMINOA?
ABOUT 500 YEARS AGO, BEFORE THE WHITE MAN CAME, THE SEMINOA TRIBE WAS SUDDENLY AND MYSTERIOUSLY WIPED OUT.
THUMP
THERE ARE ONLY A HANDFUL OF THEM AROUND TODAY. ANYWAY, HERE'S THE PART ABOUT THE PATCH.
— THE — NORTH AMERICAN INDIAN
I'LL READ IT TO YOU.

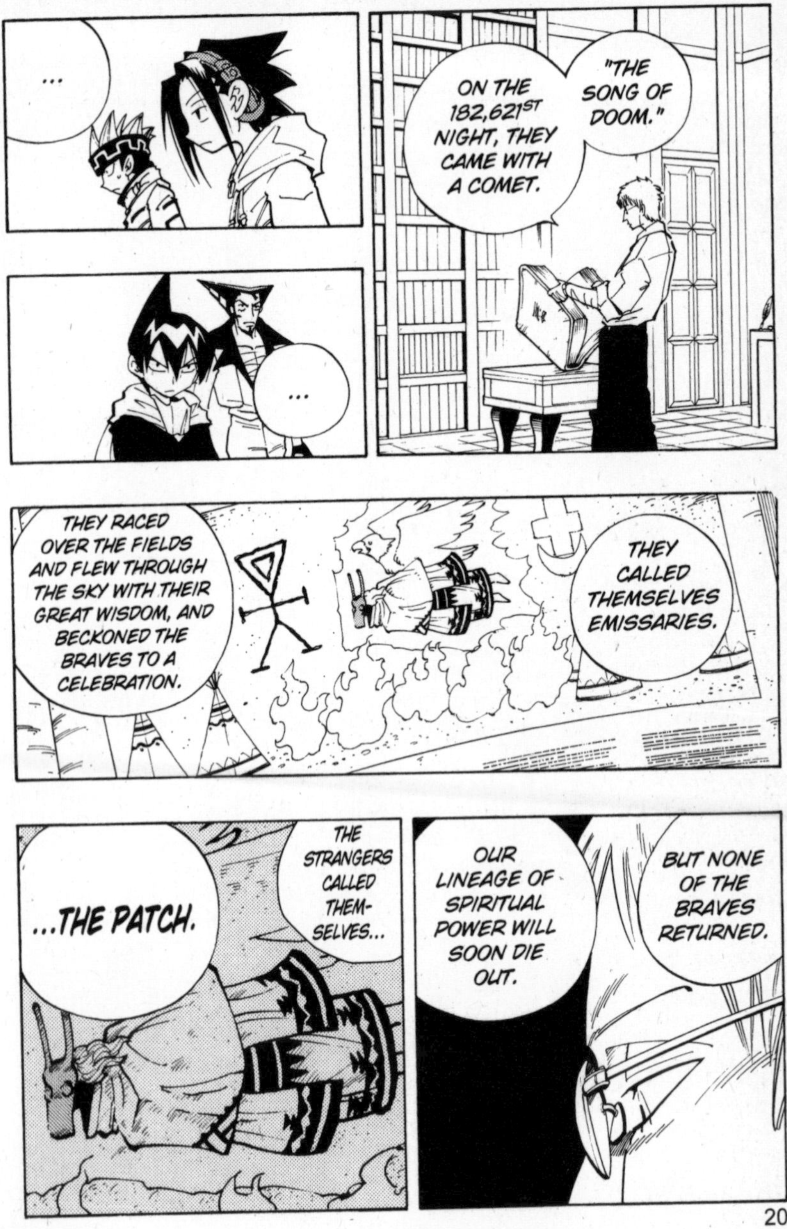
"THE SONG OF DOOM."
ON THE 182,621ST NIGHT, THEY CAME WITH A COMET.
...
...
THEY CALLED THEMSELVES EMISSARIES.
THEY RACED OVER THE FIELDS AND FLEW THROUGH THE SKY WITH THEIR GREAT WISDOM, AND BECKONED THE BRAVES TO A CELEBRATION.
BUT NONE OF THE BRAVES RETURNED.
OUR LINEAGE OF SPIRITUAL POWER WILL SOON DIE OUT.
THE STRANGERS CALLED THEM-SELVES...
...THE PATCH.

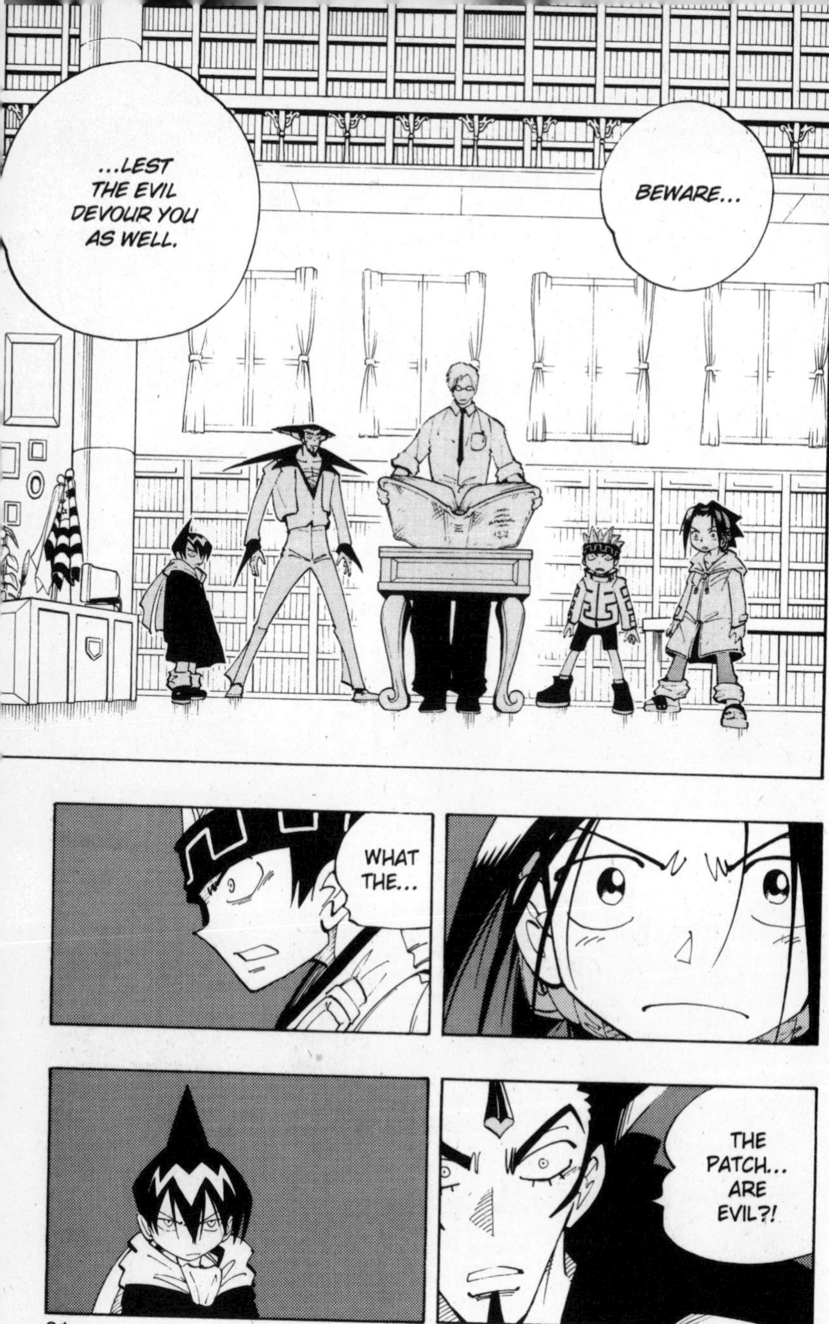
BEWARE...
...LEST THE EVIL DEVOUR YOU AS WELL.
WHAT THE...
THE PATCH... ARE EVIL?!

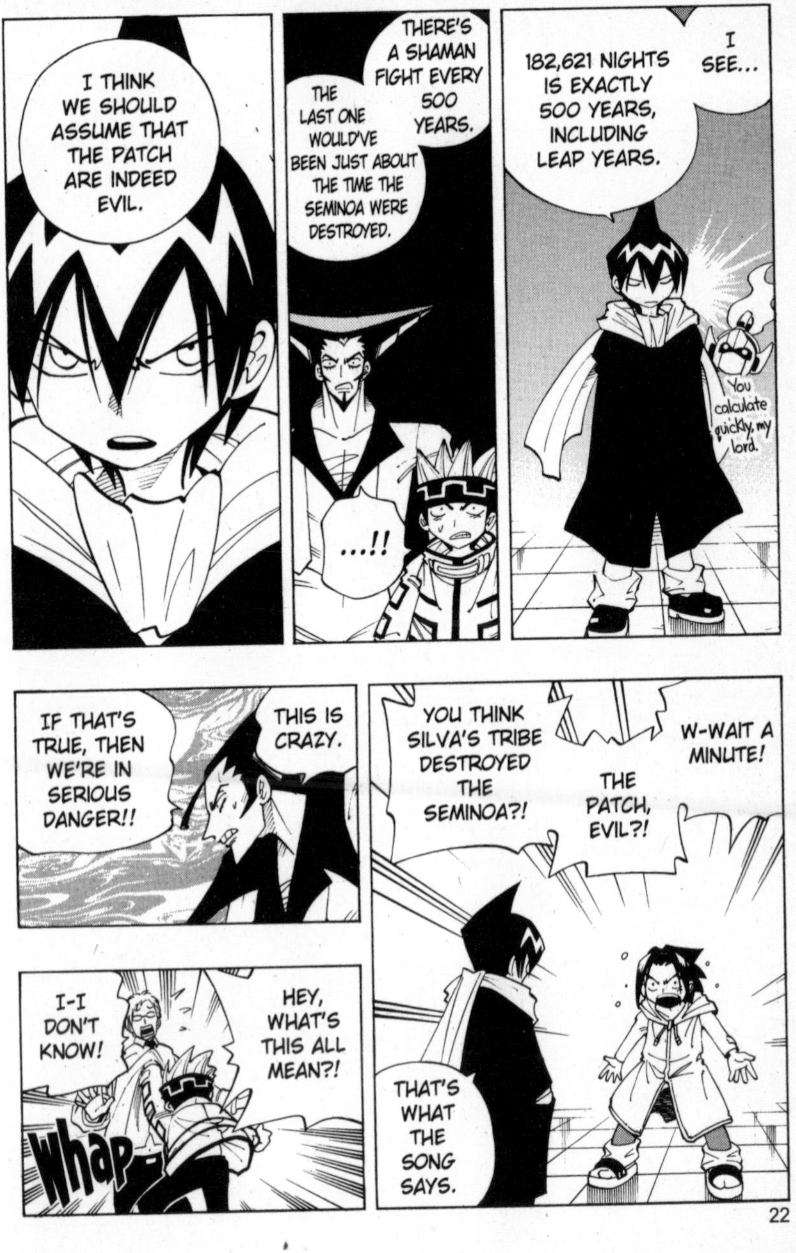

I SEE...
182,621 NIGHTS IS EXACTLY 500 YEARS, INCLUDING LEAP YEARS.
You calculate quickly, my lord.
THERE'S A SHAMAN FIGHT EVERY 500 YEARS.
THE LAST ONE WOULD'VE BEEN JUST ABOUT THE TIME THE SEMINOA WERE DESTROYED.
...!!
I THINK WE SHOULD ASSUME THAT THE PATCH ARE INDEED EVIL.
W-WAIT A MINUTE!
THE PATCH, EVIL?!
YOU THINK SILVA'S TRIBE DESTROYED THE SEMINOA?!
THAT'S WHAT THE SONG SAYS.
THIS IS CRAZY.
IF THAT'S TRUE, THEN WE'RE IN SERIOUS DANGER!!
HEY, WHAT'S THIS ALL MEAN?!
I-I DON'T KNOW!
Whap

READ THIS WAY

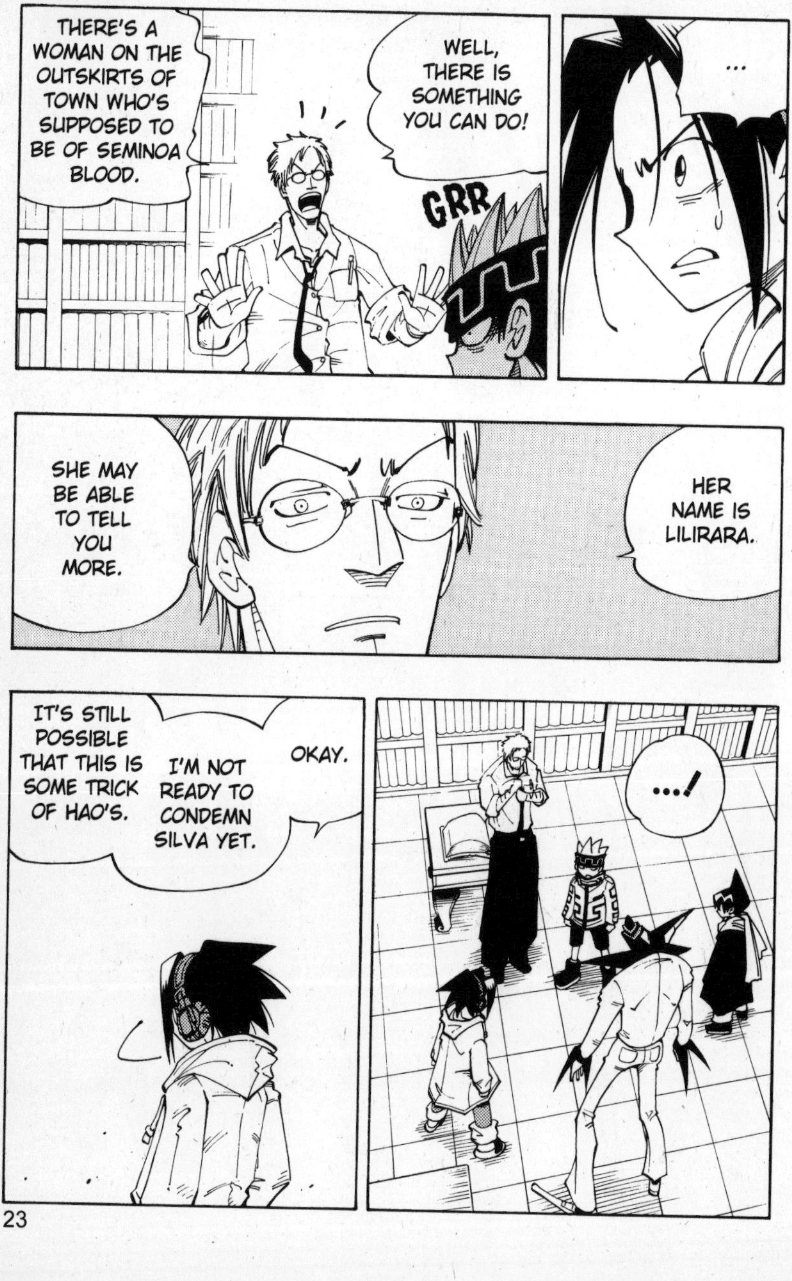
...
WELL, THERE IS SOMETHING YOU CAN DO!
THERE'S A WOMAN ON THE OUTSKIRTS OF TOWN WHO'S SUPPOSED TO BE OF SEMINOA BLOOD.
GRR
HER NAME IS LILIRARA.
SHE MAY BE ABLE TO TELL YOU MORE.
...!
OKAY.
I'M NOT READY TO CONDEMN SILVA YET.
IT'S STILL POSSIBLE THAT THIS IS SOME TRICK OF HAO'S.

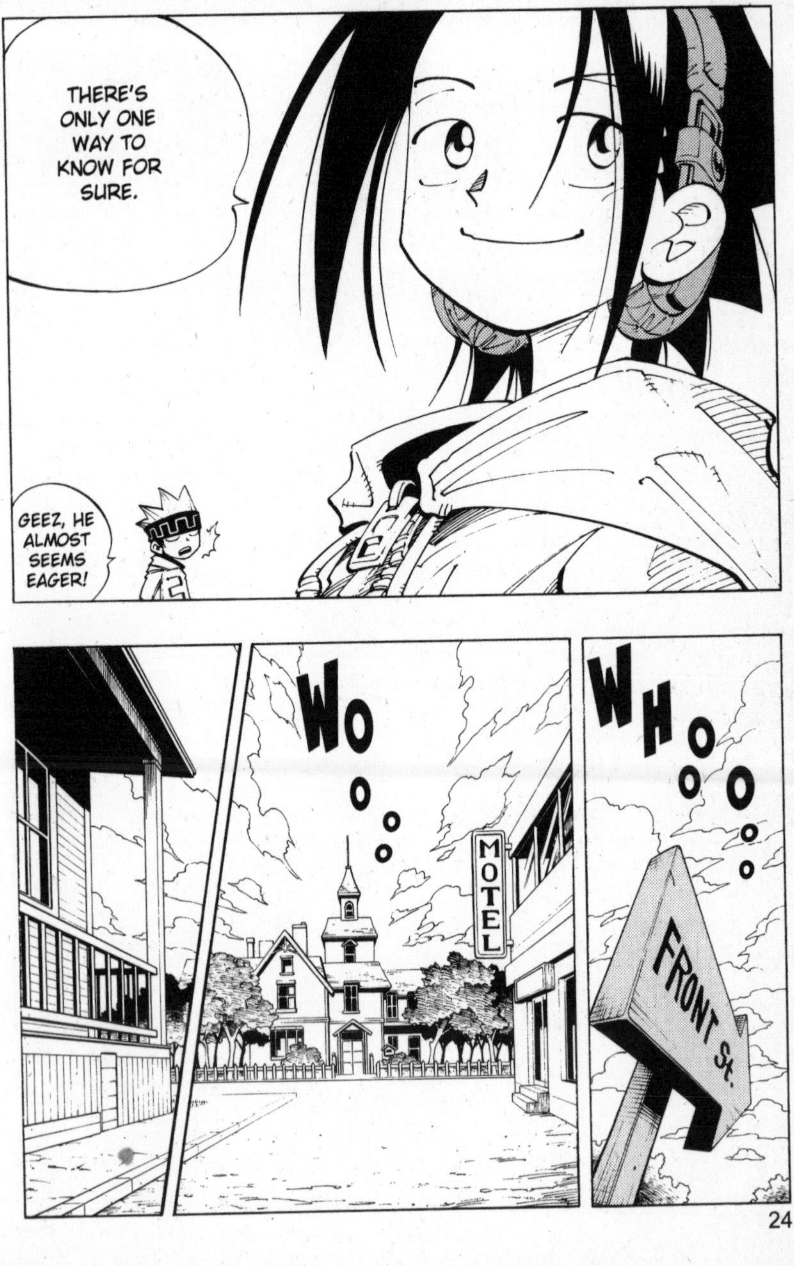
THERE'S ONLY ONE WAY TO KNOW FOR SURE.
GEEZ, HE ALMOST SEEMS EAGER!
WHOOOOOO
FRONT St.
WOOOO
MOTEL

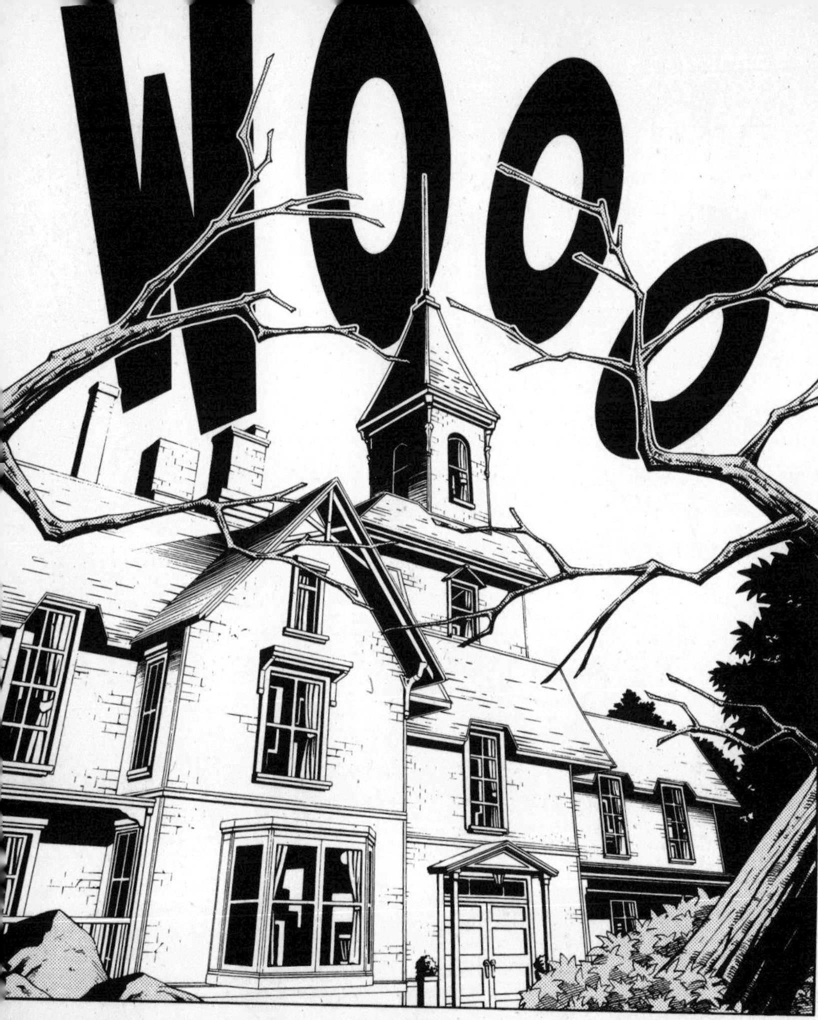
WOOO

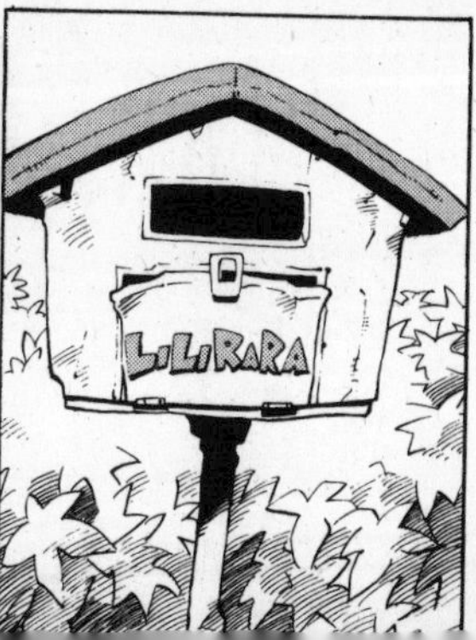
LiLiRaRa

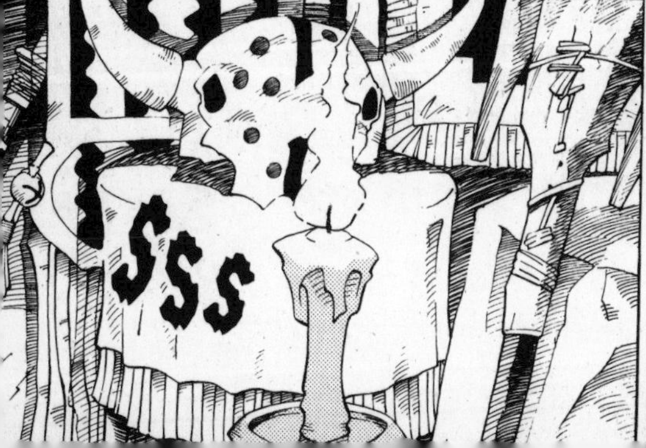
SSS

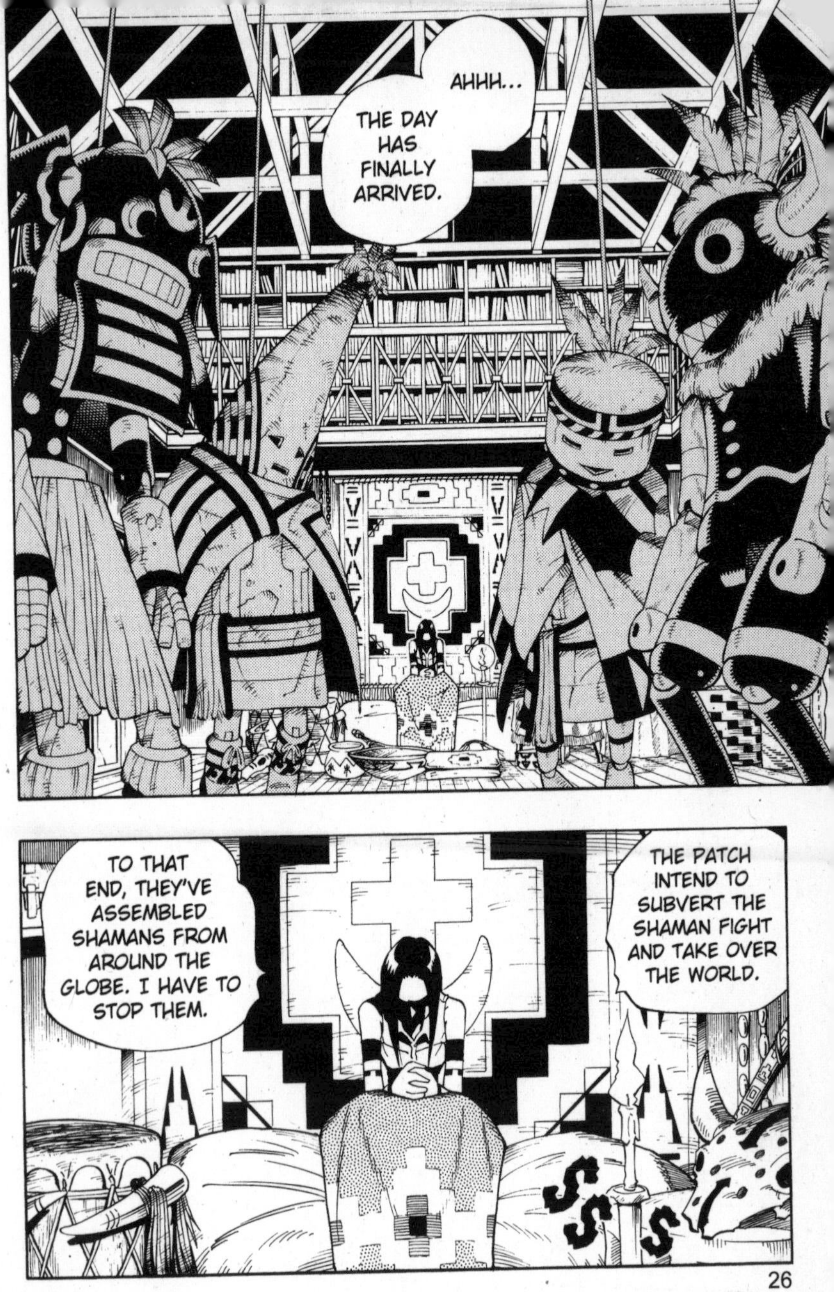
AHHH...
THE DAY HAS FINALLY ARRIVED.
THE PATCH INTEND TO SUBVERT THE SHAMAN FIGHT AND TAKE OVER THE WORLD.
TO THAT END, THEY'VE ASSEMBLED SHAMANS FROM AROUND THE GLOBE. I HAVE TO STOP THEM.

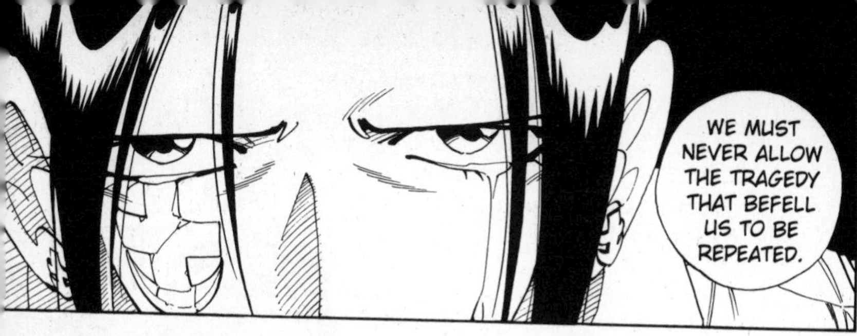
WE MUST NEVER ALLOW THE TRAGEDY THAT BEFELL US TO BE REPEATED.
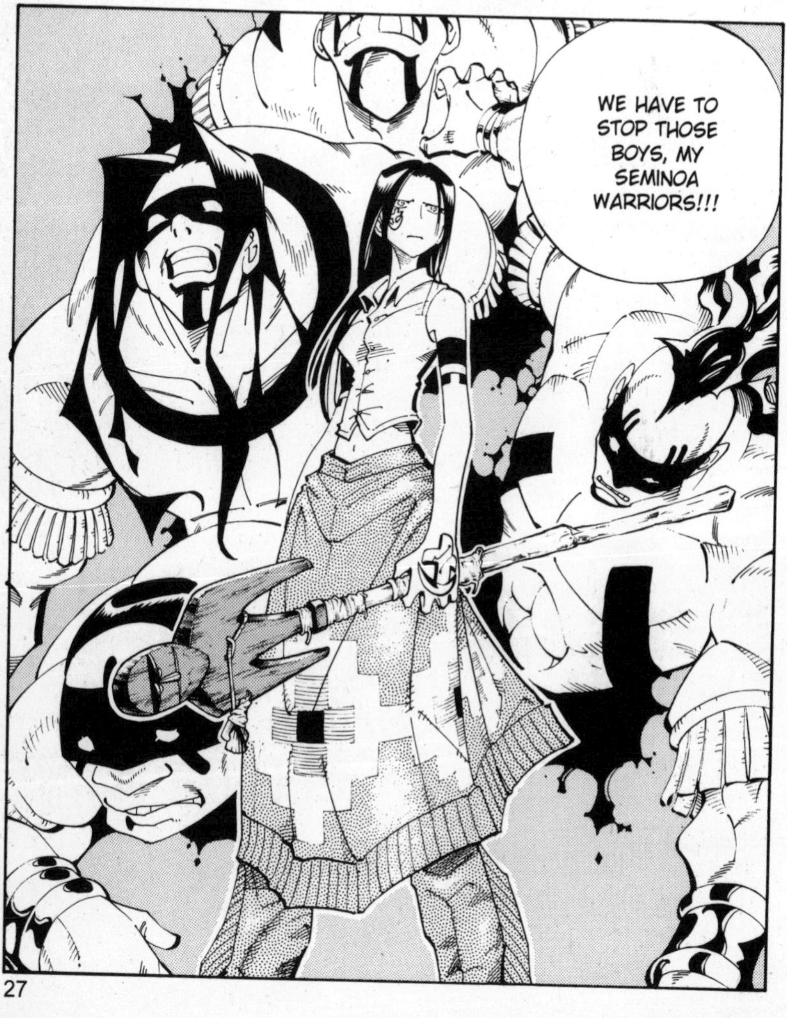
WE HAVE TO STOP THOSE BOYS, MY SEMINOA WARRIORS!!!

SHAMAN KING CHARACTER FILE No.42

2000
(SEP)

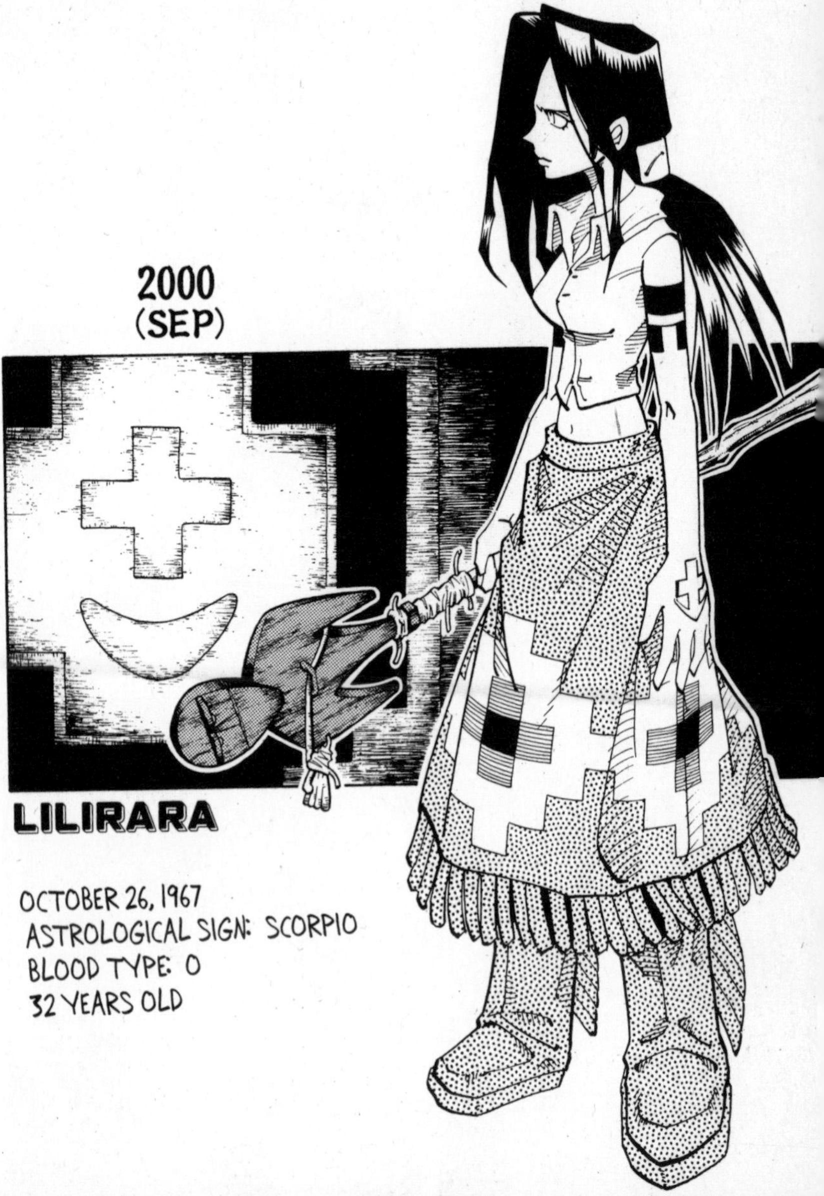

LILIRARA

OCTOBER 26, 1967
ASTROLOGICAL SIGN: SCORPIO
BLOOD TYPE: O
32 YEARS OLD

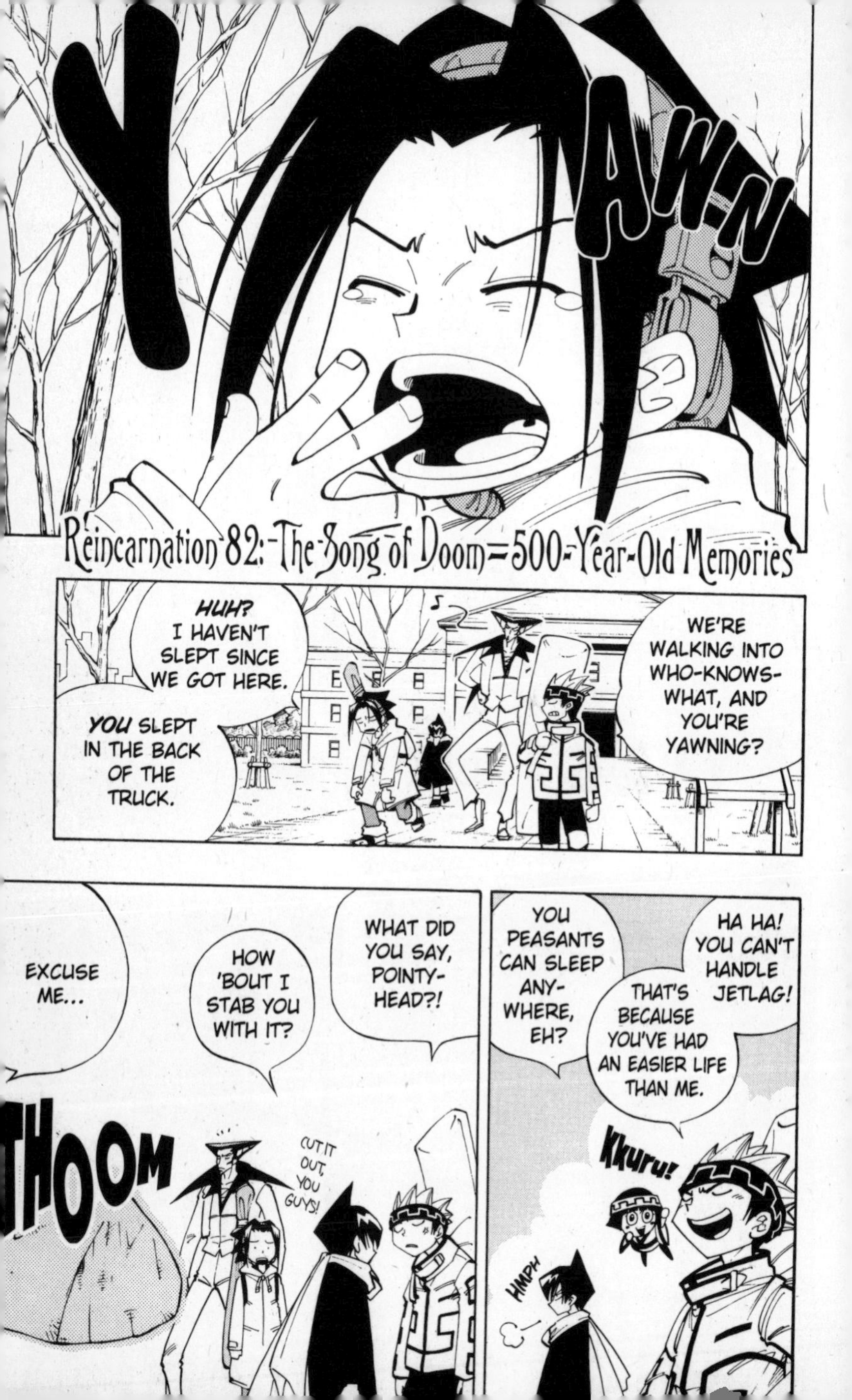
YAWN
Reincarnation 82: The Song of Doom = 500-Year-Old Memories
WE'RE WALKING INTO WHO-KNOWS-WHAT, AND YOU'RE YAWNING?
HUH? I HAVEN'T SLEPT SINCE WE GOT HERE.
YOU SLEPT IN THE BACK OF THE TRUCK.
HA HA! YOU CAN'T HANDLE JETLAG!
YOU PEASANTS CAN SLEEP ANY-WHERE, EH?
THAT'S BECAUSE YOU'VE HAD AN EASIER LIFE THAN ME.
Kkuru!
HMPH
WHAT DID YOU SAY, POINTY-HEAD?!
HOW 'BOUT I STAB YOU WITH IT?
EXCUSE ME...
CUT IT OUT, YOU GUYS!
THOOM

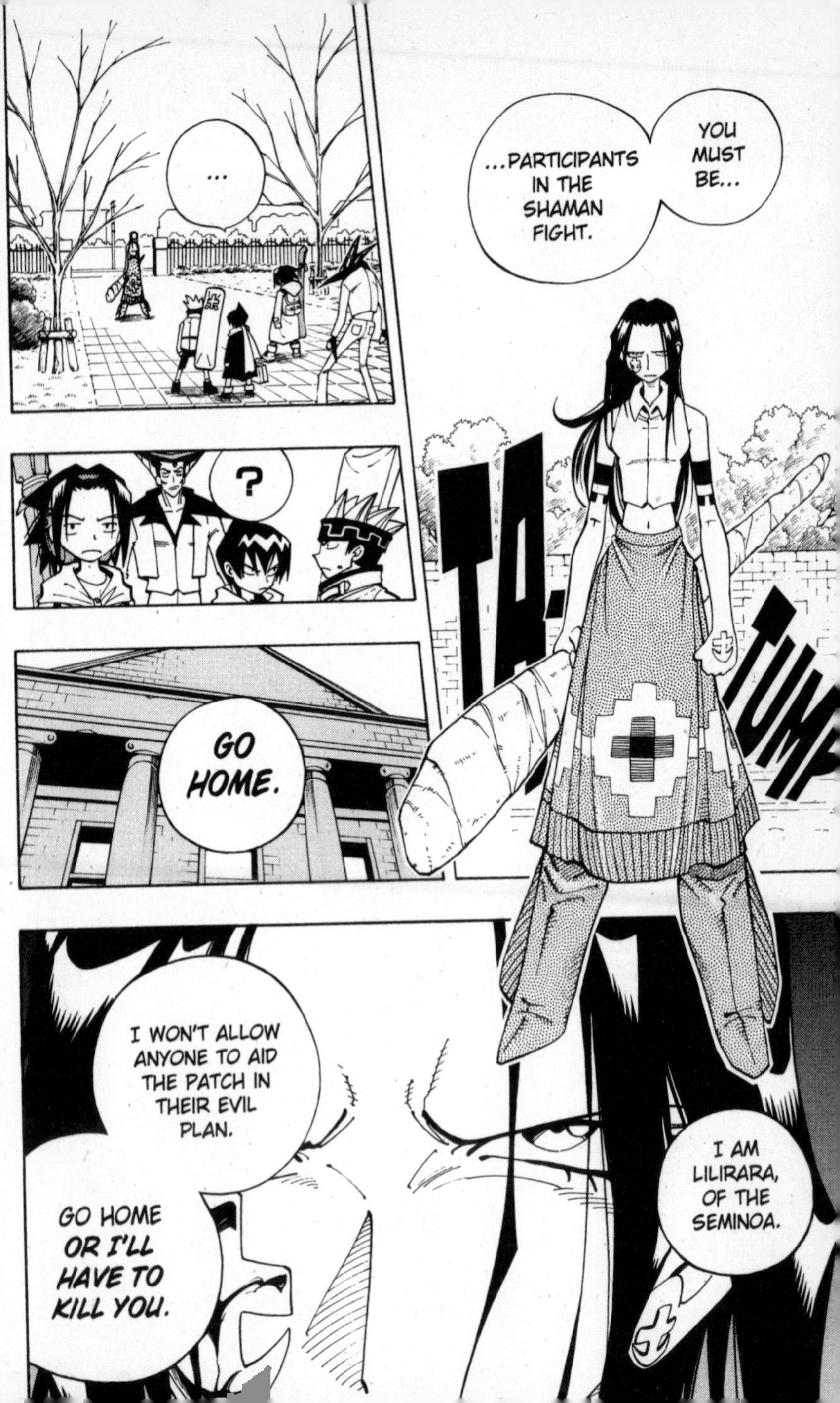
YOU MUST BE...
...PARTICIPANTS IN THE SHAMAN FIGHT.
TA-TUMP
...
?
GO HOME.
I AM LILIRARA, OF THE SEMINOA.
I WON'T ALLOW ANYONE TO AID THE PATCH IN THEIR EVIL PLAN.
GO HOME OR I'LL HAVE TO KILL YOU.

Reincarnation 82: The Song of Doom—500-Year-Old Memories

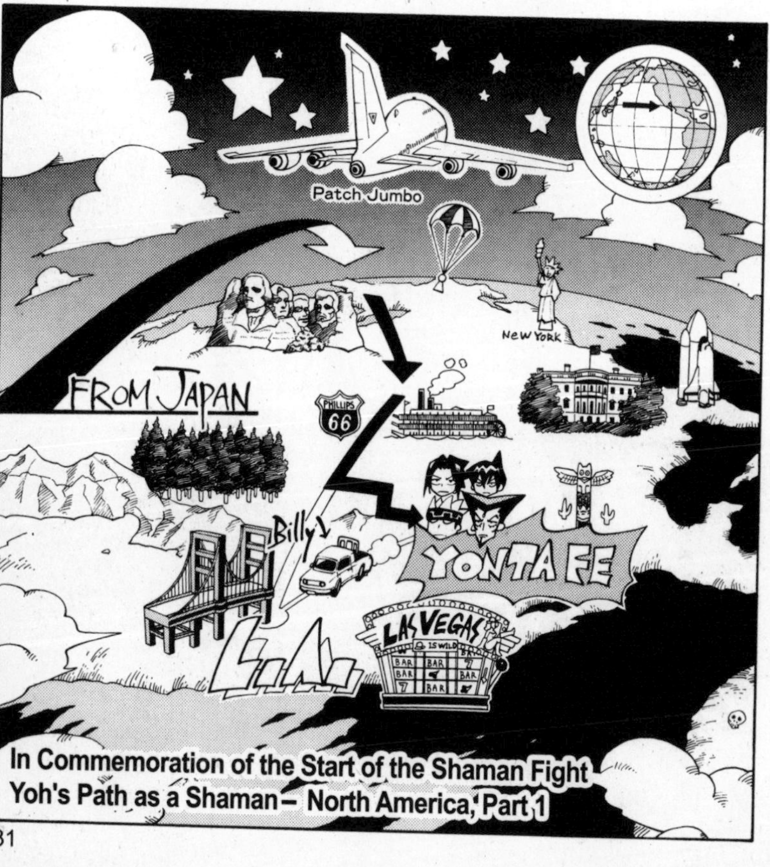
Patch Jumbo
NEW YORK
FROM JAPAN
PHILLIPS 66
Billy
YONTA FE
L.A.
LAS VEGAS
BAR
7
In Commemoration of the Start of the Shaman Fight
Yoh's Path as a Shaman— North America, Part 1

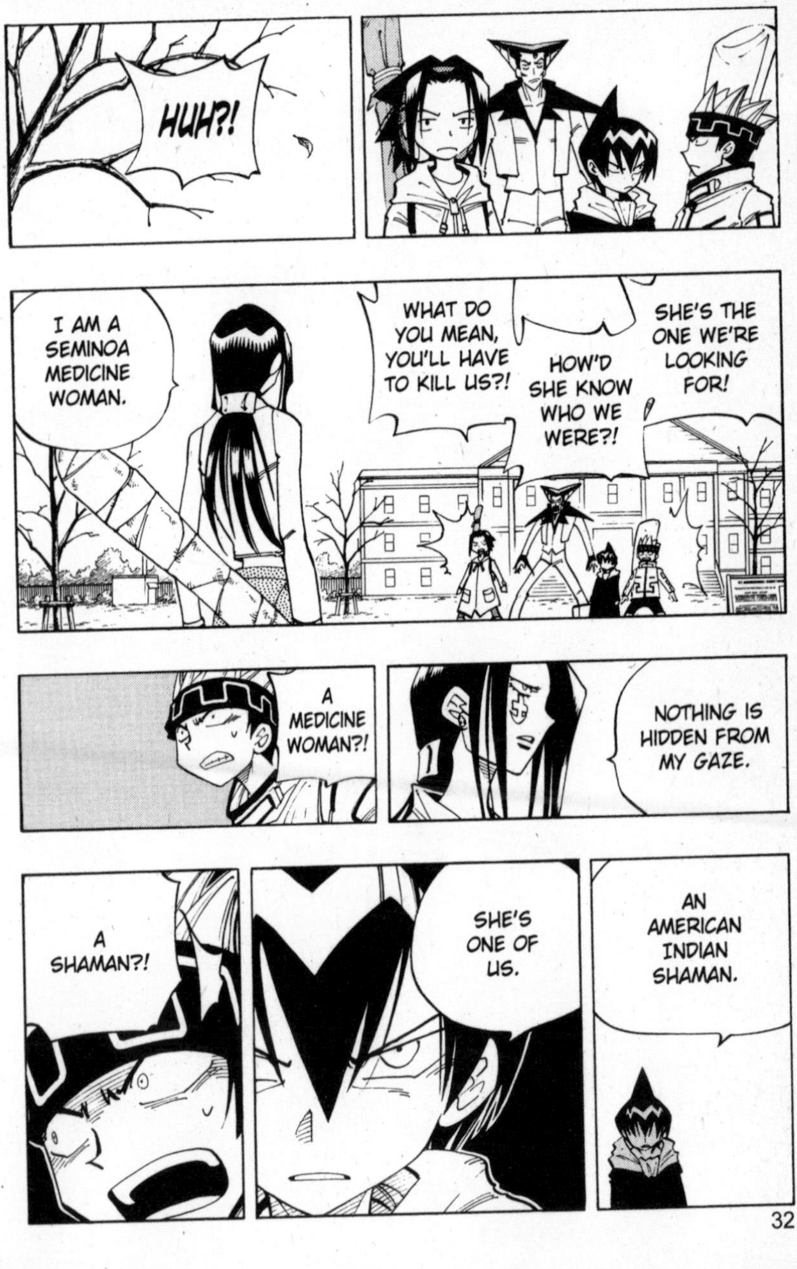
HUH?!
SHE'S THE ONE WE'RE LOOKING FOR!
HOW'D SHE KNOW WHO WE WERE?!
WHAT DO YOU MEAN, YOU'LL HAVE TO KILL US?!
I AM A SEMINOA MEDICINE WOMAN.
NOTHING IS HIDDEN FROM MY GAZE.
A MEDICINE WOMAN?!
AN AMERICAN INDIAN SHAMAN.
SHE'S ONE OF US.
A SHAMAN?!

READ THIS WAY

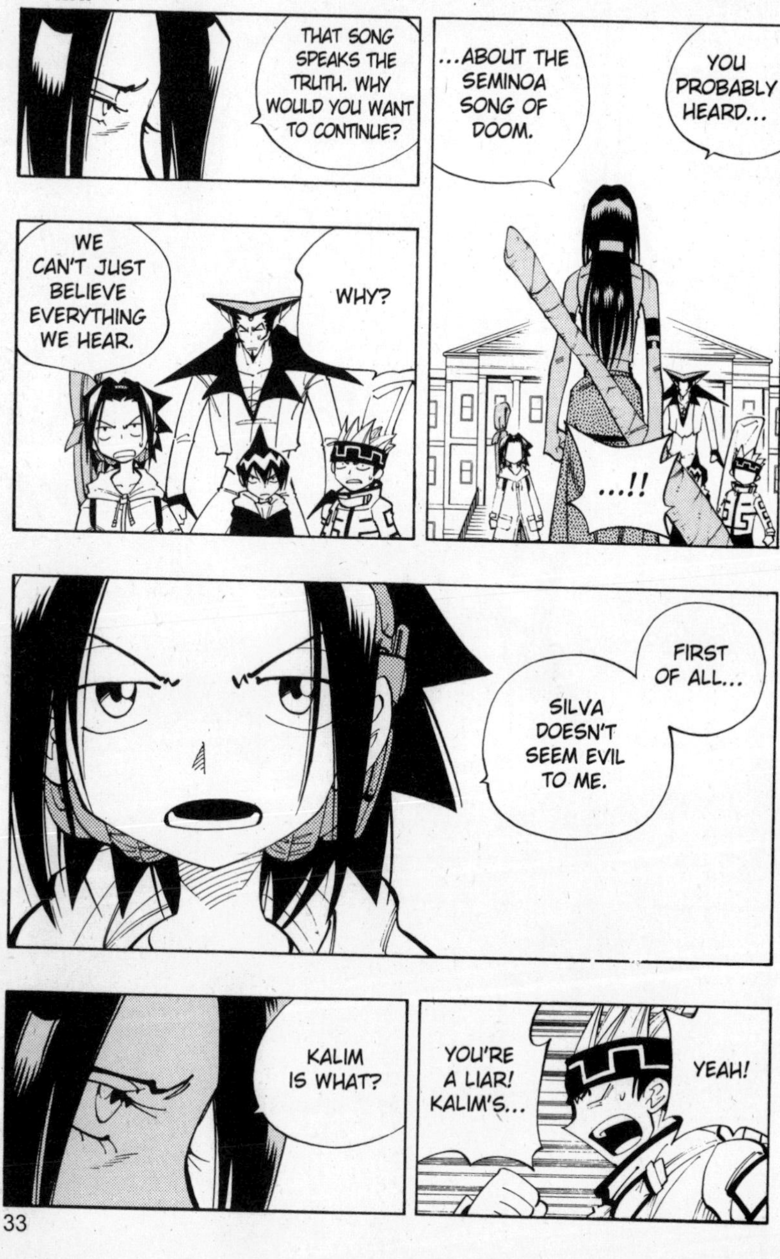
YOU PROBABLY HEARD...
...ABOUT THE SEMINOA SONG OF DOOM.
...!!
THAT SONG SPEAKS THE TRUTH. WHY WOULD YOU WANT TO CONTINUE?
WHY?
WE CAN'T JUST BELIEVE EVERYTHING WE HEAR.
FIRST OF ALL...
SILVA DOESN'T SEEM EVIL TO ME.
YEAH!
YOU'RE A LIAR! KALIM'S...
KALIM IS WHAT?

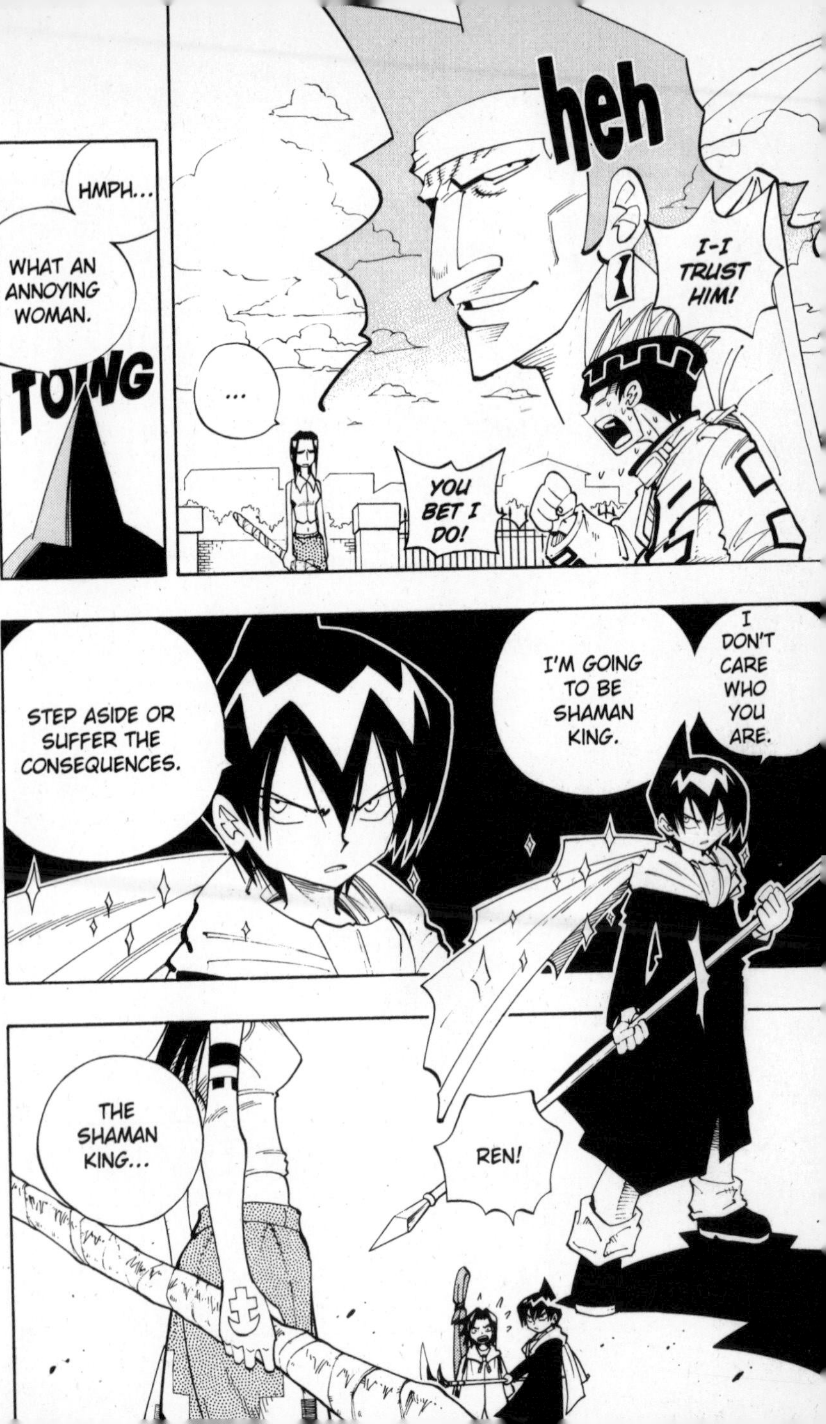
heh
I-I TRUST HIM!
YOU BET I DO!
...
HMPH...
WHAT AN ANNOYING WOMAN.
TOING
I DON'T CARE WHO YOU ARE.
I'M GOING TO BE SHAMAN KING.
STEP ASIDE OR SUFFER THE CONSEQUENCES.
REN!
THE SHAMAN KING...

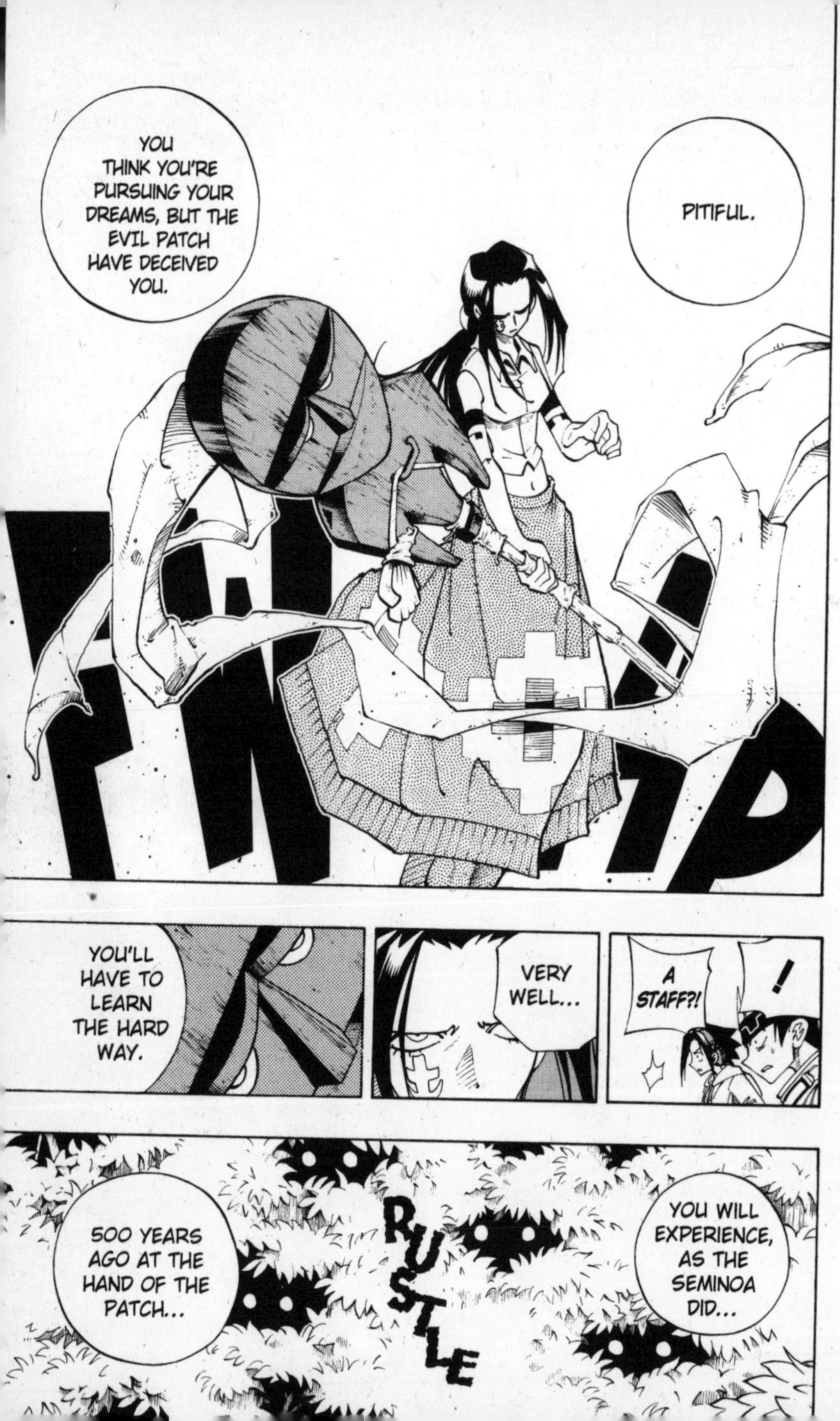
PITIFUL.
YOU THINK YOU'RE PURSUING YOUR DREAMS, BUT THE EVIL PATCH HAVE DECEIVED YOU.
!
A STAFF?!
VERY WELL...
YOU'LL HAVE TO LEARN THE HARD WAY.
YOU WILL EXPERIENCE, AS THE SEMINOA DID...
RUSTLE
500 YEARS AGO AT THE HAND OF THE PATCH...

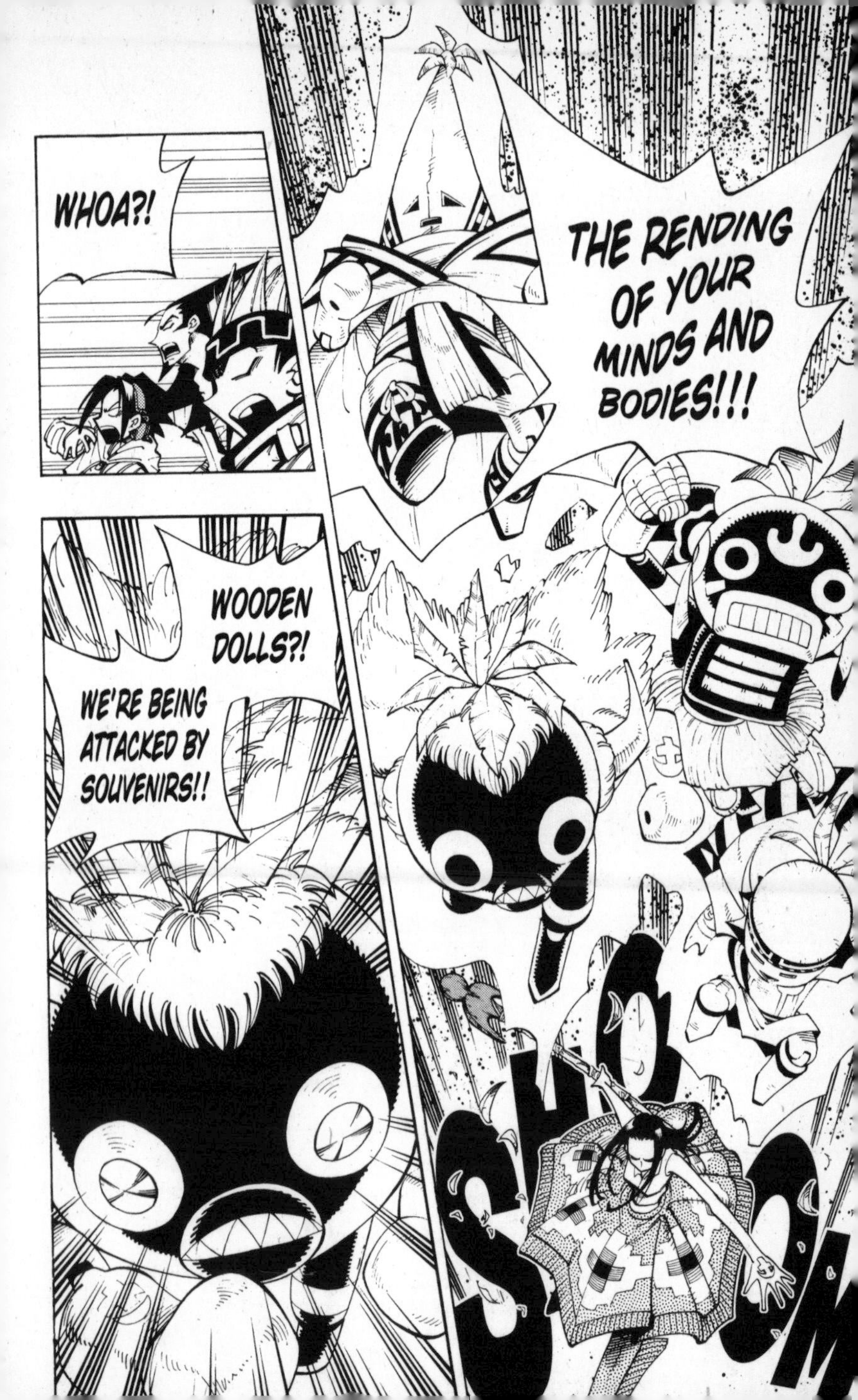
THE RENDING OF YOUR MINDS AND BODIES!!!
SHOOM
WHOA?!
WOODEN DOLLS?!
WE'RE BEING ATTACKED BY SOUVENIRS!!

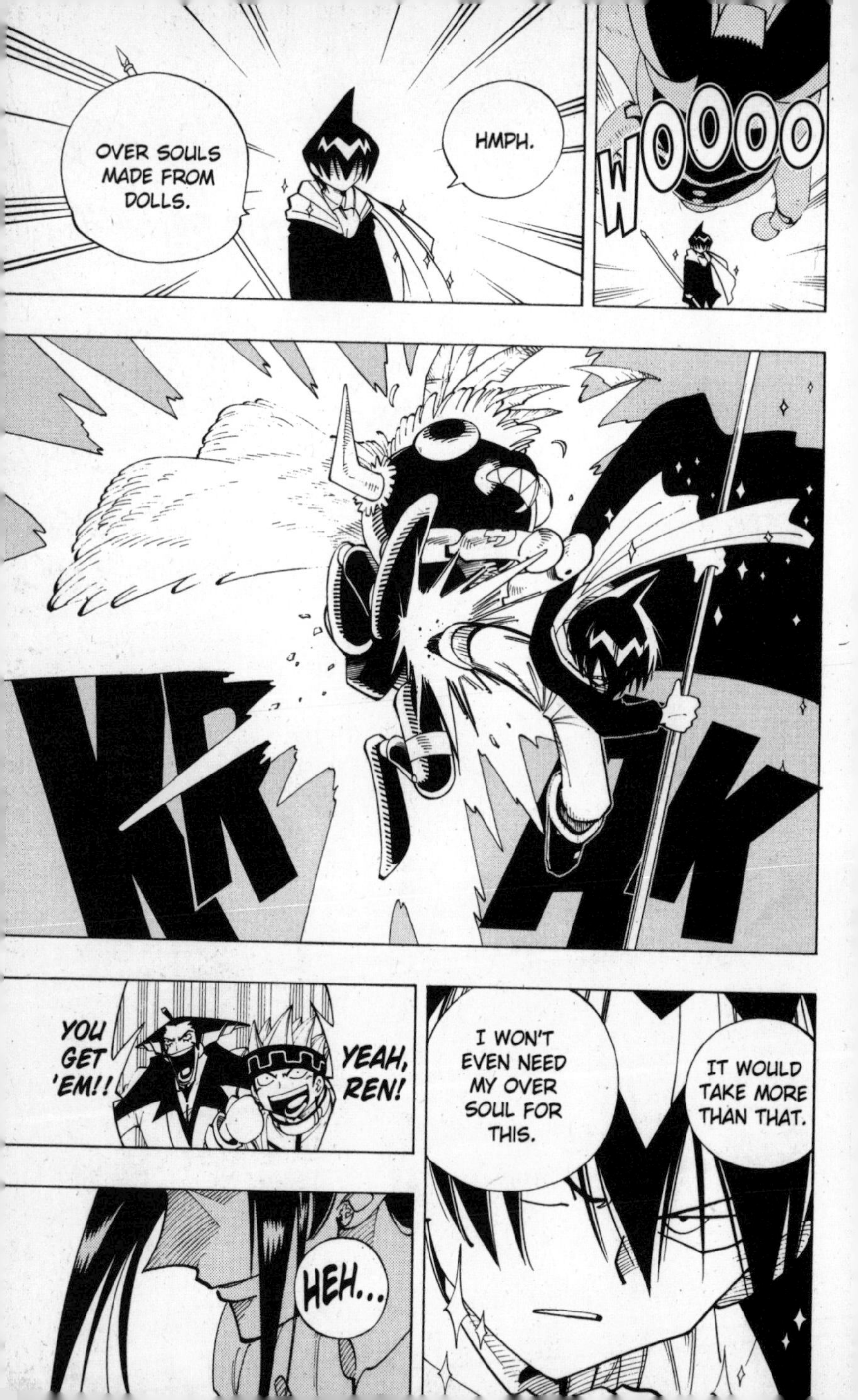
WOOOO
HMPH.
OVER SOULS MADE FROM DOLLS.
KRAK
IT WOULD TAKE MORE THAN THAT.
I WON'T EVEN NEED MY OVER SOUL FOR THIS.
YEAH, REN!
YOU GET 'EM!!
HEH...

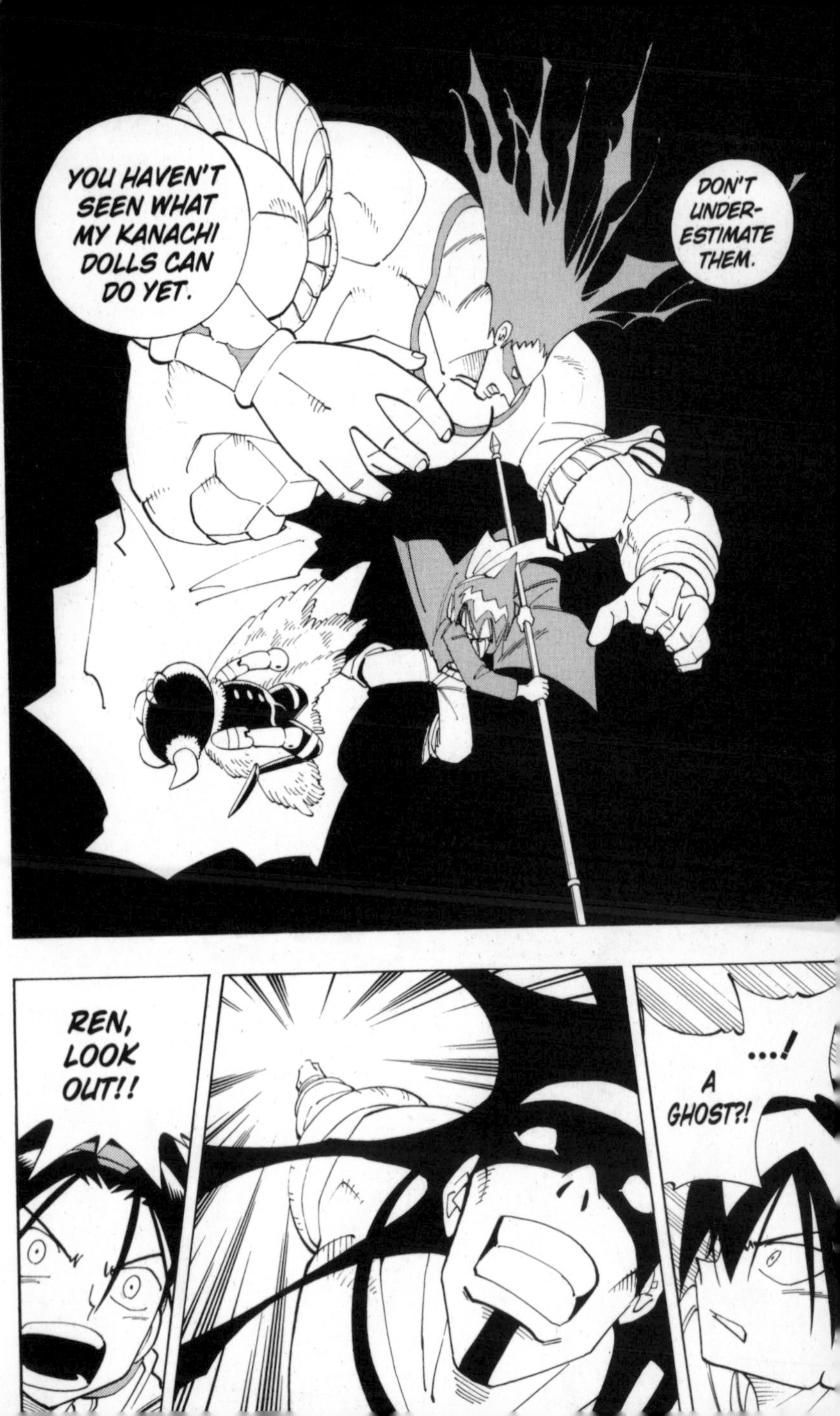
DON'T UNDER-ESTIMATE THEM.
YOU HAVEN'T SEEN WHAT MY KANACHI DOLLS CAN DO YET.
...!
A GHOST?!
REN, LOOK OUT!!

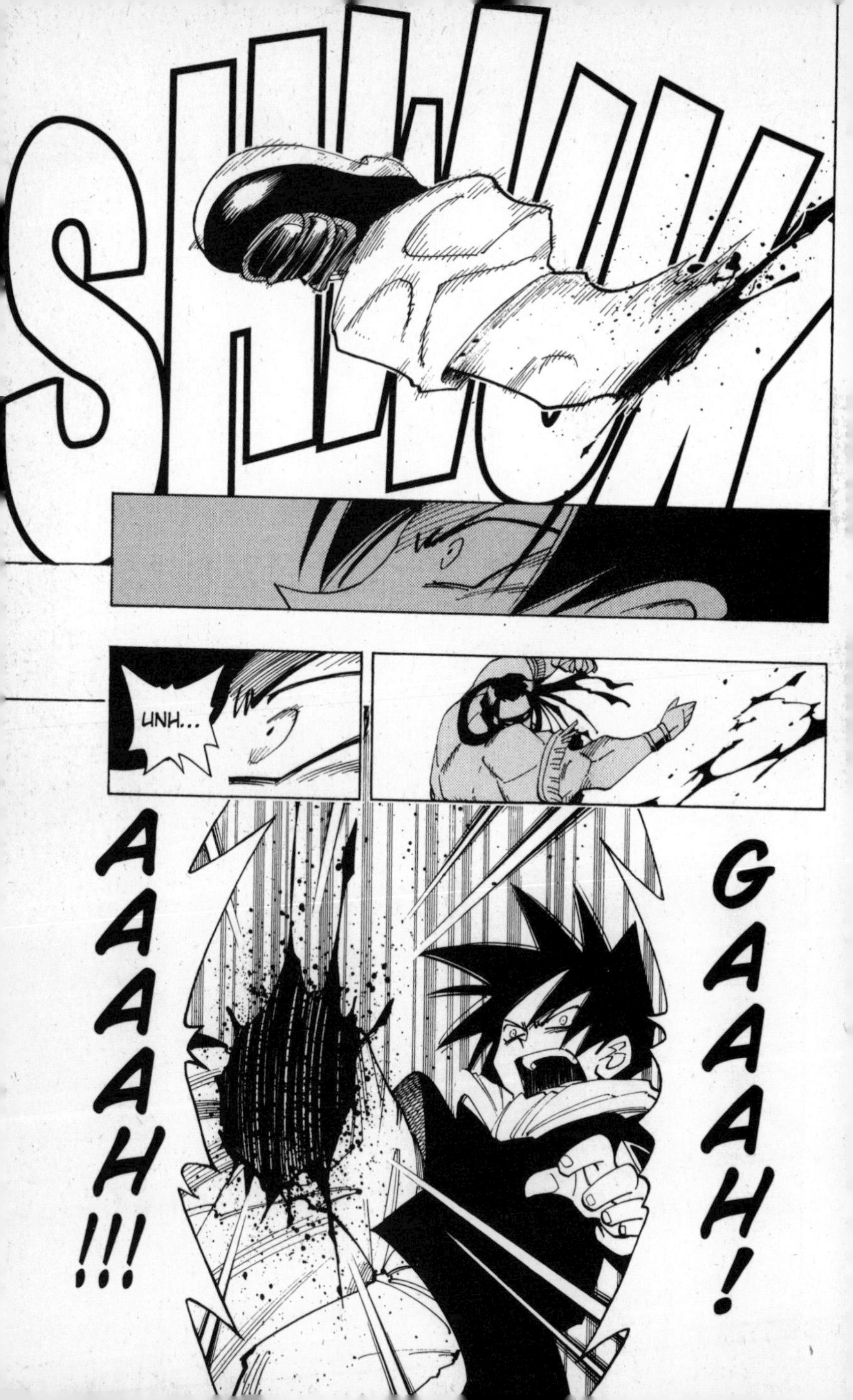
UNH...
GAAAH!
AAAAAH!!!

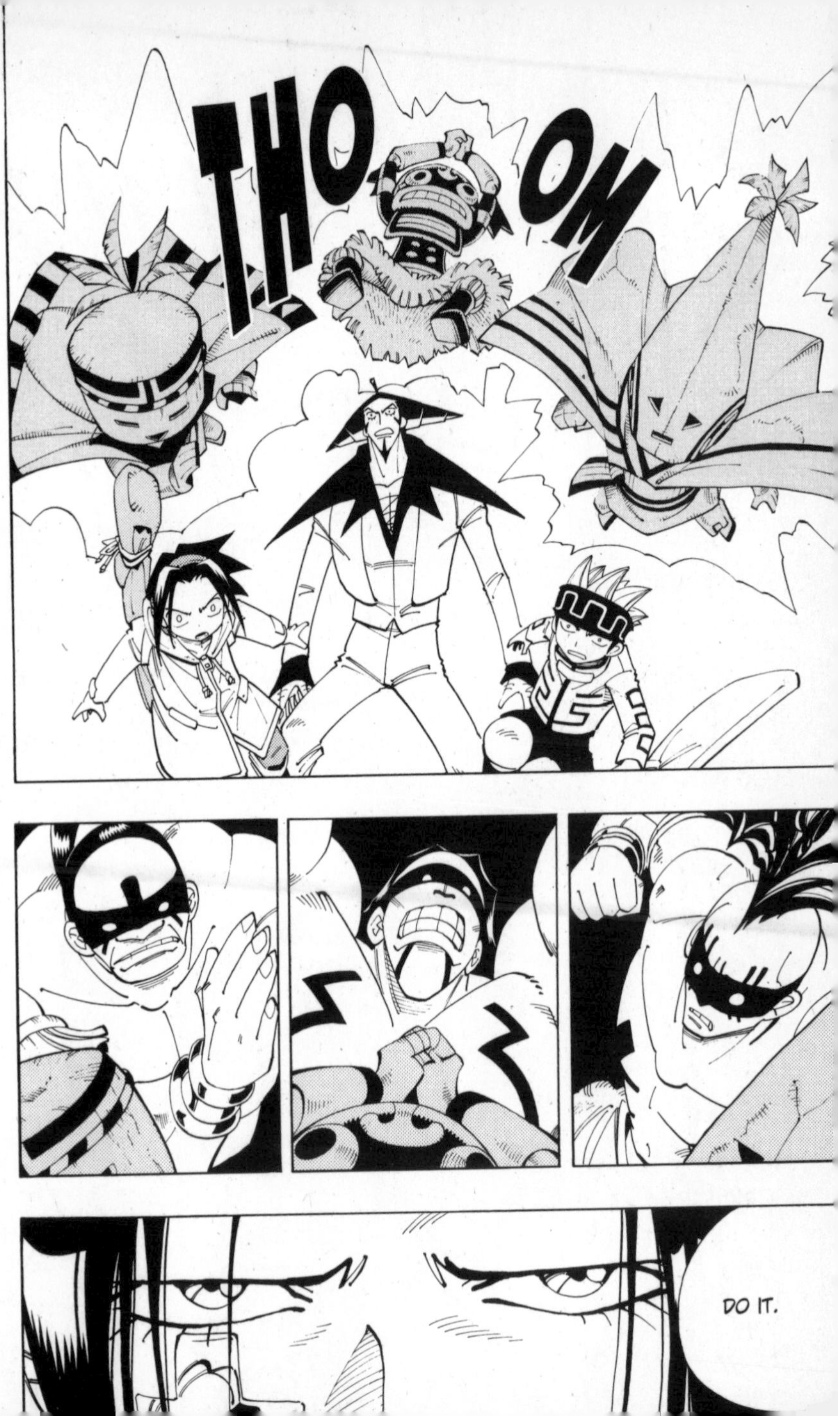
THOOM
DO IT.

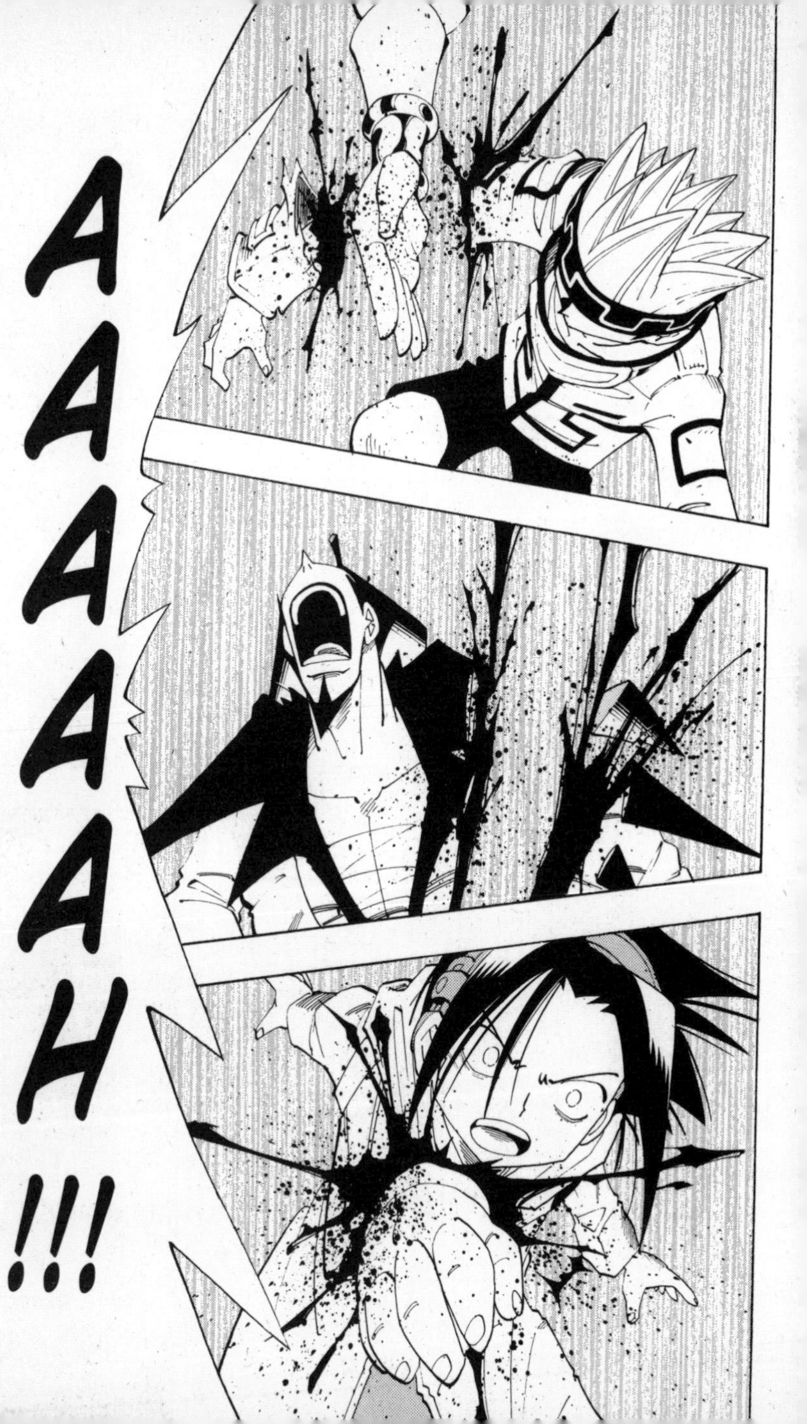
AAAAAAAH!!!

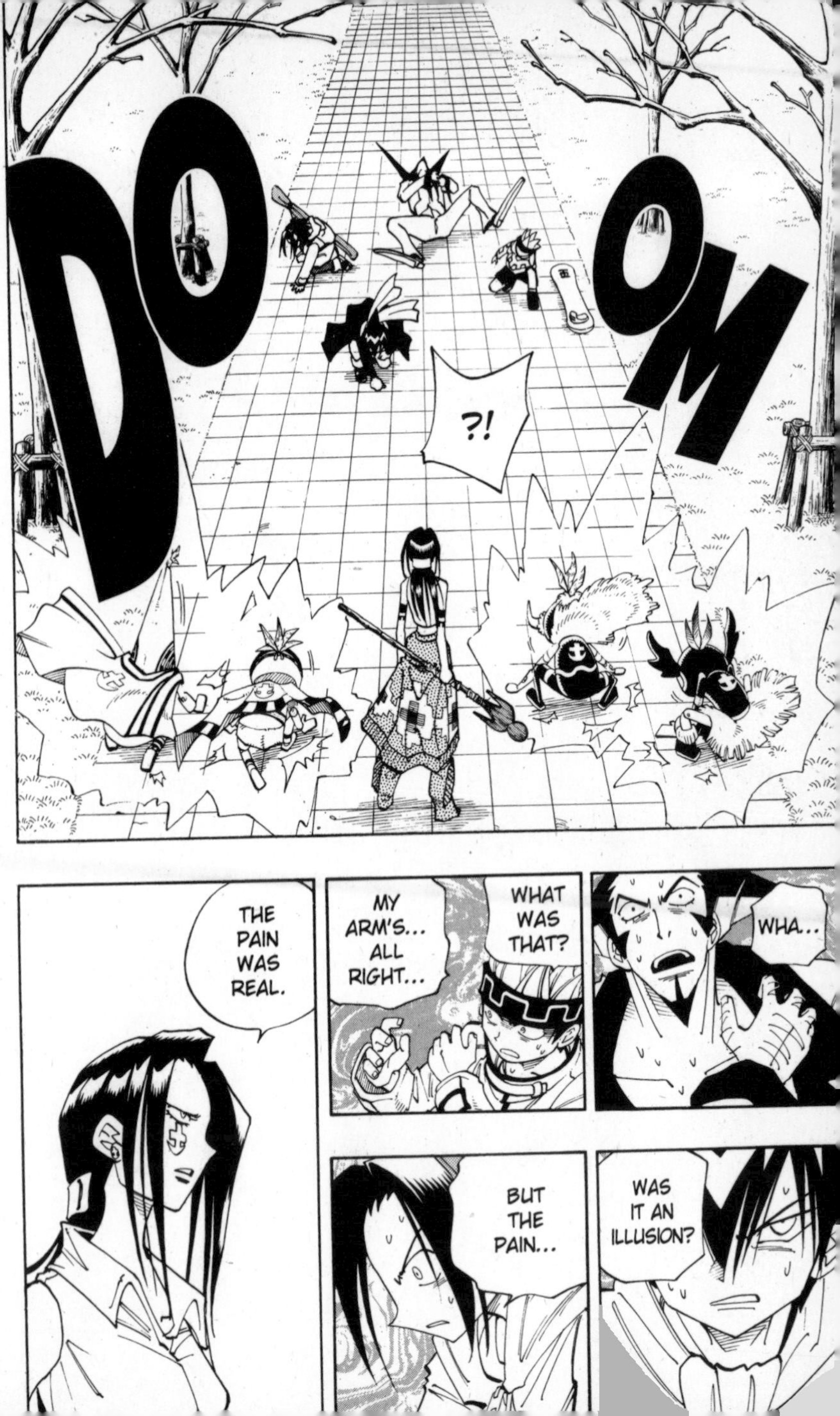
DOOM
?!
WHA...
WHAT WAS THAT?
MY ARM'S... ALL RIGHT...
WAS IT AN ILLUSION?
BUT THE PAIN...
THE PAIN WAS REAL.

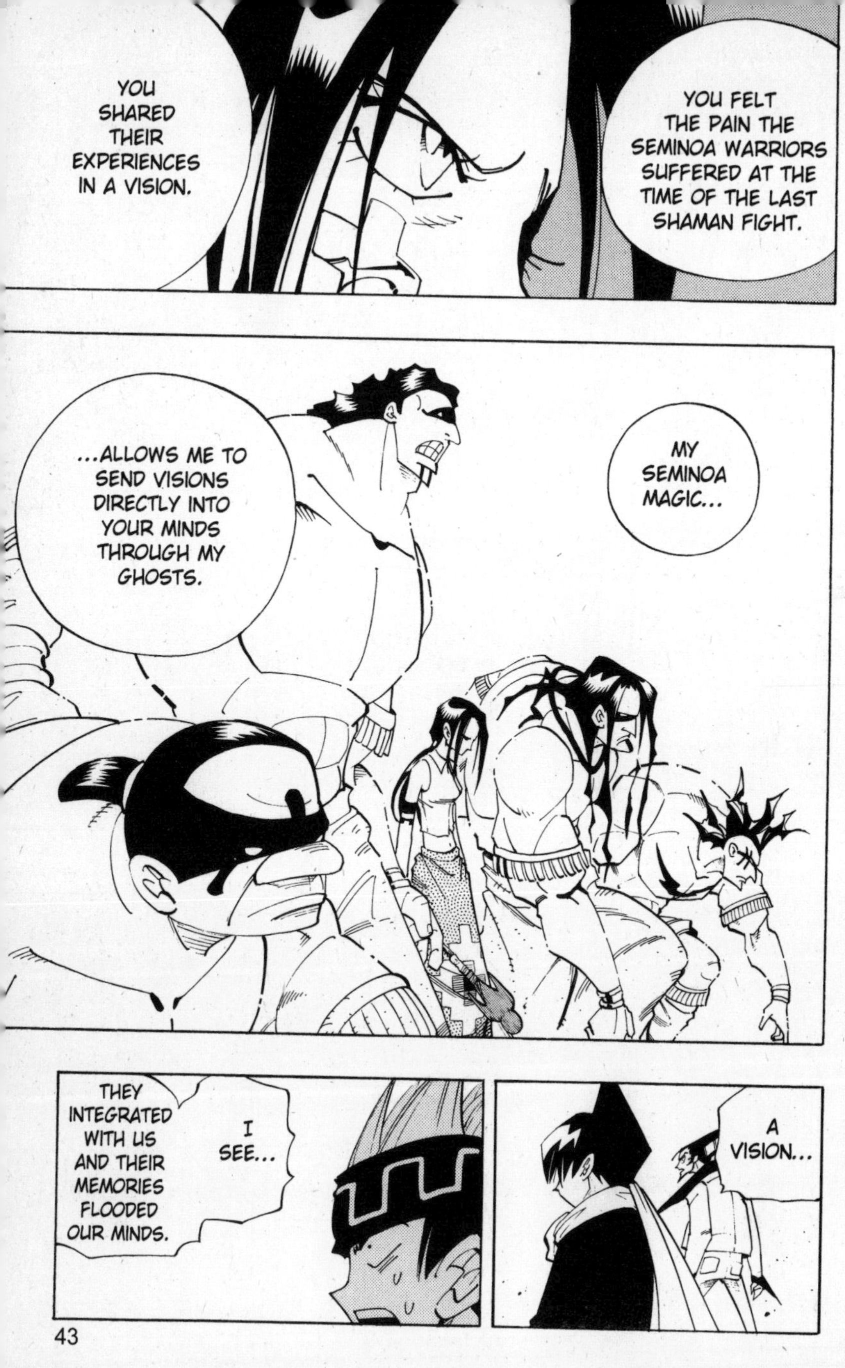
YOU FELT THE PAIN THE SEMINOA WARRIORS SUFFERED AT THE TIME OF THE LAST SHAMAN FIGHT.
YOU SHARED THEIR EXPERIENCES IN A VISION.
MY SEMINOA MAGIC...
...ALLOWS ME TO SEND VISIONS DIRECTLY INTO YOUR MINDS THROUGH MY GHOSTS.
A VISION...
I SEE...
THEY INTEGRATED WITH US AND THEIR MEMORIES FLOODED OUR MINDS.

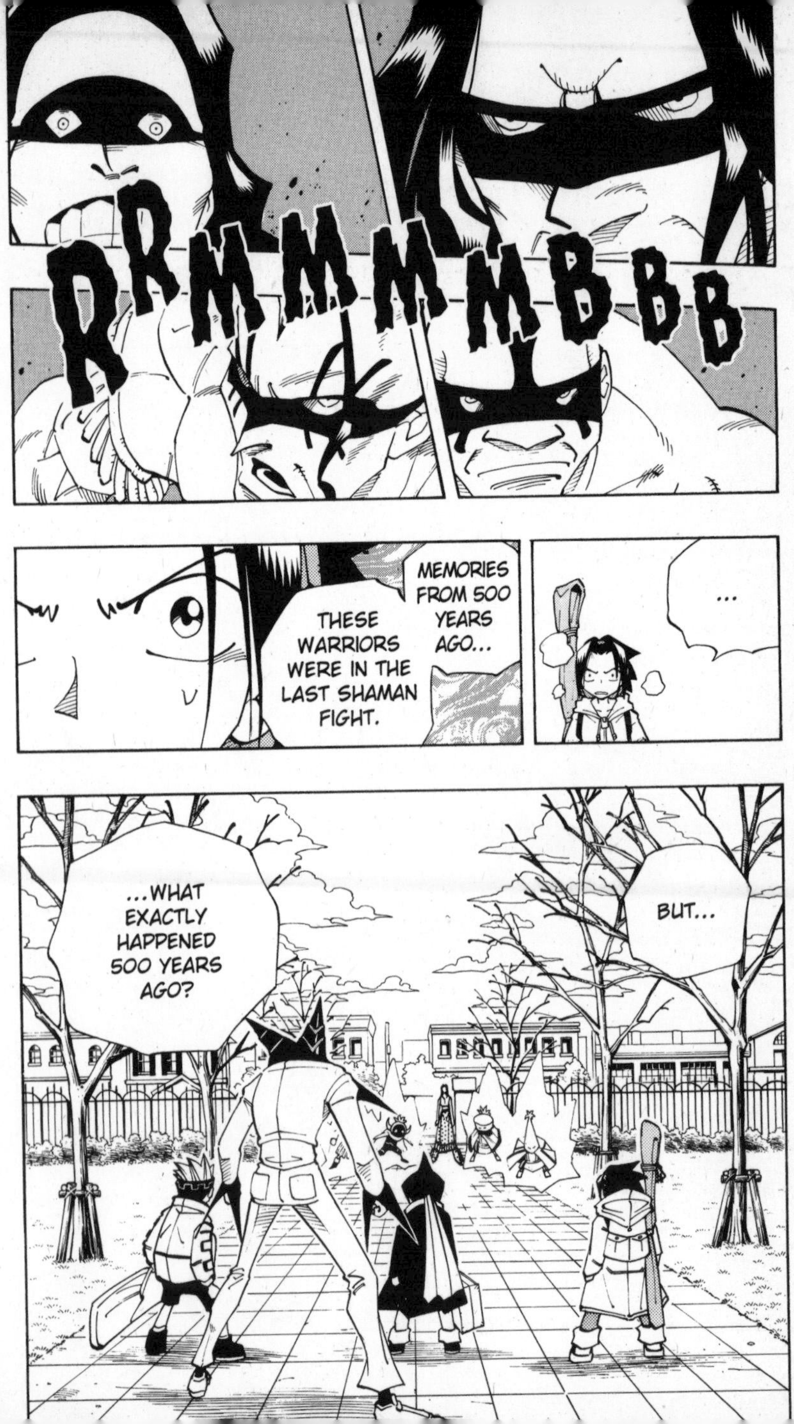
RRMMMMBBB
...
MEMORIES FROM 500 YEARS AGO...
THESE WARRIORS WERE IN THE LAST SHAMAN FIGHT.
BUT...
...WHAT EXACTLY HAPPENED 500 YEARS AGO?

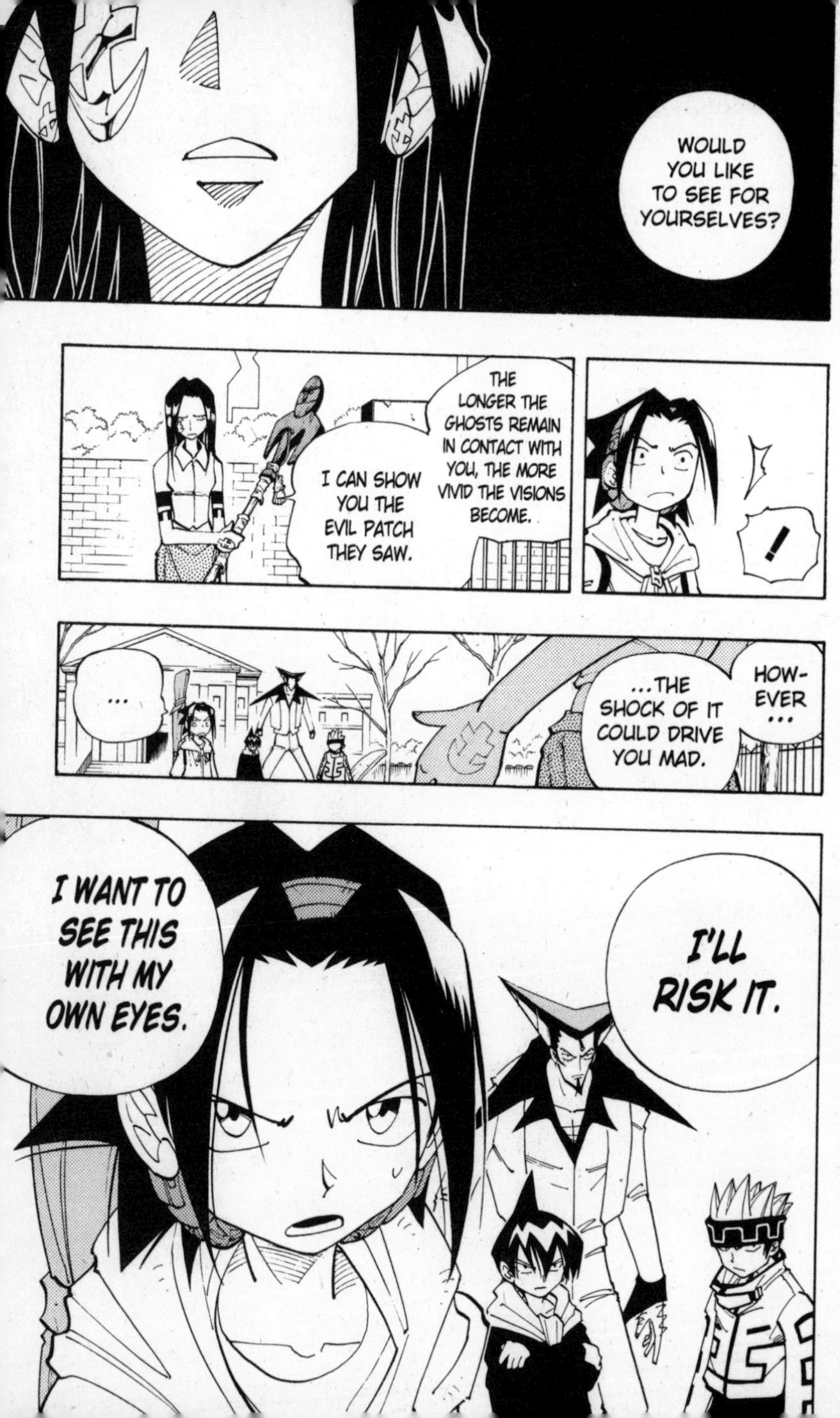
WOULD YOU LIKE TO SEE FOR YOURSELVES?
!
THE LONGER THE GHOSTS REMAIN IN CONTACT WITH YOU, THE MORE VIVID THE VISIONS BECOME.
I CAN SHOW YOU THE EVIL PATCH THEY SAW.
HOW-EVER...
...THE SHOCK OF IT COULD DRIVE YOU MAD.
...
I'LL RISK IT.
I WANT TO SEE THIS WITH MY OWN EYES.

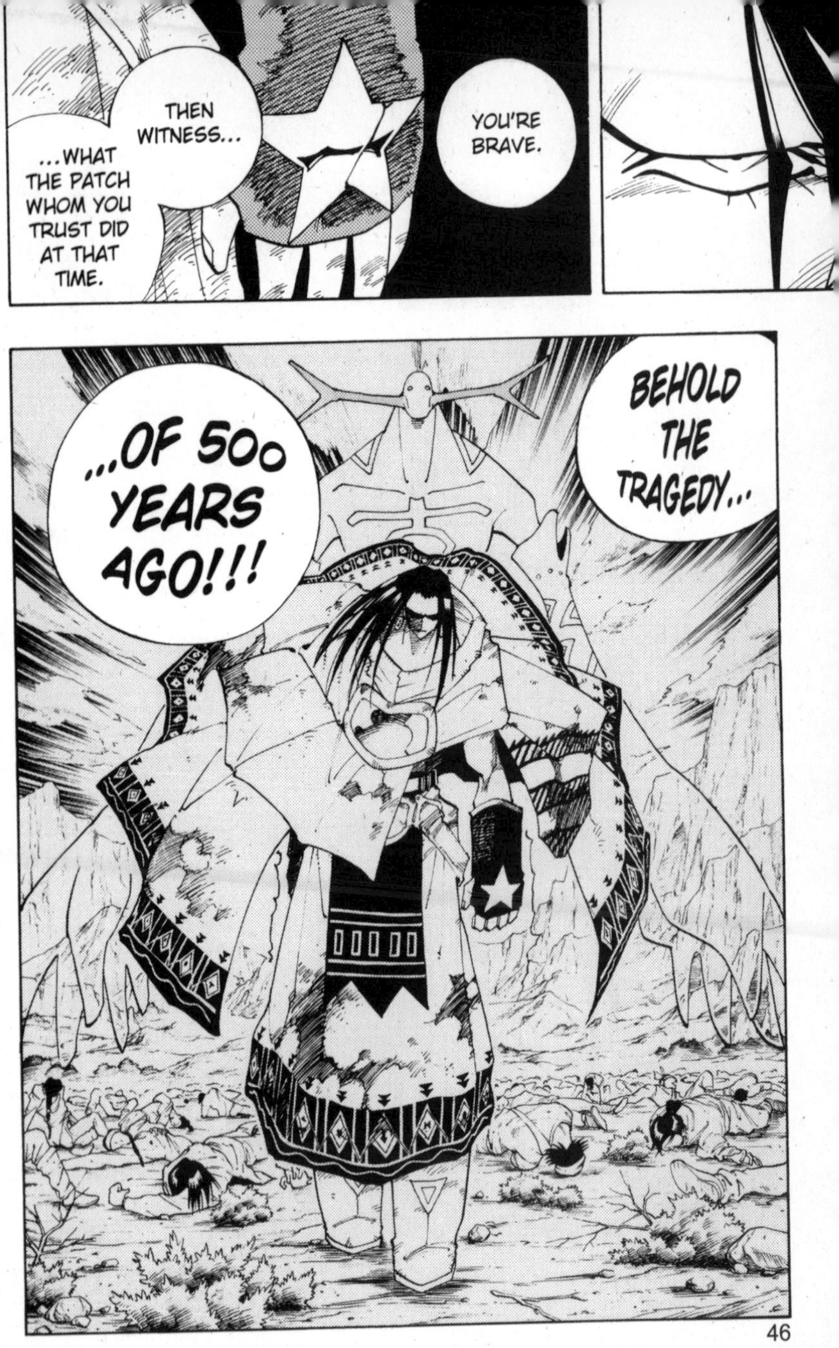
YOU'RE BRAVE.
THEN WITNESS...
...WHAT THE PATCH WHOM YOU TRUST DID AT THAT TIME.
BEHOLD THE TRAGEDY...
...OF 500 YEARS AGO!!!

Shaman King™

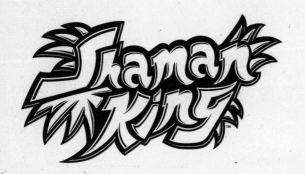

SHAMAN
KING
10

LILIRARA'S STAFF

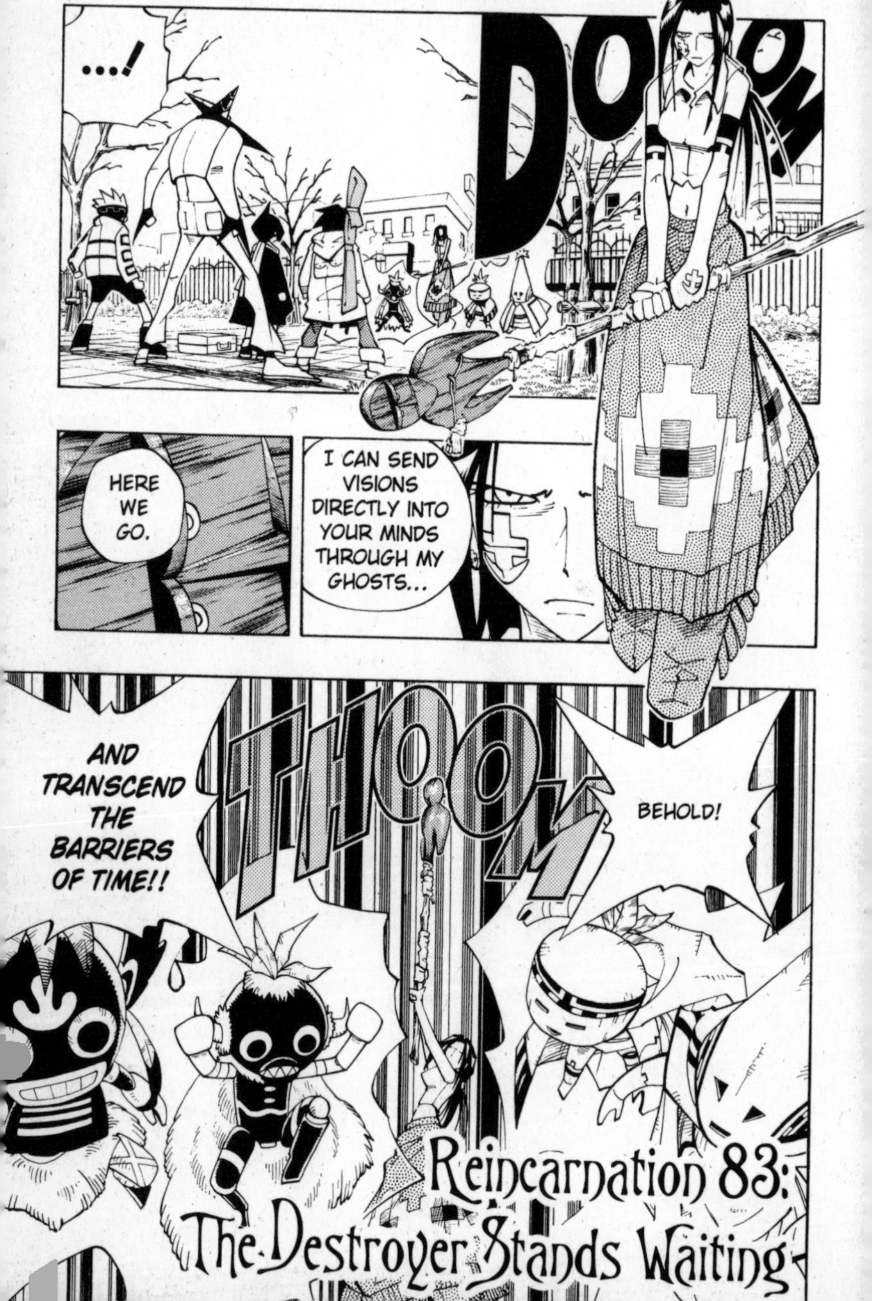
DOOM
...!
I CAN SEND VISIONS DIRECTLY INTO YOUR MINDS THROUGH MY GHOSTS...
HERE WE GO.
BEHOLD!
THOOM
AND TRANSCEND THE BARRIERS OF TIME!!
Reincarnation 83:
The Destroyer Stands Waiting

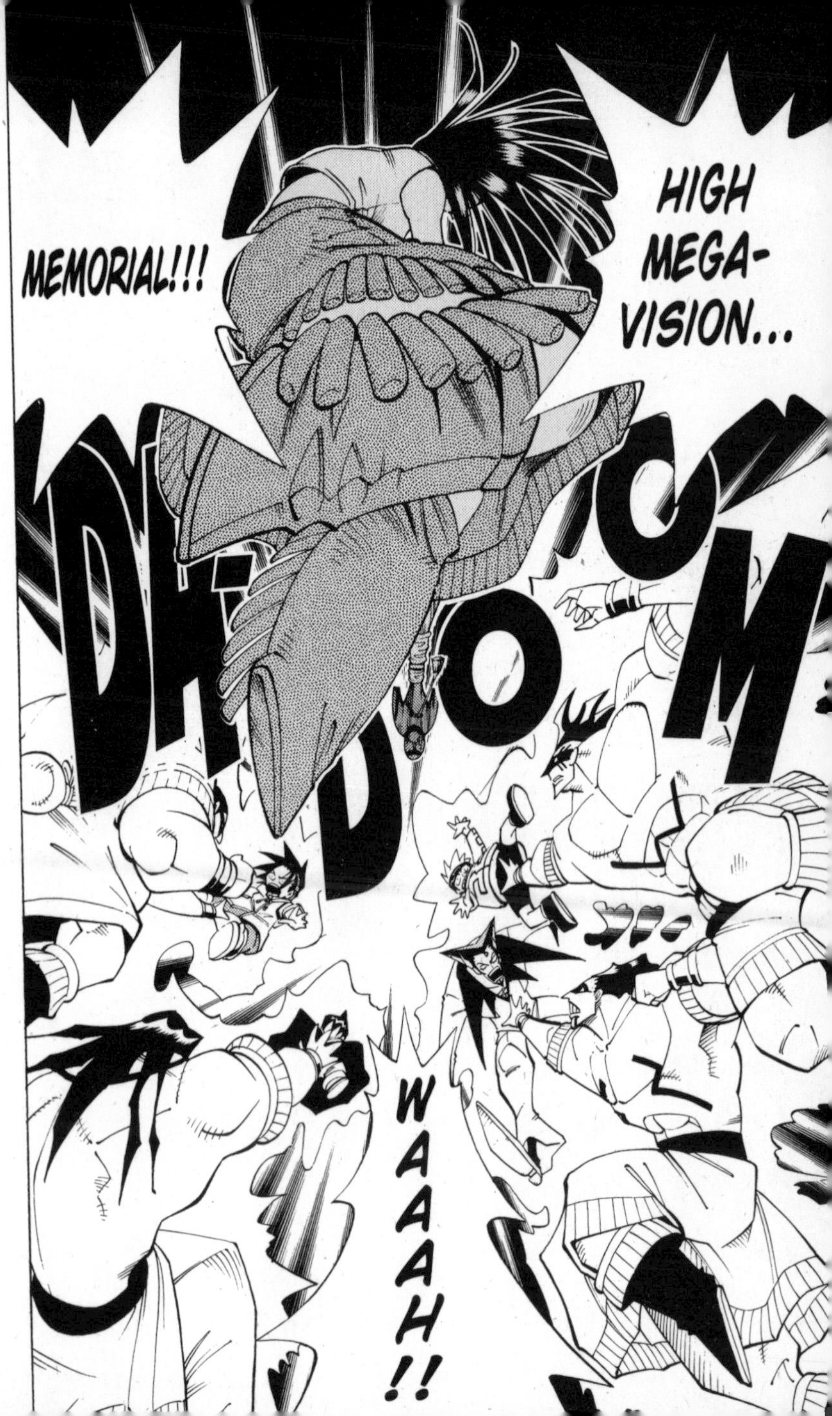
HIGH MEGA-VISION...
MEMORIAL!!!
WAAAH!!

Reincarnation 83: The Destroyer Stands Waiting

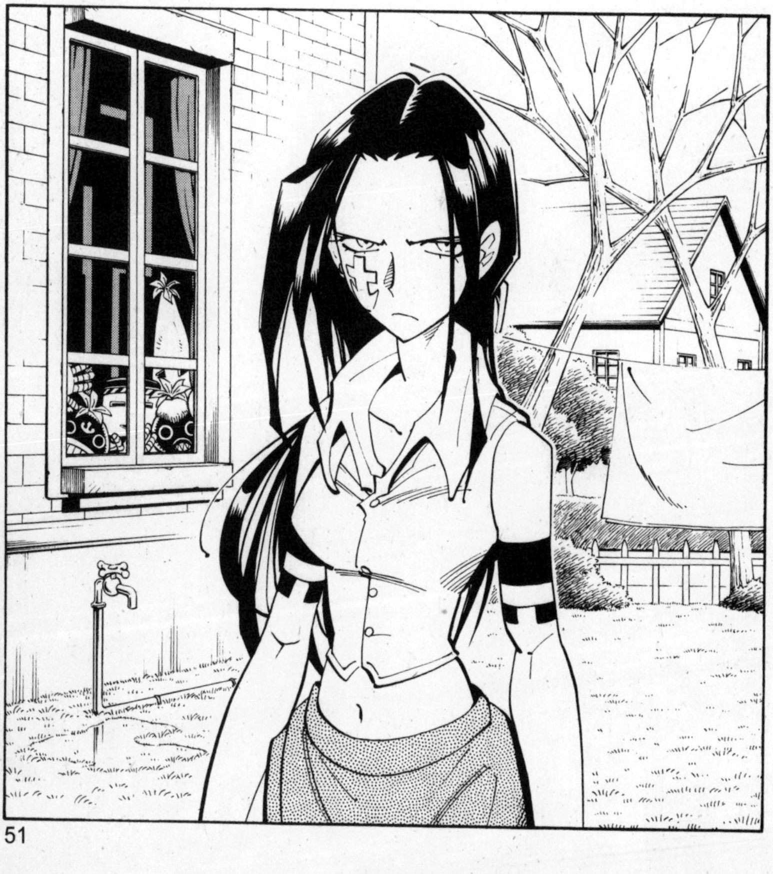

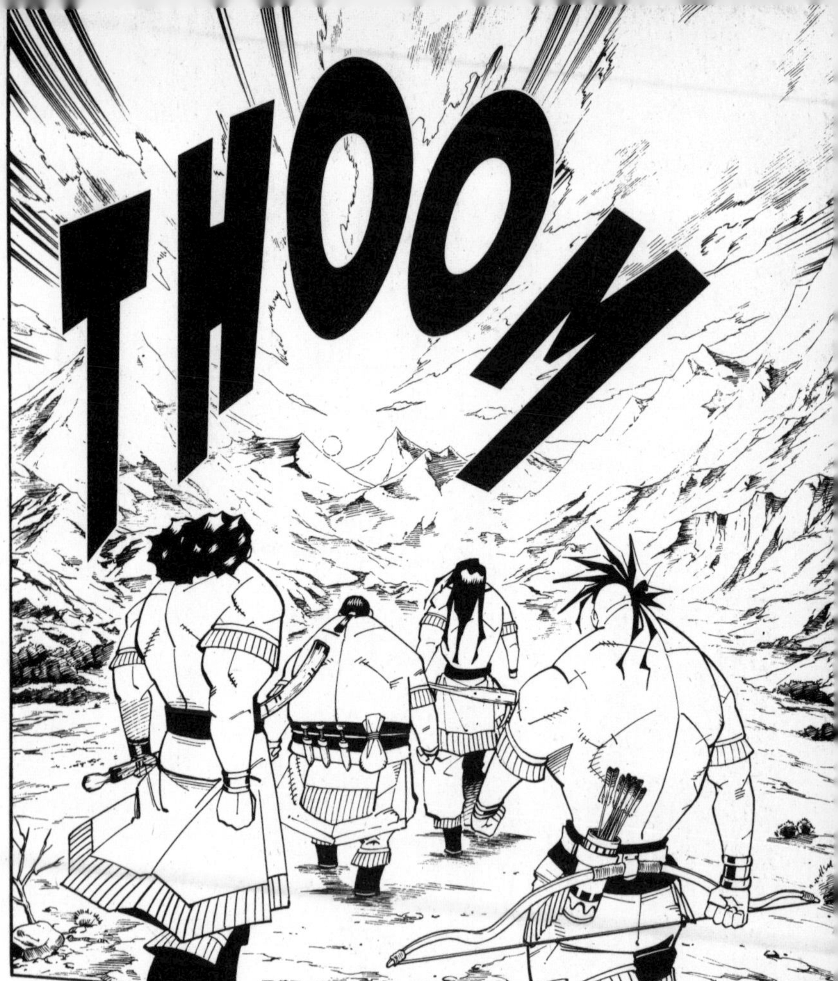
THOOM
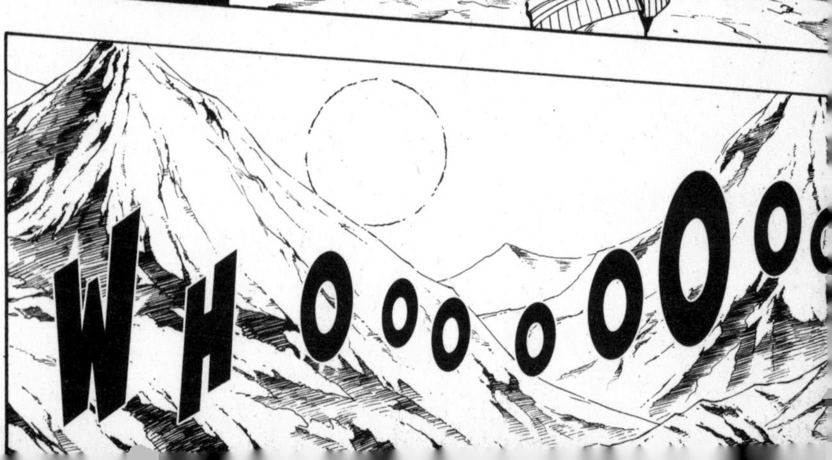
WHOOOOOOO

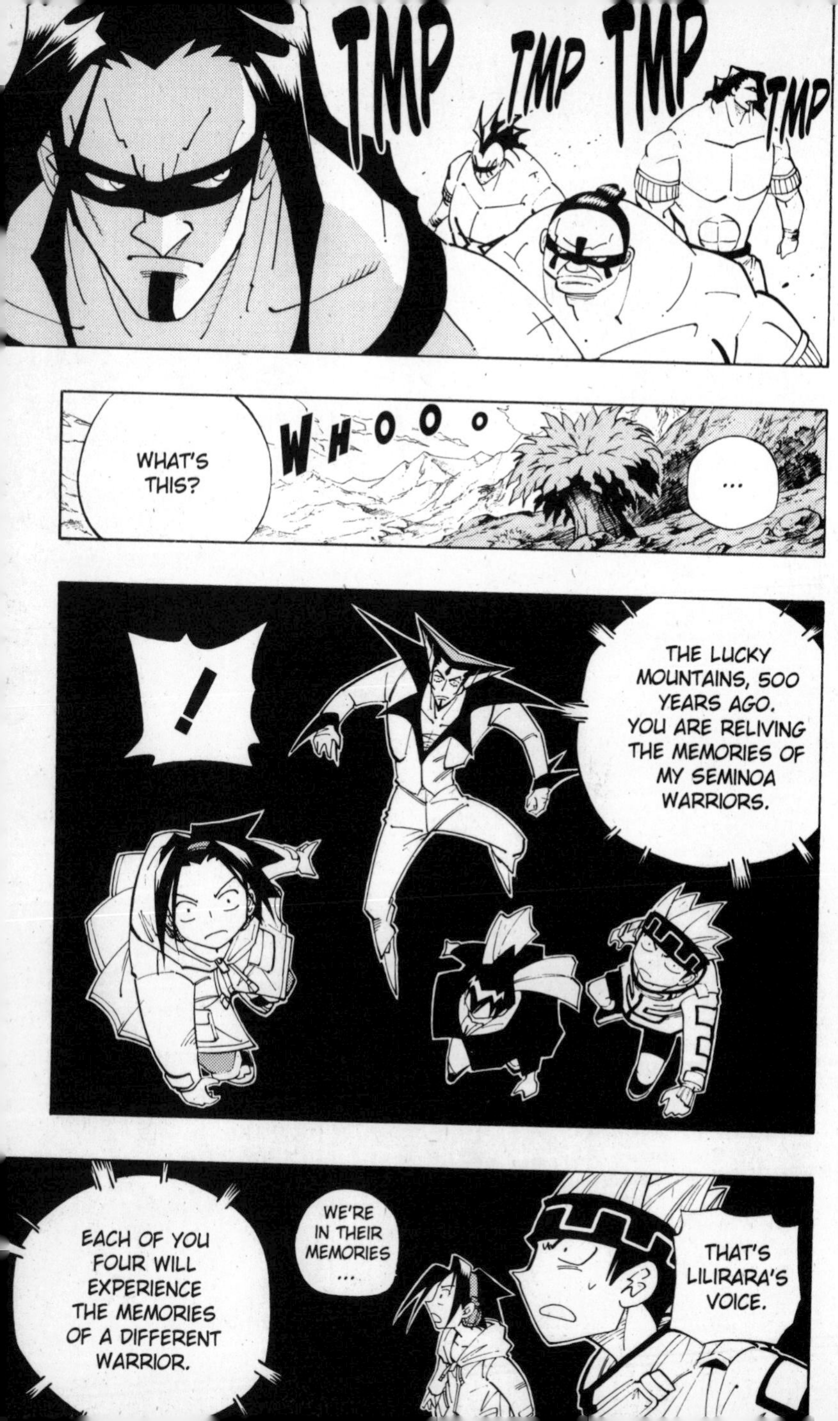
TMP TMP TMP TMP
...
WHOOO
WHAT'S THIS?
THE LUCKY MOUNTAINS, 500 YEARS AGO. YOU ARE RELIVING THE MEMORIES OF MY SEMINOA WARRIORS.
!
THAT'S LILIRARA'S VOICE.
WE'RE IN THEIR MEMORIES...
EACH OF YOU FOUR WILL EXPERIENCE THE MEMORIES OF A DIFFERENT WARRIOR.

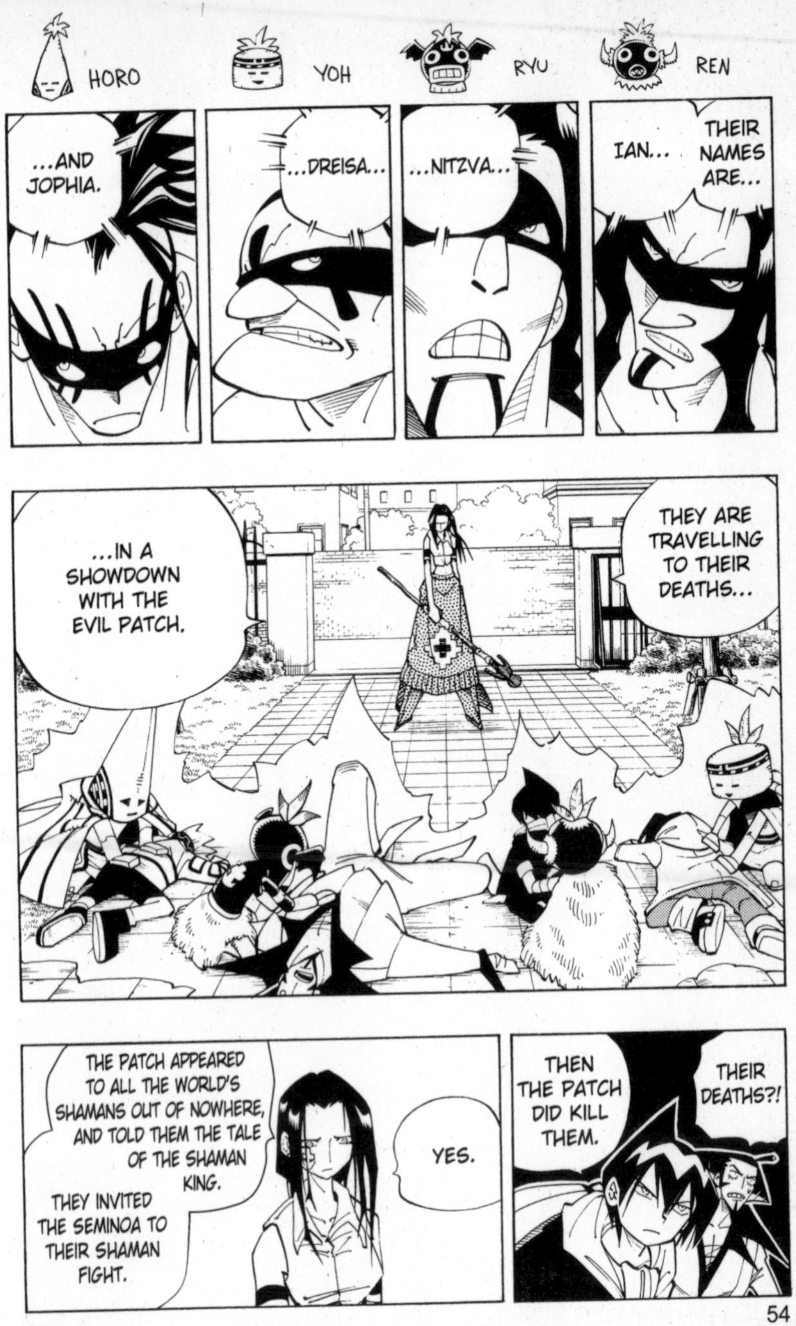
REN
RYU
YOH
HORO
THEIR NAMES ARE...
IAN...
...NITZVA...
...DREISA...
...AND JOPHIA.
THEY ARE TRAVELLING TO THEIR DEATHS...
...IN A SHOWDOWN WITH THE EVIL PATCH.
THEIR DEATHS?!
THEN THE PATCH DID KILL THEM.
YES.
THE PATCH APPEARED TO ALL THE WORLD'S SHAMANS OUT OF NOWHERE, AND TOLD THEM THE TALE OF THE SHAMAN KING.
THEY INVITED THE SEMINOA TO THEIR SHAMAN FIGHT.

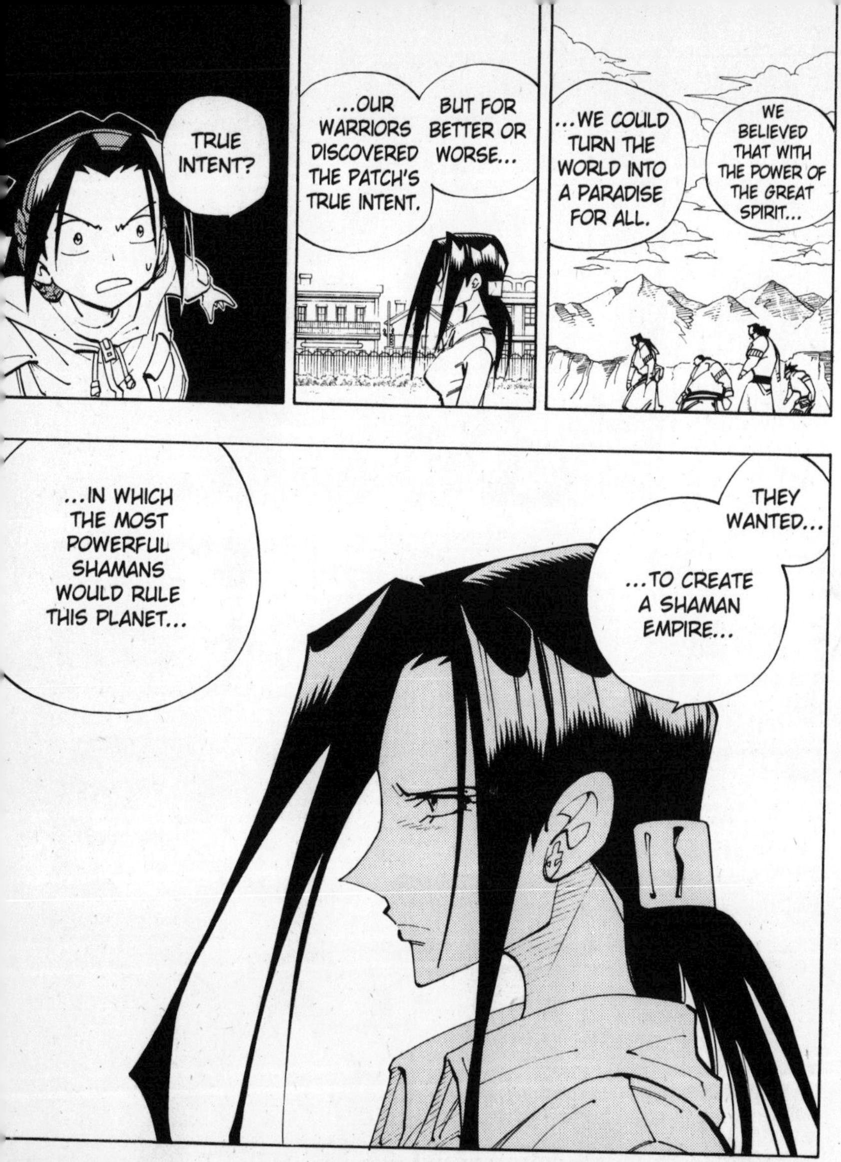
WE BELIEVED THAT WITH THE POWER OF THE GREAT SPIRIT...
...WE COULD TURN THE WORLD INTO A PARADISE FOR ALL.
BUT FOR BETTER OR WORSE...
...OUR WARRIORS DISCOVERED THE PATCH'S TRUE INTENT.
TRUE INTENT?
THEY WANTED...
...TO CREATE A SHAMAN EMPIRE...
...IN WHICH THE MOST POWERFUL SHAMANS WOULD RULE THIS PLANET...

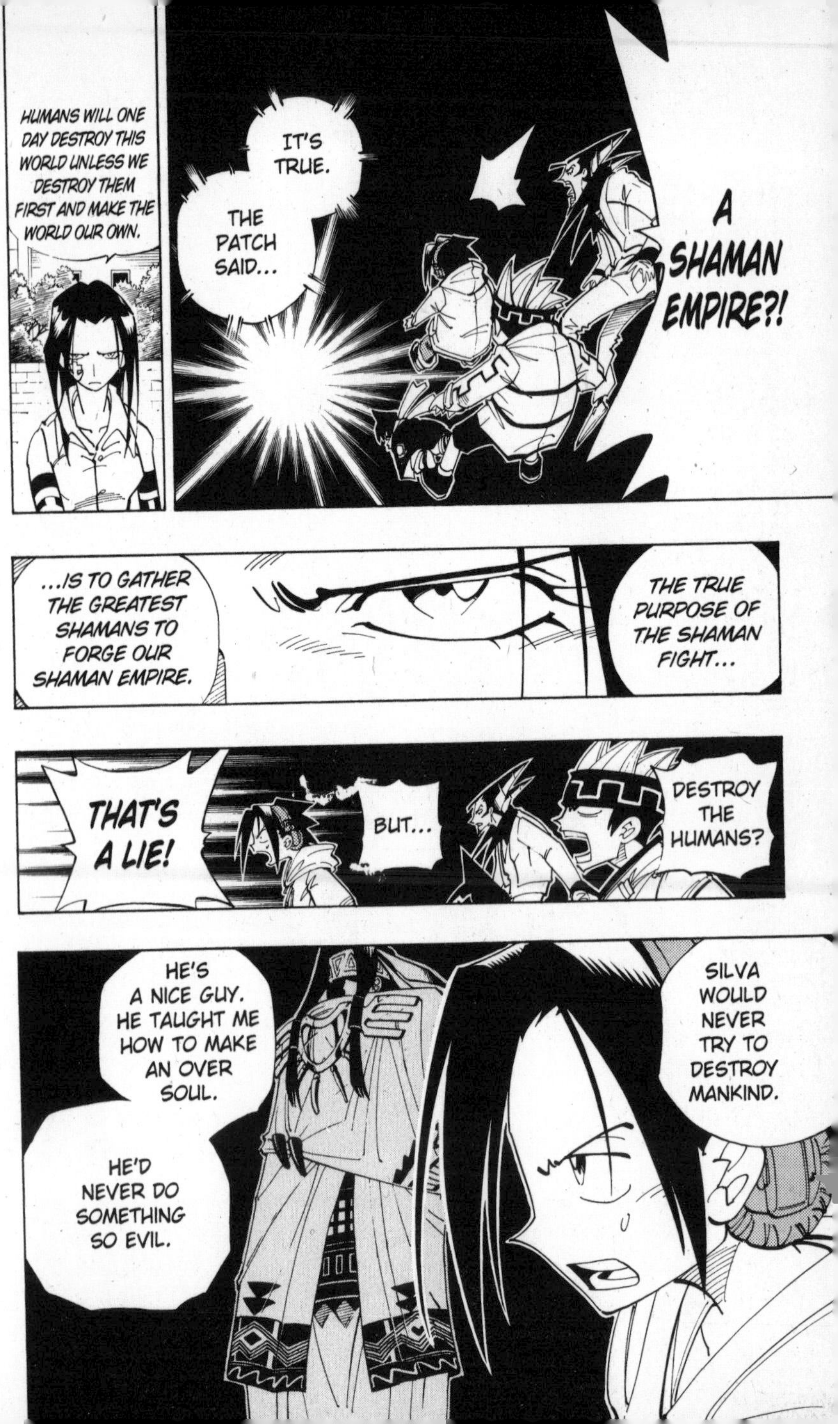
A SHAMAN EMPIRE?!
IT'S TRUE.
THE PATCH SAID...
HUMANS WILL ONE DAY DESTROY THIS WORLD UNLESS WE DESTROY THEM FIRST AND MAKE THE WORLD OUR OWN.
THE TRUE PURPOSE OF THE SHAMAN FIGHT...
...IS TO GATHER THE GREATEST SHAMANS TO FORGE OUR SHAMAN EMPIRE.
DESTROY THE HUMANS?
BUT...
THAT'S A LIE!
SILVA WOULD NEVER TRY TO DESTROY MANKIND.
HE'S A NICE GUY. HE TAUGHT ME HOW TO MAKE AN OVER SOUL.
HE'D NEVER DO SOMETHING SO EVIL.

READ THIS WAY

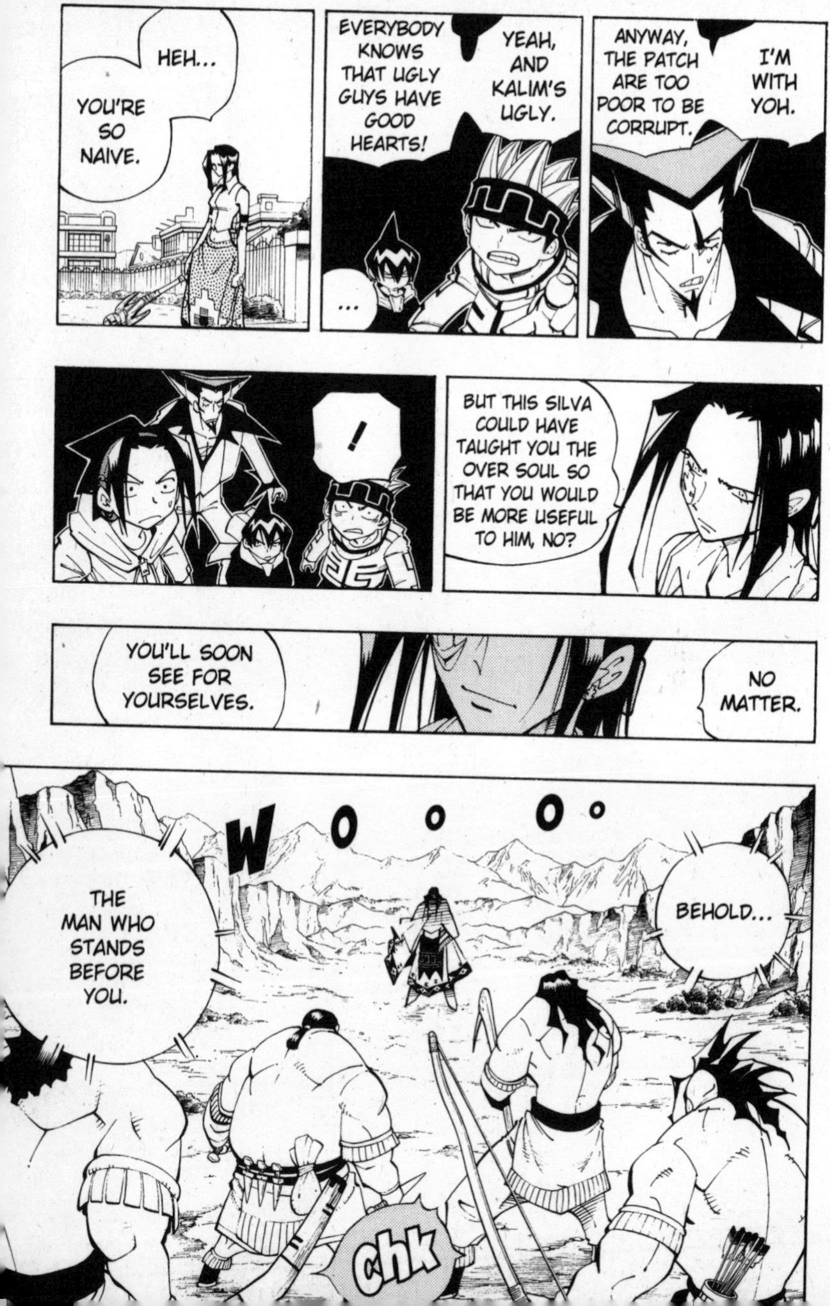
I'M WITH YOH.
ANYWAY, THE PATCH ARE TOO POOR TO BE CORRUPT.
EVERYBODY KNOWS THAT UGLY GUYS HAVE GOOD HEARTS!
YEAH, AND KALIM'S UGLY.
...
HEH...
YOU'RE SO NAIVE.
BUT THIS SILVA COULD HAVE TAUGHT YOU THE OVER SOUL SO THAT YOU WOULD BE MORE USEFUL TO HIM, NO?
!
NO MATTER.
YOU'LL SOON SEE FOR YOURSELVES.
BEHOLD...
WOOOO
THE MAN WHO STANDS BEFORE YOU.
chk

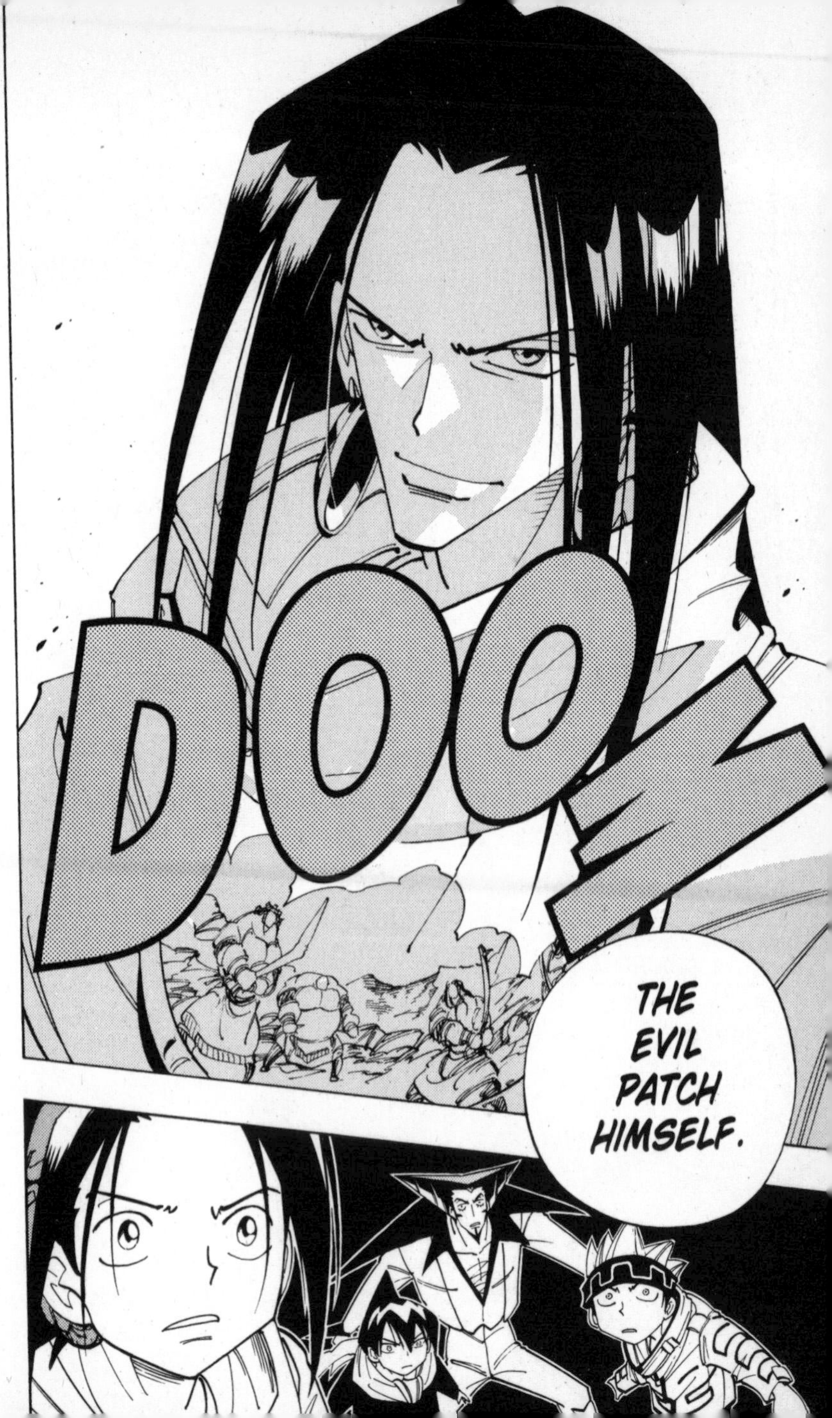
DOOM
THE EVIL PATCH HIMSELF.

READ THIS WAY

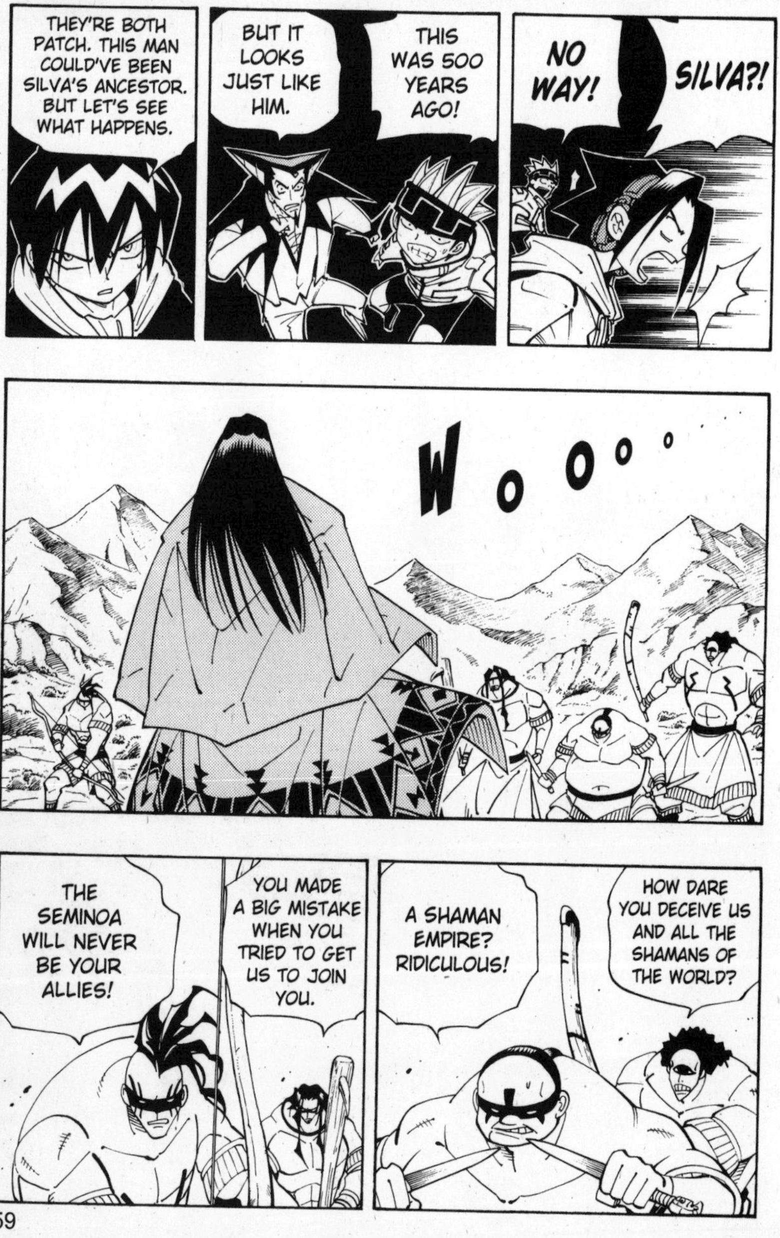
SILVA?!
NO WAY!
THIS WAS 500 YEARS AGO!
BUT IT LOOKS JUST LIKE HIM.
THEY'RE BOTH PATCH. THIS MAN COULD'VE BEEN SILVA'S ANCESTOR. BUT LET'S SEE WHAT HAPPENS.
WOooo
HOW DARE YOU DECEIVE US AND ALL THE SHAMANS OF THE WORLD?
A SHAMAN EMPIRE? RIDICULOUS!
YOU MADE A BIG MISTAKE WHEN YOU TRIED TO GET US TO JOIN YOU.
THE SEMINOA WILL NEVER BE YOUR ALLIES!

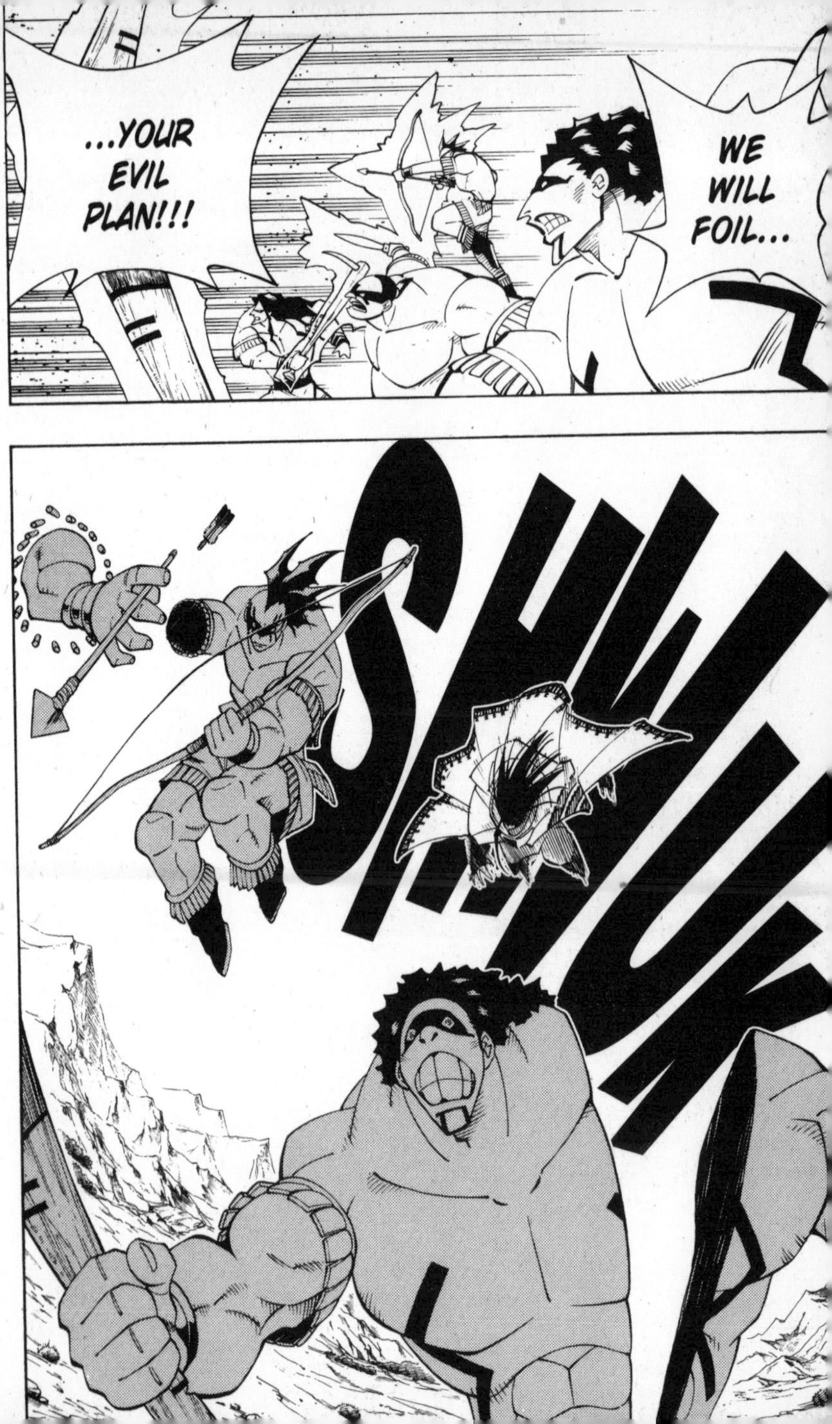
WE WILL FOIL...
...YOUR EVIL PLAN!!!

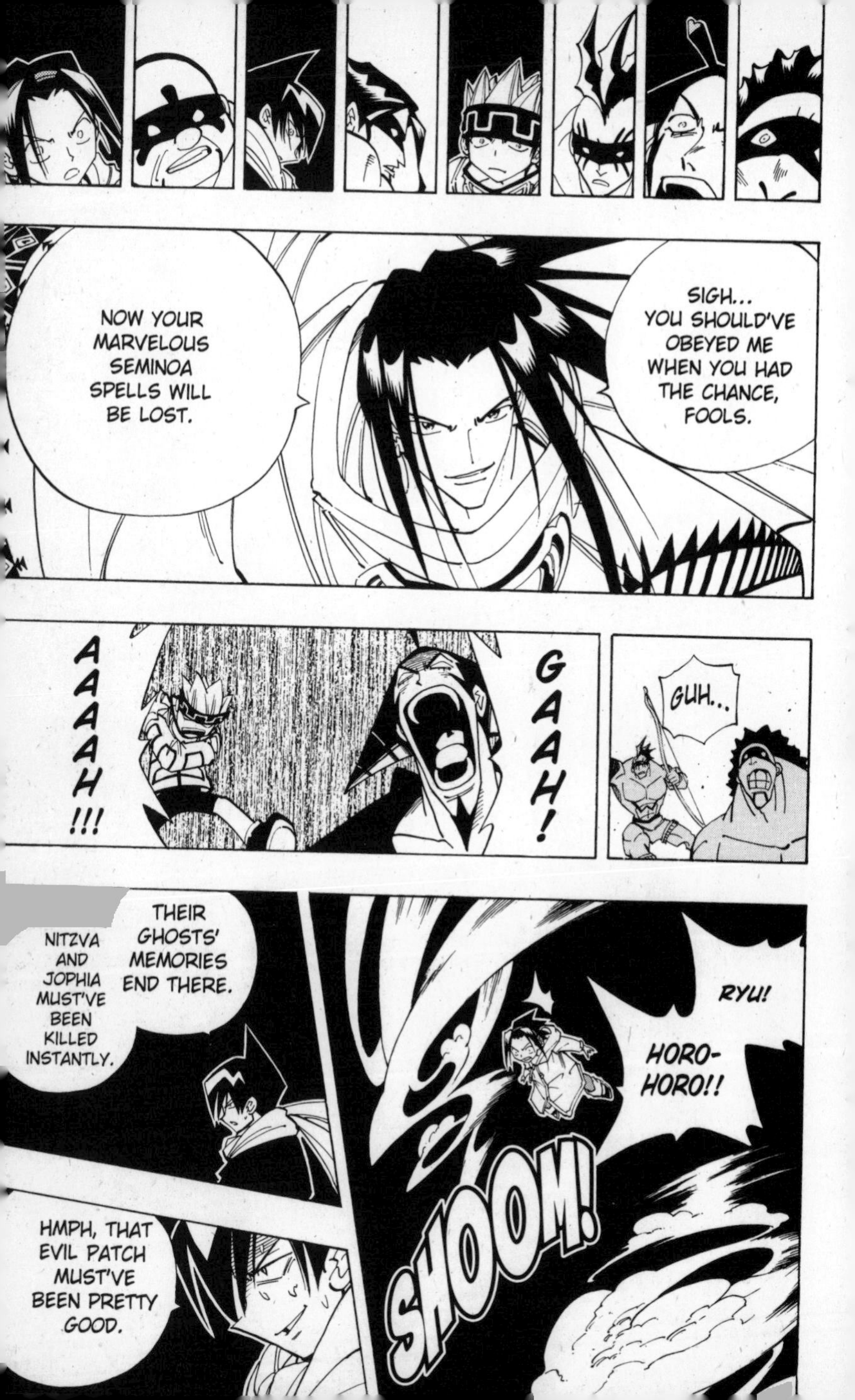
SIGH... YOU SHOULD'VE OBEYED ME WHEN YOU HAD THE CHANCE, FOOLS.
NOW YOUR MARVELOUS SEMINOA SPELLS WILL BE LOST.
GUH...
GAAAH!
AAAAAH!!!
RYU!
HORO-HORO!!
SHOOM!
THEIR GHOSTS' MEMORIES END THERE.
NITZVA AND JOPHIA MUST'VE BEEN KILLED INSTANTLY.
HMPH, THAT EVIL PATCH MUST'VE BEEN PRETTY GOOD.

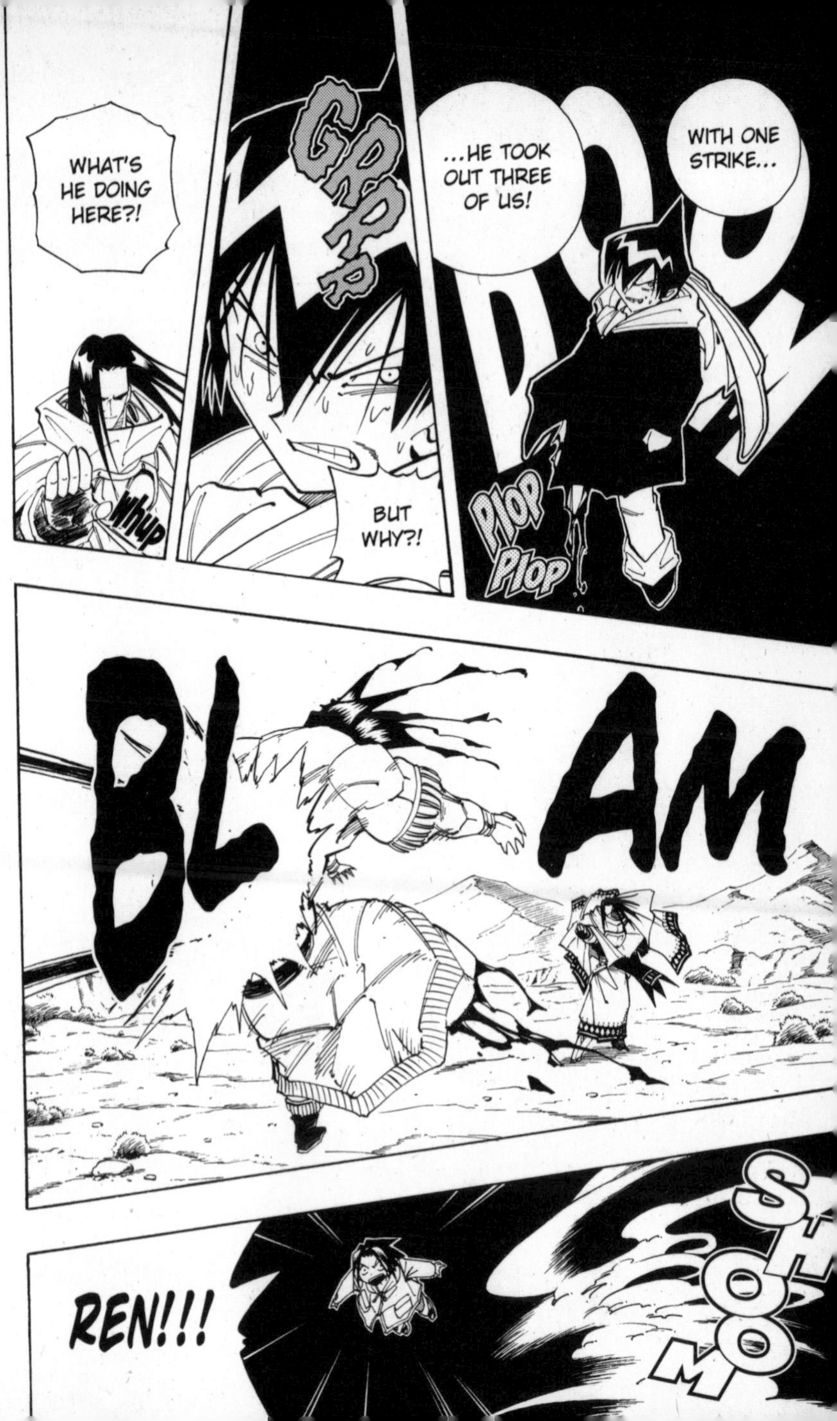
WITH ONE STRIKE...
...HE TOOK OUT THREE OF US!
DOOM
PLOP PLOP
GRRR
BUT WHY?!
WHAT'S HE DOING HERE?!
whup
BLAM
SHOOM
REN!!!

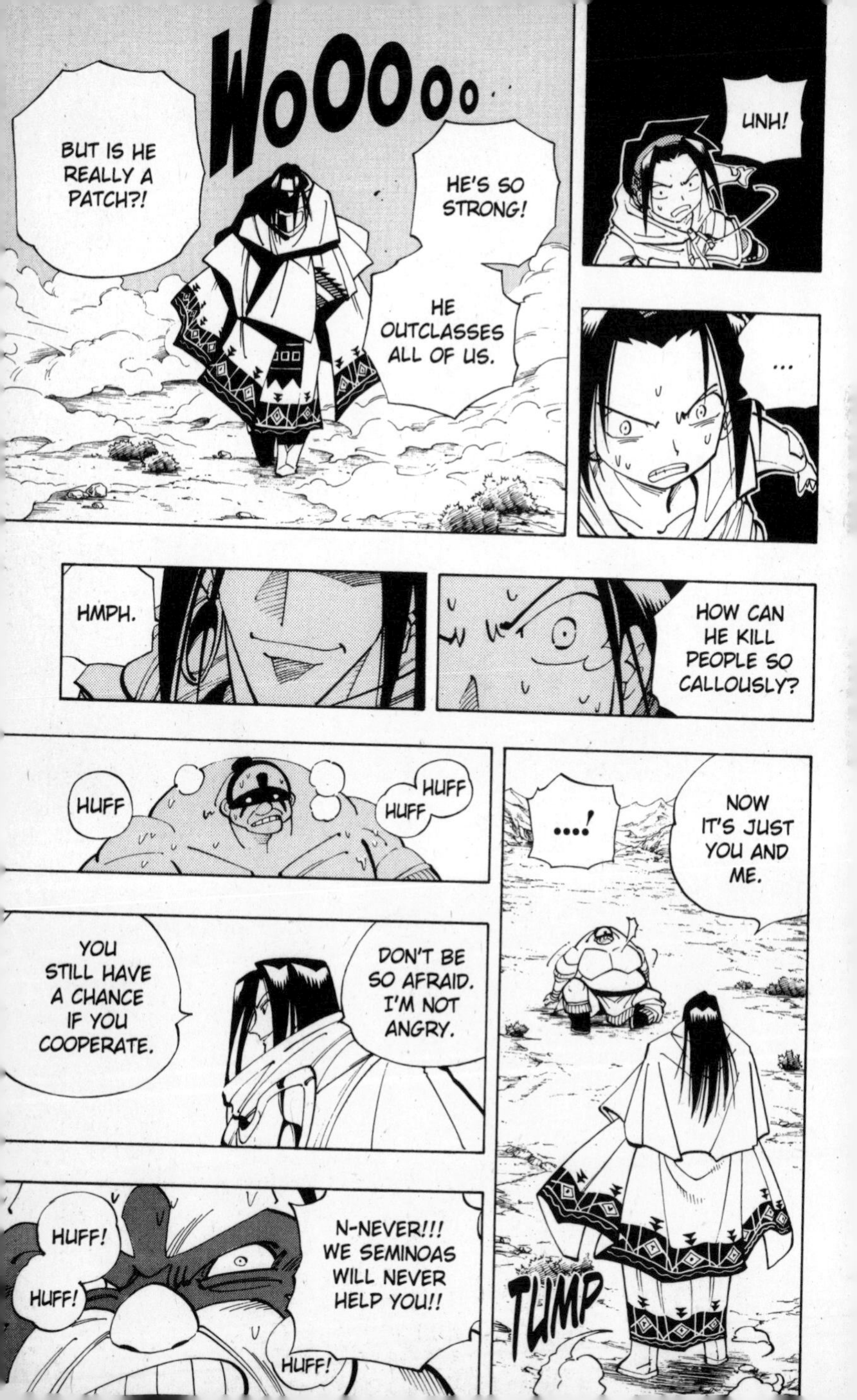
UNH!
...
WoOOOoo...
HE'S SO STRONG!
HE OUTCLASSES ALL OF US.
BUT IS HE REALLY A PATCH?!
HOW CAN HE KILL PEOPLE SO CALLOUSLY?
HMPH.
NOW IT'S JUST YOU AND ME.
....!
TUMP
HUFF HUFF
HUFF
DON'T BE SO AFRAID. I'M NOT ANGRY.
YOU STILL HAVE A CHANCE IF YOU COOPERATE.
N-NEVER!!! WE SEMINOAS WILL NEVER HELP YOU!!
HUFF!
HUFF!
HUFF!

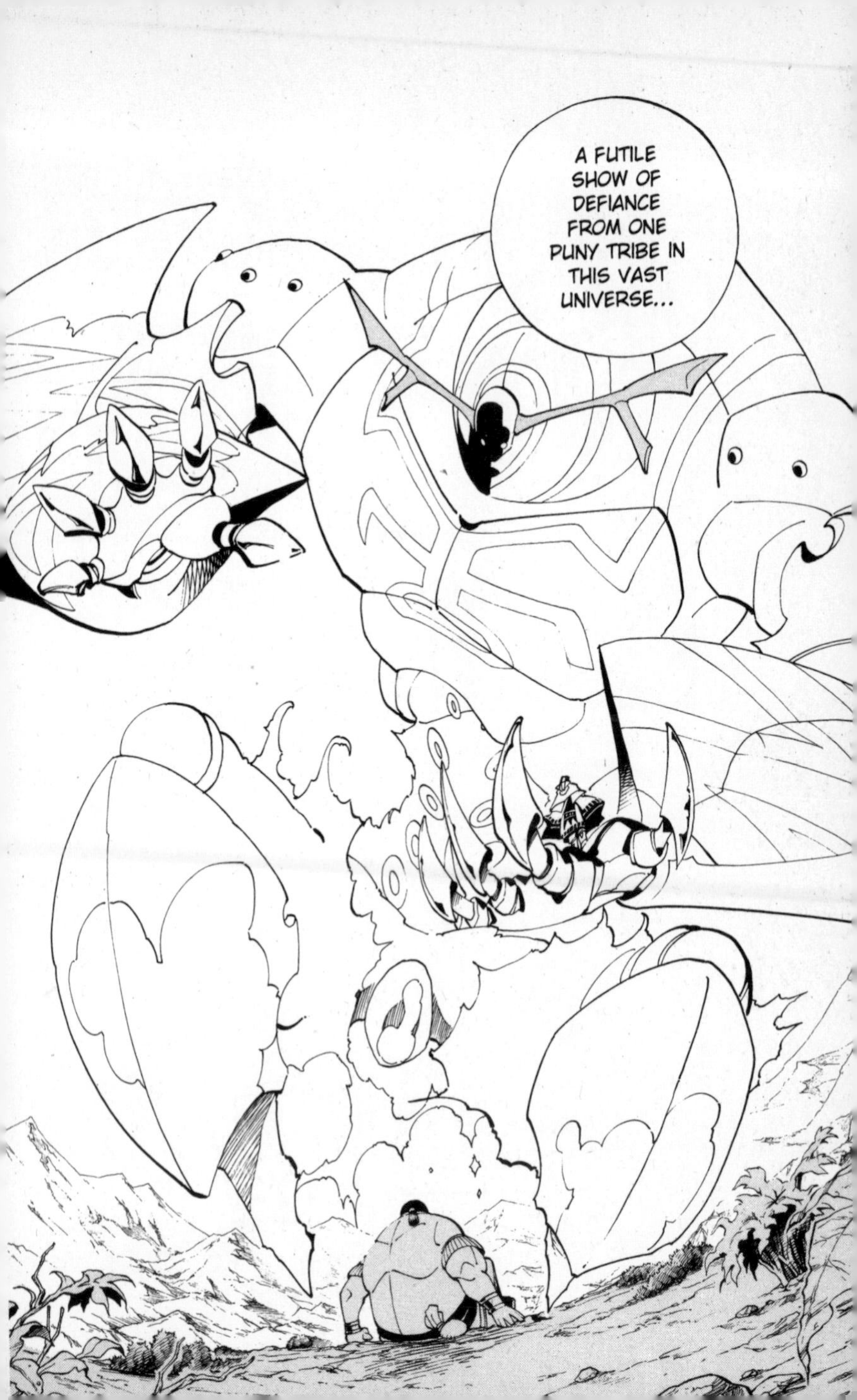
A FUTILE SHOW OF DEFIANCE FROM ONE PUNY TRIBE IN THIS VAST UNIVERSE...

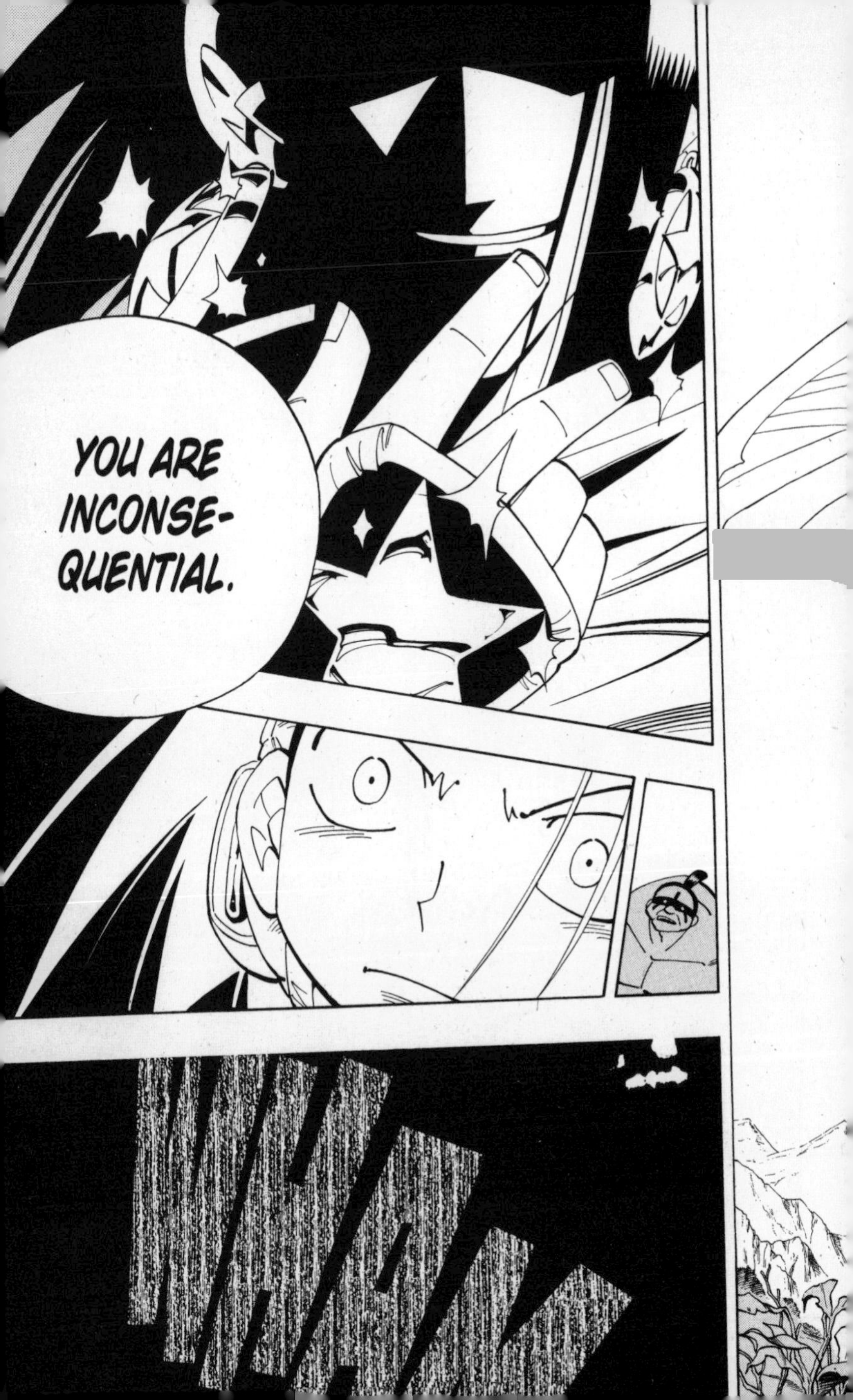
YOU ARE INCONSE-QUENTIAL.

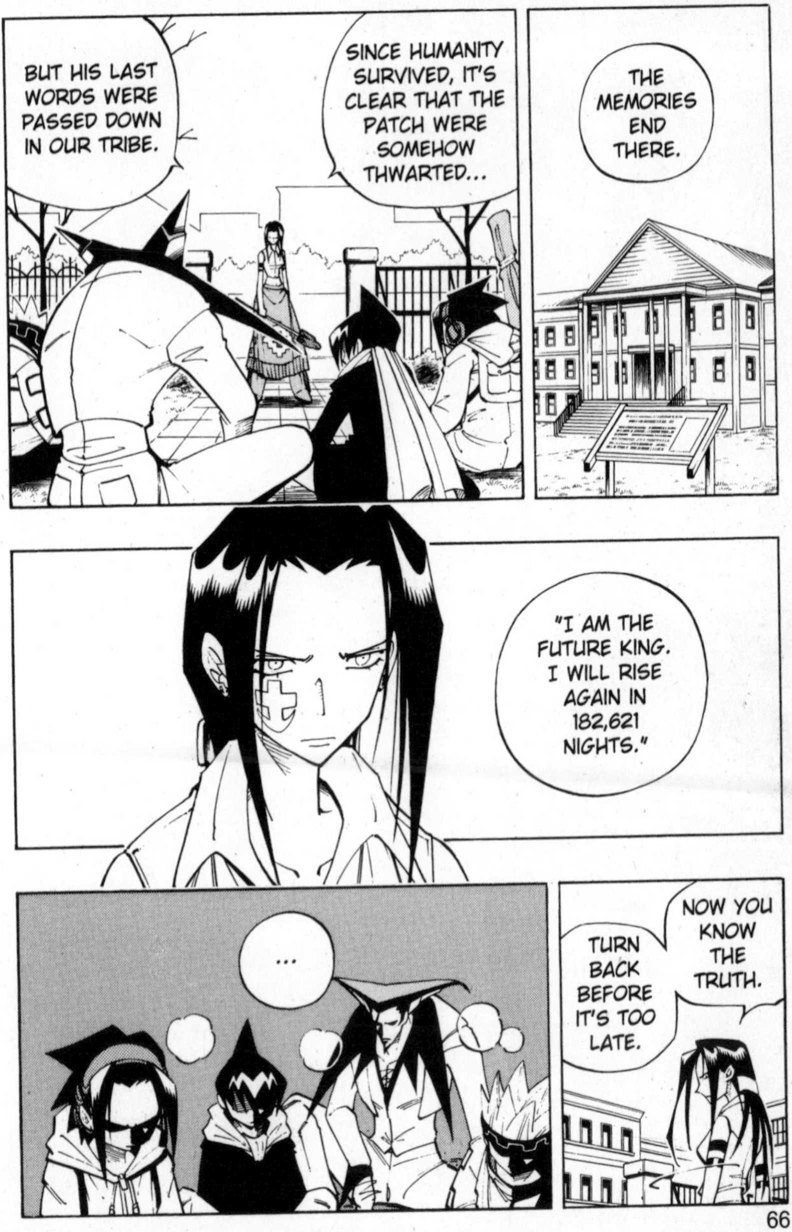
THE MEMORIES END THERE.
SINCE HUMANITY SURVIVED, IT'S CLEAR THAT THE PATCH WERE SOMEHOW THWARTED...
BUT HIS LAST WORDS WERE PASSED DOWN IN OUR TRIBE.
"I AM THE FUTURE KING. I WILL RISE AGAIN IN 182,621 NIGHTS."
NOW YOU KNOW THE TRUTH.
TURN BACK BEFORE IT'S TOO LATE.
...

READ THIS WAY

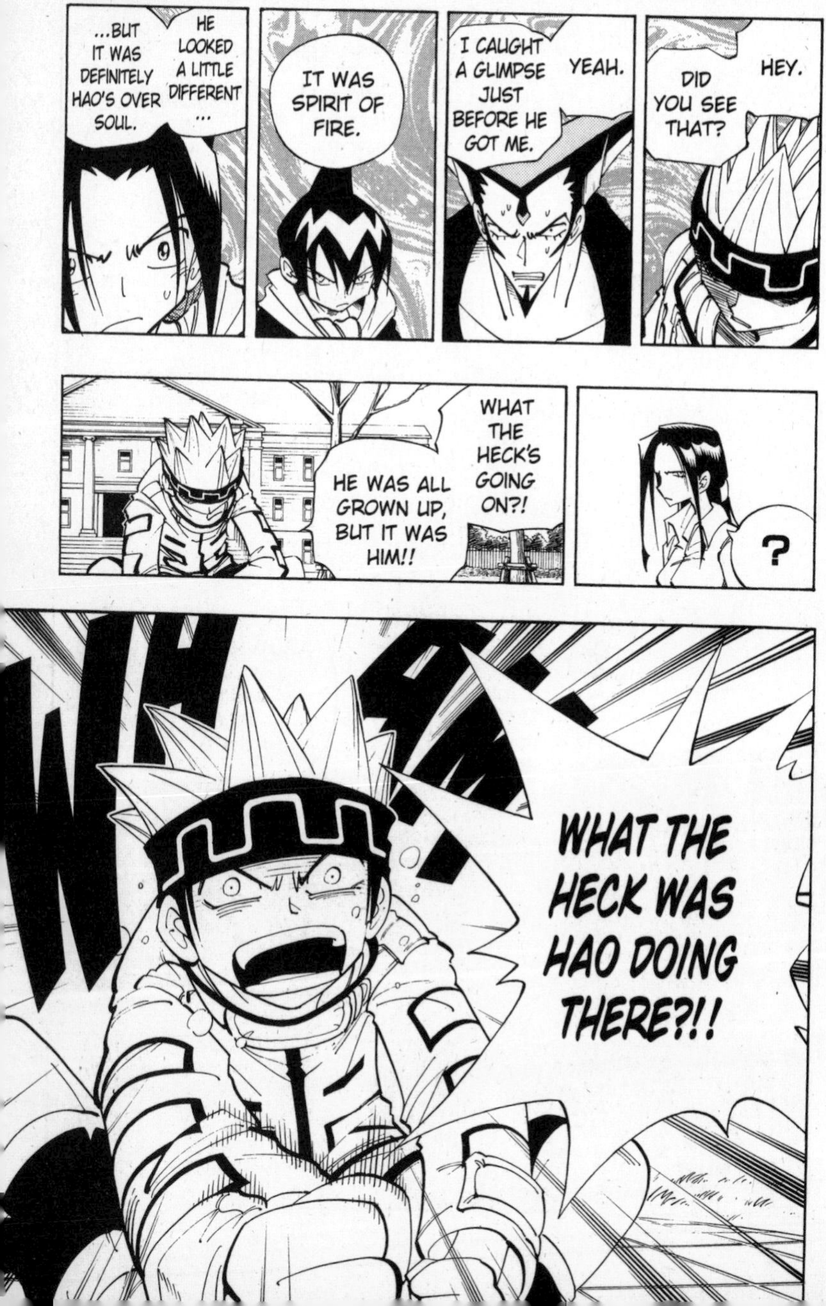
HEY.
DID YOU SEE THAT?
YEAH.
I CAUGHT A GLIMPSE JUST BEFORE HE GOT ME.
IT WAS SPIRIT OF FIRE.
HE LOOKED A LITTLE DIFFERENT ...
...BUT IT WAS DEFINITELY HAO'S OVER SOUL.
?
WHAT THE HECK'S GOING ON?!
HE WAS ALL GROWN UP, BUT IT WAS HIM!!
WHAM
WHAT THE HECK WAS HAO DOING THERE?!!

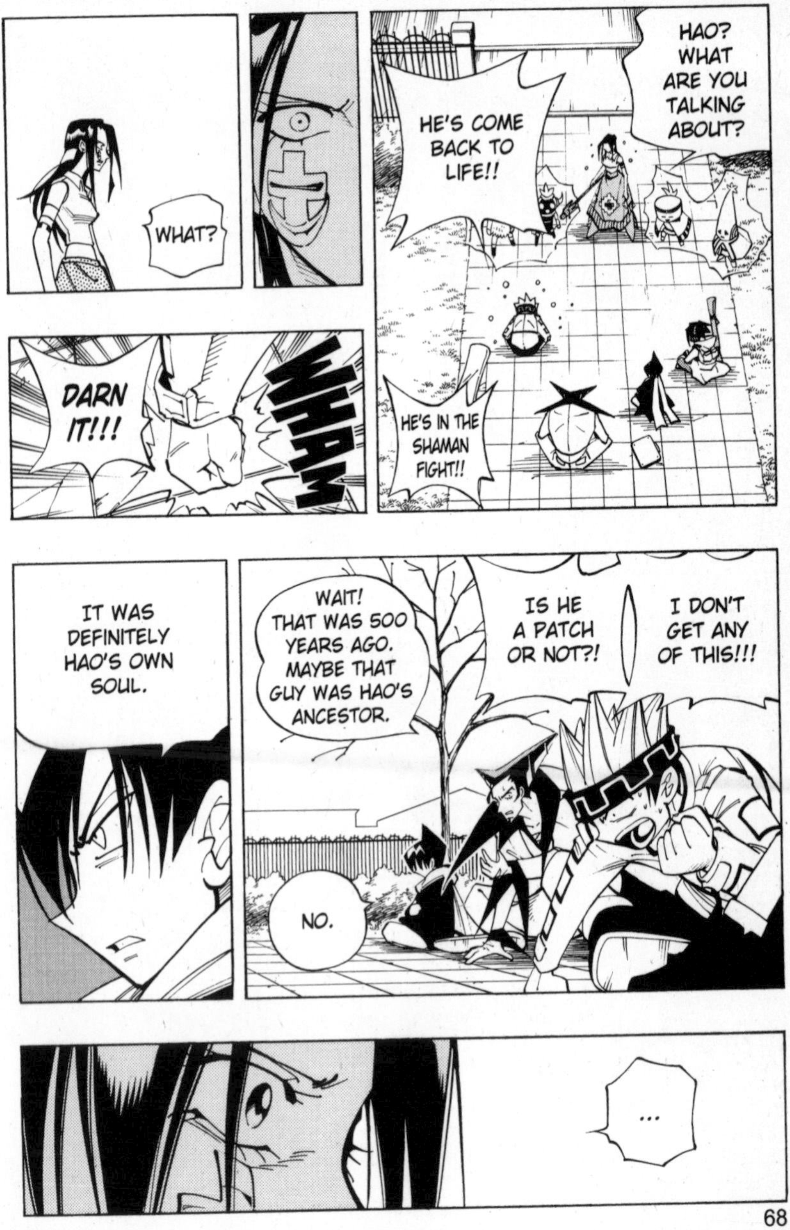
HAO? WHAT ARE YOU TALKING ABOUT?
HE'S COME BACK TO LIFE!!
HE'S IN THE SHAMAN FIGHT!!
WHAT?
WHAM
DARN IT!!!
I DON'T GET ANY OF THIS!!!
IS HE A PATCH OR NOT?!
WAIT! THAT WAS 500 YEARS AGO. MAYBE THAT GUY WAS HAO'S ANCESTOR.
NO.
IT WAS DEFINITELY HAO'S OWN SOUL.
...

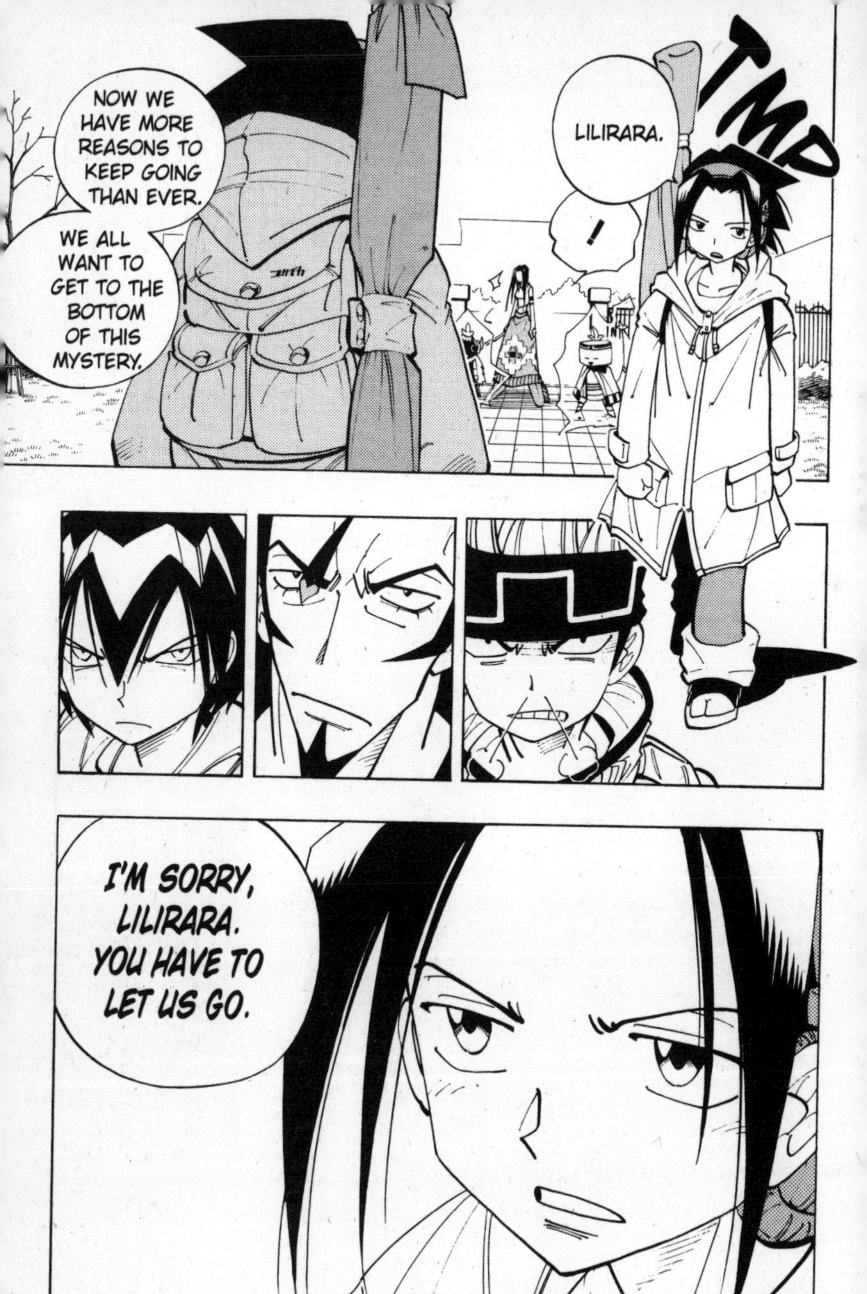
TMP
LILIRARA.
!
NOW WE HAVE MORE REASONS TO KEEP GOING THAN EVER.
WE ALL WANT TO GET TO THE BOTTOM OF THIS MYSTERY.
I'M SORRY, LILIRARA. YOU HAVE TO LET US GO.

SHAMAN KING CHARACTER FILE No.43

THE KANACHI DOLLS & THE SEMINOA WARRIORS

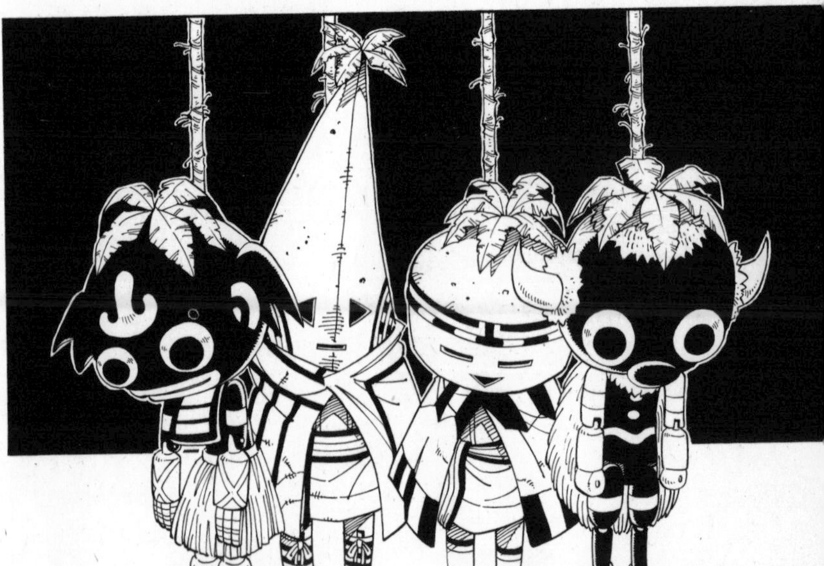

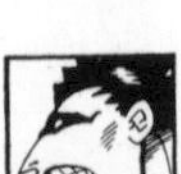

NITZVA

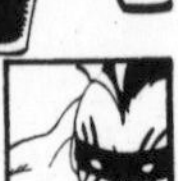

JOPHIA

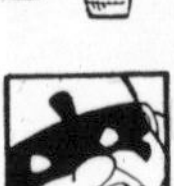

DREISA

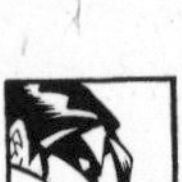

IAN

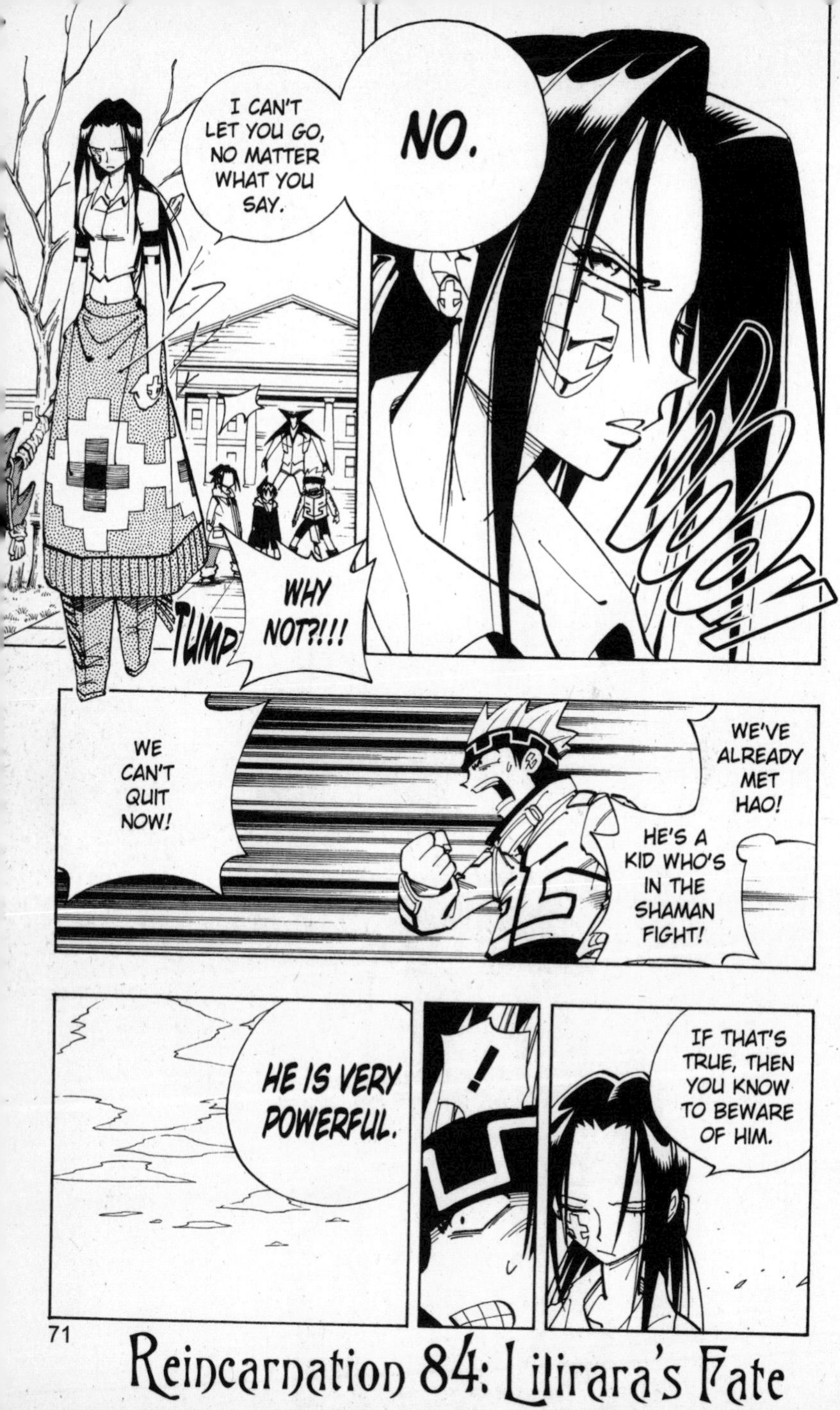
NO.
I CAN'T LET YOU GO, NO MATTER WHAT YOU SAY.
WHY NOT?!!!
TUMP
WE'VE ALREADY MET HAO!
HE'S A KID WHO'S IN THE SHAMAN FIGHT!
WE CAN'T QUIT NOW!
IF THAT'S TRUE, THEN YOU KNOW TO BEWARE OF HIM.
!
HE IS VERY POWERFUL.

Reincarnation 84: Lilirara's Fate

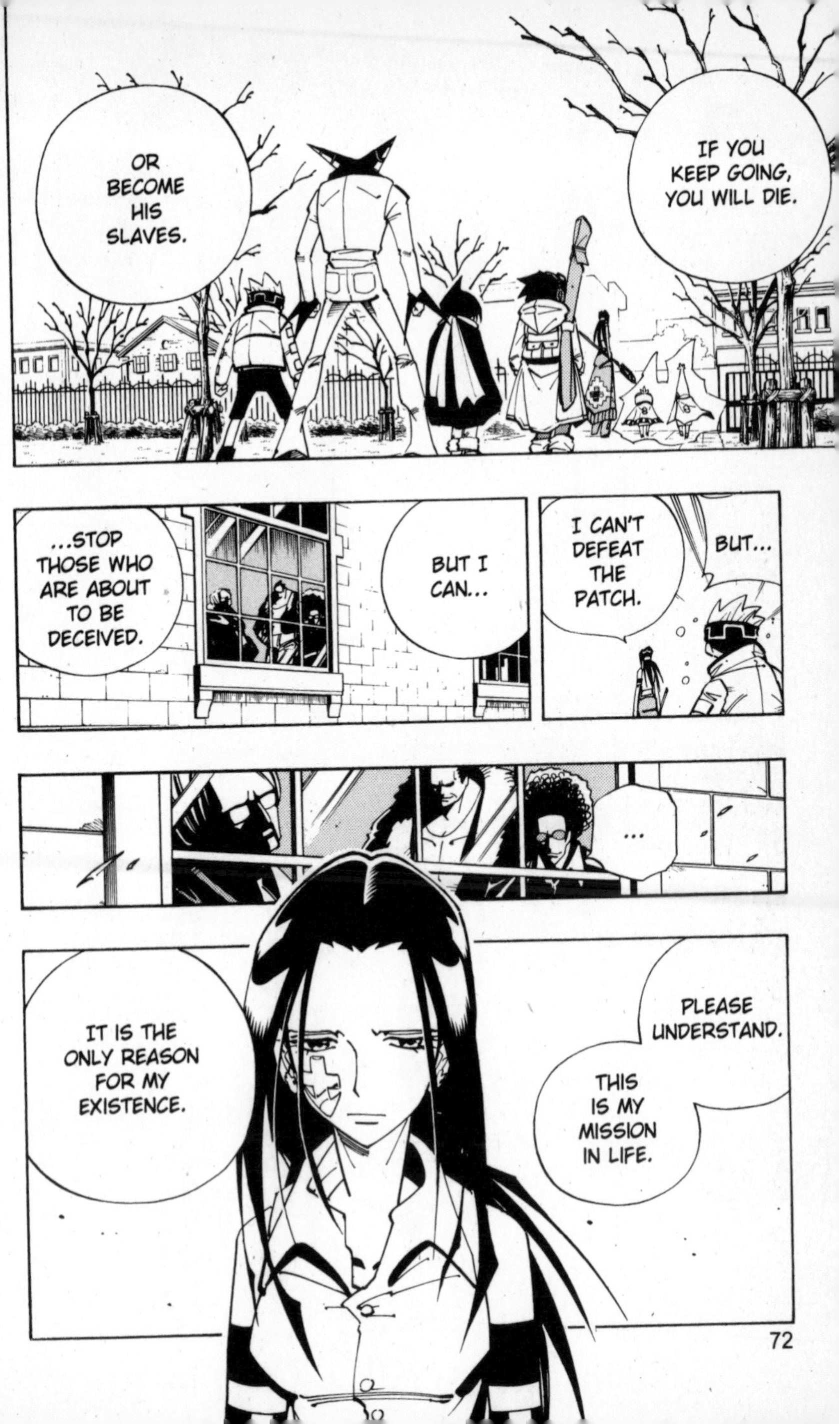
IF YOU KEEP GOING, YOU WILL DIE.
OR BECOME HIS SLAVES.
BUT...
I CAN'T DEFEAT THE PATCH.
BUT I CAN...
...STOP THOSE WHO ARE ABOUT TO BE DECEIVED.
...
PLEASE UNDERSTAND.
THIS IS MY MISSION IN LIFE.
IT IS THE ONLY REASON FOR MY EXISTENCE.

Reincarnation 84: Lilirara's Fate

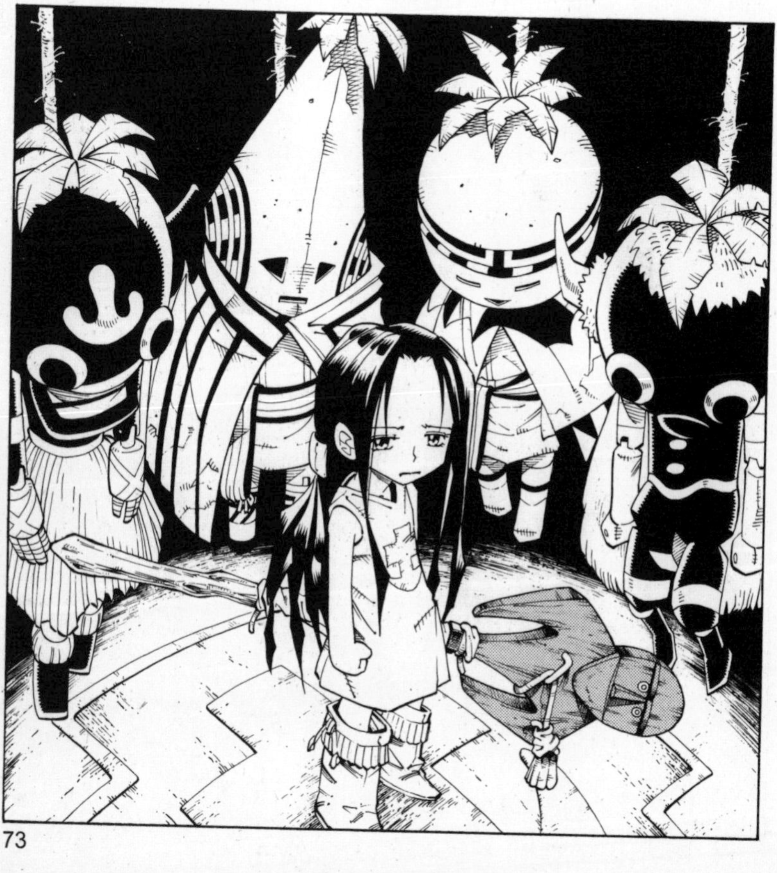

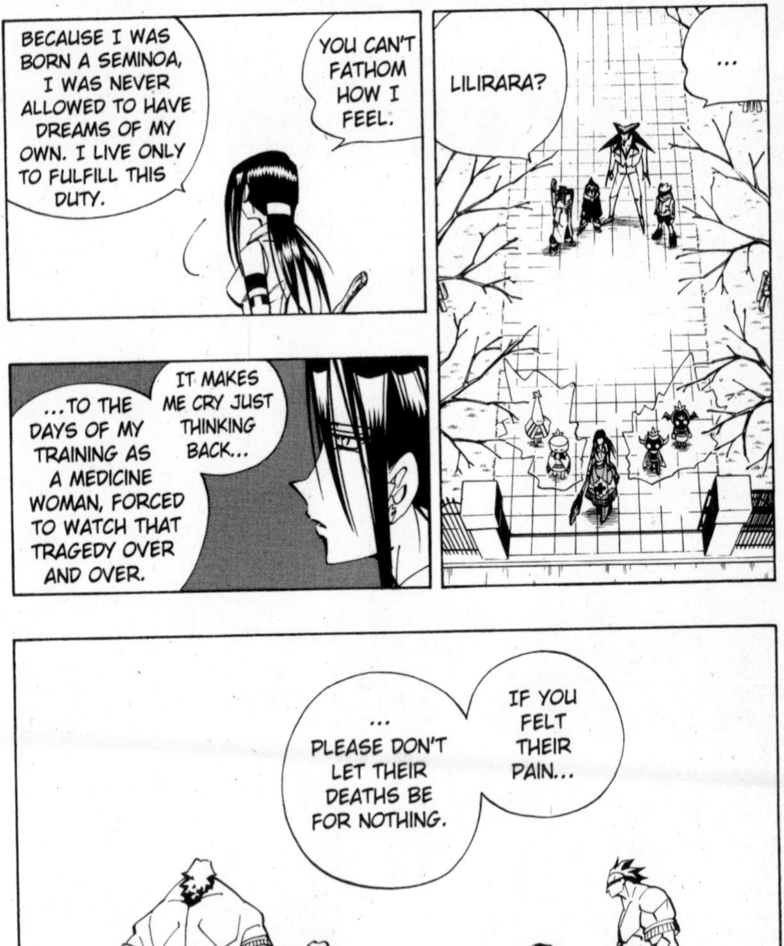
...
LILIRARA?
YOU CAN'T FATHOM HOW I FEEL.
BECAUSE I WAS BORN A SEMINOA, I WAS NEVER ALLOWED TO HAVE DREAMS OF MY OWN. I LIVE ONLY TO FULFILL THIS DUTY.
IT MAKES ME CRY JUST THINKING BACK...
...TO THE DAYS OF MY TRAINING AS A MEDICINE WOMAN, FORCED TO WATCH THAT TRAGEDY OVER AND OVER.
IF YOU FELT THEIR PAIN...
... PLEASE DON'T LET THEIR DEATHS BE FOR NOTHING.

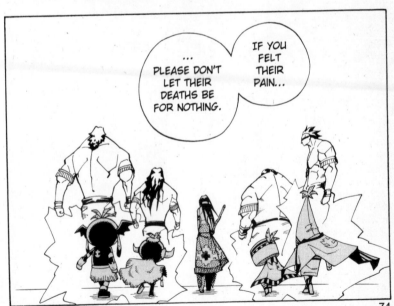

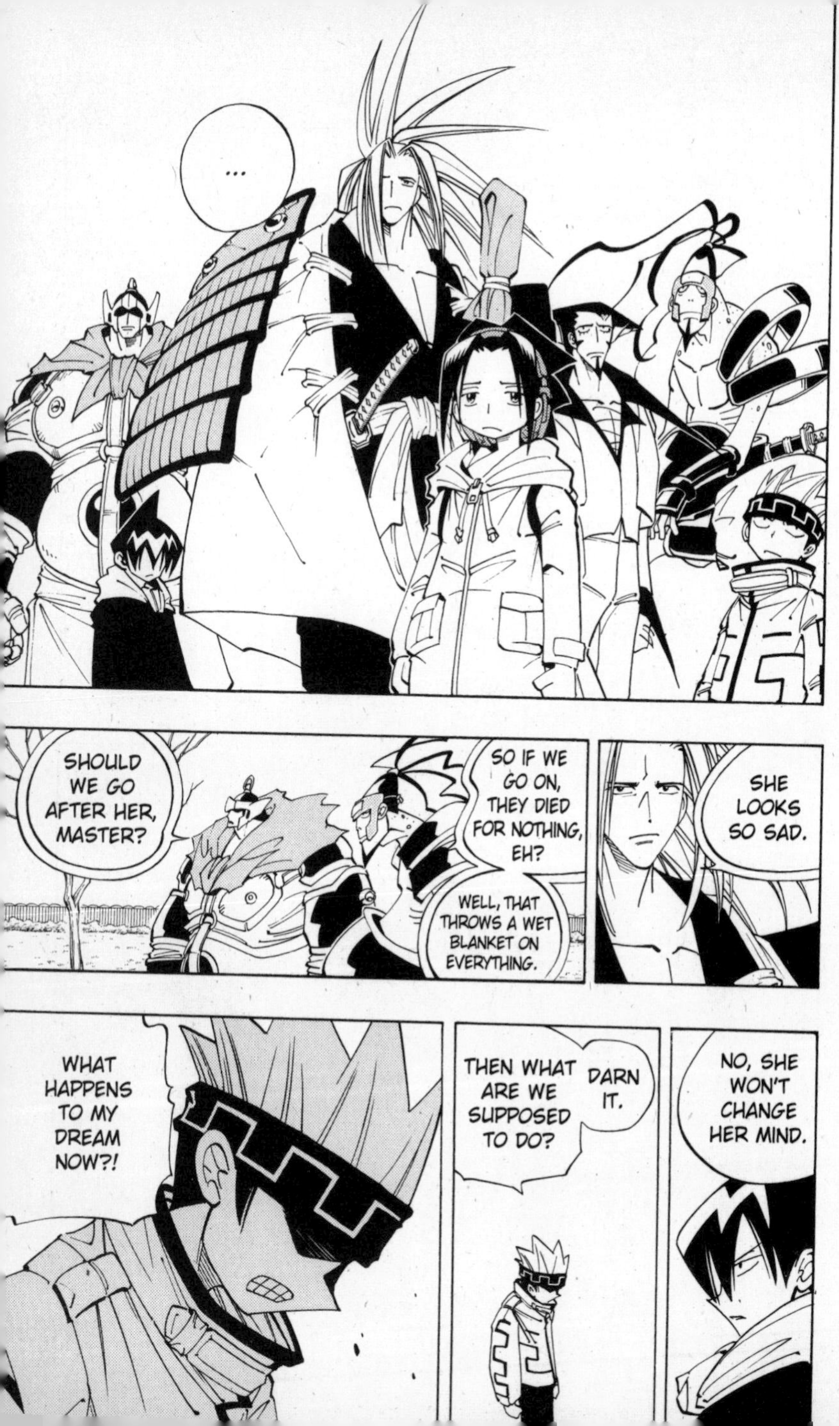
...
SHE LOOKS SO SAD.
SO IF WE GO ON, THEY DIED FOR NOTHING, EH?
WELL, THAT THROWS A WET BLANKET ON EVERYTHING.
SHOULD WE GO AFTER HER, MASTER?
NO, SHE WON'T CHANGE HER MIND.
DARN IT.
THEN WHAT ARE WE SUPPOSED TO DO?
WHAT HAPPENS TO MY DREAM NOW?!

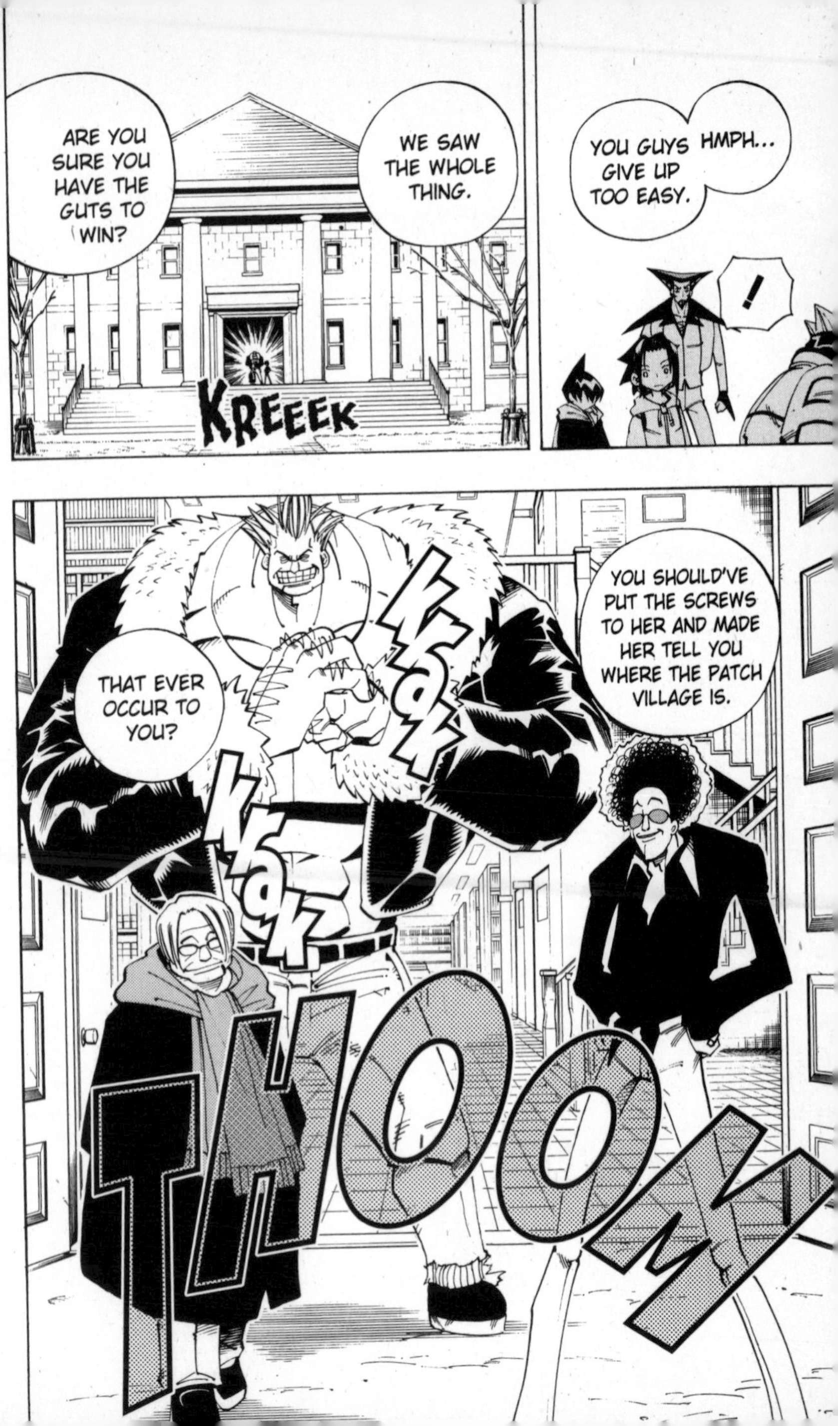
HMPH...
YOU GUYS GIVE UP TOO EASY.
!
WE SAW THE WHOLE THING.
ARE YOU SURE YOU HAVE THE GUTS TO WIN?
KREEEK
YOU SHOULD'VE PUT THE SCREWS TO HER AND MADE HER TELL YOU WHERE THE PATCH VILLAGE IS.
KRAK
KRAK
THAT EVER OCCUR TO YOU?
THOOM

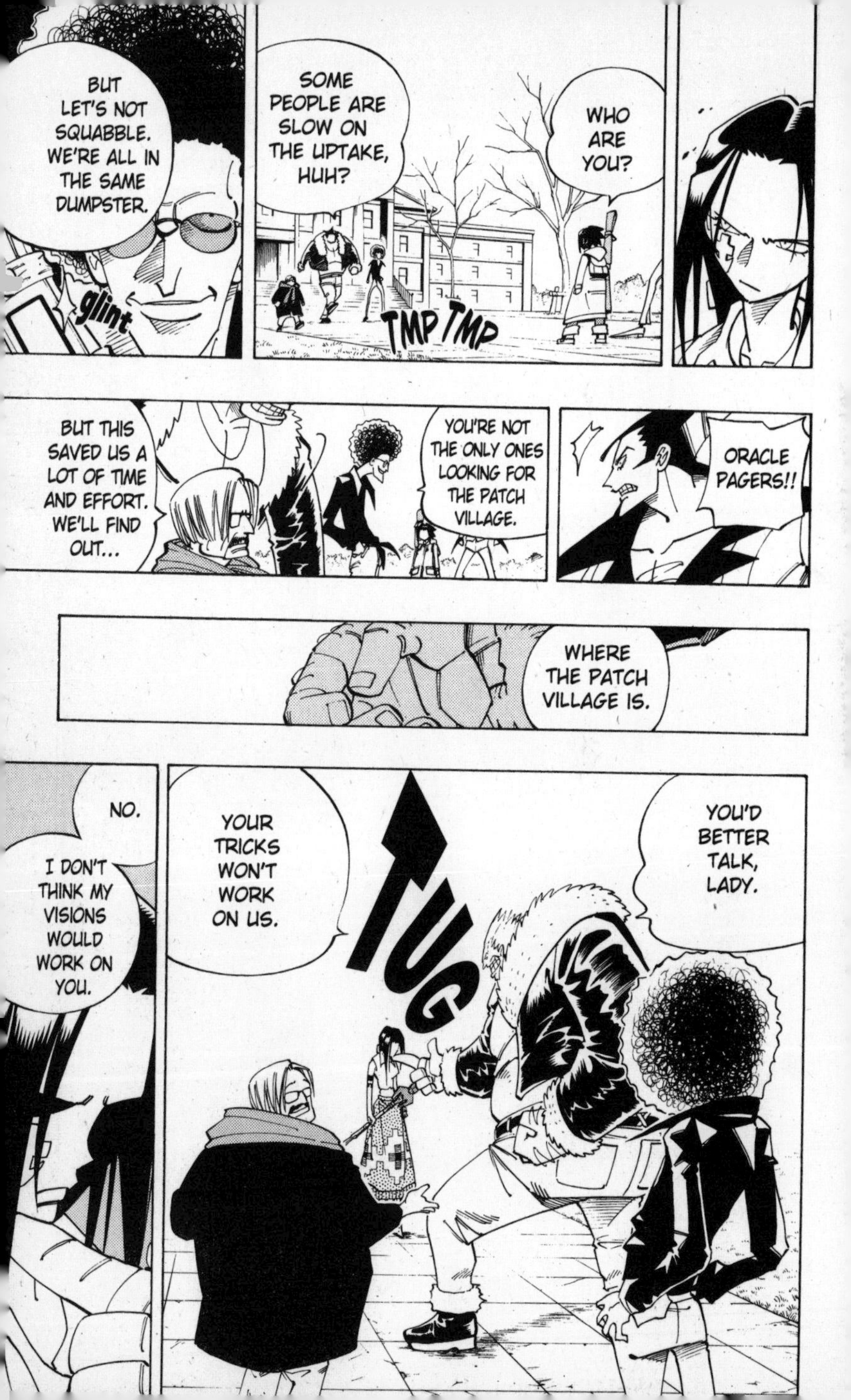
WHO ARE YOU?
SOME PEOPLE ARE SLOW ON THE UPTAKE, HUH?
TMP TMP
BUT LET'S NOT SQUABBLE. WE'RE ALL IN THE SAME DUMPSTER.
glint
ORACLE PAGERS!!
YOU'RE NOT THE ONLY ONES LOOKING FOR THE PATCH VILLAGE.
BUT THIS SAVED US A LOT OF TIME AND EFFORT. WE'LL FIND OUT...
WHERE THE PATCH VILLAGE IS.
YOU'D BETTER TALK, LADY.
TUG
YOUR TRICKS WON'T WORK ON US.
NO.
I DON'T THINK MY VISIONS WOULD WORK ON YOU.

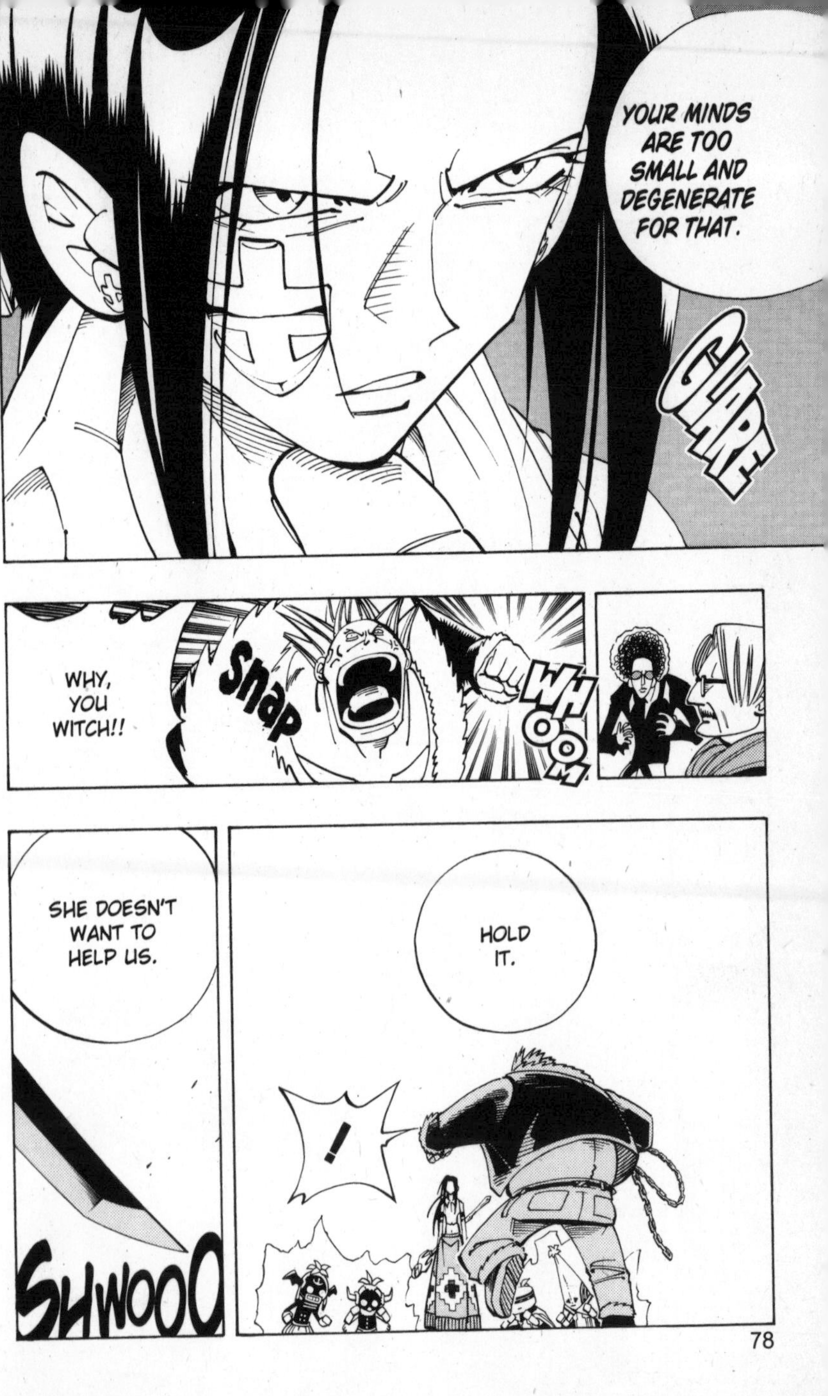

YOUR MINDS ARE TOO SMALL AND DEGENERATE FOR THAT.
GLARE
WHOOM
Snap
WHY, YOU WITCH!!
HOLD IT.
!
SHE DOESN'T WANT TO HELP US.
SHWOOO

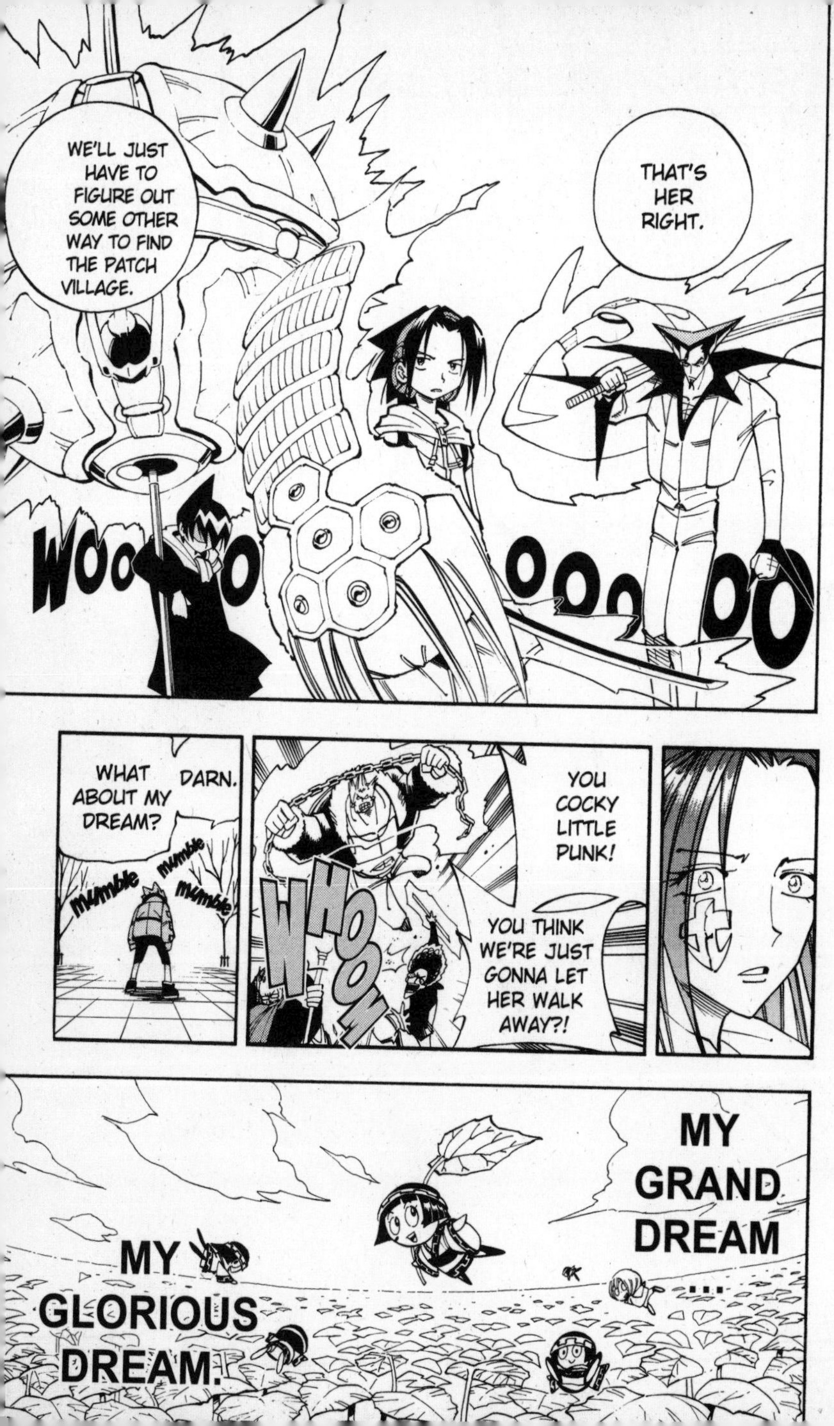
THAT'S HER RIGHT.
WE'LL JUST HAVE TO FIGURE OUT SOME OTHER WAY TO FIND THE PATCH VILLAGE.
WOOOOOOOOOO
YOU COCKY LITTLE PUNK!
YOU THINK WE'RE JUST GONNA LET HER WALK AWAY?!
WHOOOM
DARN.
WHAT ABOUT MY DREAM?
mumble mumble mumble
MY GRAND DREAM...
MY GLORIOUS DREAM.

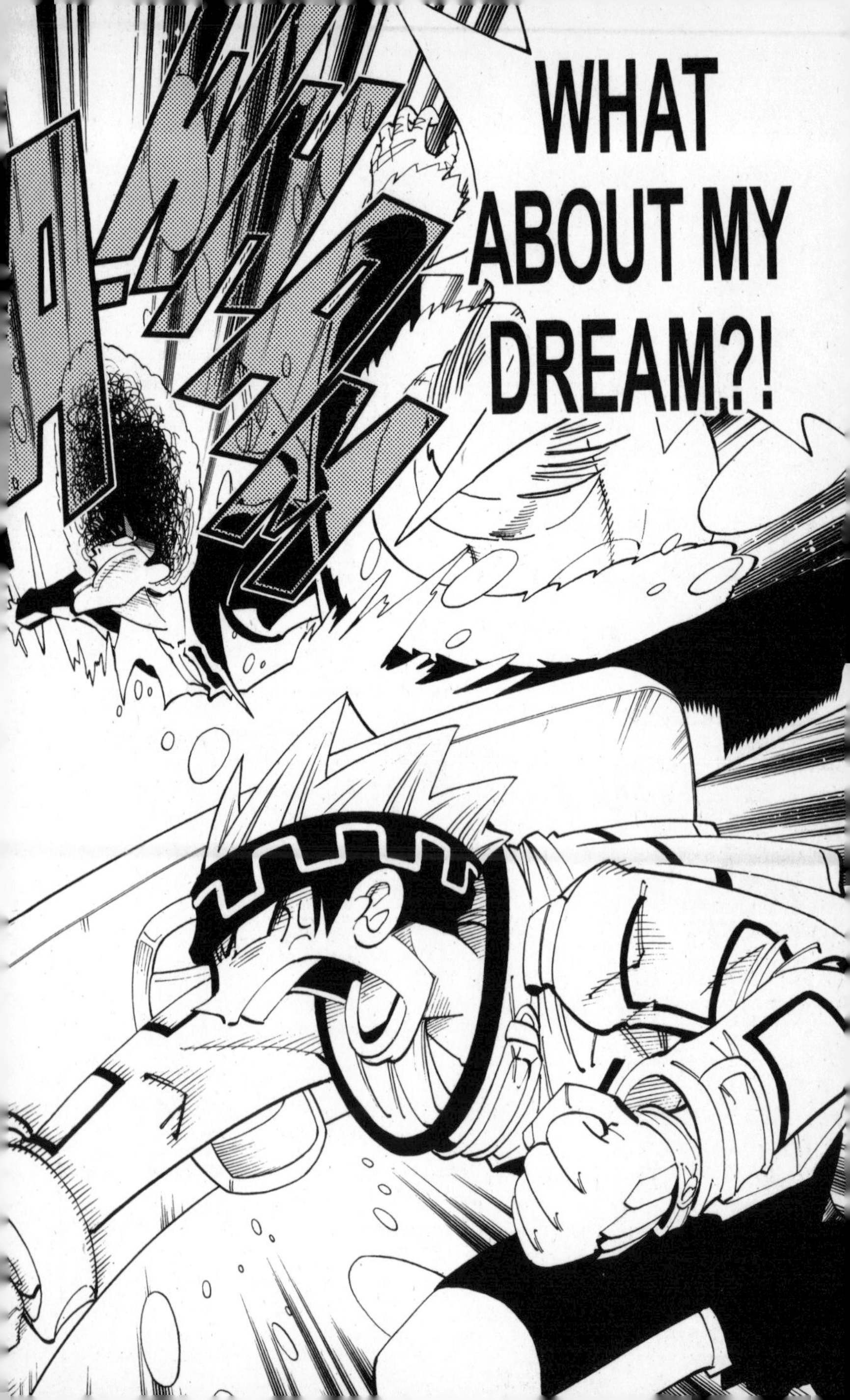
WHAT ABOUT MY DREAM?!

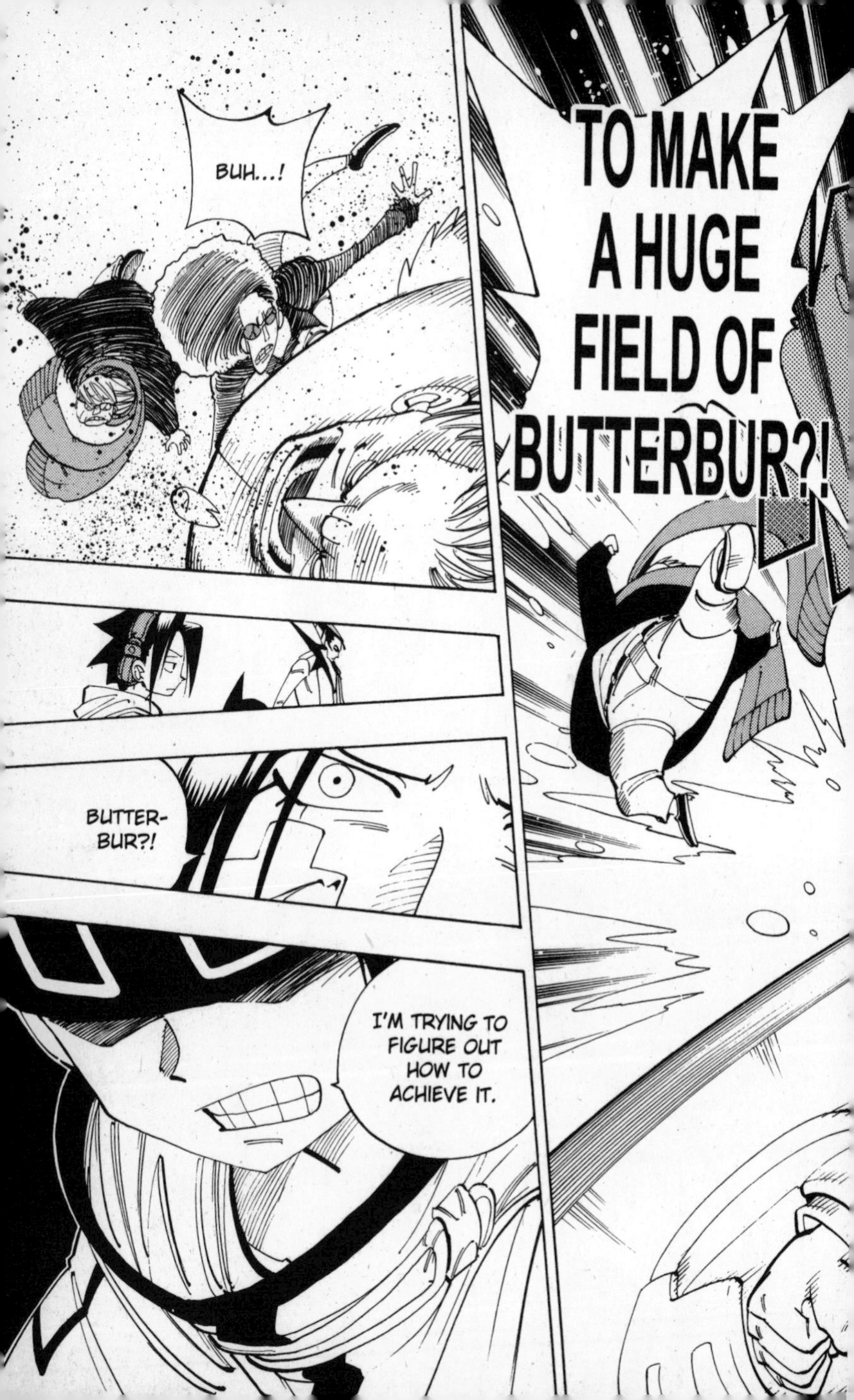
TO MAKE A HUGE FIELD OF BUTTERBUR?!
BUH...!
BUTTER-BUR?!
I'M TRYING TO FIGURE OUT HOW TO ACHIEVE IT.

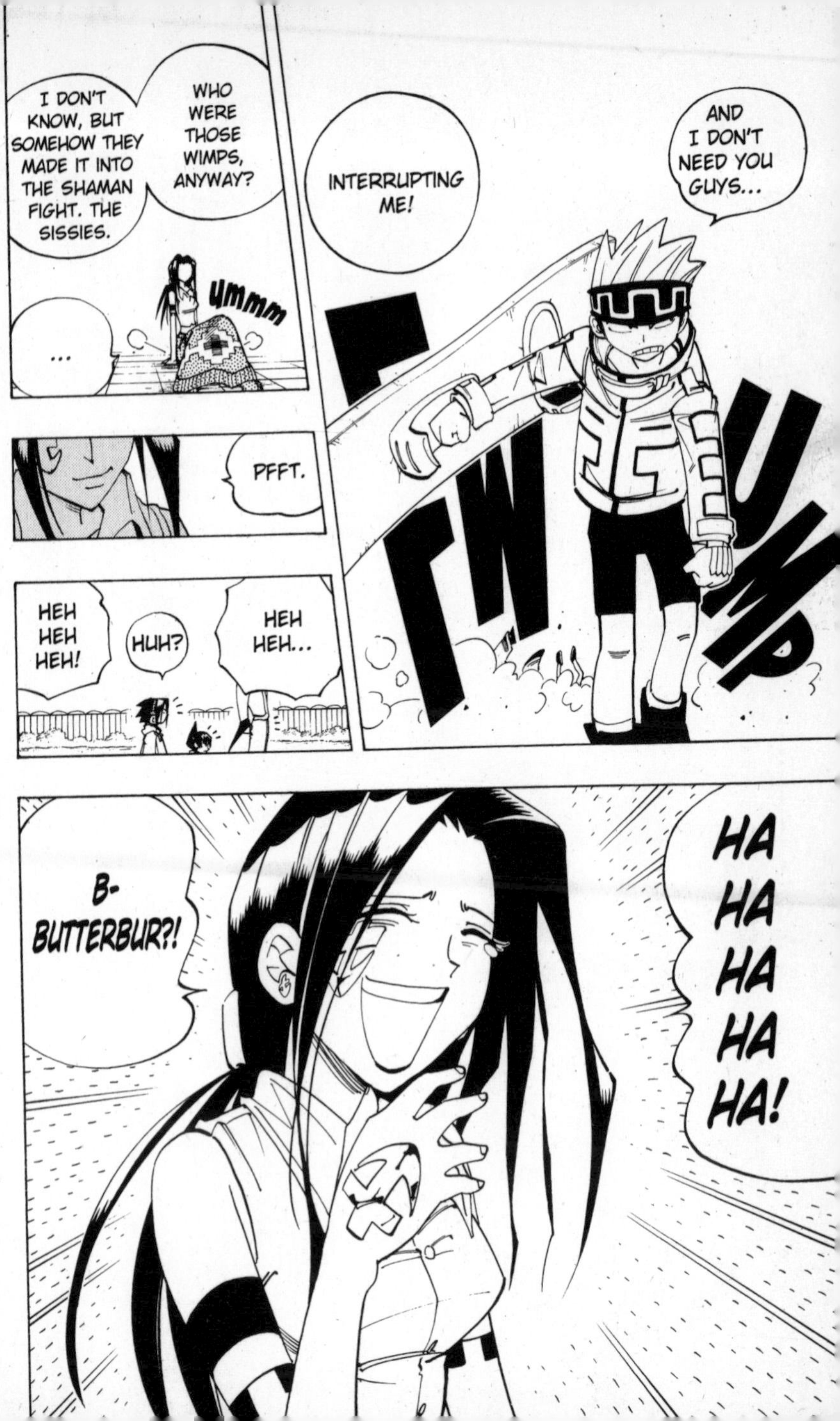
AND I DON'T NEED YOU GUYS...
INTERRUPTING ME!
FWUMP
WHO WERE THOSE WIMPS, ANYWAY?
I DON'T KNOW, BUT SOMEHOW THEY MADE IT INTO THE SHAMAN FIGHT. THE SISSIES.
UMMM
...
PFFT.
HEH HEH...
HUH?
HEH HEH HEH!
HA HA HA HA HA HA!
B- BUTTERBUR?!

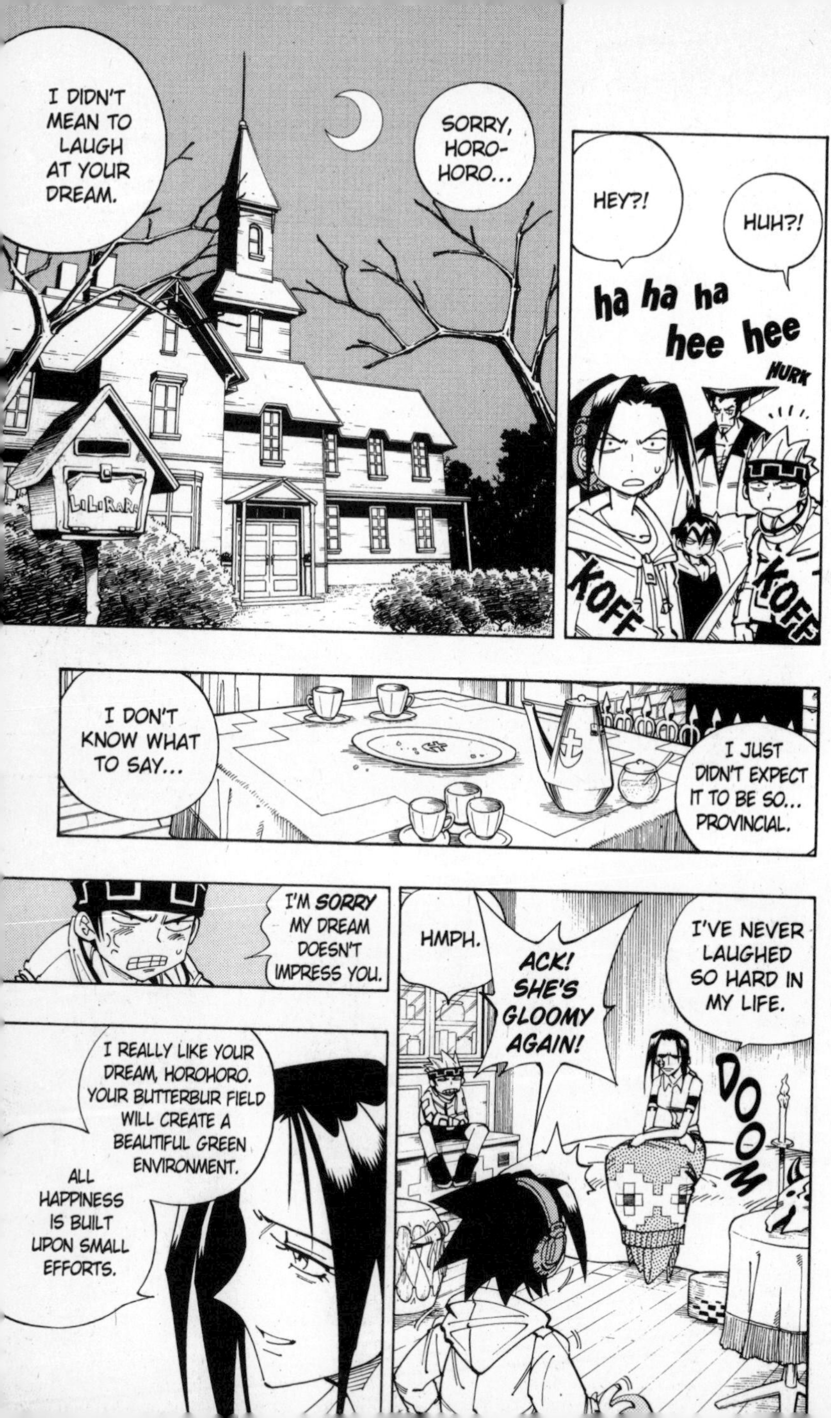
HUH?!
HEY?!
ha ha ha
hee hee
HURK
KOFF
KOFF
SORRY, HORO-HORO...
I DIDN'T MEAN TO LAUGH AT YOUR DREAM.
LILIRARA
I JUST DIDN'T EXPECT IT TO BE SO... PROVINCIAL.
I DON'T KNOW WHAT TO SAY...
I'VE NEVER LAUGHED SO HARD IN MY LIFE.
ACK! SHE'S GLOOMY AGAIN!
HMPH.
DOOOM
I'M SORRY MY DREAM DOESN'T IMPRESS YOU.
I REALLY LIKE YOUR DREAM, HOROHORO. YOUR BUTTERBUR FIELD WILL CREATE A BEAUTIFUL GREEN ENVIRONMENT.
ALL HAPPINESS IS BUILT UPON SMALL EFFORTS.

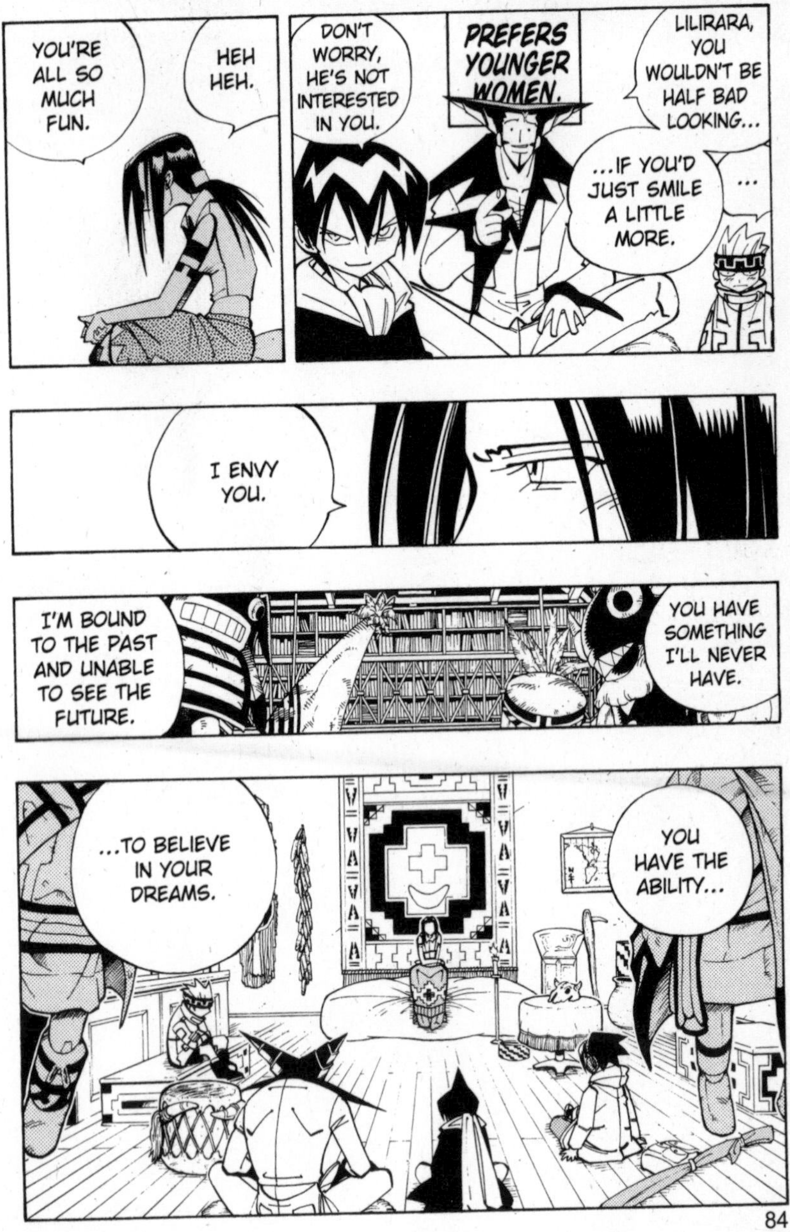
LILIRARA, YOU WOULDN'T BE HALF BAD LOOKING...
...
...IF YOU'D JUST SMILE A LITTLE MORE.
PREFERS YOUNGER WOMEN.
DON'T WORRY, HE'S NOT INTERESTED IN YOU.
HEH HEH.
YOU'RE ALL SO MUCH FUN.
I ENVY YOU.
YOU HAVE SOMETHING I'LL NEVER HAVE.
I'M BOUND TO THE PAST AND UNABLE TO SEE THE FUTURE.
YOU HAVE THE ABILITY...
...TO BELIEVE IN YOUR DREAMS.

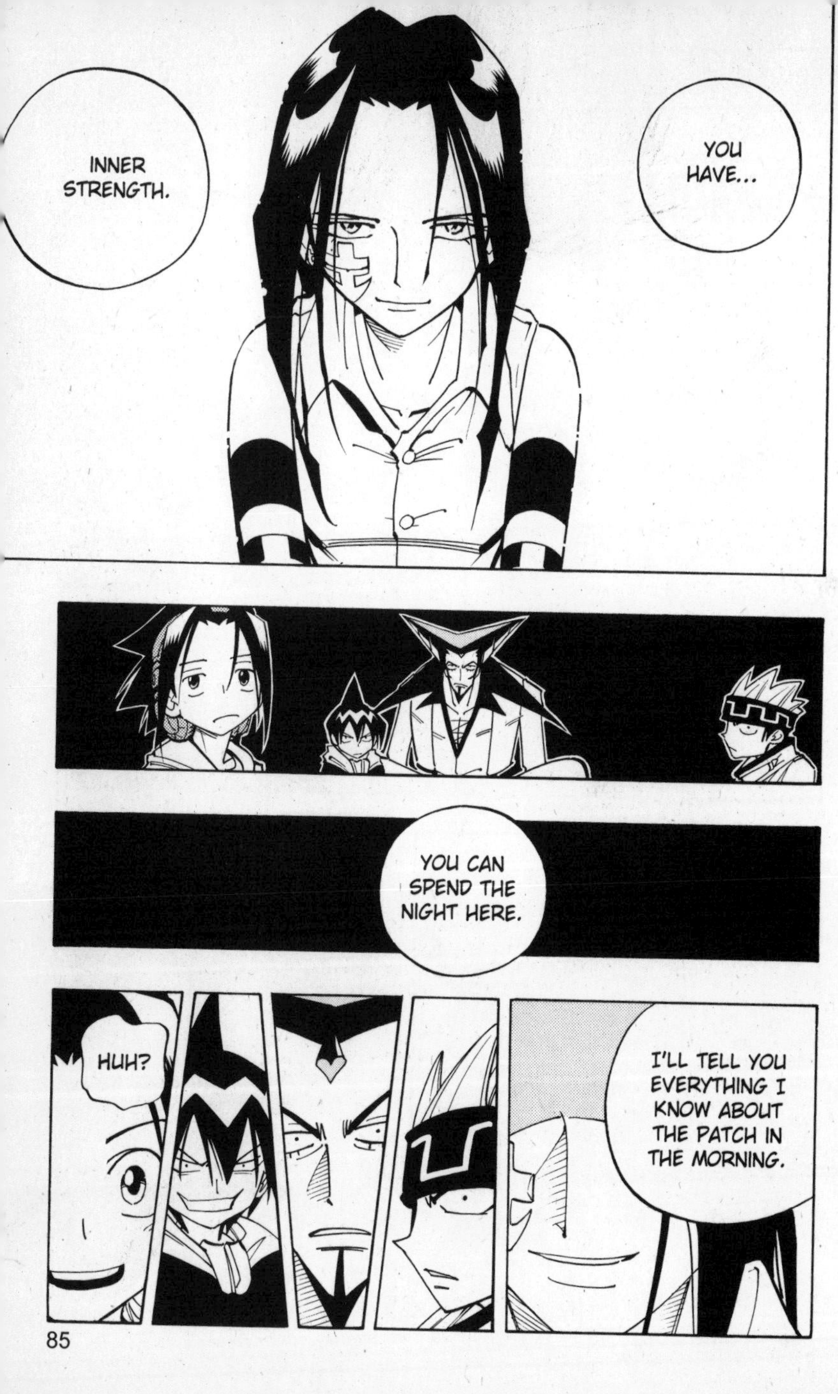
YOU HAVE...
INNER STRENGTH.
YOU CAN SPEND THE NIGHT HERE.
I'LL TELL YOU EVERYTHING I KNOW ABOUT THE PATCH IN THE MORNING.
HUH?

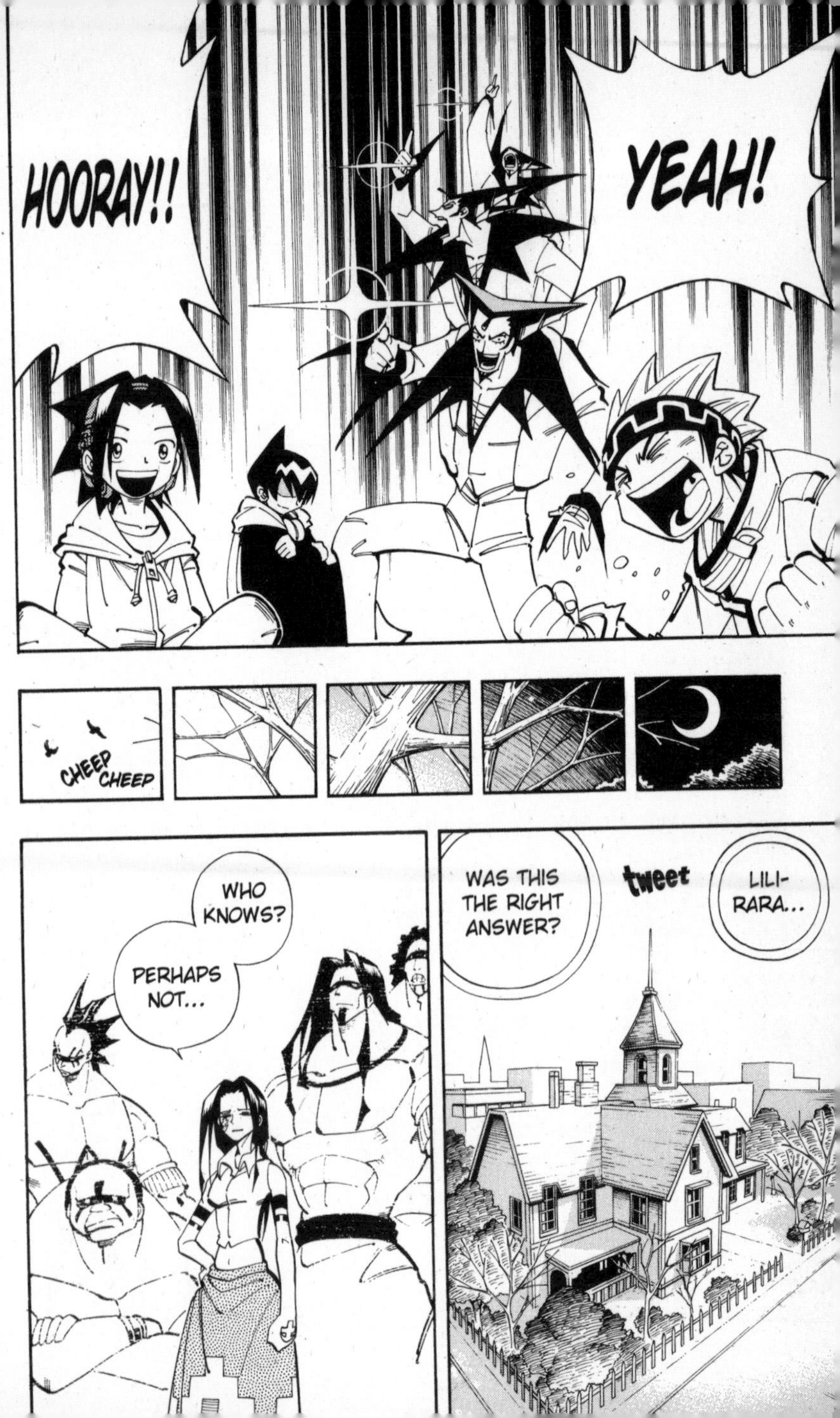
YEAH!
HOORAY!!
CHEEP CHEEP
LILI-RARA...
tweet
WAS THIS THE RIGHT ANSWER?
WHO KNOWS?
PERHAPS NOT...

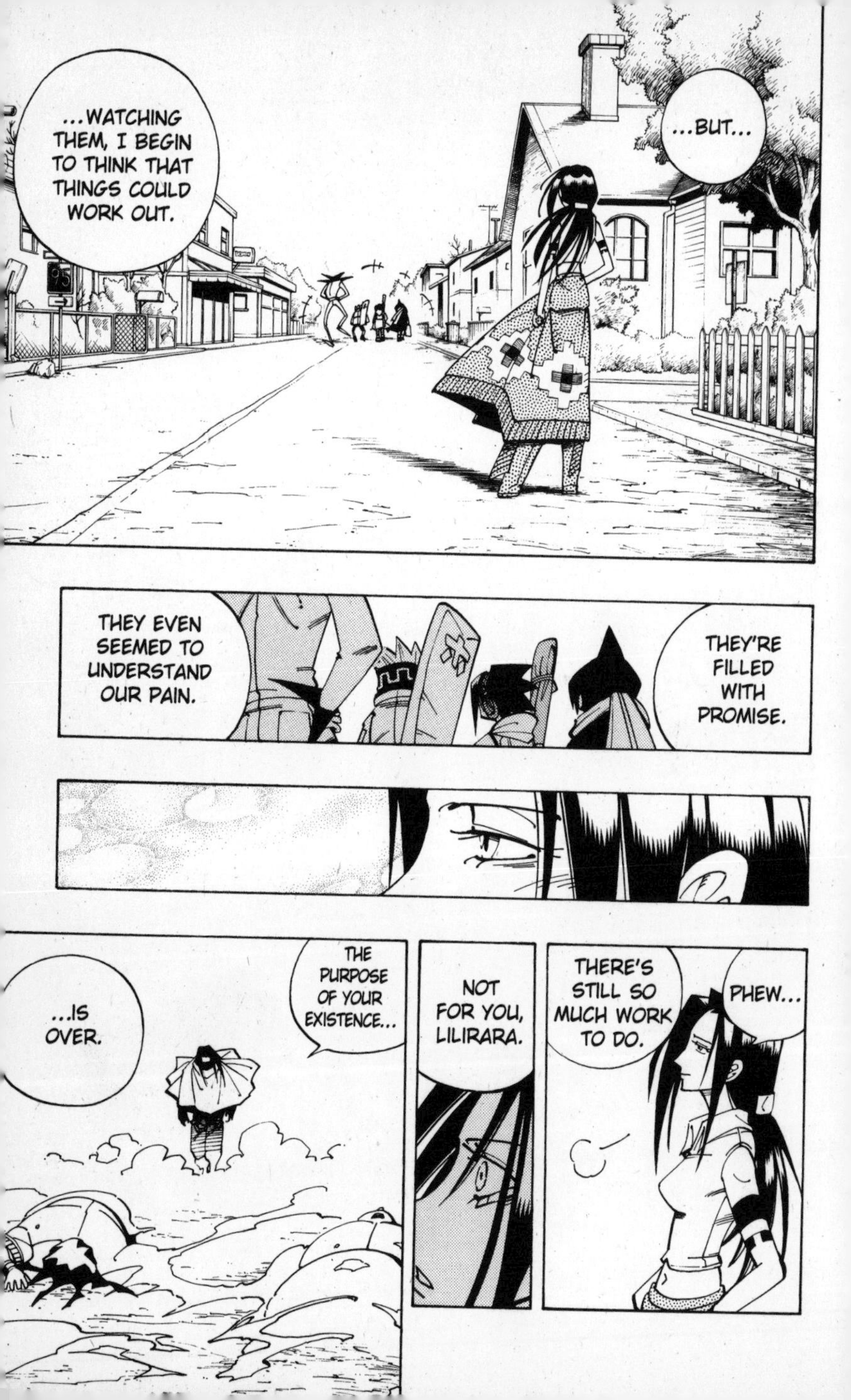
...BUT...
...WATCHING THEM, I BEGIN TO THINK THAT THINGS COULD WORK OUT.
THEY'RE FILLED WITH PROMISE.
THEY EVEN SEEMED TO UNDERSTAND OUR PAIN.
PHEW...
THERE'S STILL SO MUCH WORK TO DO.
NOT FOR YOU, LILIRARA.
THE PURPOSE OF YOUR EXISTENCE...
...IS OVER.

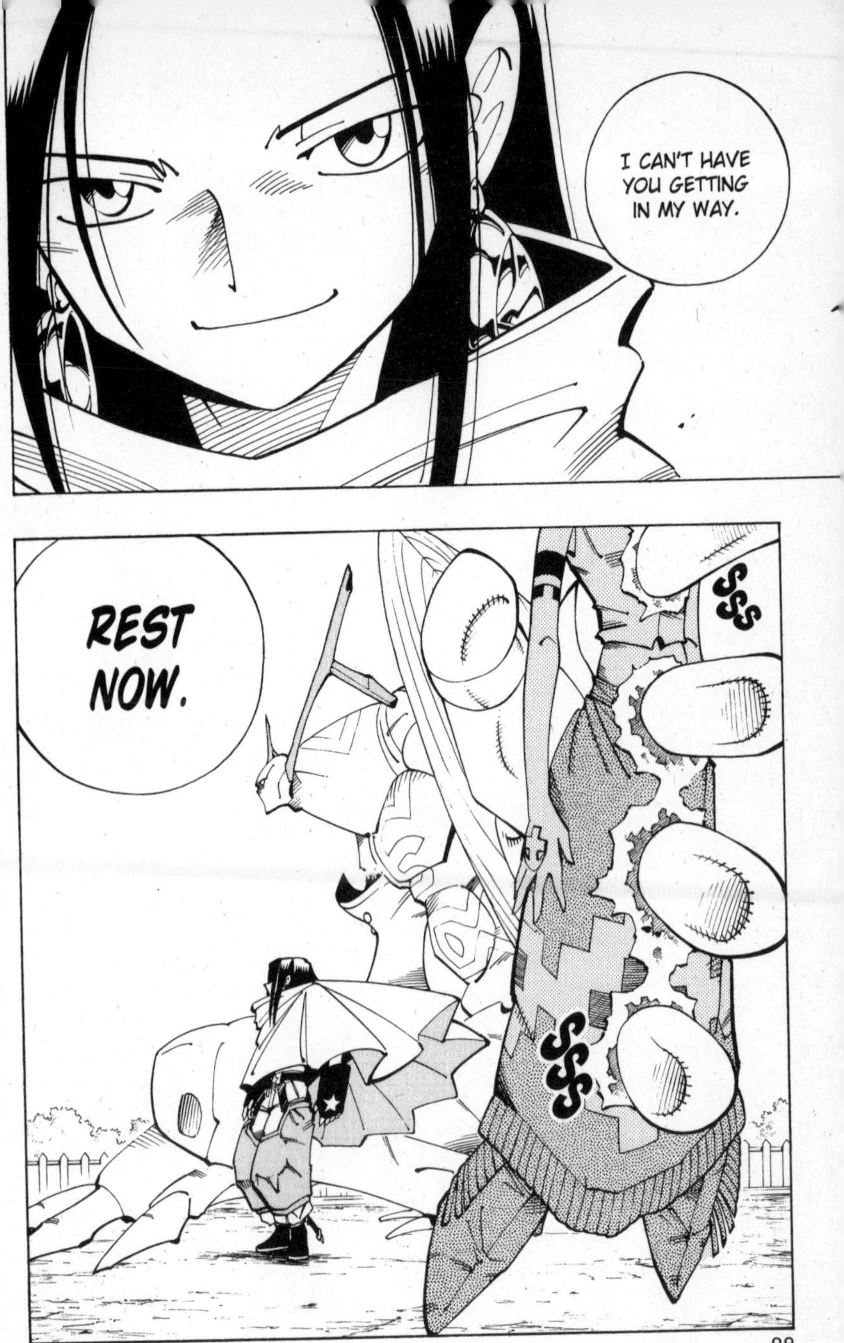
I CAN'T HAVE YOU GETTING IN MY WAY.
REST NOW.
SSS
SSS

Shaman King™

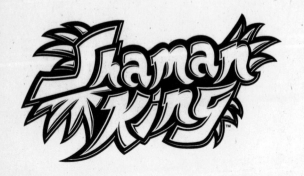

SHAMAN KING CHARACTER FILE No.44

リゼルグ・ダイゼル

2000
(SEP)

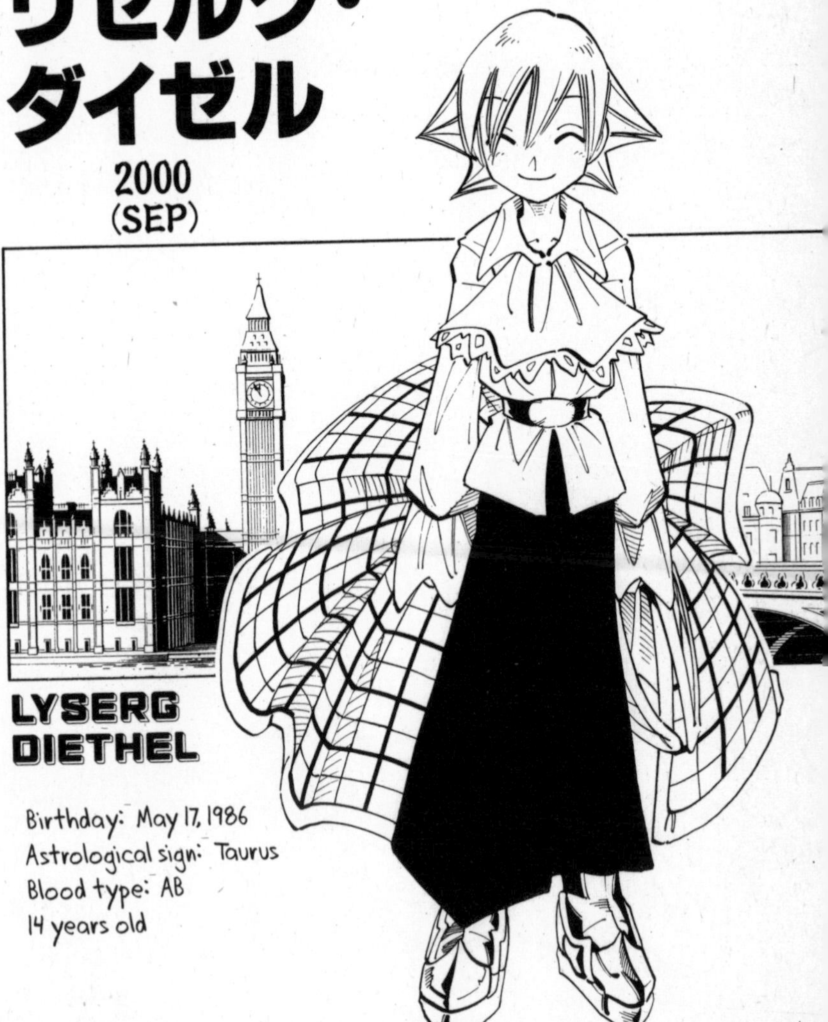

LYSERG DIETHEL

Birthday: May 17, 1986
Astrological sign: Taurus
Blood type: AB
14 years old

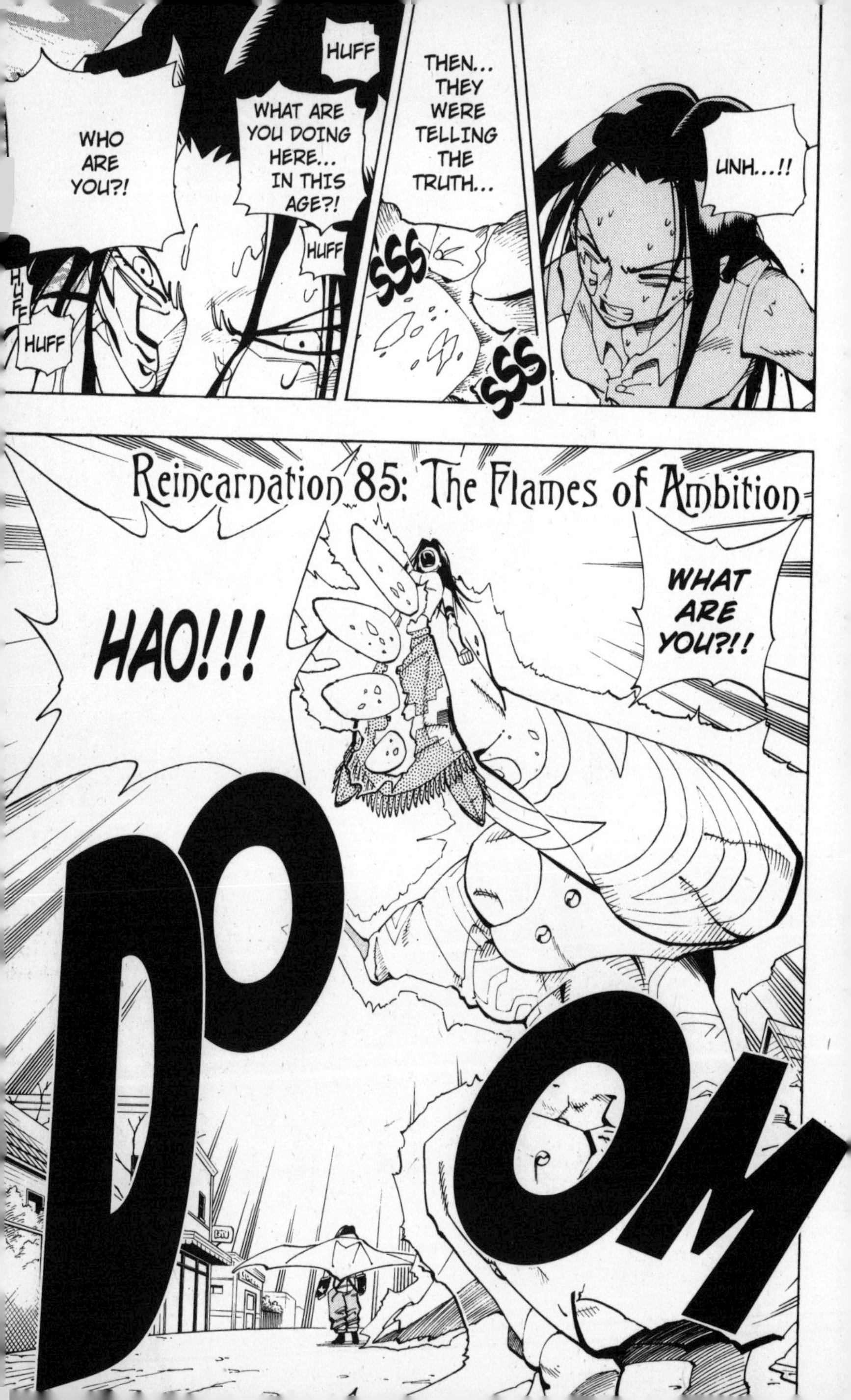
UNH...!!
THEN... THEY WERE TELLING THE TRUTH...
SSS
SSS
HUFF
WHAT ARE YOU DOING HERE... IN THIS AGE?!
HUFF
WHO ARE YOU?!
HUFF
HUFF
Reincarnation 85: The Flames of Ambition
WHAT ARE YOU?!!
HAO!!!
DOOM

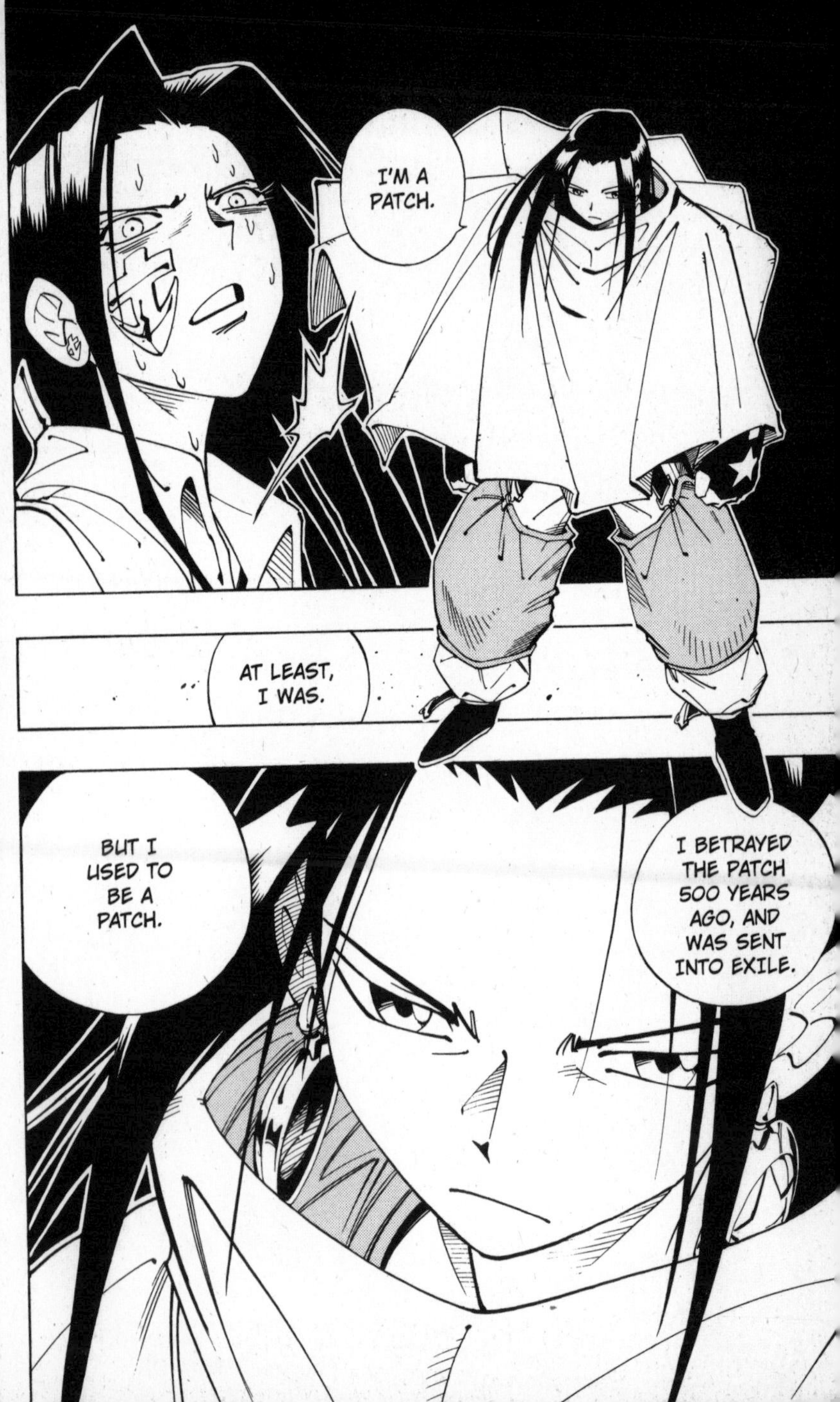
I'M A PATCH.
AT LEAST, I WAS.
BUT I USED TO BE A PATCH.
I BETRAYED THE PATCH 500 YEARS AGO, AND WAS SENT INTO EXILE.

Reincarnation 85:
The Flames of Ambition

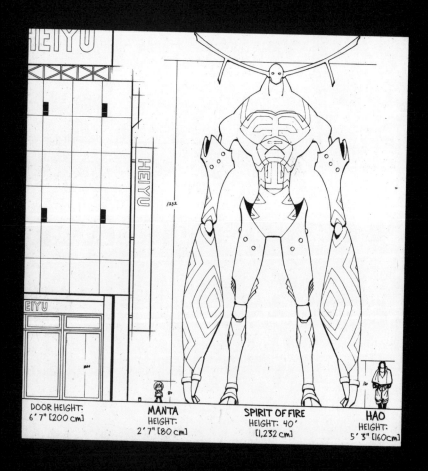

DOOR HEIGHT:
6' 7" [200 cm]

MANTA
HEIGHT:
2' 7" [80 cm]

SPIRIT OF FIRE
HEIGHT: 40'
[1,232 cm]

HAO
HEIGHT:
5' 3" [160cm]

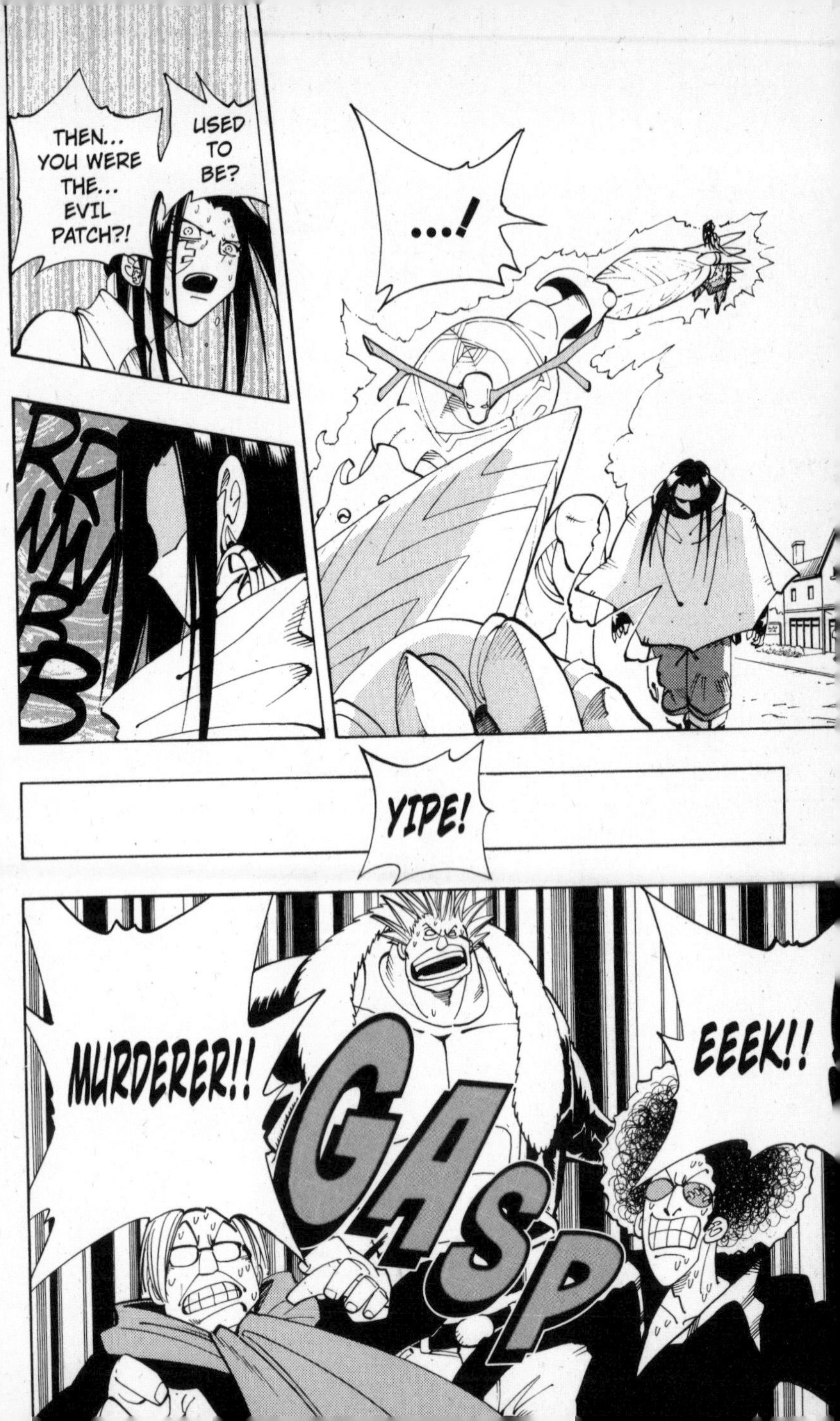
...!
USED TO BE?
THEN... YOU WERE THE... EVIL PATCH?!
RRMMBB
YIPE!
EEEK!!
GASP
MURDERER!!

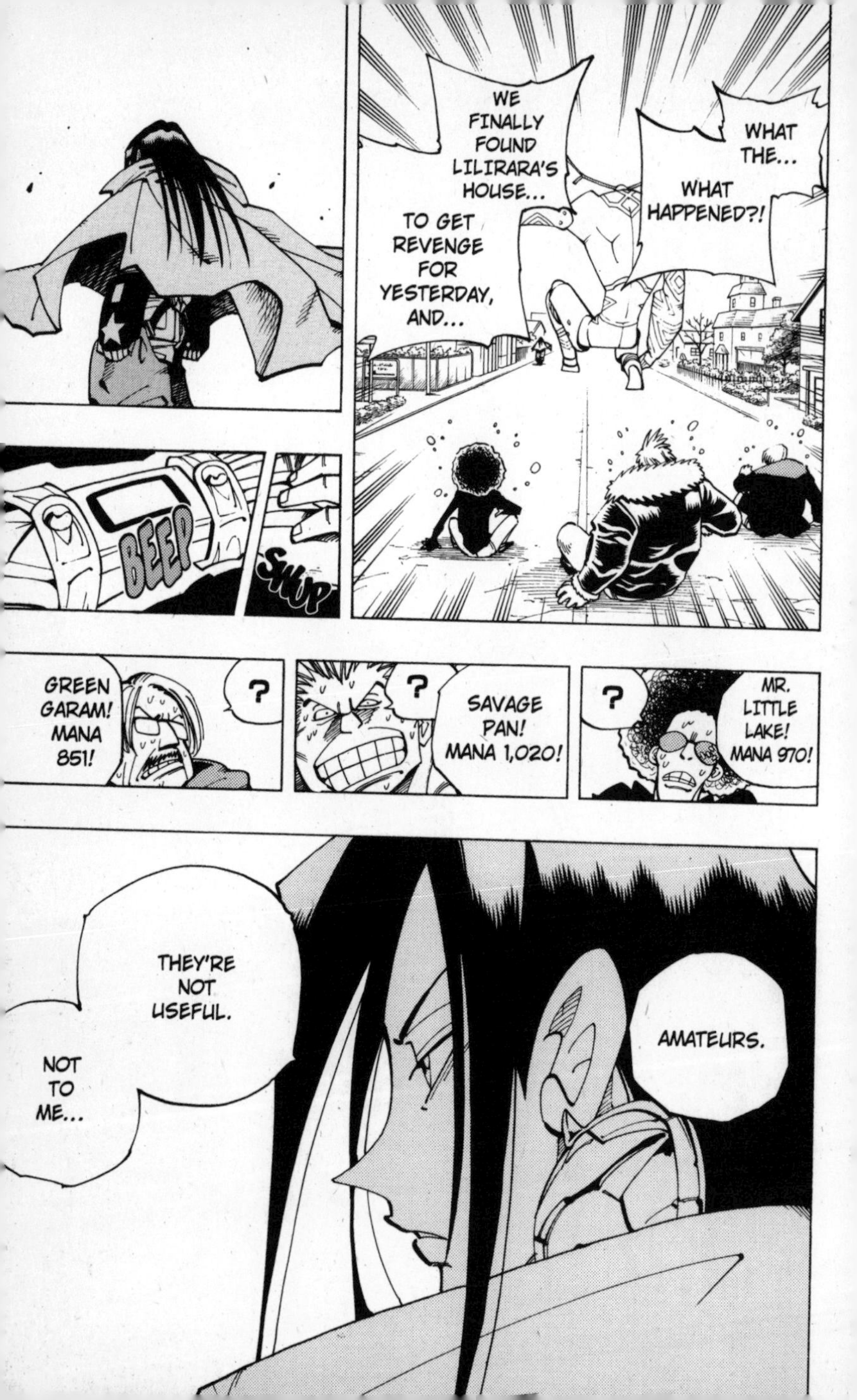
WE FINALLY FOUND LILIRARA'S HOUSE...
TO GET REVENGE FOR YESTERDAY, AND...
WHAT THE...
WHAT HAPPENED?!
BEEP
MR. LITTLE LAKE! MANA 970!
?
SAVAGE PAN! MANA 1,020!
?
?
GREEN GARAM! MANA 851!
AMATEURS.
THEY'RE NOT USEFUL.
NOT TO ME...

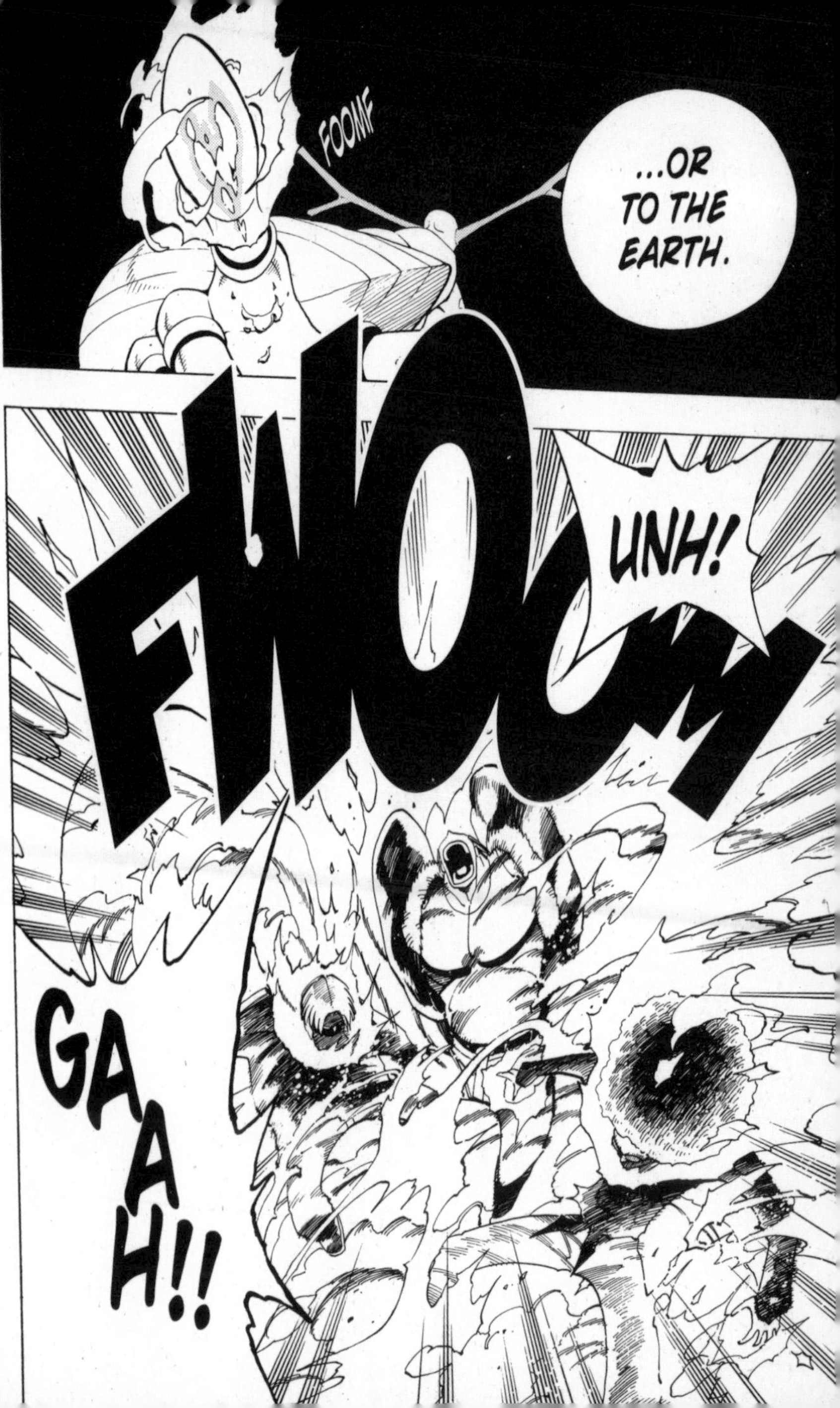

...OR TO THE EARTH.
FOOMF
FWOOM
UNH!
GAAAH!!

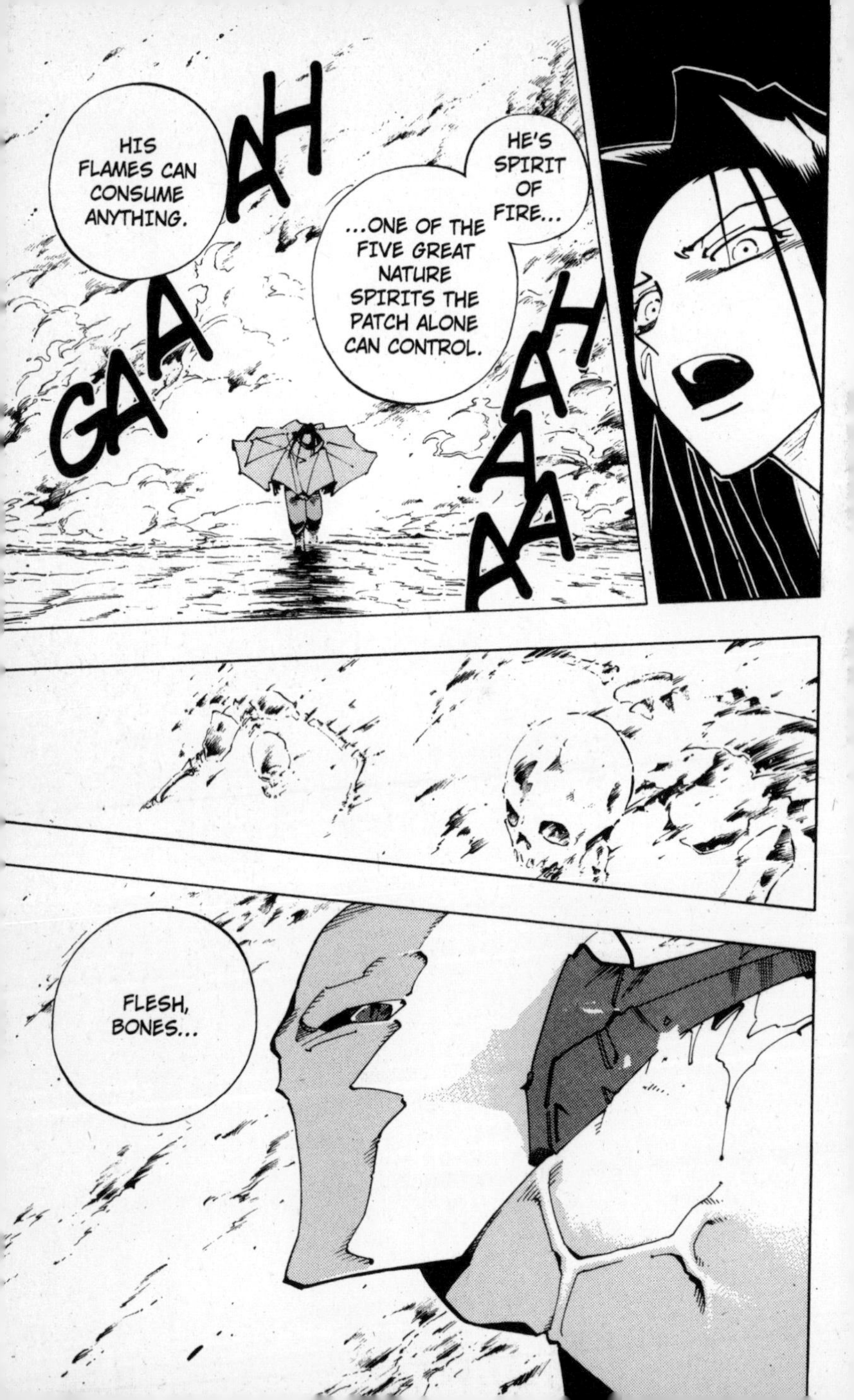
HAHAHAAA
HE'S SPIRIT OF FIRE...
...ONE OF THE FIVE GREAT NATURE SPIRITS THE PATCH ALONE CAN CONTROL.
GAAAH
HIS FLAMES CAN CONSUME ANYTHING.
FLESH, BONES...

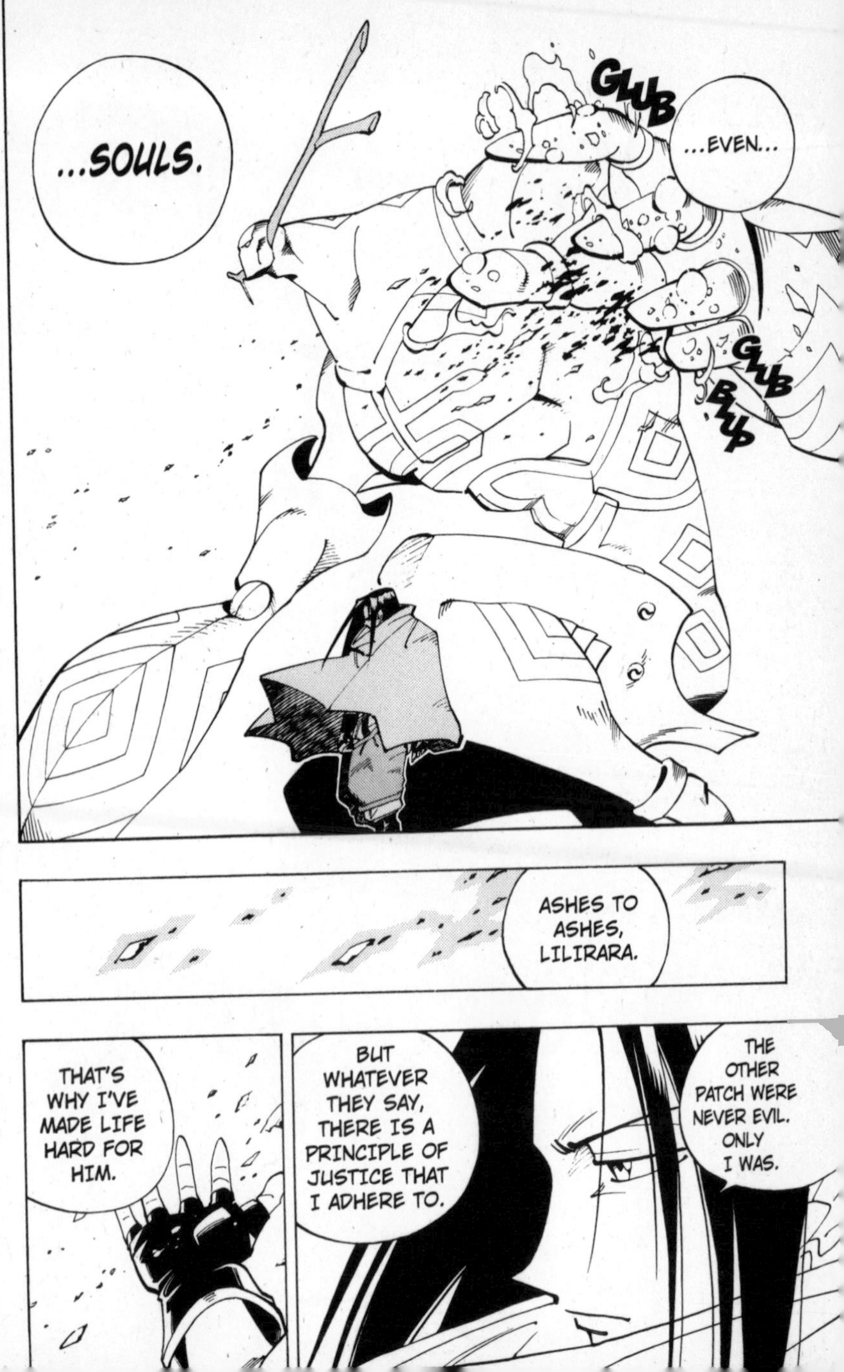
GLUB
...EVEN...
GLUB
BLUP
...SOULS.
ASHES TO ASHES, LILIRARA.
THE OTHER PATCH WERE NEVER EVIL. ONLY I WAS.
BUT WHATEVER THEY SAY, THERE IS A PRINCIPLE OF JUSTICE THAT I ADHERE TO.
THAT'S WHY I'VE MADE LIFE HARD FOR HIM.

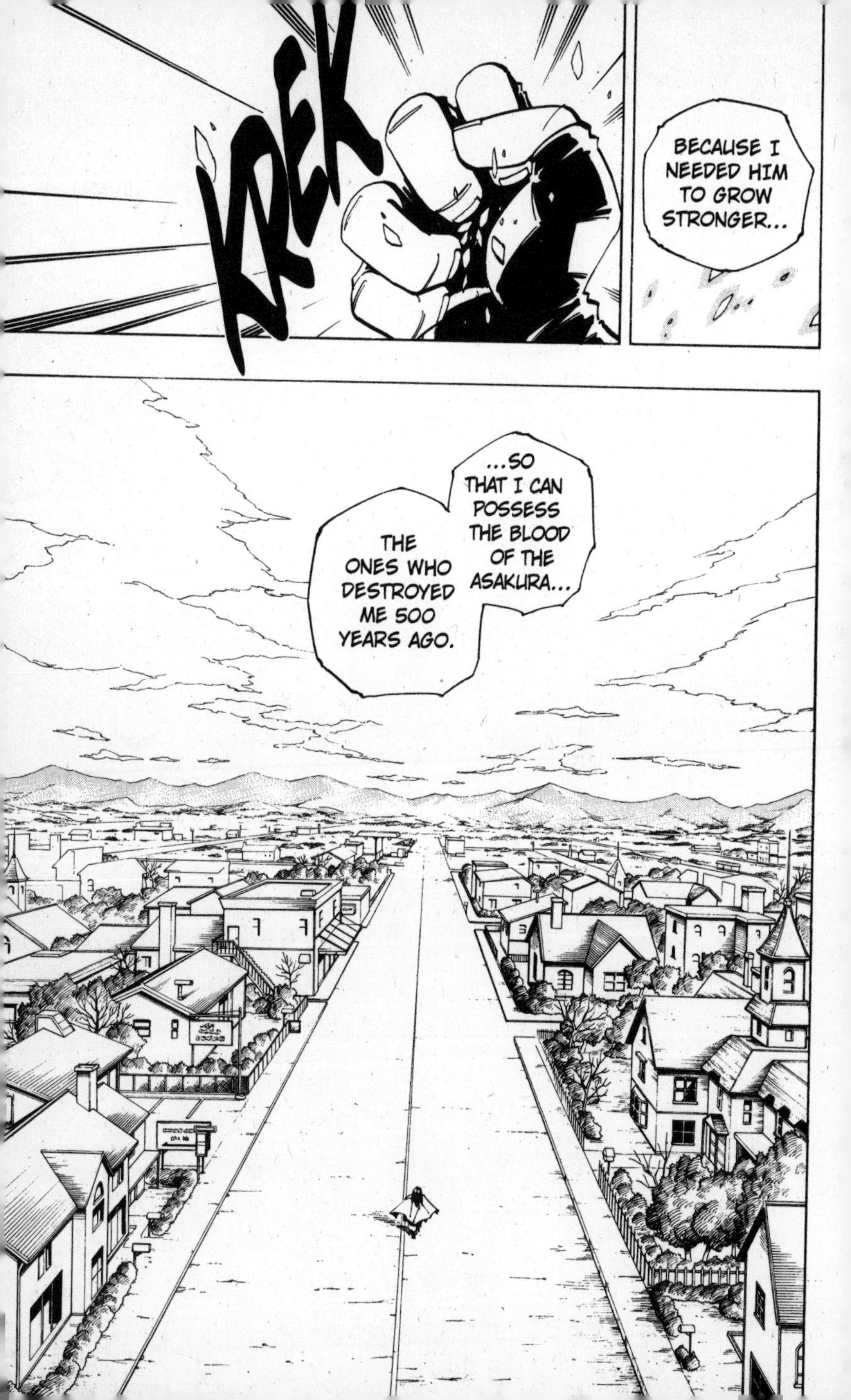
BECAUSE I NEEDED HIM TO GROW STRONGER...
KREK
...SO THAT I CAN POSSESS THE BLOOD OF THE ASAKURA...
THE ONES WHO DESTROYED ME 500 YEARS AGO.

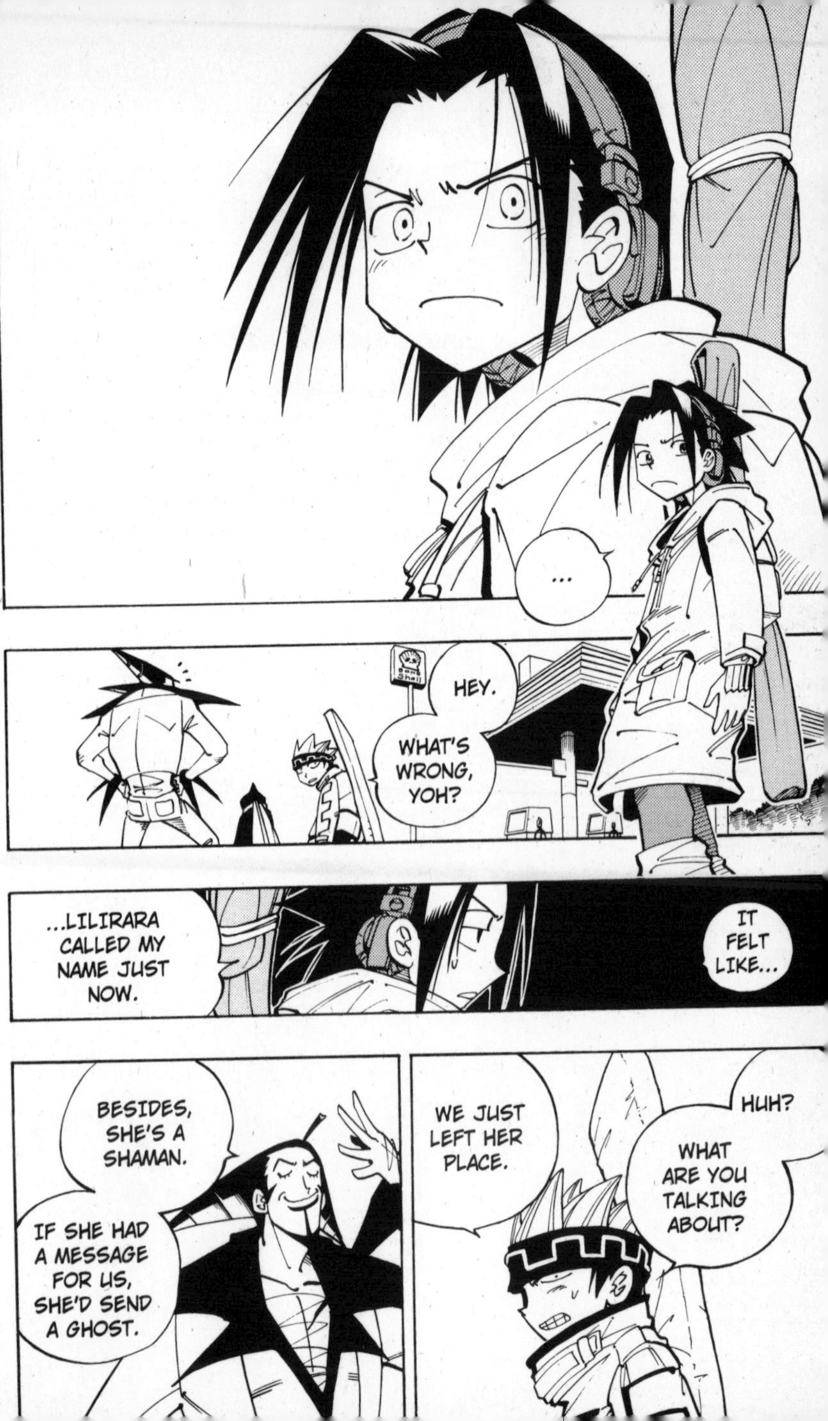
...
HEY.
WHAT'S WRONG, YOH?
IT FELT LIKE...
...LILIRARA CALLED MY NAME JUST NOW.
HUH?
WHAT ARE YOU TALKING ABOUT?
WE JUST LEFT HER PLACE.
BESIDES, SHE'S A SHAMAN.
IF SHE HAD A MESSAGE FOR US, SHE'D SEND A GHOST.

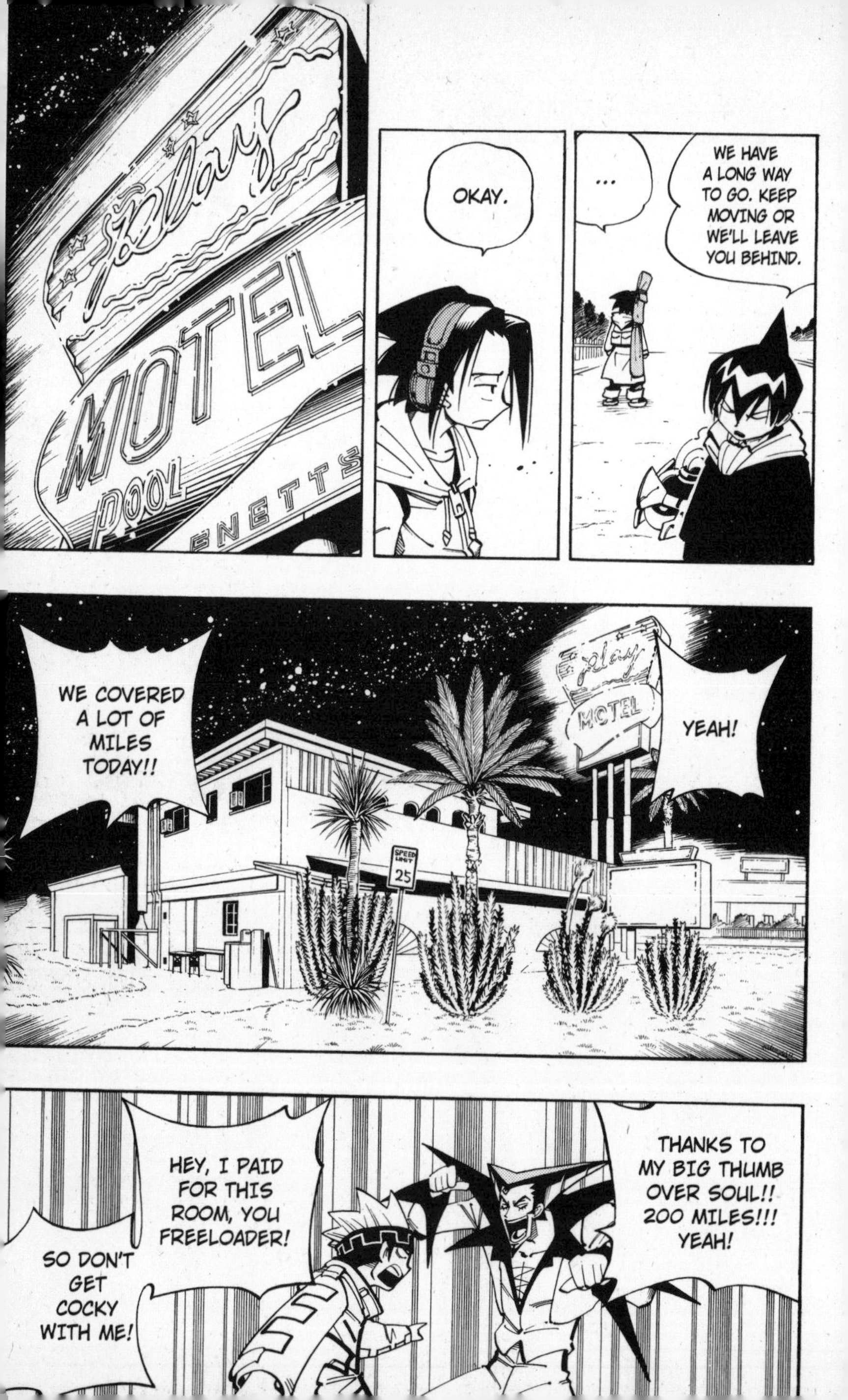

Play
MOTEL
POOL
WE HAVE A LONG WAY TO GO. KEEP MOVING OR WE'LL LEAVE YOU BEHIND.
...
OKAY.
WE COVERED A LOT OF MILES TODAY!!
YEAH!
SPEED LIMIT 25
THANKS TO MY BIG THUMB OVER SOUL!! 200 MILES!!! YEAH!
HEY, I PAID FOR THIS ROOM, YOU FREELOADER!
SO DON'T GET COCKY WITH ME!

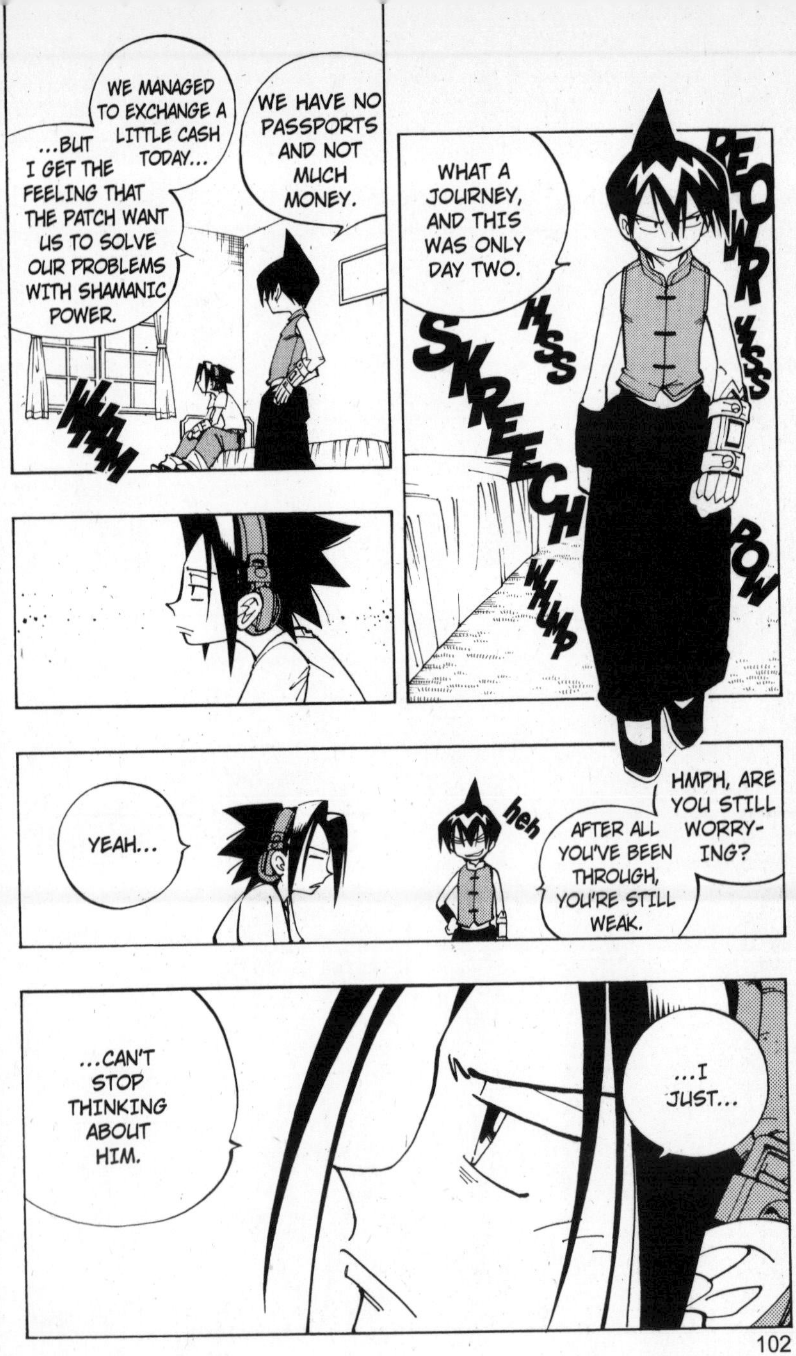
WHAT A JOURNEY, AND THIS WAS ONLY DAY TWO.
REOWR
HISS
HISS
SKREEECH
POW
WHUMP
WE HAVE NO PASSPORTS AND NOT MUCH MONEY.
WE MANAGED TO EXCHANGE A LITTLE CASH TODAY...
...BUT I GET THE FEELING THAT THE PATCH WANT US TO SOLVE OUR PROBLEMS WITH SHAMANIC POWER.
WHAM
HMPH, ARE YOU STILL WORRYING?
AFTER ALL YOU'VE BEEN THROUGH, YOU'RE STILL WEAK.
heh
YEAH...
...I JUST...
...CAN'T STOP THINKING ABOUT HIM.

READ THIS WAY

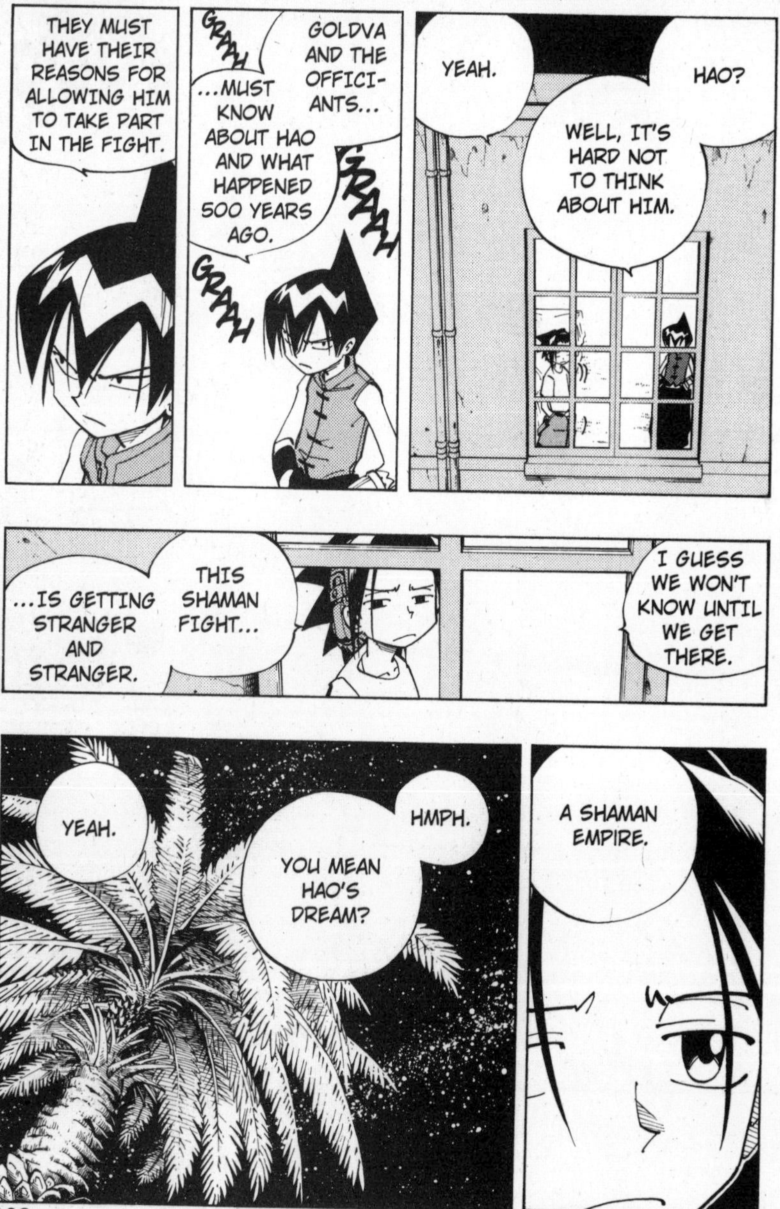
HAO?
YEAH.
WELL, IT'S HARD NOT TO THINK ABOUT HIM.
GOLDVA AND THE OFFICI- ANTS...
...MUST KNOW ABOUT HAO AND WHAT HAPPENED 500 YEARS AGO.
GRAAAH
GRAAAH
GRAAAH
THEY MUST HAVE THEIR REASONS FOR ALLOWING HIM TO TAKE PART IN THE FIGHT.
I GUESS WE WON'T KNOW UNTIL WE GET THERE.
THIS SHAMAN FIGHT...
...IS GETTING STRANGER AND STRANGER.
A SHAMAN EMPIRE.
HMPH.
YOU MEAN HAO'S DREAM?
YEAH.

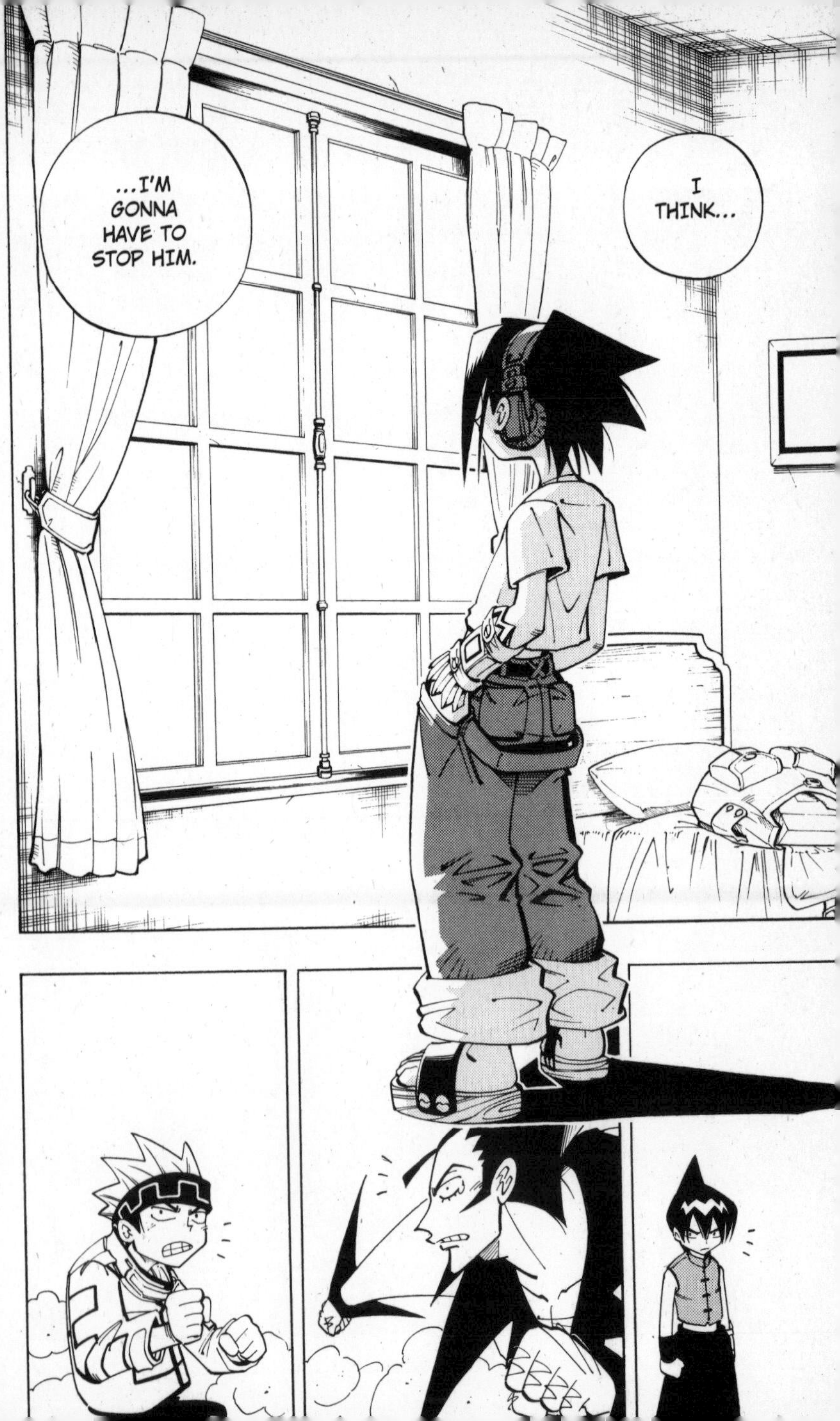
I THINK...
...I'M GONNA HAVE TO STOP HIM.

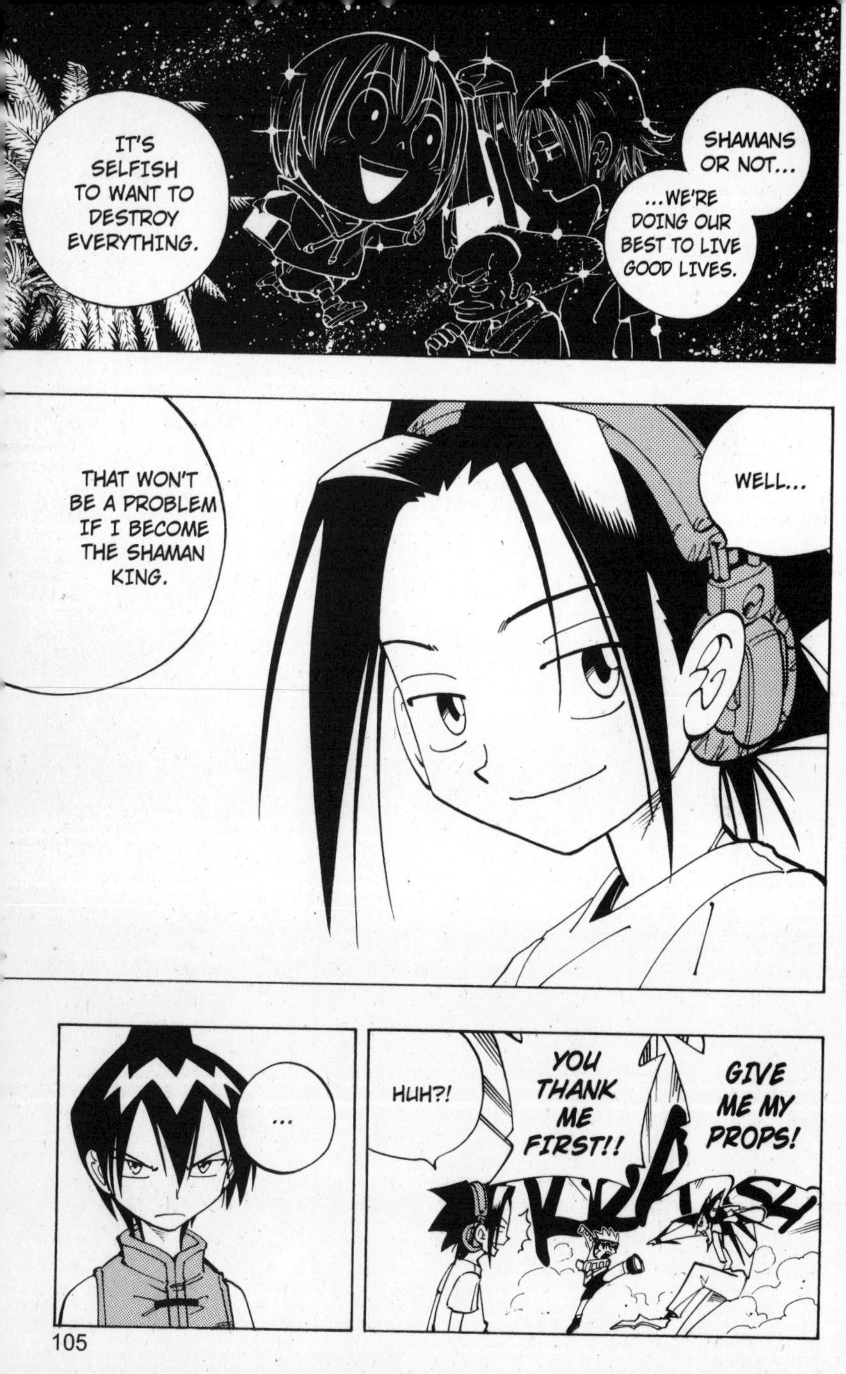
SHAMANS OR NOT...
...WE'RE DOING OUR BEST TO LIVE GOOD LIVES.
IT'S SELFISH TO WANT TO DESTROY EVERYTHING.
WELL...
THAT WON'T BE A PROBLEM IF I BECOME THE SHAMAN KING.
GIVE ME MY PROPS!
YOU THANK ME FIRST!!
HUH?!
...

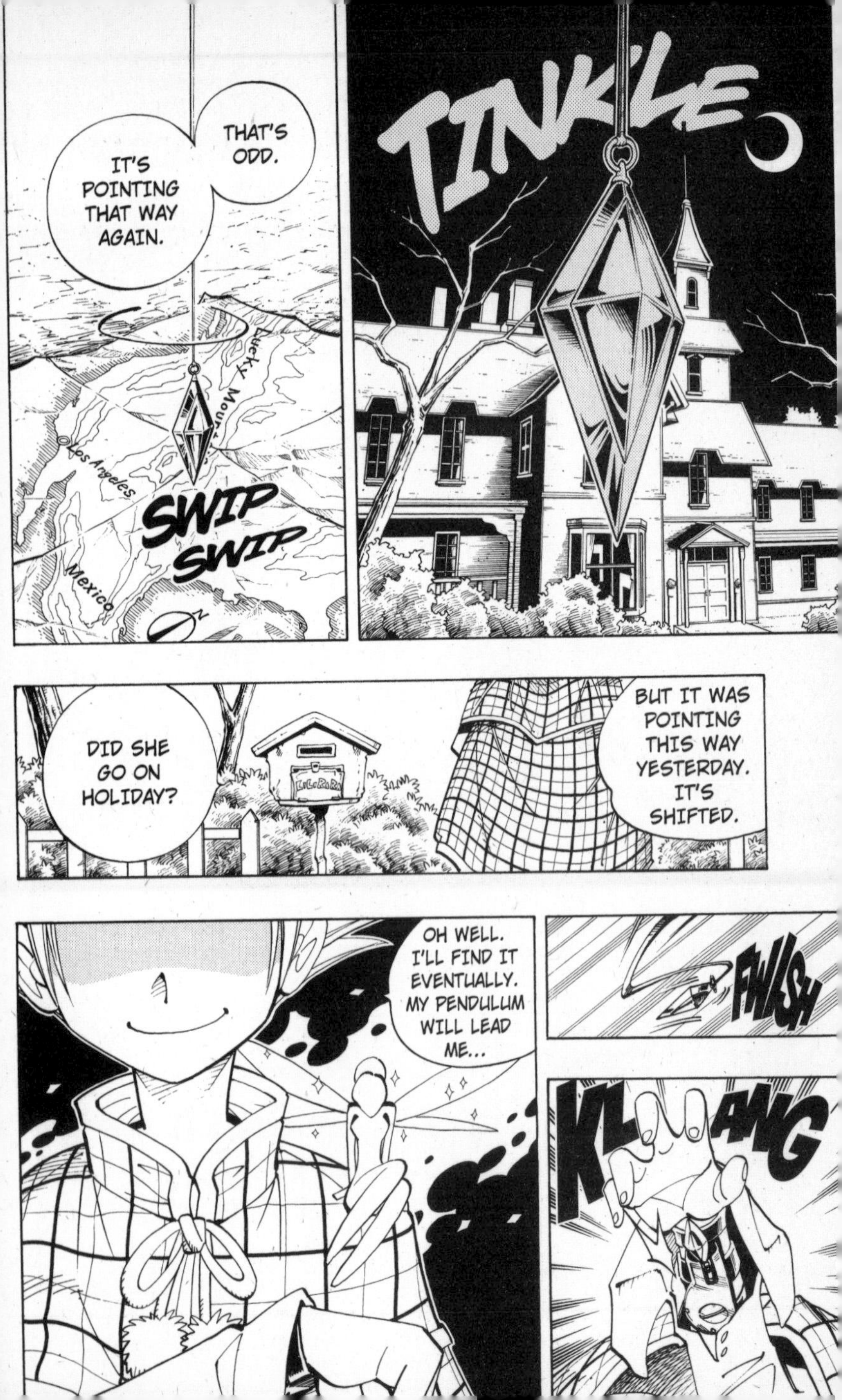
TINKLE
THAT'S ODD.
IT'S POINTING THAT WAY AGAIN.
Los Angeles
Mexico
SWIP SWIP
BUT IT WAS POINTING THIS WAY YESTERDAY. IT'S SHIFTED.
DID SHE GO ON HOLIDAY?
FWISH
KLANG
OH WELL. I'LL FIND IT EVENTUALLY. MY PENDULUM WILL LEAD ME...

READ THIS WAY

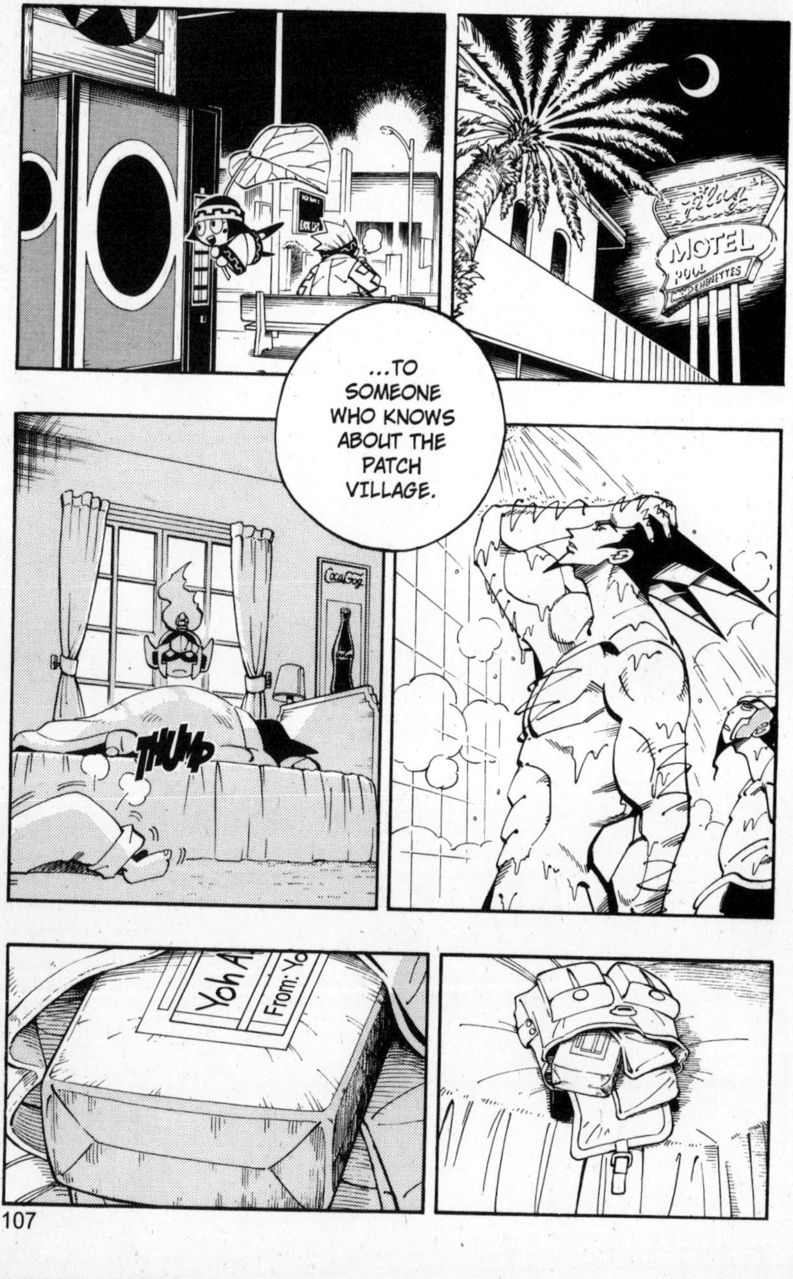
MOTEL
POOL
...TO SOMEONE WHO KNOWS ABOUT THE PATCH VILLAGE.
THUMP

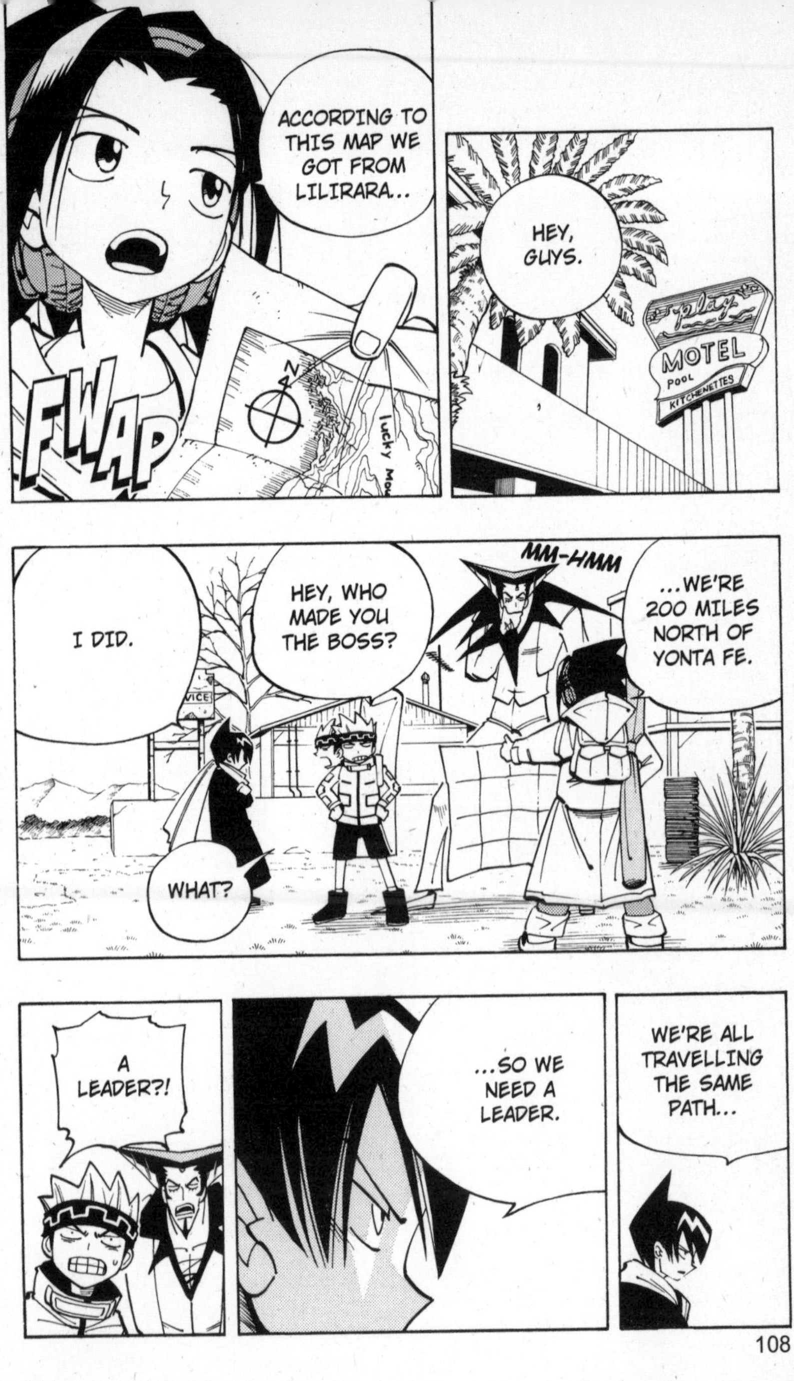
HEY, GUYS.
play
MOTEL
POOL
KITCHENETTES
ACCORDING TO THIS MAP WE GOT FROM LILIRARA...
FWAP
...WE'RE 200 MILES NORTH OF YONTA FE.
MM-HMM
HEY, WHO MADE YOU THE BOSS?
I DID.
WHAT?
WE'RE ALL TRAVELLING THE SAME PATH...
...SO WE NEED A LEADER.
A LEADER?!

READ THIS WAY

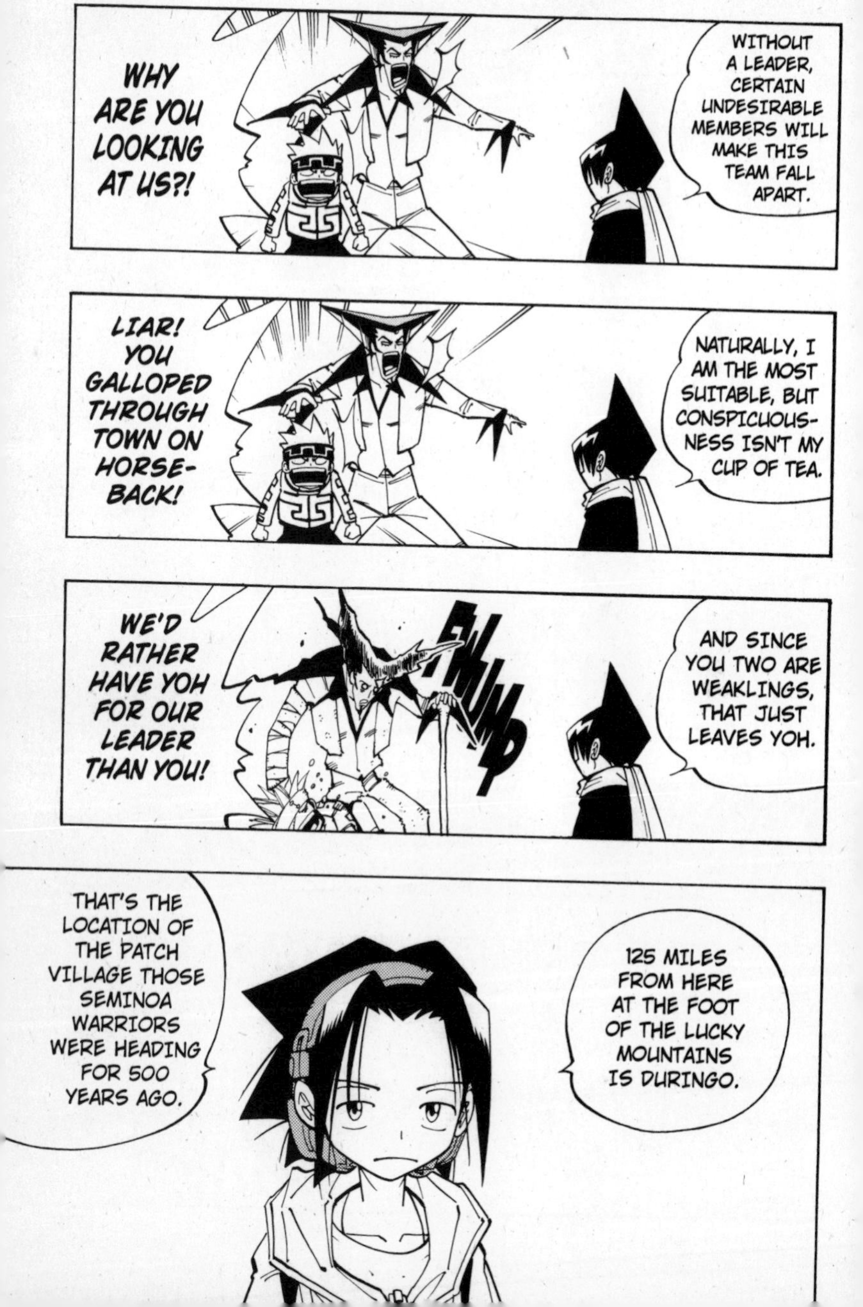

WITHOUT A LEADER, CERTAIN UNDESIRABLE MEMBERS WILL MAKE THIS TEAM FALL APART.
WHY ARE YOU LOOKING AT US?!
NATURALLY, I AM THE MOST SUITABLE, BUT CONSPICUOUS-NESS ISN'T MY CUP OF TEA.
LIAR! YOU GALLOPED THROUGH TOWN ON HORSE-BACK!
AND SINCE YOU TWO ARE WEAKLINGS, THAT JUST LEAVES YOH.
FWUMP
WE'D RATHER HAVE YOH FOR OUR LEADER THAN YOU!
125 MILES FROM HERE AT THE FOOT OF THE LUCKY MOUNTAINS IS DURINGO.
THAT'S THE LOCATION OF THE PATCH VILLAGE THOSE SEMINOA WARRIORS WERE HEADING FOR 500 YEARS AGO.

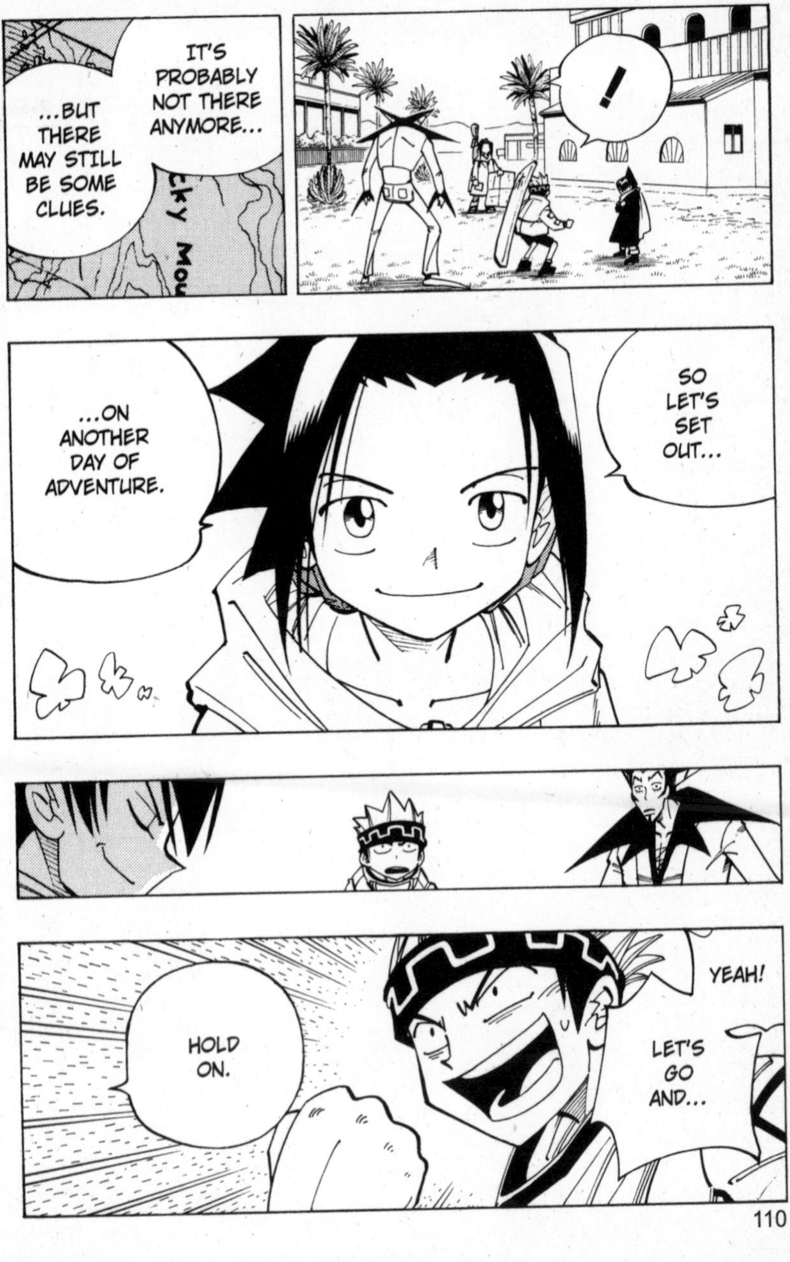
!
IT'S PROBABLY NOT THERE ANYMORE...
...BUT THERE MAY STILL BE SOME CLUES.
SO LET'S SET OUT...
...ON ANOTHER DAY OF ADVENTURE.
YEAH!
LET'S GO AND...
HOLD ON.

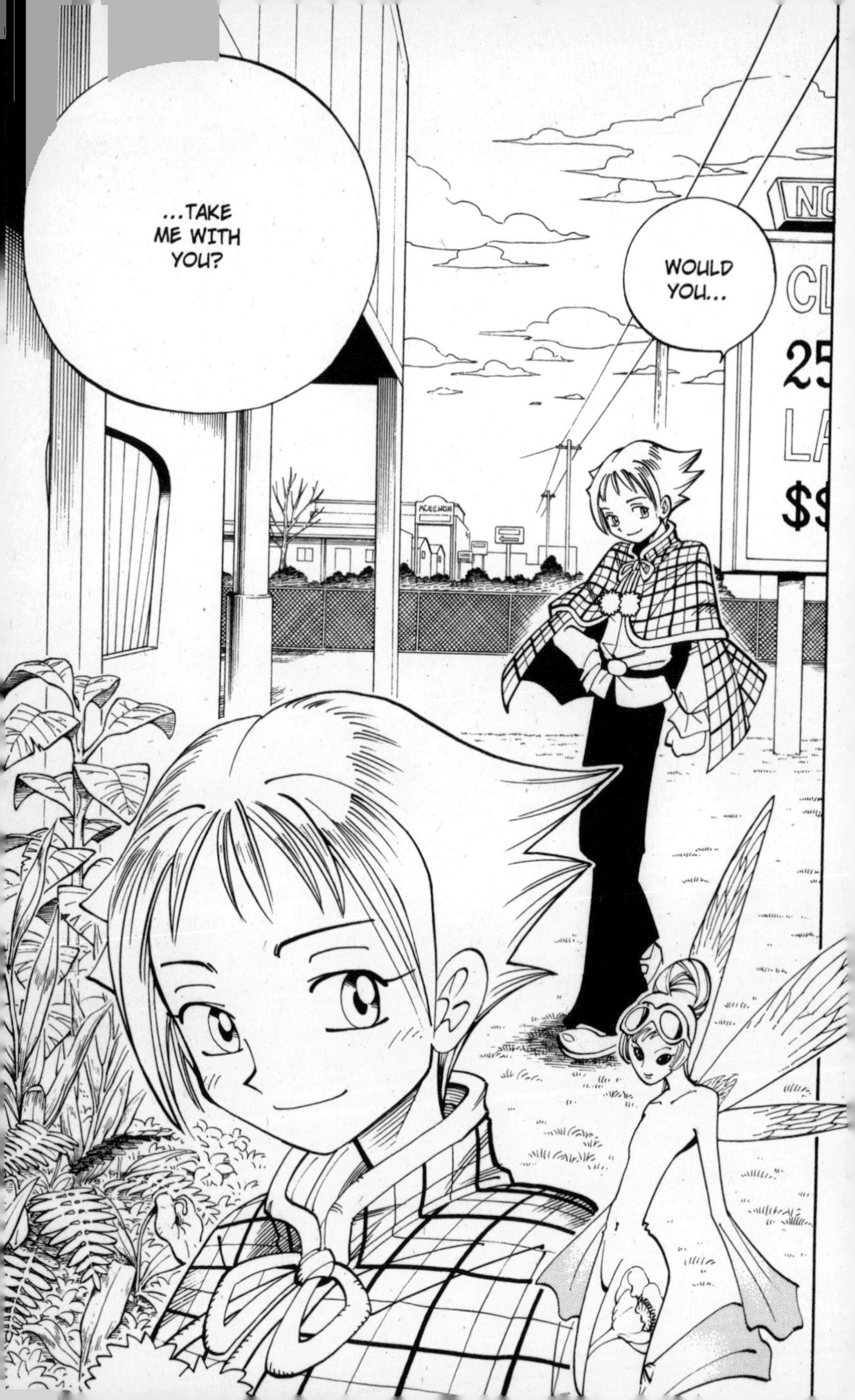
WOULD YOU...
...TAKE ME WITH YOU?

SHAMAN KING CHARACTER FILE No.45

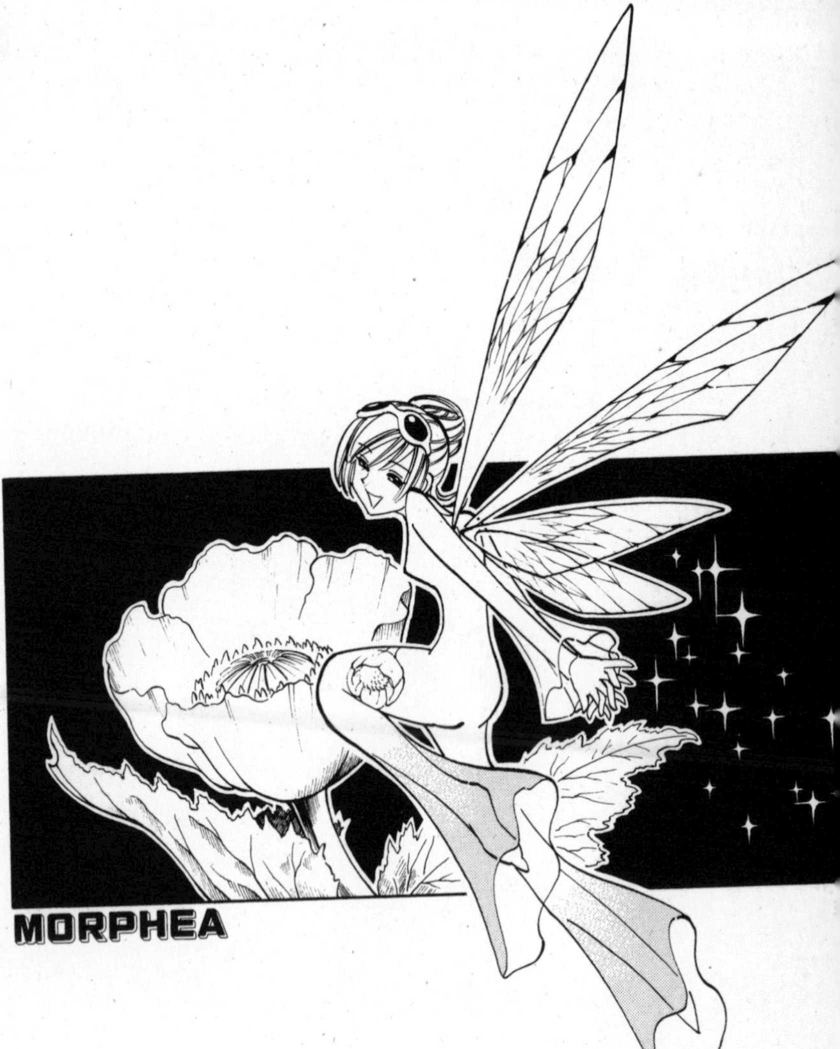

MORPHEA

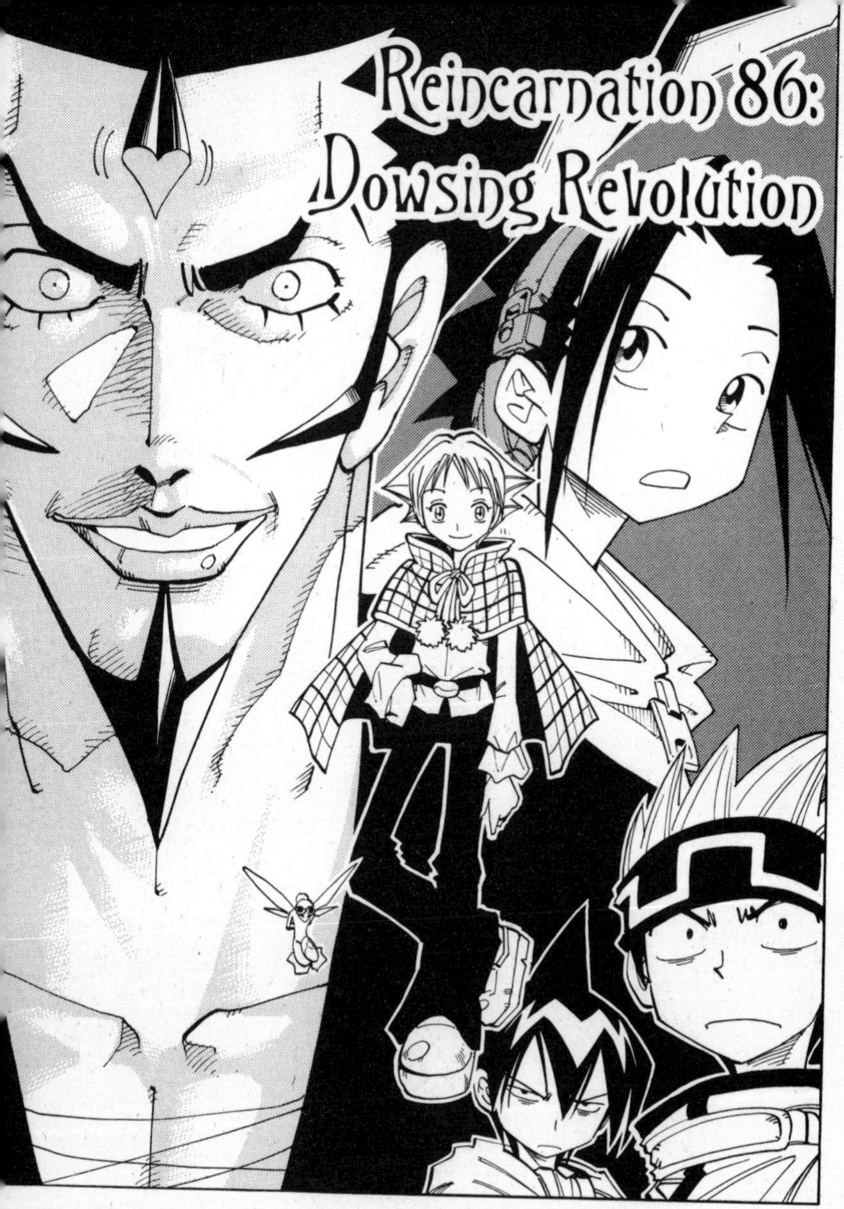
Reincarnation 86:
Dowsing Revolution
WHAT THE...?

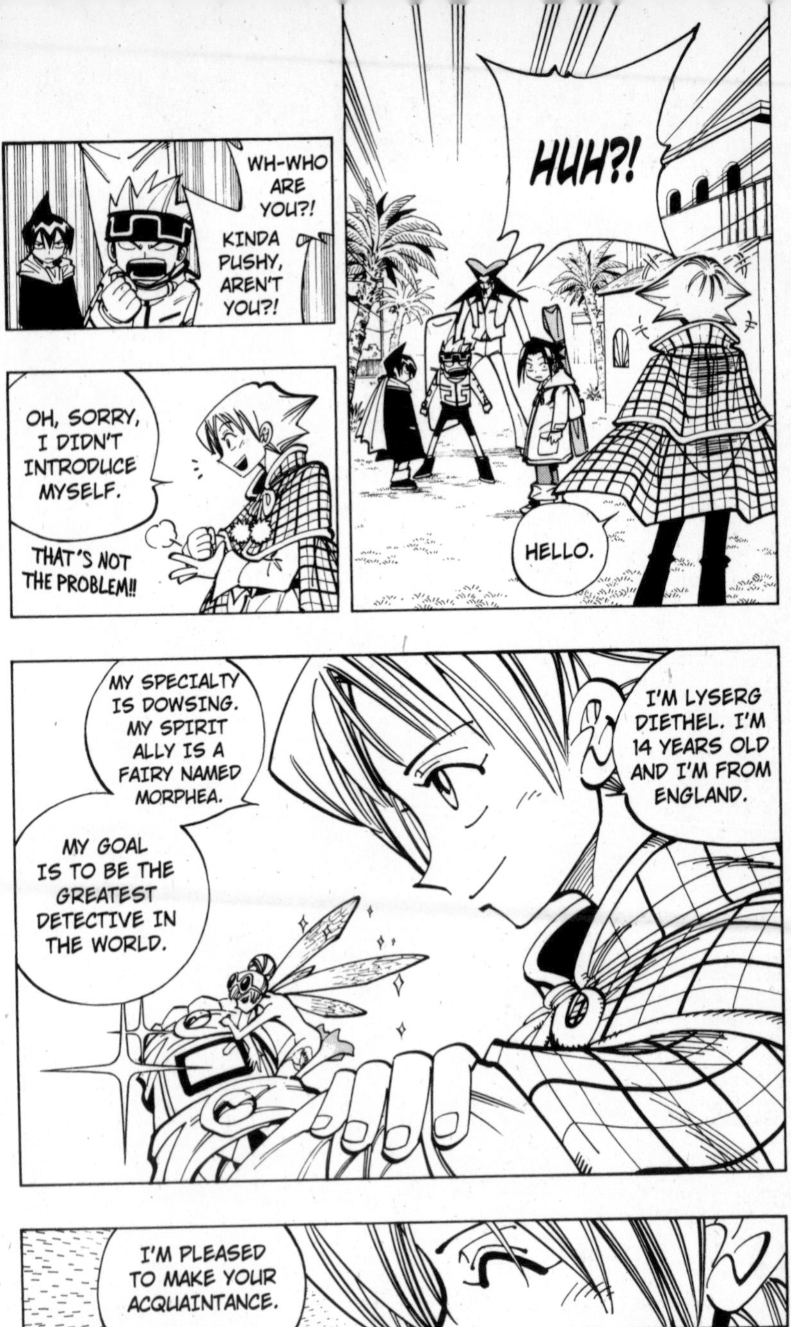
HUH?!
HELLO.
WH-WHO ARE YOU?!
KINDA PUSHY, AREN'T YOU?!
OH, SORRY, I DIDN'T INTRODUCE MYSELF.
THAT'S NOT THE PROBLEM!!
I'M LYSERG DIETHEL. I'M 14 YEARS OLD AND I'M FROM ENGLAND.
MY SPECIALTY IS DOWSING. MY SPIRIT ALLY IS A FAIRY NAMED MORPHEA.
MY GOAL IS TO BE THE GREATEST DETECTIVE IN THE WORLD.
I'M PLEASED TO MAKE YOUR ACQUAINTANCE.

Reincarnation 86: Dowsing Revolution

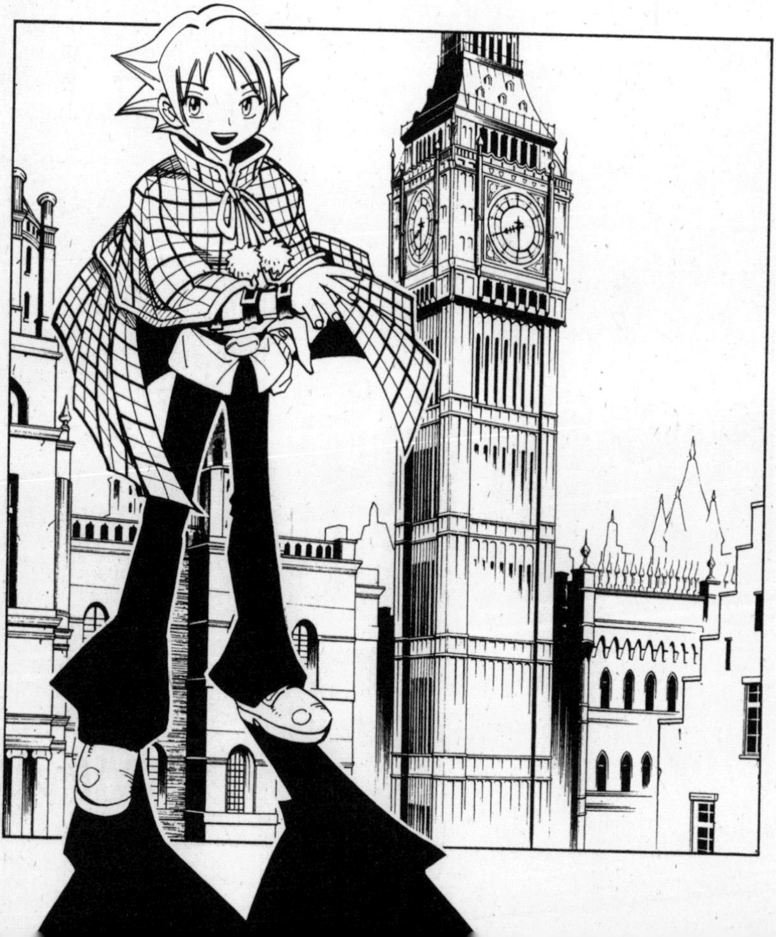

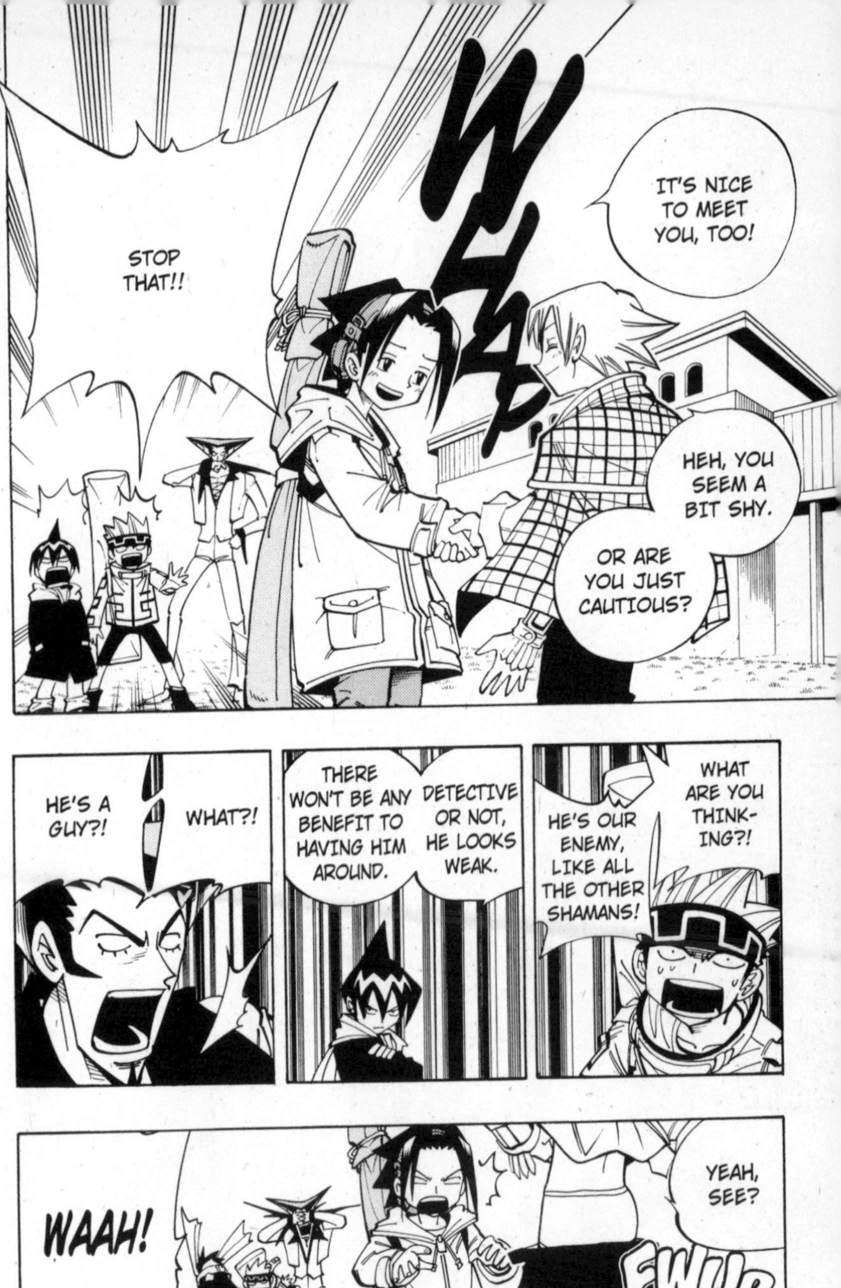
IT'S NICE TO MEET YOU, TOO!
WHAP
HEH, YOU SEEM A BIT SHY.
OR ARE YOU JUST CAUTIOUS?
STOP THAT!!
WHAT ARE YOU THINK-ING?!
HE'S OUR ENEMY, LIKE ALL THE OTHER SHAMANS!
DETECTIVE OR NOT, HE LOOKS WEAK.
THERE WON'T BE ANY BENEFIT TO HAVING HIM AROUND.
WHAT?!
HE'S A GUY?!
YEAH, SEE?
FWUP
WAAH!

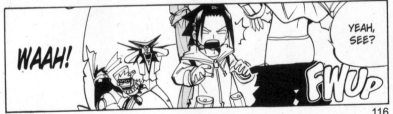

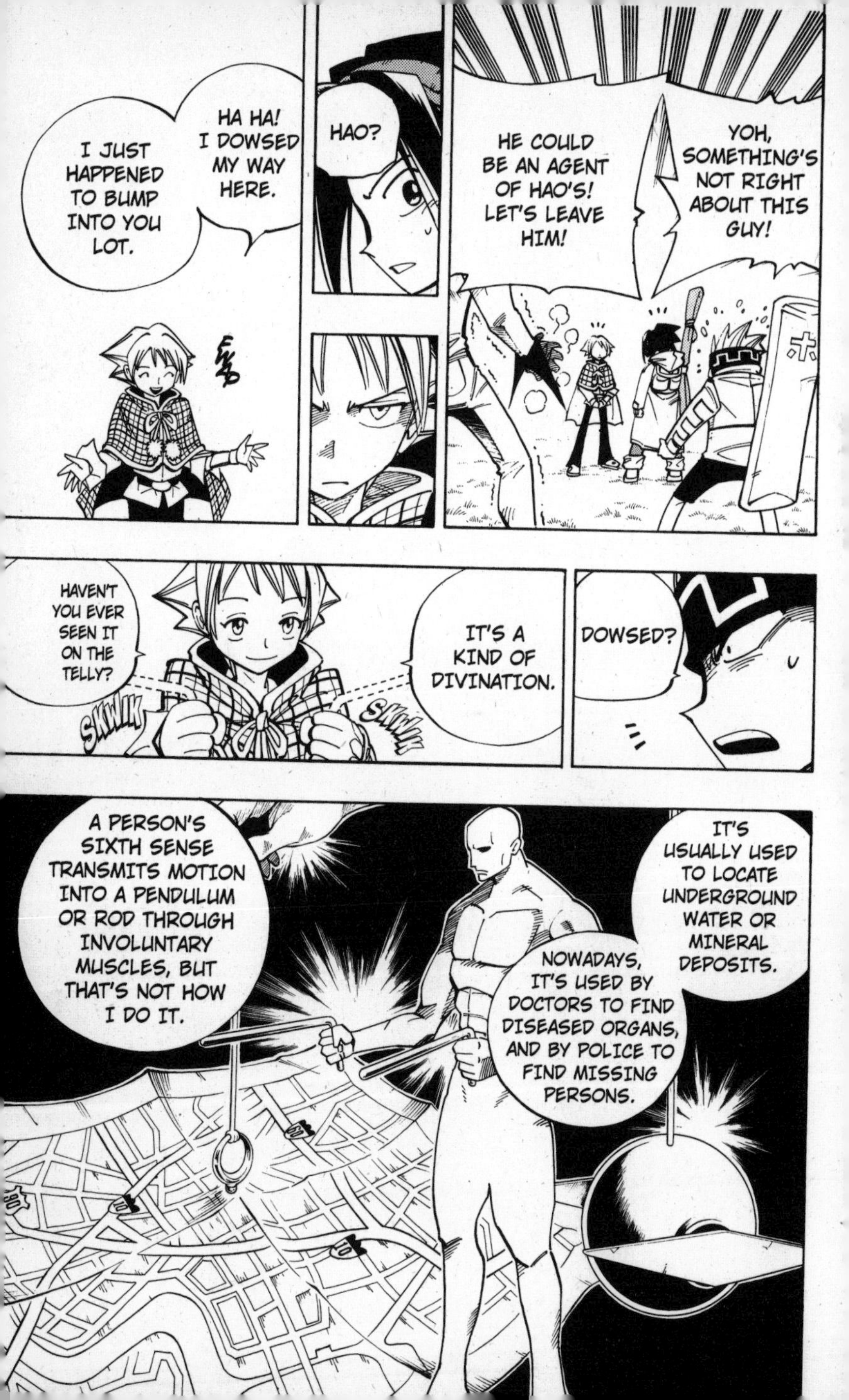
YOH, SOMETHING'S NOT RIGHT ABOUT THIS GUY!
HE COULD BE AN AGENT OF HAO'S! LET'S LEAVE HIM!
HAO?
HA HA! I DOWSED MY WAY HERE.
I JUST HAPPENED TO BUMP INTO YOU LOT.
DOWSED?
IT'S A KIND OF DIVINATION.
SKWIK
HAVEN'T YOU EVER SEEN IT ON THE TELLY?
SKWIK
IT'S USUALLY USED TO LOCATE UNDERGROUND WATER OR MINERAL DEPOSITS.
NOWADAYS, IT'S USED BY DOCTORS TO FIND DISEASED ORGANS, AND BY POLICE TO FIND MISSING PERSONS.
A PERSON'S SIXTH SENSE TRANSMITS MOTION INTO A PENDULUM OR ROD THROUGH INVOLUNTARY MUSCLES, BUT THAT'S NOT HOW I DO IT.

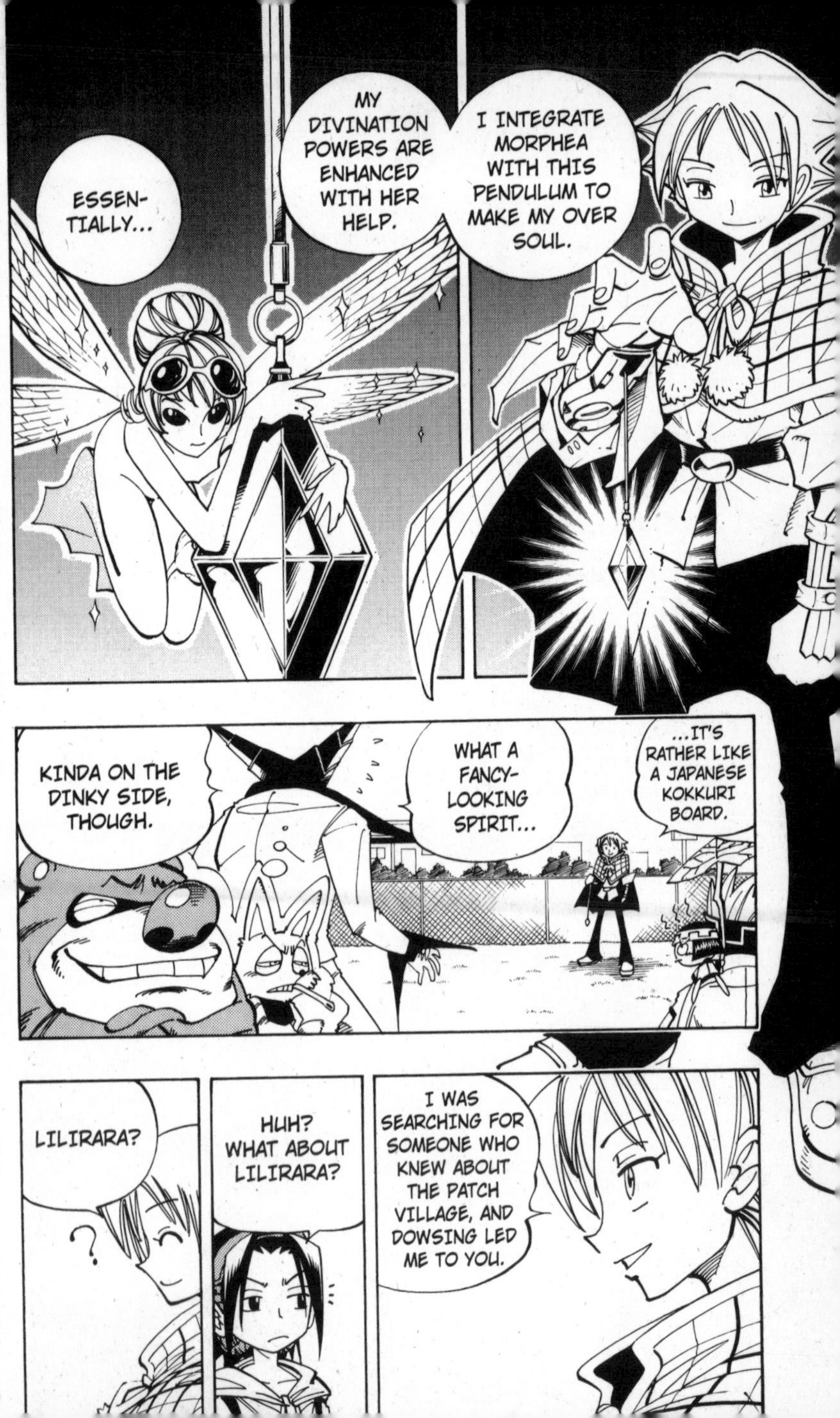
I INTEGRATE MORPHEA WITH THIS PENDULUM TO MAKE MY OVER SOUL.
MY DIVINATION POWERS ARE ENHANCED WITH HER HELP.
ESSEN-TIALLY...
...IT'S RATHER LIKE A JAPANESE KOKKURI BOARD.
WHAT A FANCY-LOOKING SPIRIT...
KINDA ON THE DINKY SIDE, THOUGH.
I WAS SEARCHING FOR SOMEONE WHO KNEW ABOUT THE PATCH VILLAGE, AND DOWSING LED ME TO YOU.
HUH? WHAT ABOUT LILIRARA?
LILIRARA?

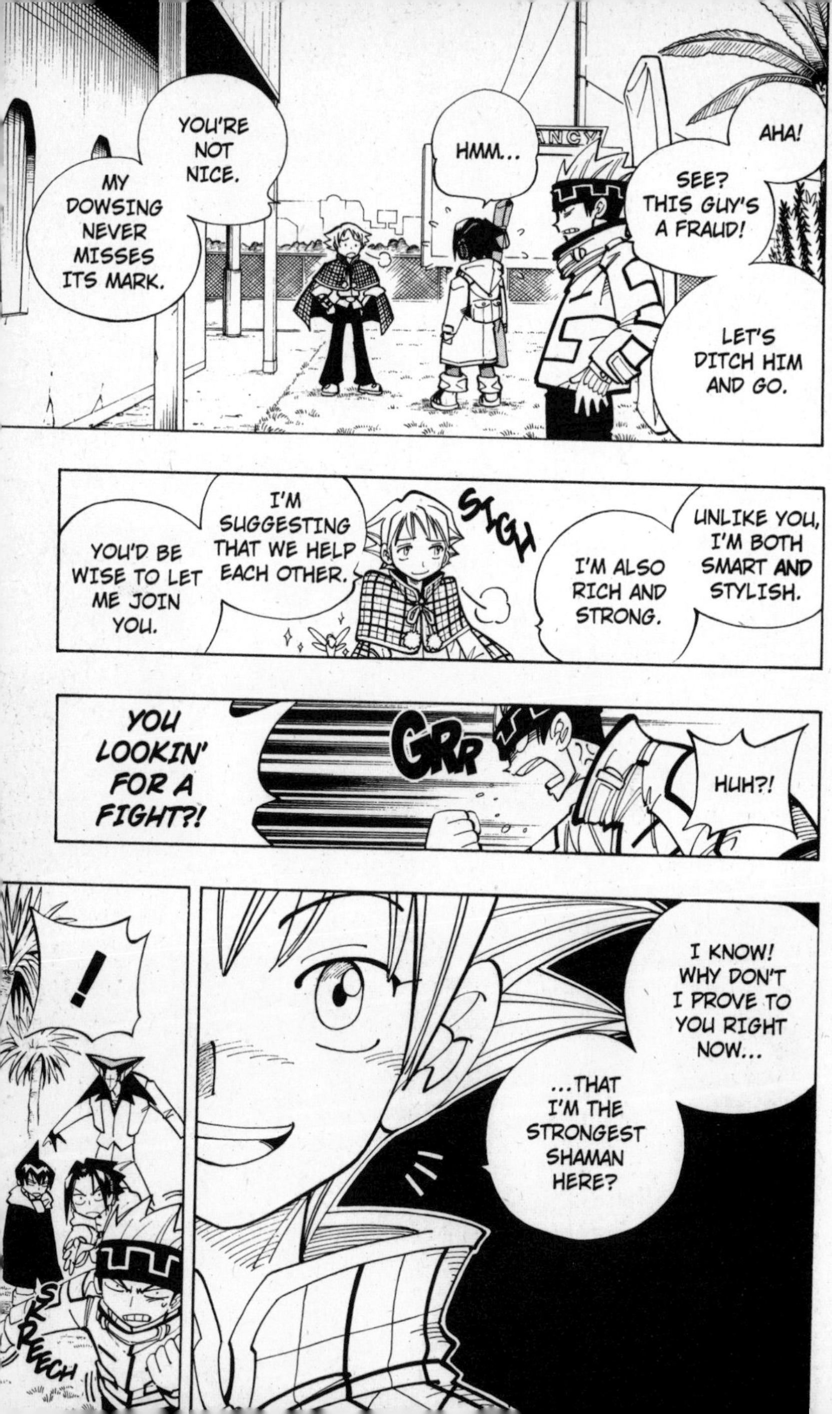
AHA!
SEE? THIS GUY'S A FRAUD!
LET'S DITCH HIM AND GO.
HMM...
YOU'RE NOT NICE.
MY DOWSING NEVER MISSES ITS MARK.
UNLIKE YOU, I'M BOTH SMART AND STYLISH.
I'M ALSO RICH AND STRONG.
SIGH
I'M SUGGESTING THAT WE HELP EACH OTHER.
YOU'D BE WISE TO LET ME JOIN YOU.
HUH?!
GRR
YOU LOOKIN' FOR A FIGHT?!
I KNOW! WHY DON'T I PROVE TO YOU RIGHT NOW...
...THAT I'M THE STRONGEST SHAMAN HERE?
!
SKREECH

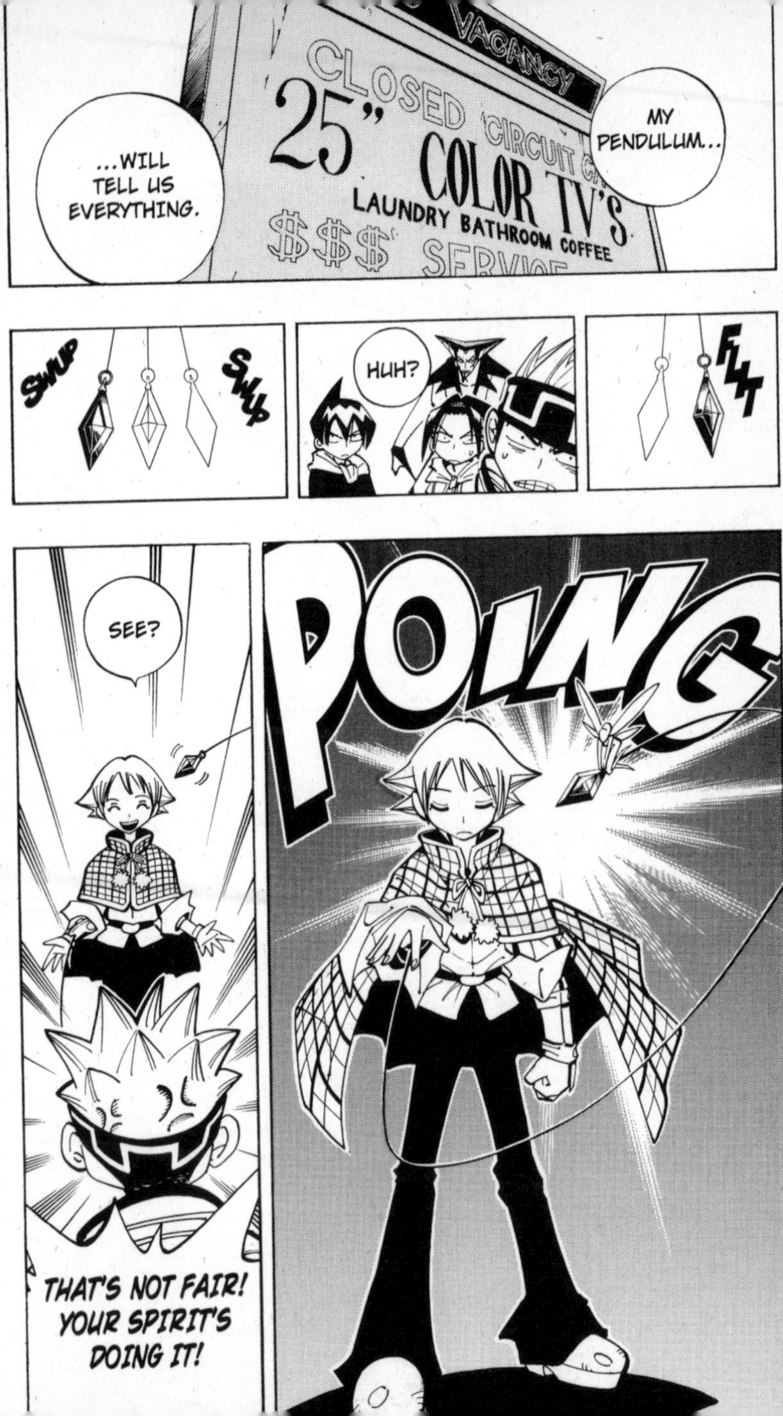
VACANCY
CLOSED CIRCUIT
25" COLOR TV'S
LAUNDRY BATHROOM COFFEE
MY PENDULUM...
...WILL TELL US EVERYTHING.
FLKT
HUH?
SWUP
SWUP
POING
SEE?
THAT'S NOT FAIR! YOUR SPIRIT'S DOING IT!

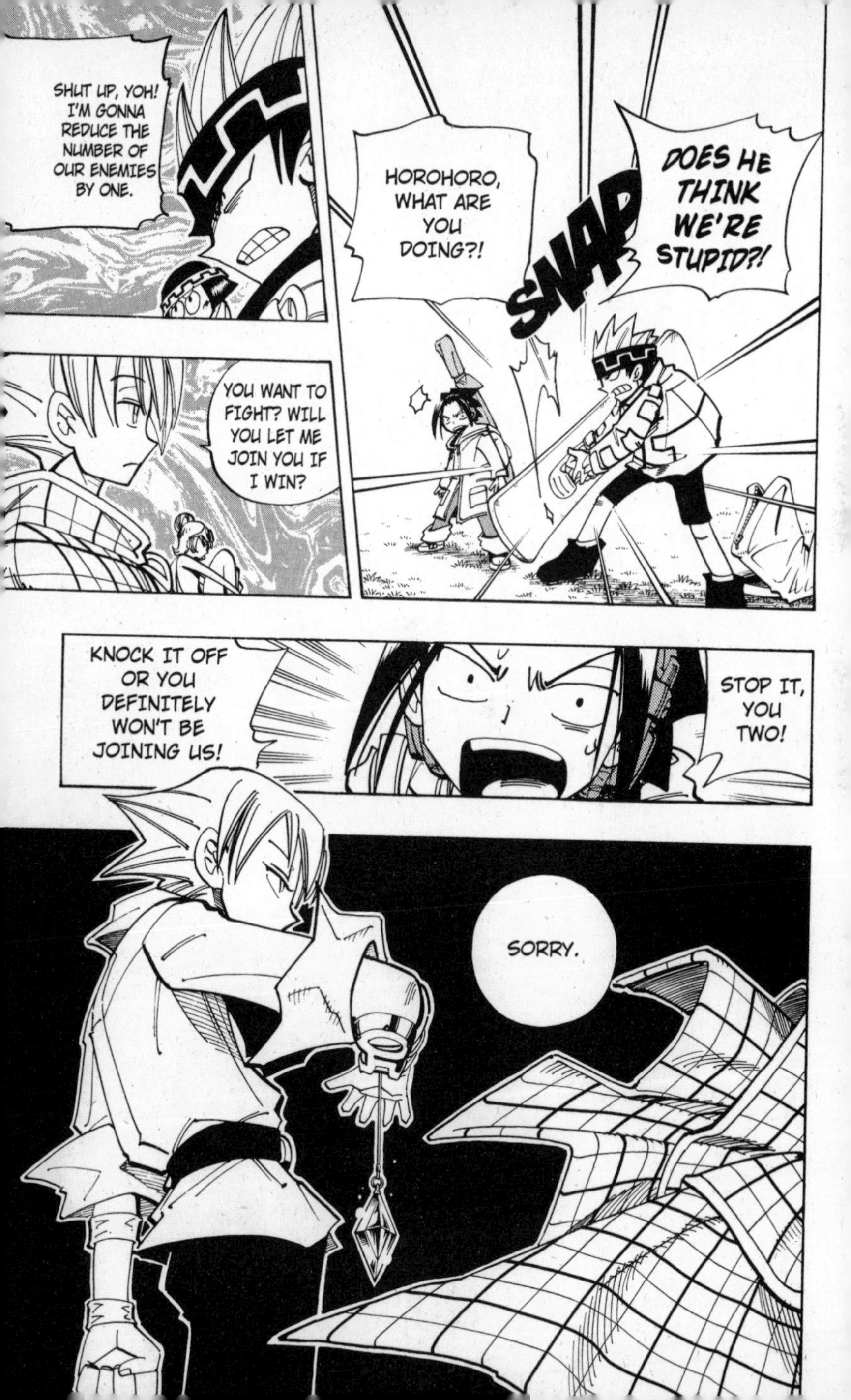

DOES HE THINK WE'RE STUPID?!
HOROHORO, WHAT ARE YOU DOING?!
SNAP
SHUT UP, YOH! I'M GONNA REDUCE THE NUMBER OF OUR ENEMIES BY ONE.
YOU WANT TO FIGHT? WILL YOU LET ME JOIN YOU IF I WIN?
STOP IT, YOU TWO!
KNOCK IT OFF OR YOU DEFINITELY WON'T BE JOINING US!
SORRY.

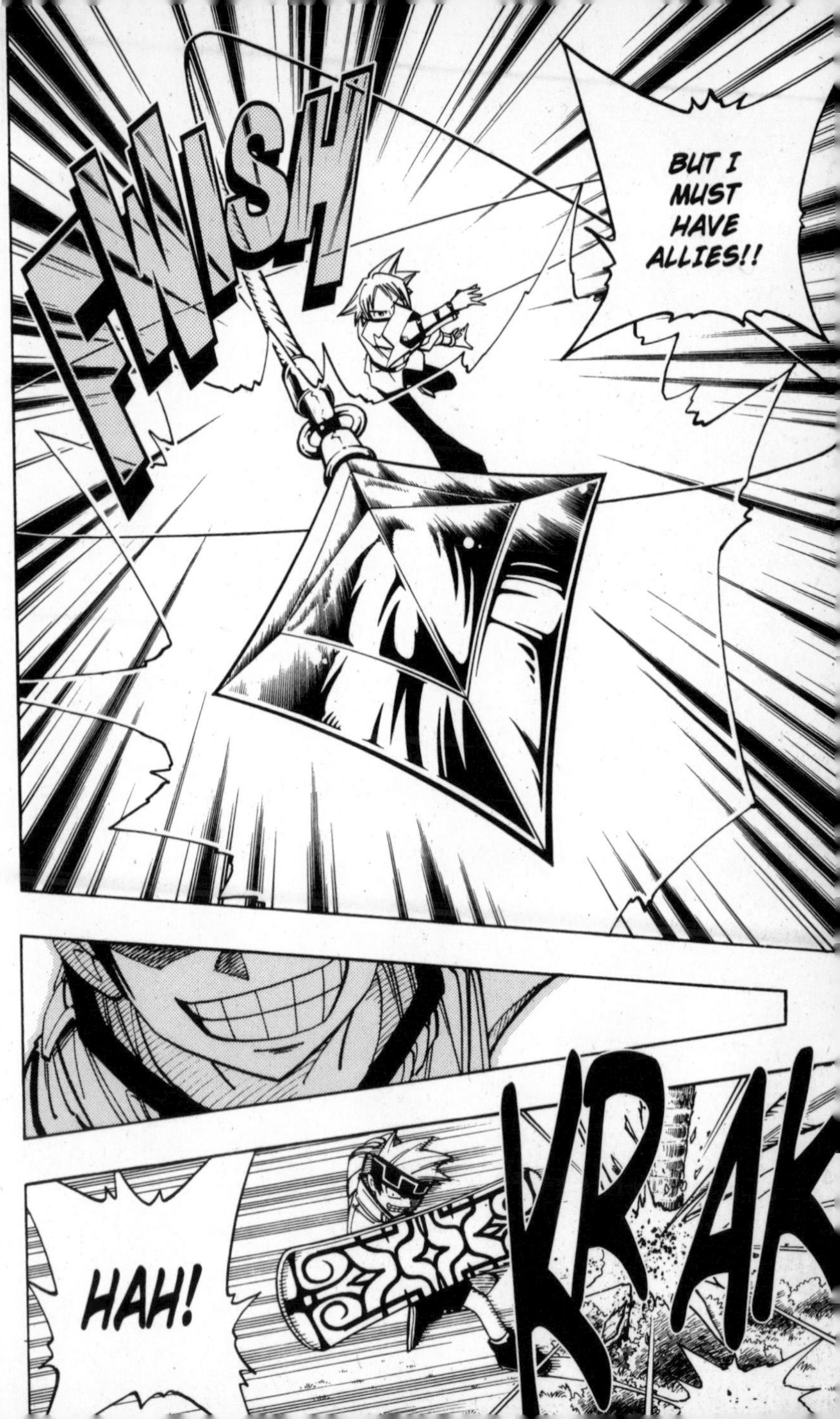
BUT I MUST HAVE ALLIES!!
FWISH
KRAK
HAH!

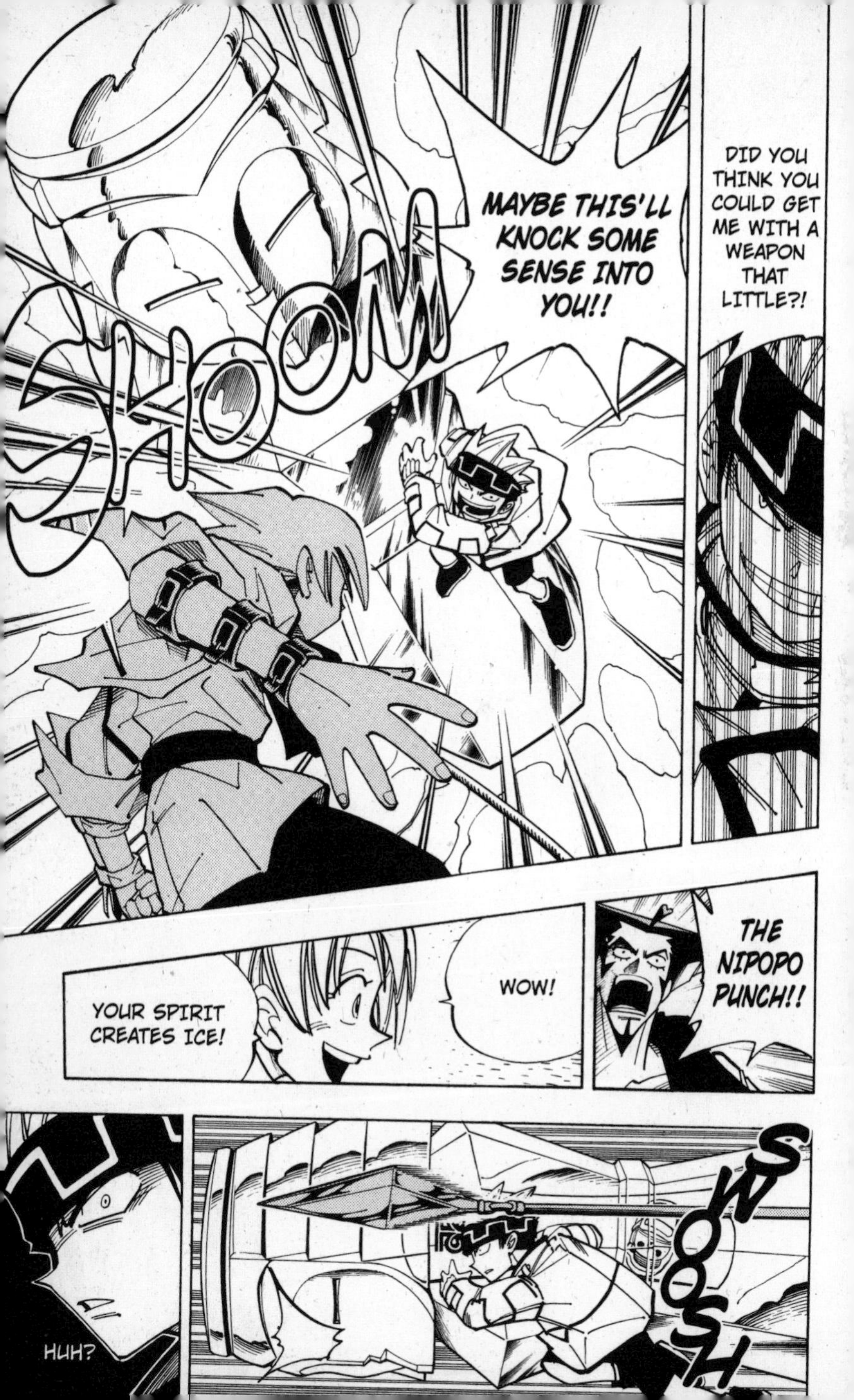
DID YOU THINK YOU COULD GET ME WITH A WEAPON THAT LITTLE?!
MAYBE THIS'LL KNOCK SOME SENSE INTO YOU!!
SHOOM
THE NIPOPO PUNCH!!
WOW!
YOUR SPIRIT CREATES ICE!
SWOOSH
HUH?

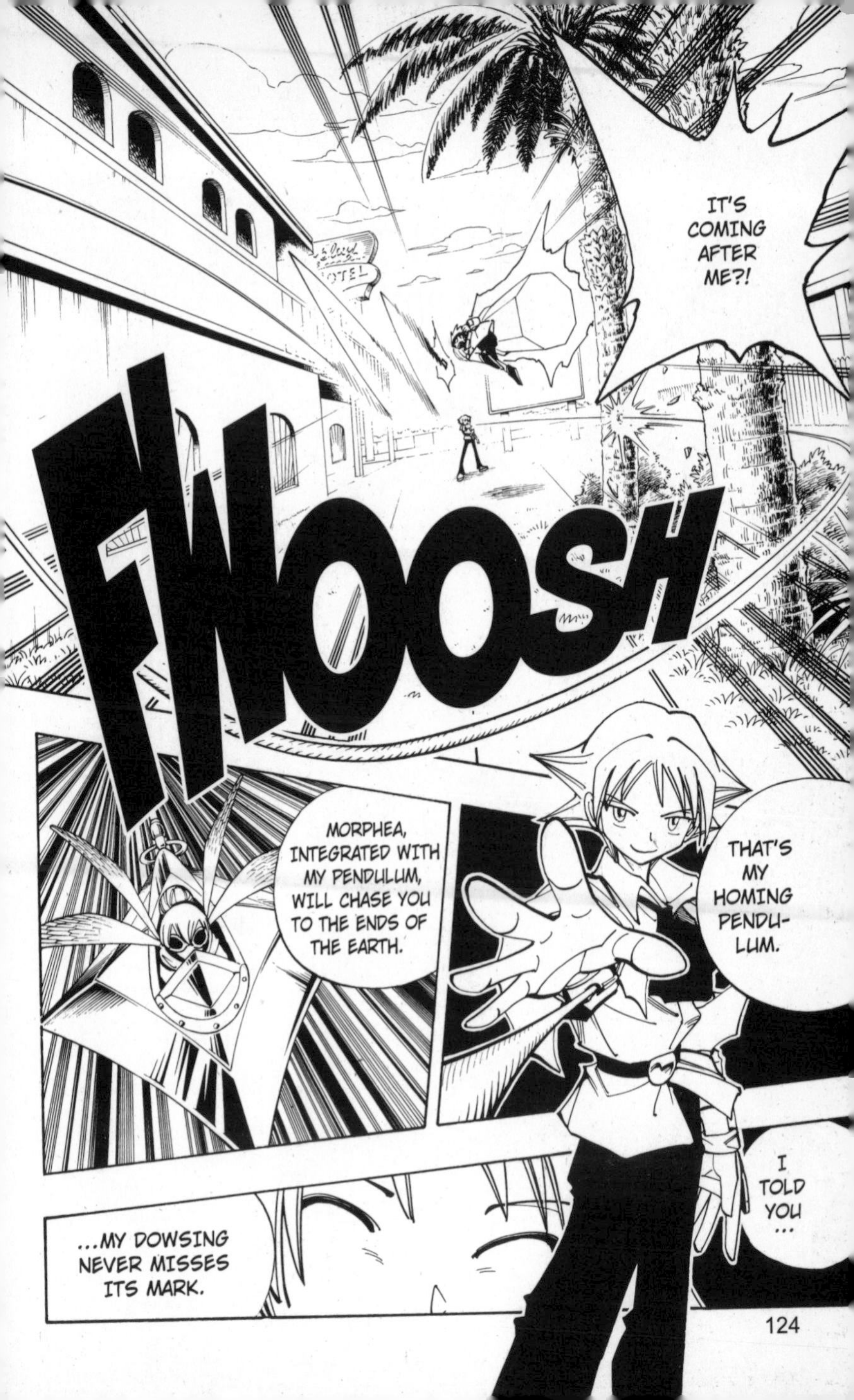
IT'S COMING AFTER ME?!
HOTEL
FWOOSH
THAT'S MY HOMING PENDULUM.
MORPHEA, INTEGRATED WITH MY PENDULUM, WILL CHASE YOU TO THE ENDS OF THE EARTH.
I TOLD YOU...
...MY DOWSING NEVER MISSES ITS MARK.

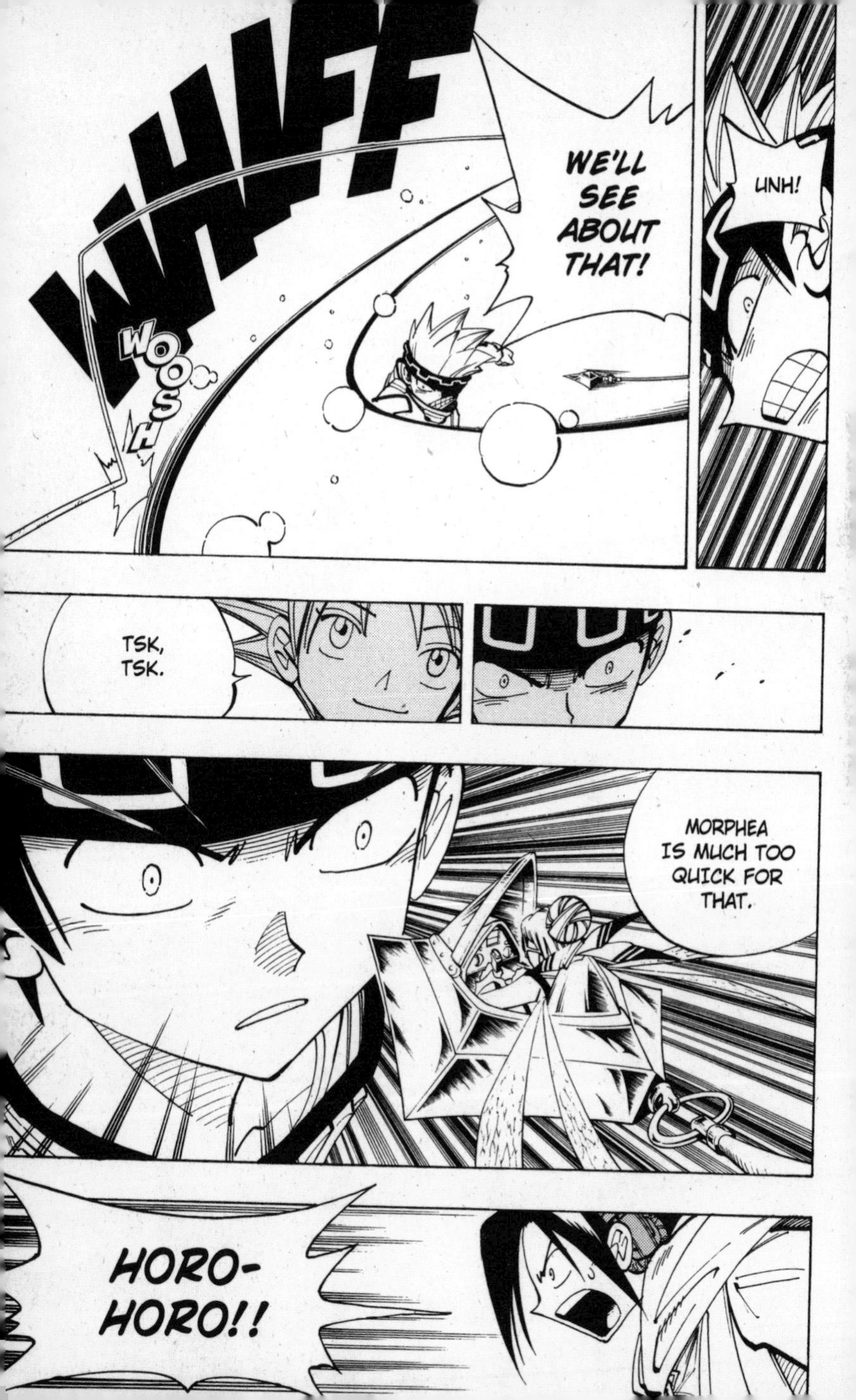
UNH!
WE'LL SEE ABOUT THAT!
WHIFF
WOOSH
TSK, TSK.
MORPHEA IS MUCH TOO QUICK FOR THAT.
HORO-HORO!!

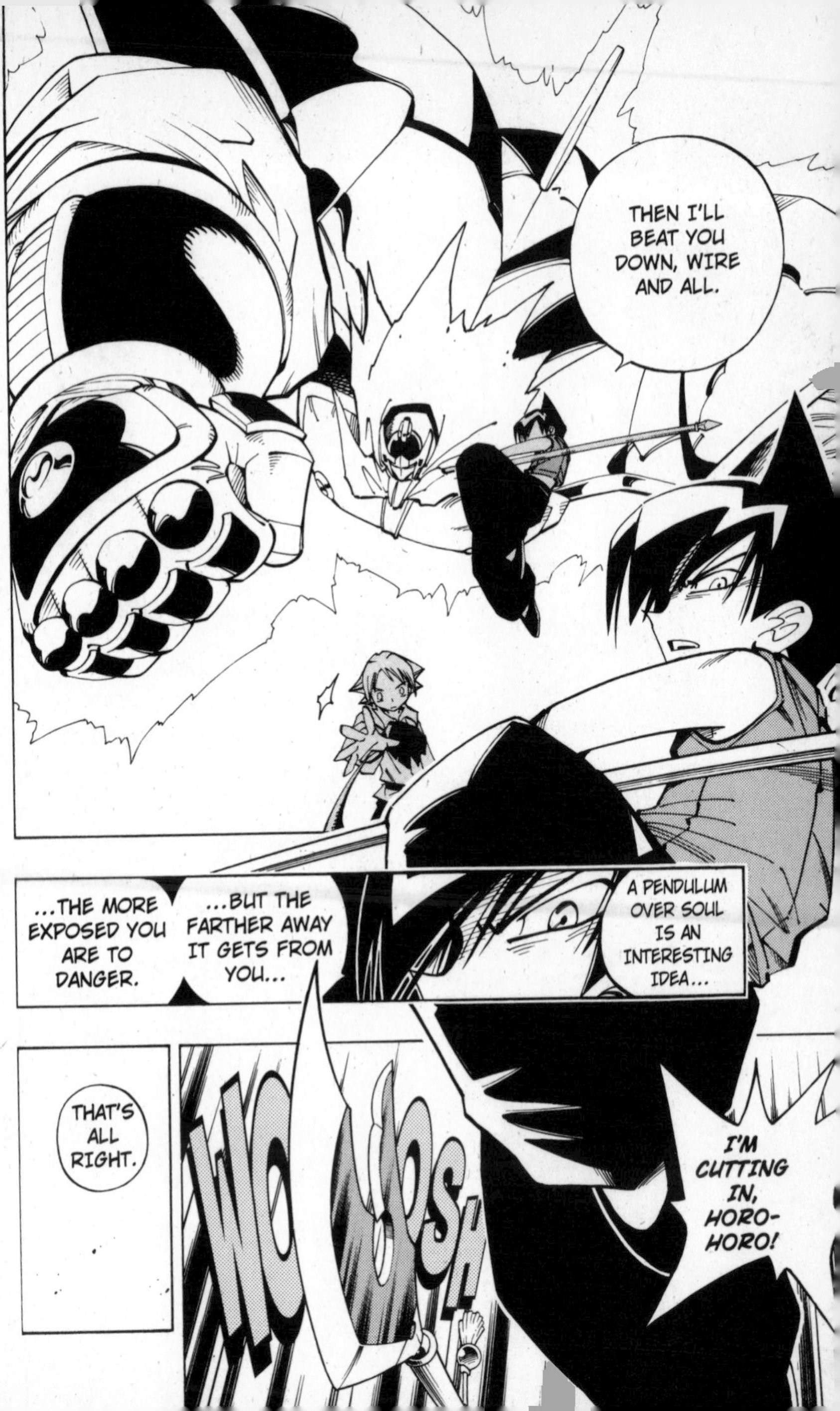
THEN I'LL BEAT YOU DOWN, WIRE AND ALL.
A PENDULUM OVER SOUL IS AN INTERESTING IDEA...
...BUT THE FARTHER AWAY IT GETS FROM YOU...
...THE MORE EXPOSED YOU ARE TO DANGER.
I'M CUTTING IN, HORO-HORO!
THAT'S ALL RIGHT.

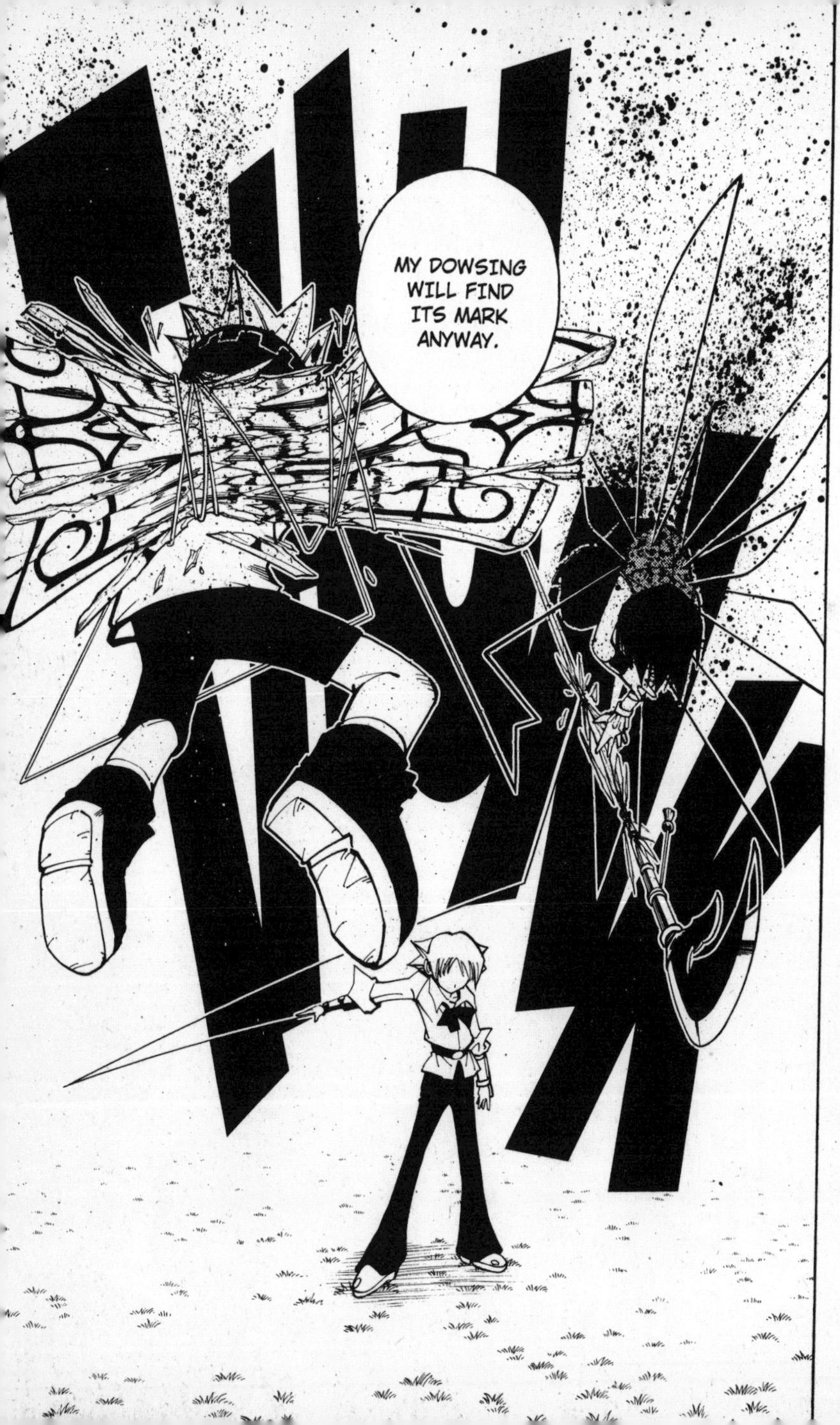
MY DOWSING WILL FIND ITS MARK ANYWAY.

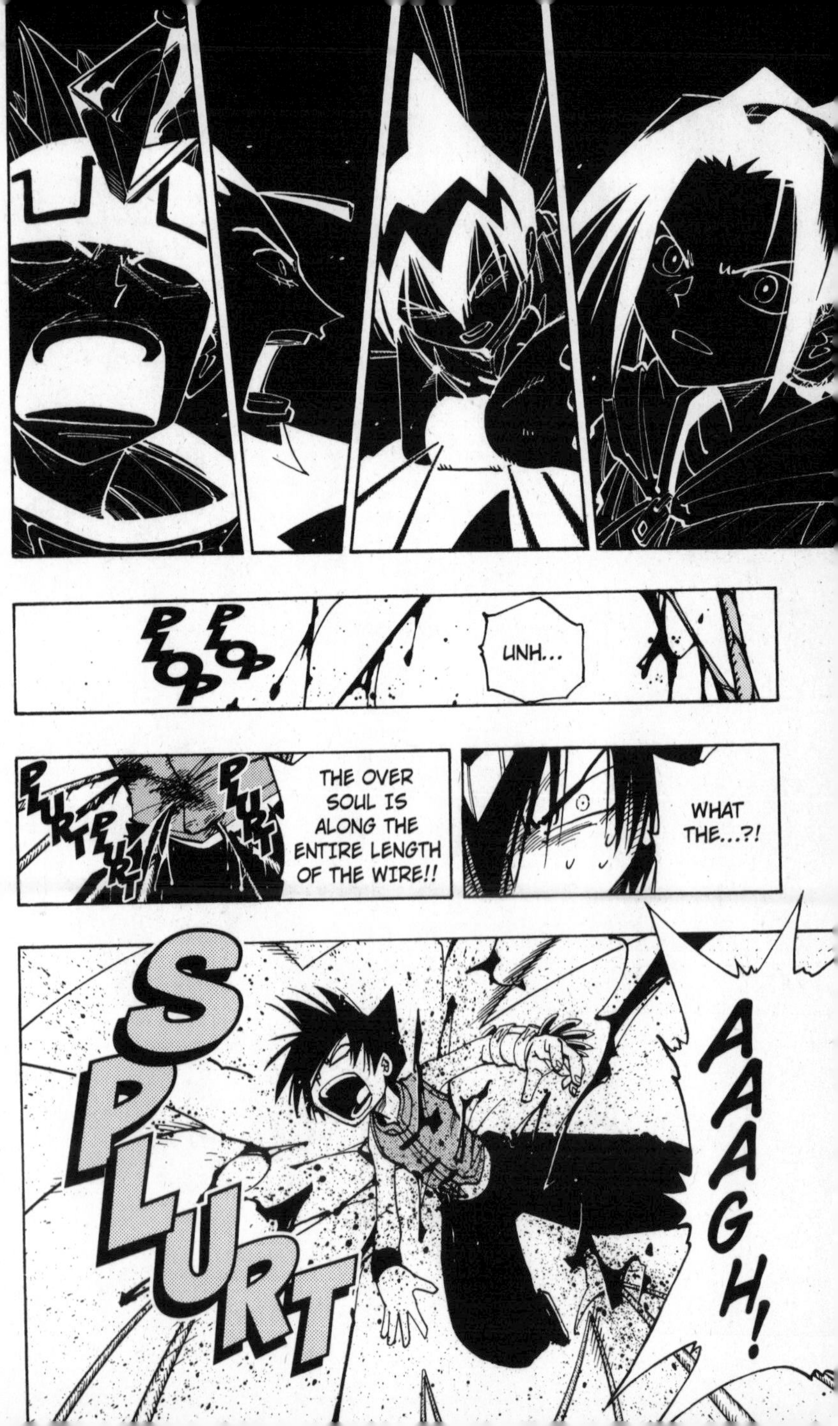
UNH...
PLOP PLOP
WHAT THE...?!
THE OVER SOUL IS ALONG THE ENTIRE LENGTH OF THE WIRE!!
PLURT PLURT
AAAGH!
SPLURT

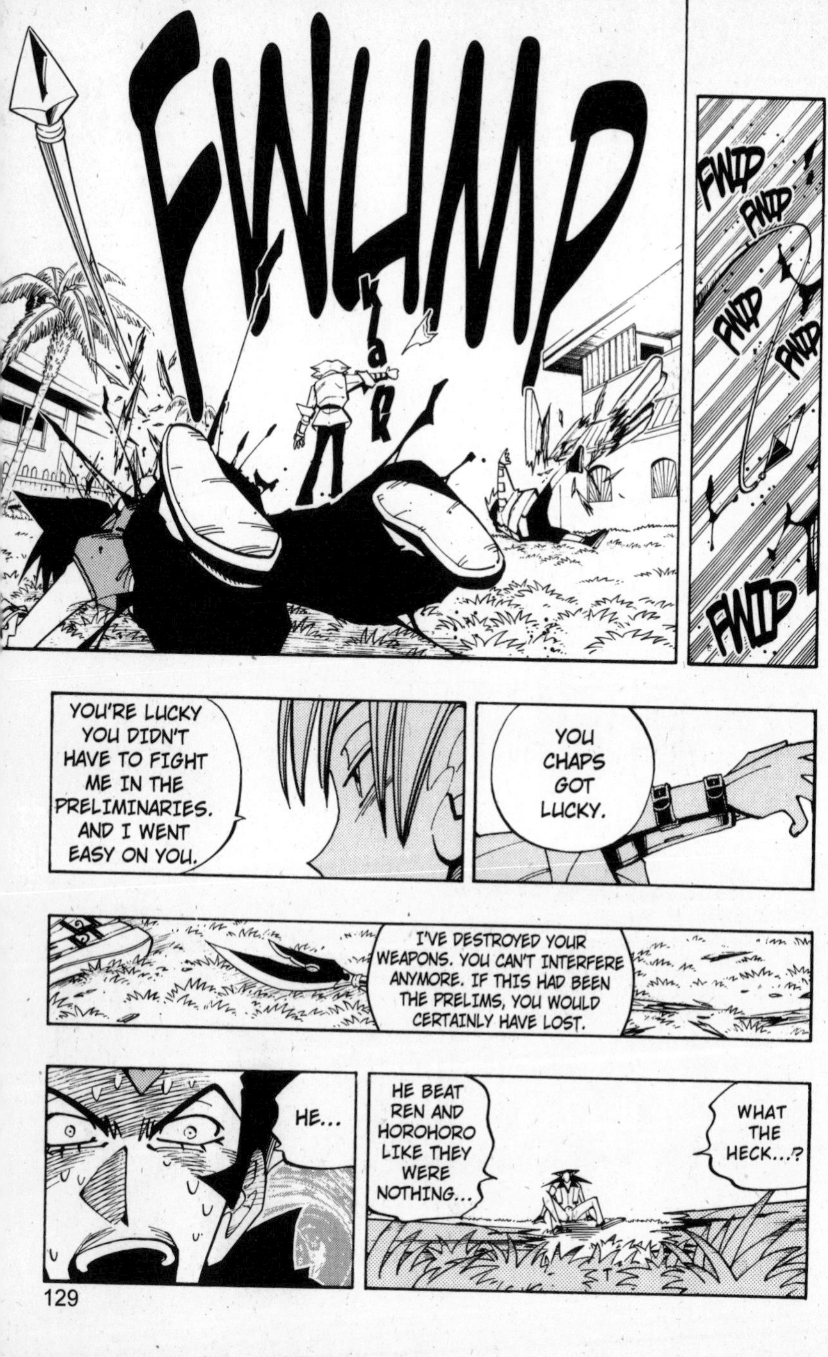
FWIP
FWIP
FWIP
FWIP
FWIP
FWUMP
KLAK
YOU CHAPS GOT LUCKY.
YOU'RE LUCKY YOU DIDN'T HAVE TO FIGHT ME IN THE PRELIMINARIES. AND I WENT EASY ON YOU.
I'VE DESTROYED YOUR WEAPONS. YOU CAN'T INTERFERE ANYMORE. IF THIS HAD BEEN THE PRELIMS, YOU WOULD CERTAINLY HAVE LOST.
WHAT THE HECK...?
HE BEAT REN AND HOROHORO LIKE THEY WERE NOTHING...
HE...

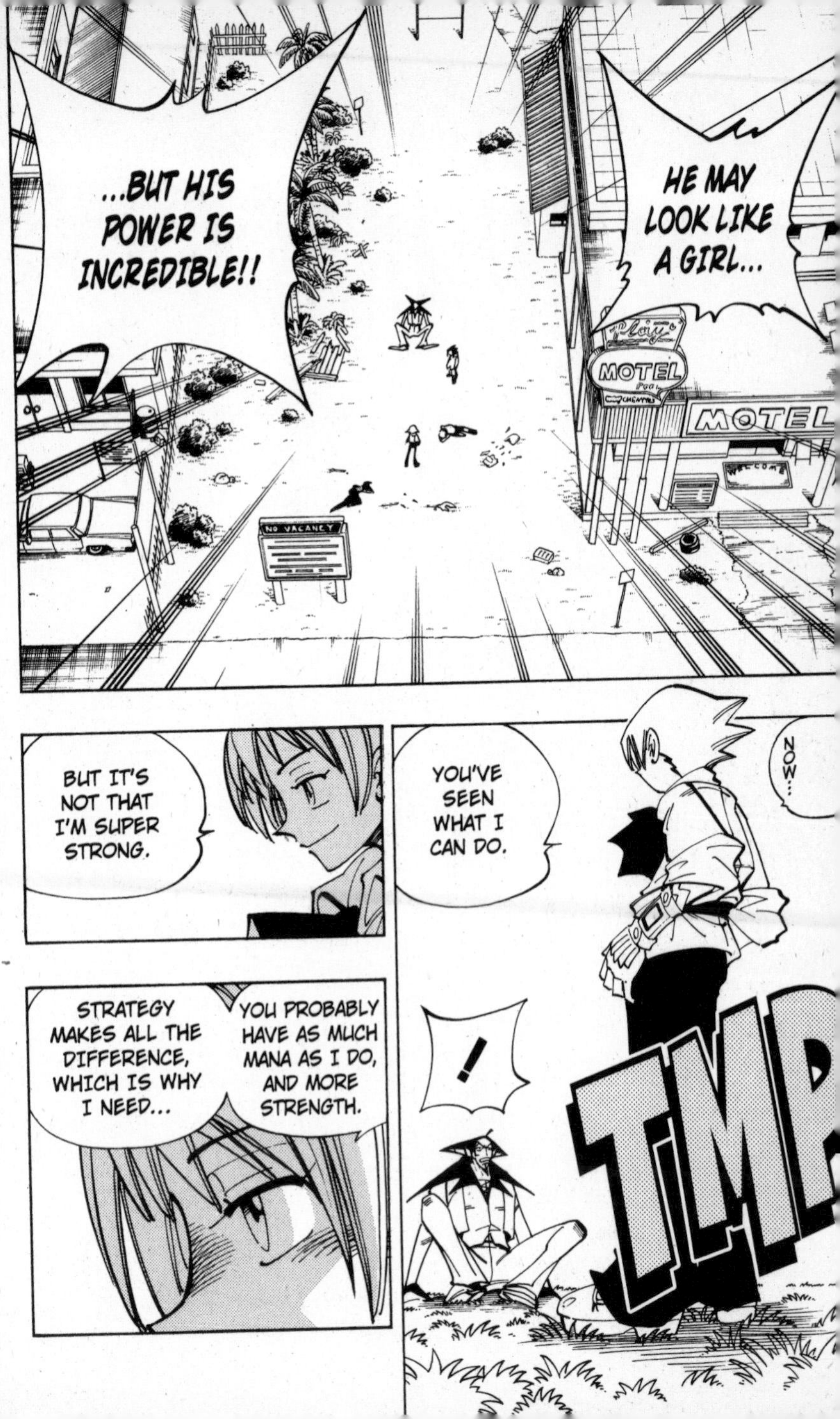
HE MAY LOOK LIKE A GIRL...
...BUT HIS POWER IS INCREDIBLE!!
MOTEL
MOTEL
NO VACANCY
NOW...
YOU'VE SEEN WHAT I CAN DO.
!
TMP
BUT IT'S NOT THAT I'M SUPER STRONG.
YOU PROBABLY HAVE AS MUCH MANA AS I DO, AND MORE STRENGTH.
STRATEGY MAKES ALL THE DIFFERENCE, WHICH IS WHY I NEED...

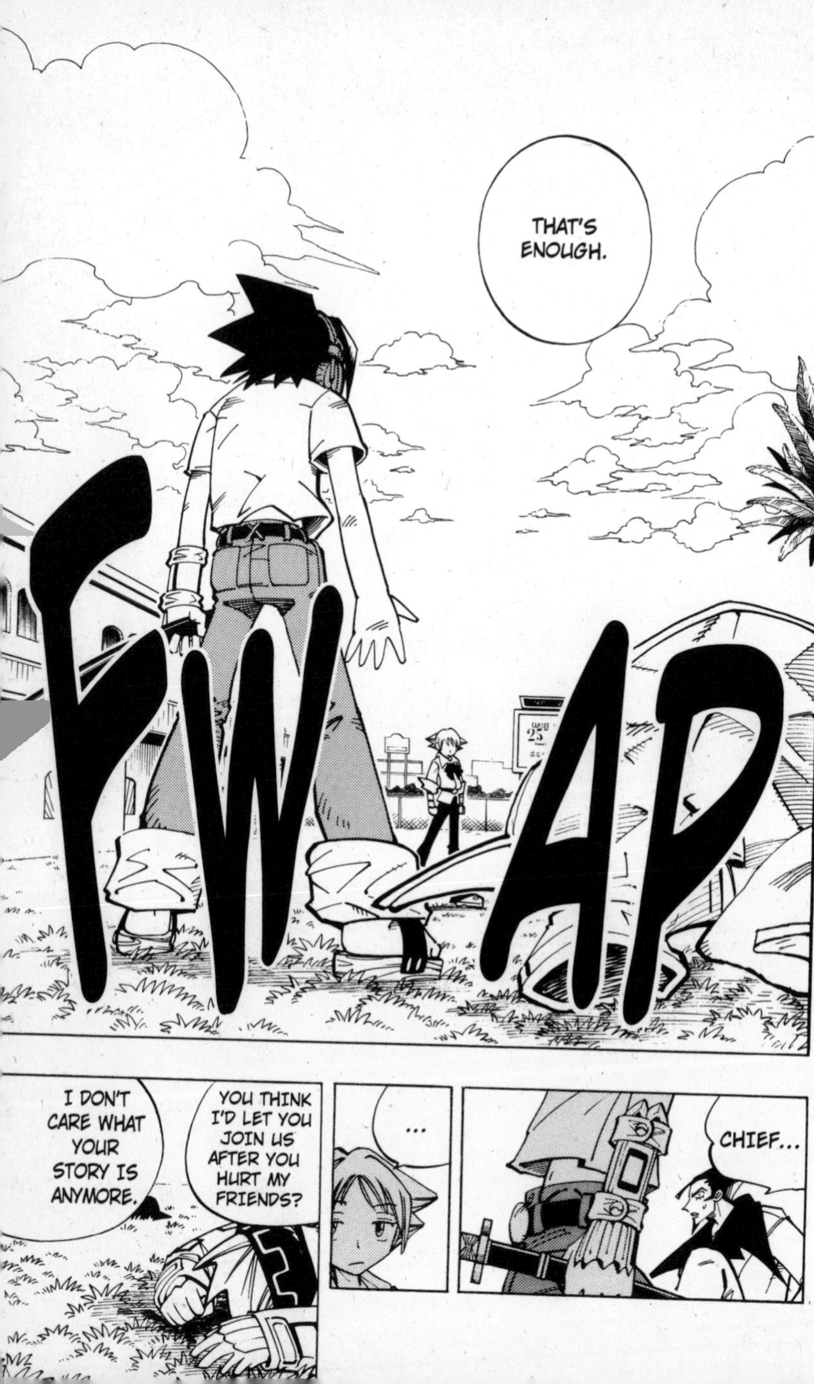
THAT'S ENOUGH.
FWAP
CHIEF...
...
YOU THINK I'D LET YOU JOIN US AFTER YOU HURT MY FRIENDS?
I DON'T CARE WHAT YOUR STORY IS ANYMORE.

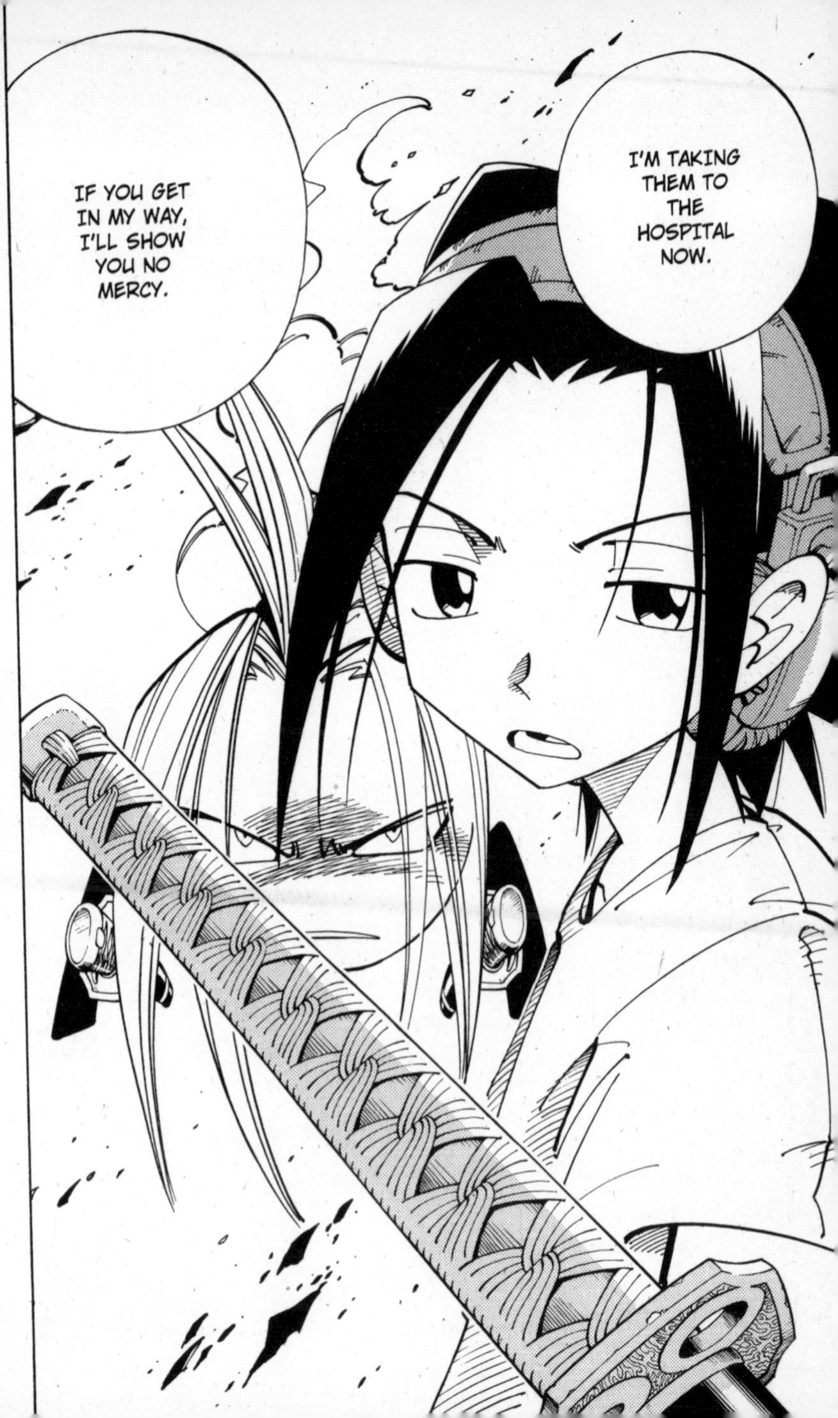
I'M TAKING THEM TO THE HOSPITAL NOW.
IF YOU GET IN MY WAY, I'LL SHOW YOU NO MERCY.

READ THIS WAY

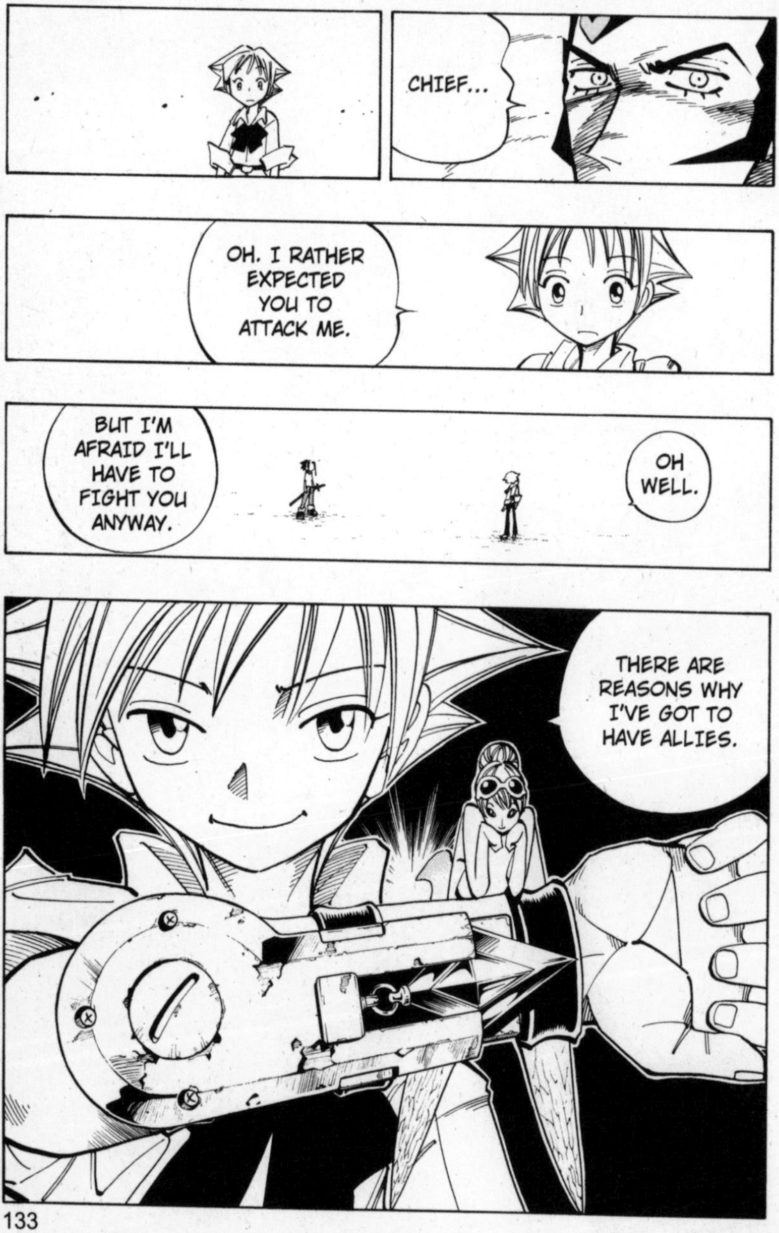
CHIEF...
OH. I RATHER EXPECTED YOU TO ATTACK ME.
OH WELL.
BUT I'M AFRAID I'LL HAVE TO FIGHT YOU ANYWAY.
THERE ARE REASONS WHY I'VE GOT TO HAVE ALLIES.

SHAMAN KING
10

**PENDULUM BAY
"ELIZABETH"**

Shaman King™

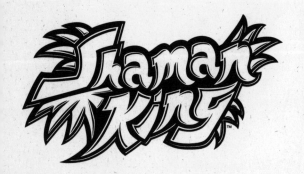

Reincarnation 87: Lyserg the Avenger

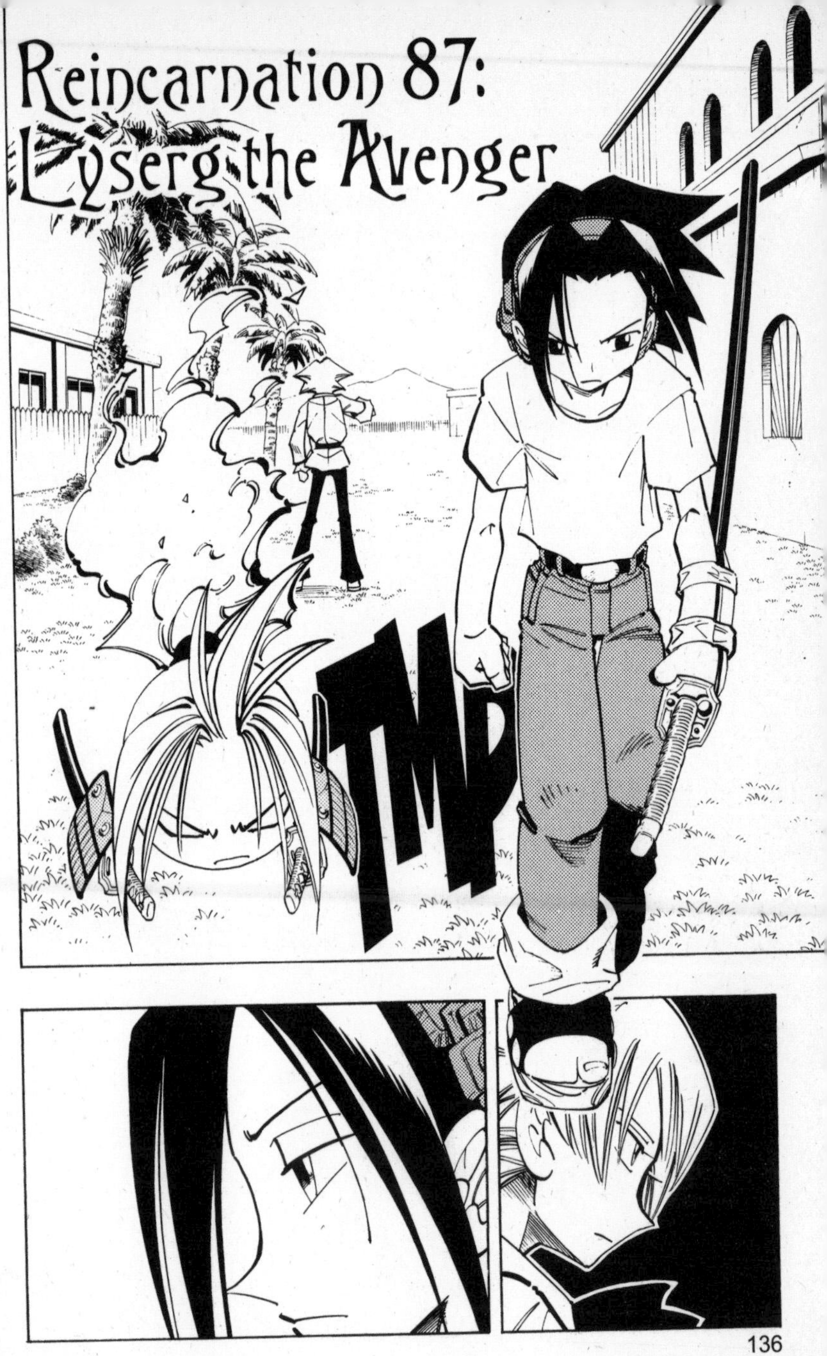
TMP

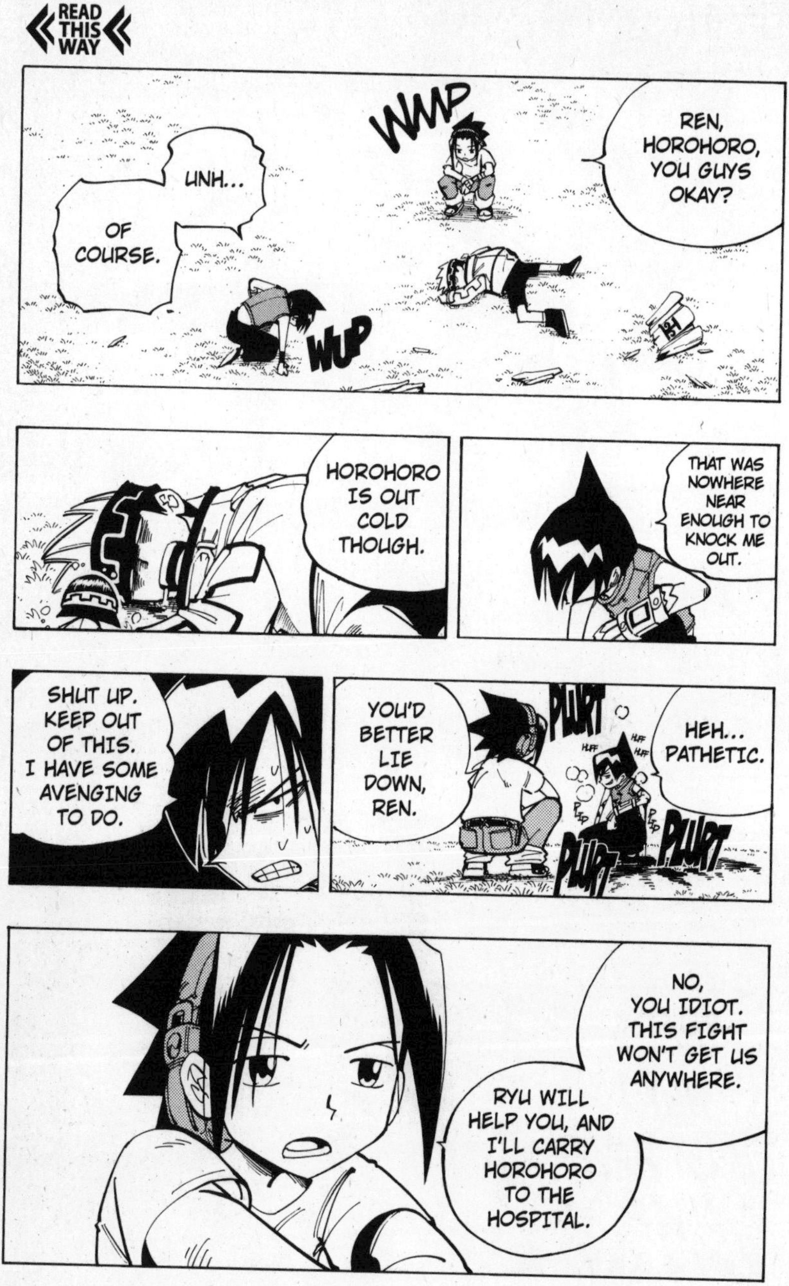
READ THIS WAY
REN, HOROHORO, YOU GUYS OKAY?
WMP
UNH...
OF COURSE.
WUP
THAT WAS NOWHERE NEAR ENOUGH TO KNOCK ME OUT.
HOROHORO IS OUT COLD THOUGH.
HEH... PATHETIC.
HUFF HUFF
HUFF
PLURT
PLURT
PLURT
YOU'D BETTER LIE DOWN, REN.
SHUT UP. KEEP OUT OF THIS. I HAVE SOME AVENGING TO DO.
NO, YOU IDIOT. THIS FIGHT WON'T GET US ANYWHERE.
RYU WILL HELP YOU, AND I'LL CARRY HOROHORO TO THE HOSPITAL.

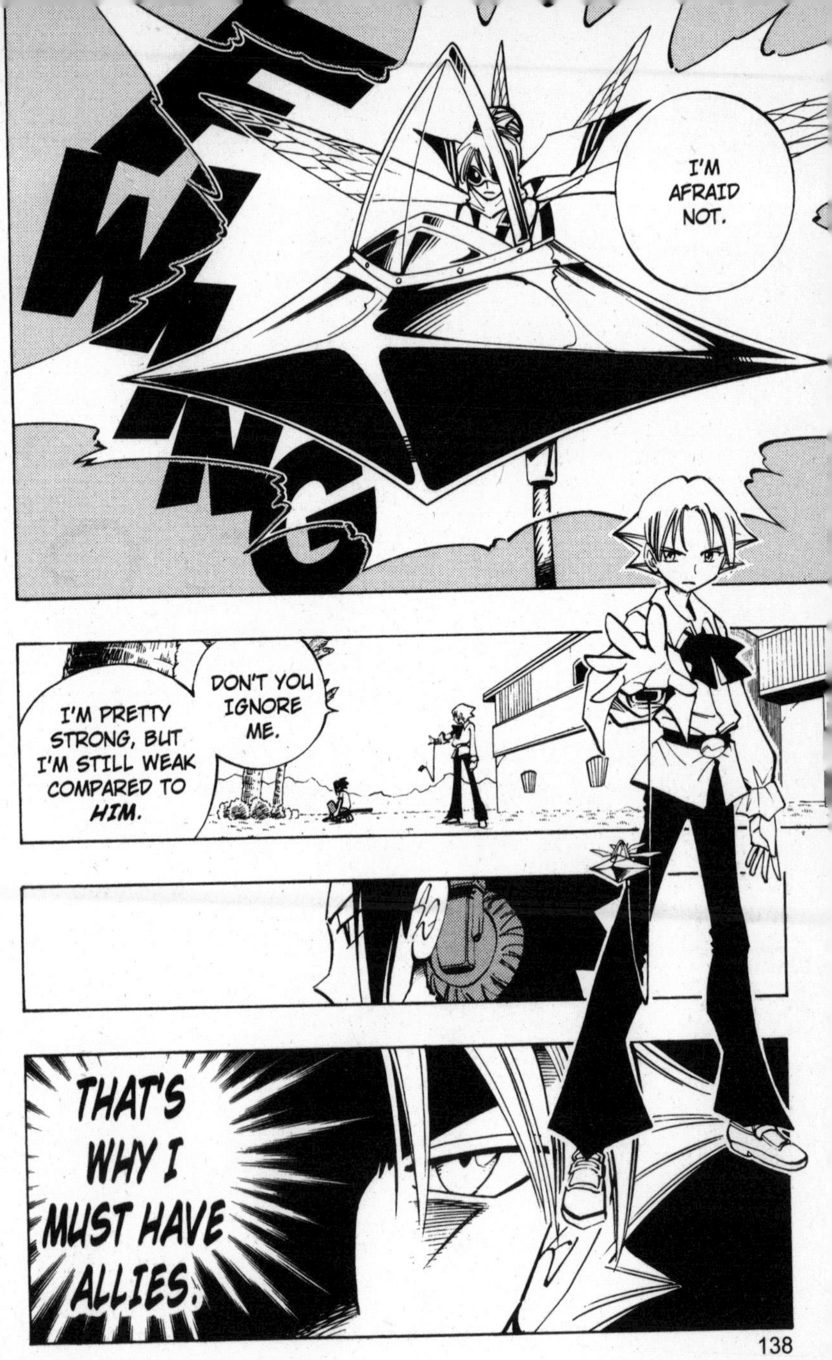
I'M AFRAID NOT.
FWWWING
DON'T YOU IGNORE ME.
I'M PRETTY STRONG, BUT I'M STILL WEAK COMPARED TO HIM.
THAT'S WHY I MUST HAVE ALLIES.

Reincarnation 87: Lyserg the Avenger

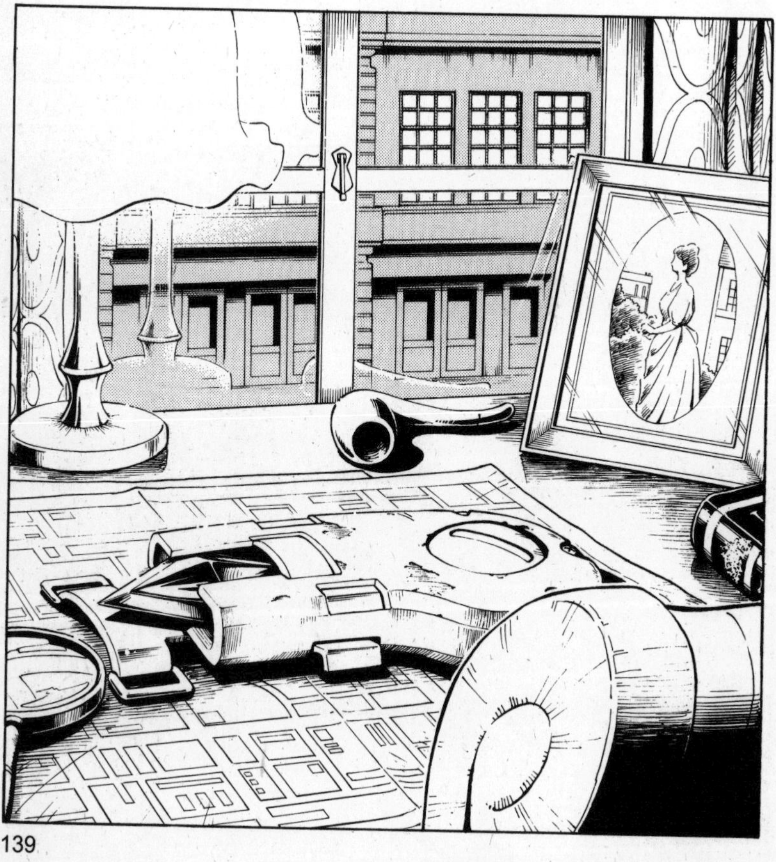

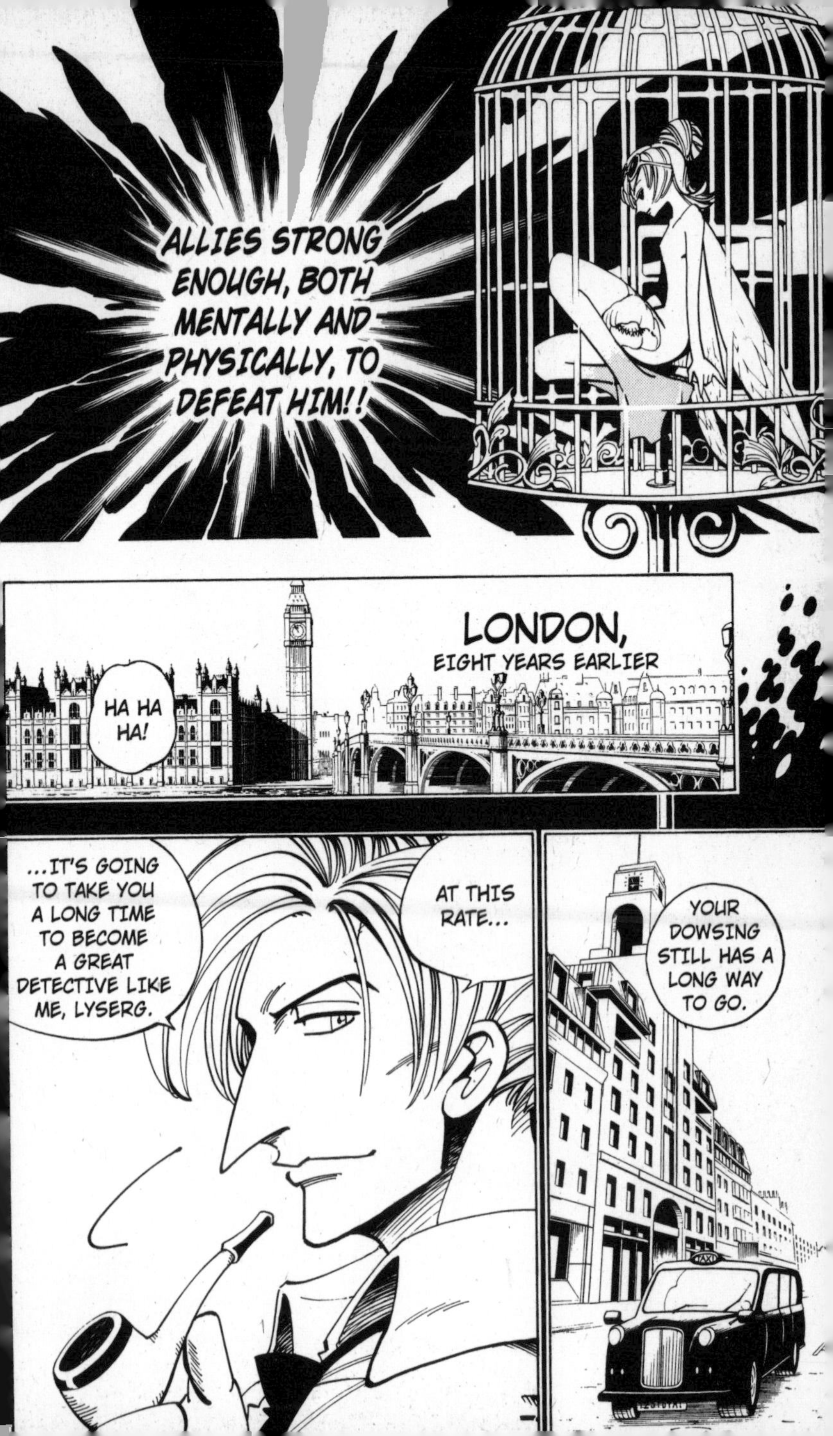
ALLIES STRONG ENOUGH, BOTH MENTALLY AND PHYSICALLY, TO DEFEAT HIM!!
LONDON, EIGHT YEARS EARLIER
HA HA HA!
YOUR DOWSING STILL HAS A LONG WAY TO GO.
AT THIS RATE...
...IT'S GOING TO TAKE YOU A LONG TIME TO BECOME A GREAT DETECTIVE LIKE ME, LYSERG.

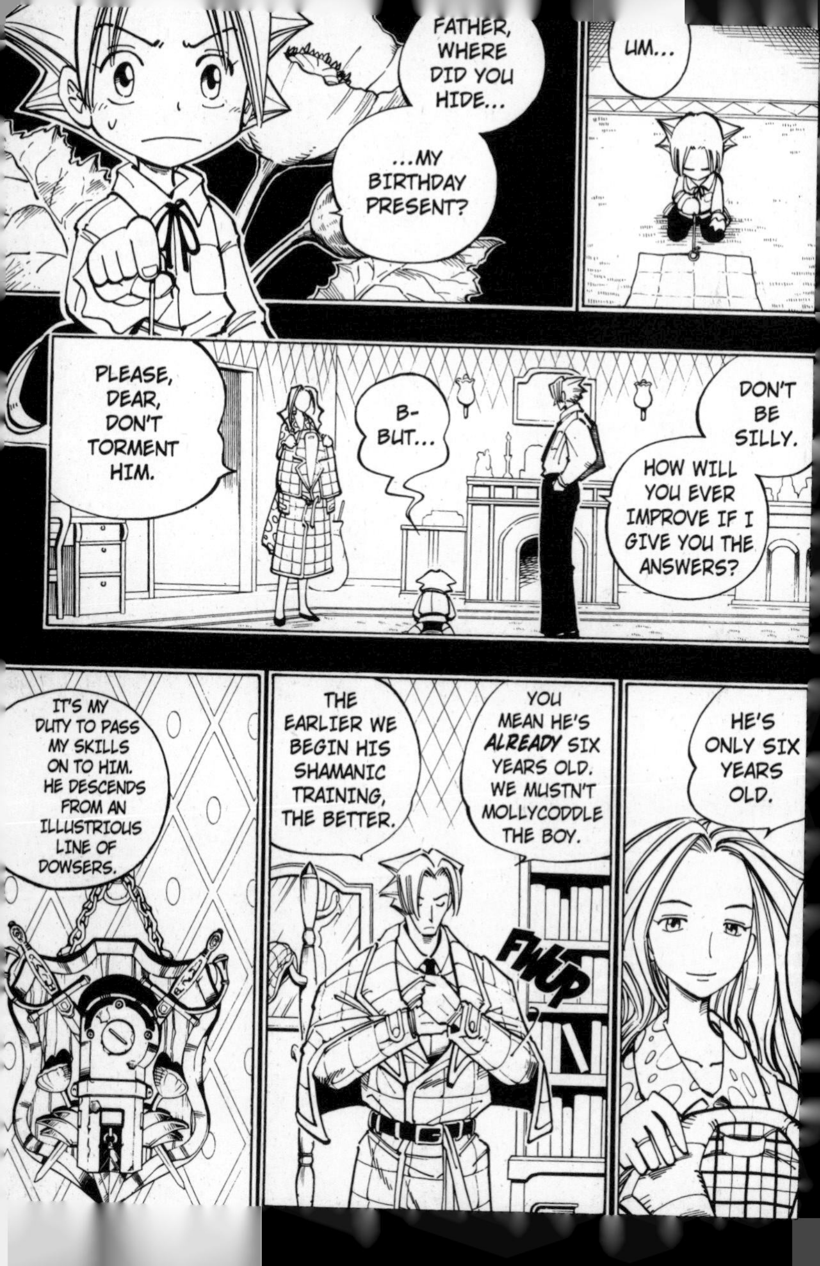
UM...
FATHER, WHERE DID YOU HIDE...
...MY BIRTHDAY PRESENT?
DON'T BE SILLY.
HOW WILL YOU EVER IMPROVE IF I GIVE YOU THE ANSWERS?
B-BUT...
PLEASE, DEAR, DON'T TORMENT HIM.
HE'S ONLY SIX YEARS OLD.
YOU MEAN HE'S ALREADY SIX YEARS OLD. WE MUSTN'T MOLLYCODDLE THE BOY.
THE EARLIER WE BEGIN HIS SHAMANIC TRAINING, THE BETTER.
FWUP
IT'S MY DUTY TO PASS MY SKILLS ON TO HIM. HE DESCENDS FROM AN ILLUSTRIOUS LINE OF DOWSERS.

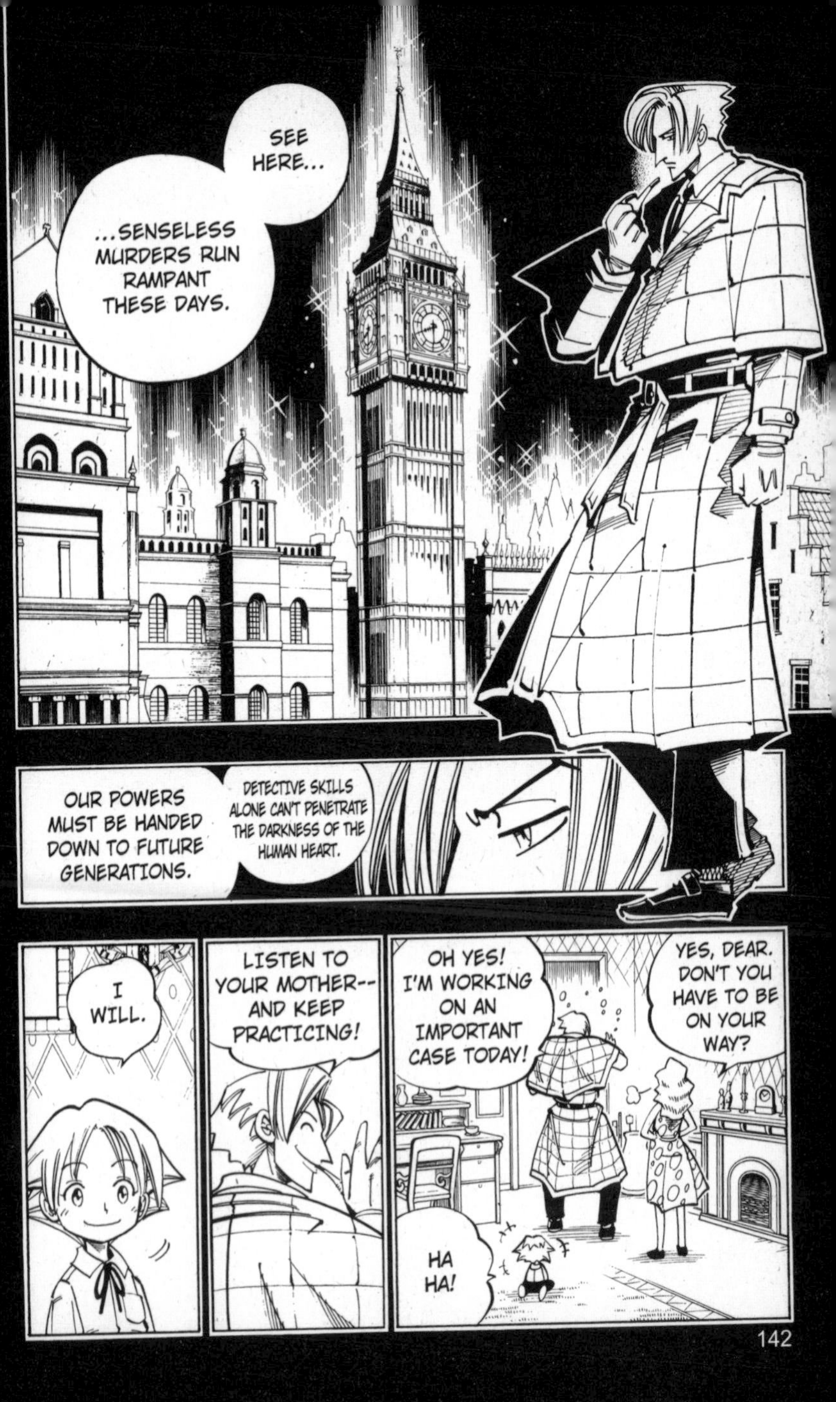
SEE HERE...
...SENSELESS MURDERS RUN RAMPANT THESE DAYS.
DETECTIVE SKILLS ALONE CAN'T PENETRATE THE DARKNESS OF THE HUMAN HEART.
OUR POWERS MUST BE HANDED DOWN TO FUTURE GENERATIONS.
YES, DEAR. DON'T YOU HAVE TO BE ON YOUR WAY?
OH YES! I'M WORKING ON AN IMPORTANT CASE TODAY!
HA HA!
LISTEN TO YOUR MOTHER--AND KEEP PRACTICING!
I WILL.

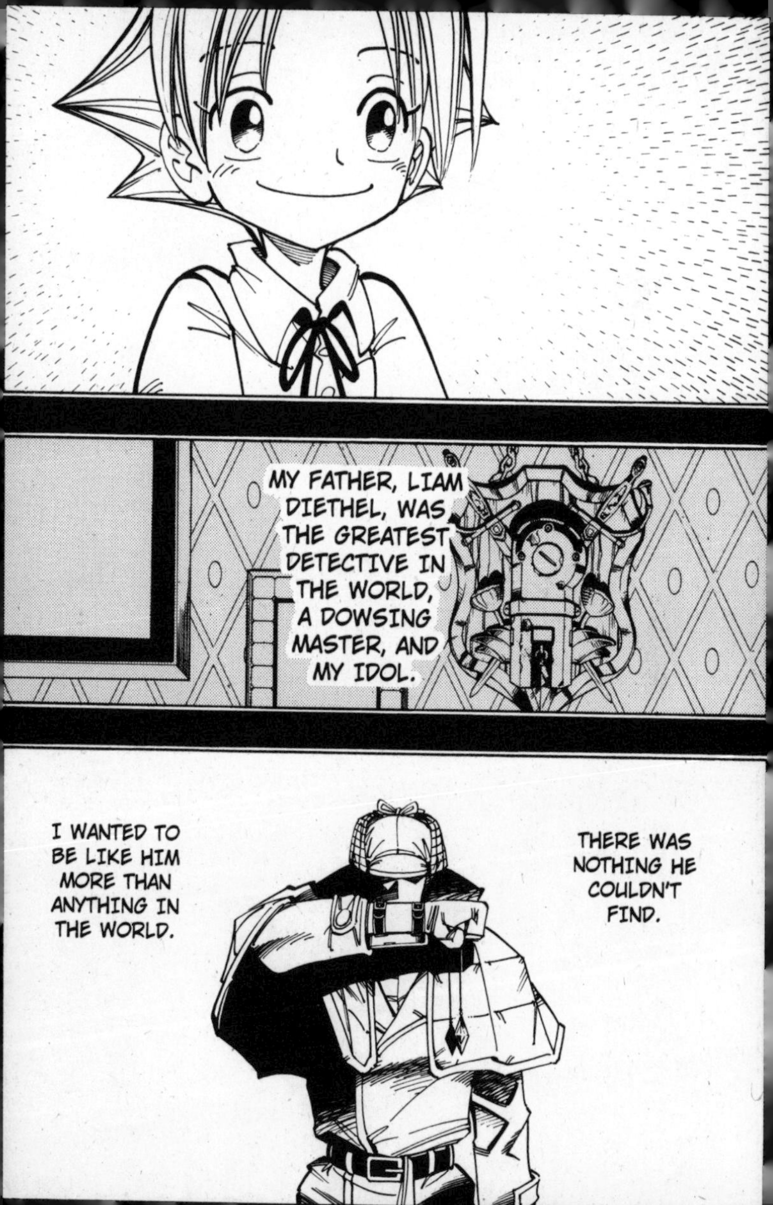
MY FATHER, LIAM DIETHEL, WAS THE GREATEST DETECTIVE IN THE WORLD, A DOWSING MASTER, AND MY IDOL.
THERE WAS NOTHING HE COULDN'T FIND.
I WANTED TO BE LIKE HIM MORE THAN ANYTHING IN THE WORLD.

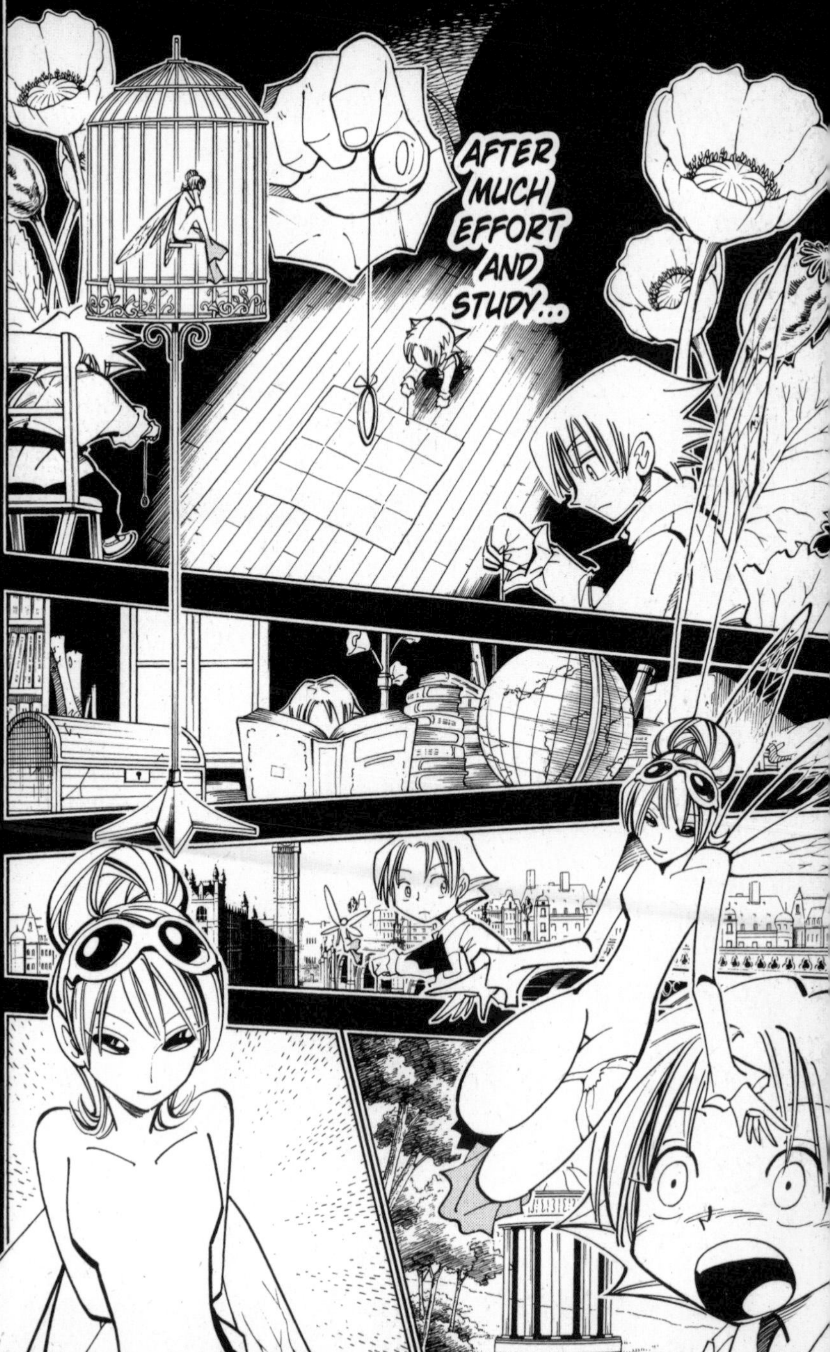
AFTER MUCH EFFORT AND STUDY...

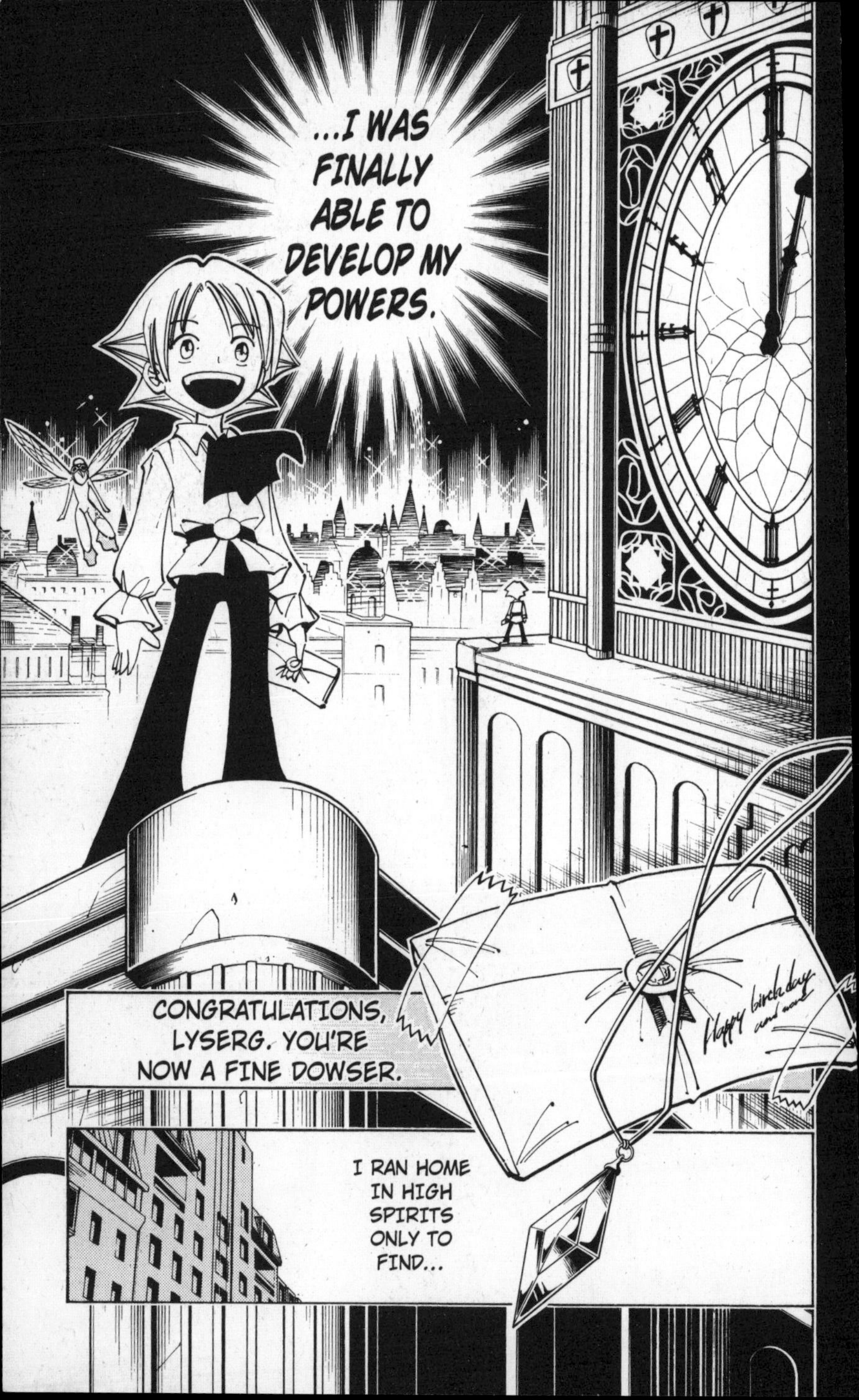
...I WAS FINALLY ABLE TO DEVELOP MY POWERS.
CONGRATULATIONS, LYSERG. YOU'RE NOW A FINE DOWSER.
I RAN HOME IN HIGH SPIRITS ONLY TO FIND...

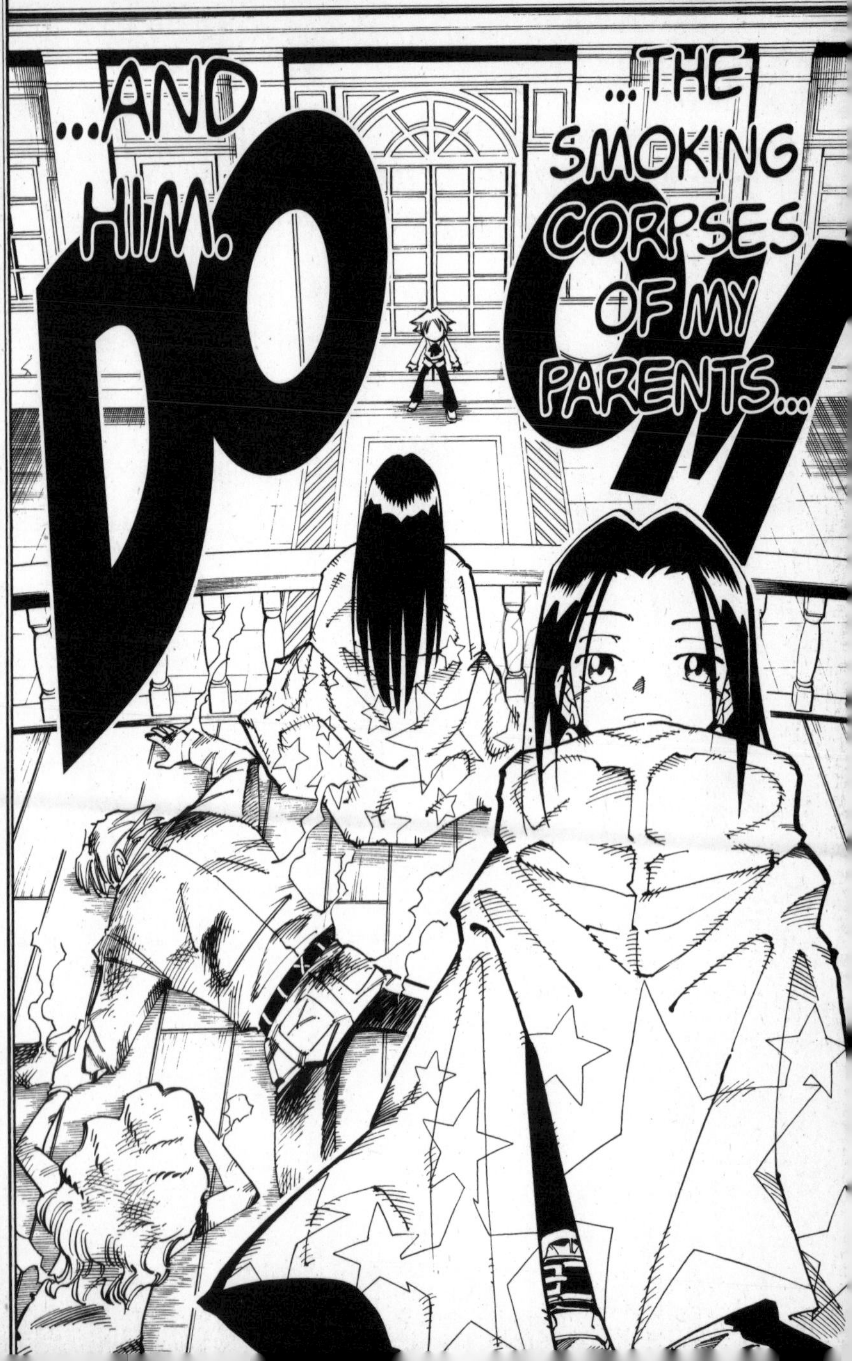
...THE SMOKING CORPSES OF MY PARENTS...
...AND HIM.
DOOM

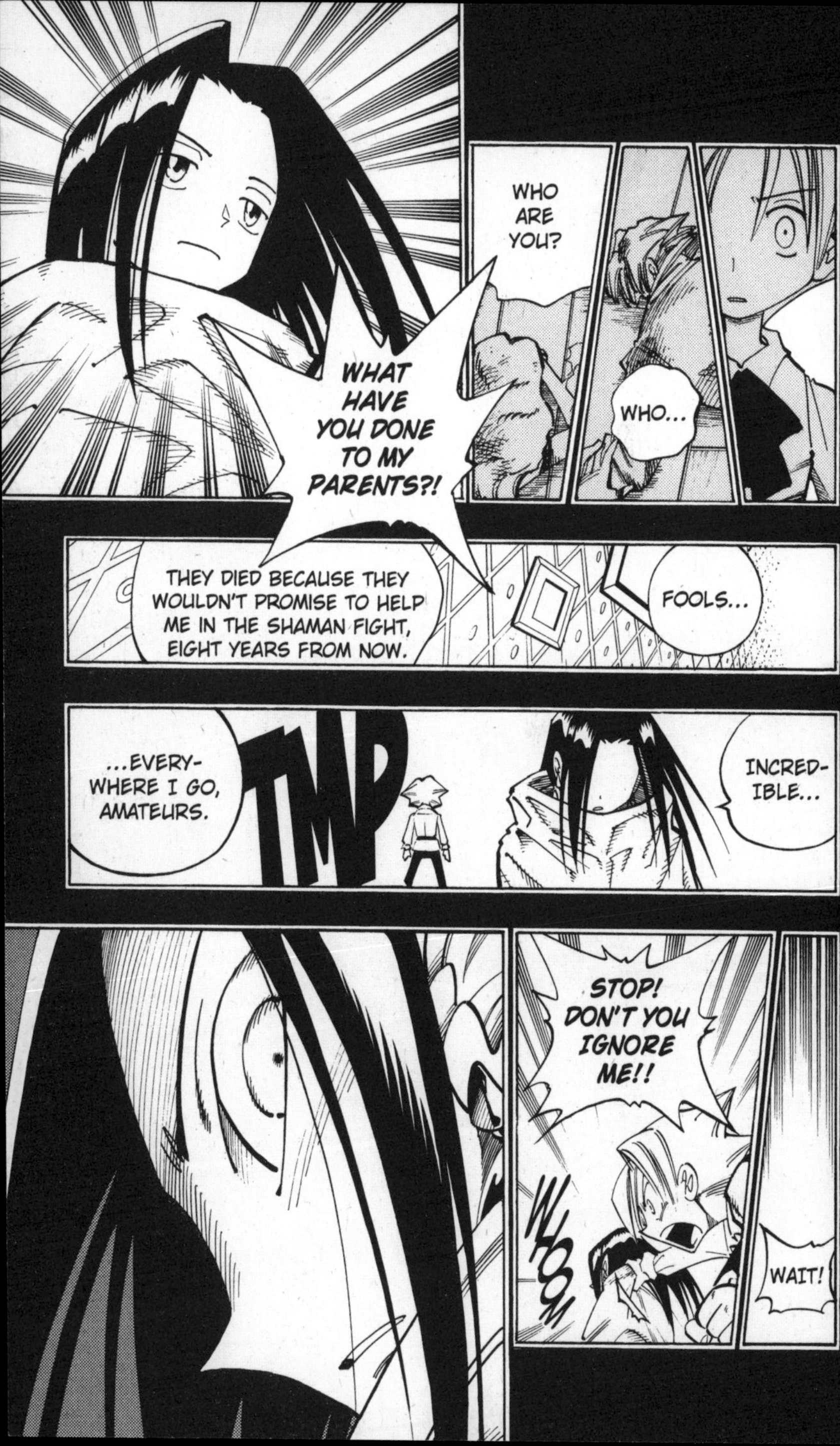
WHO...
WHO ARE YOU?
WHAT HAVE YOU DONE TO MY PARENTS?!
FOOLS...
THEY DIED BECAUSE THEY WOULDN'T PROMISE TO HELP ME IN THE SHAMAN FIGHT, EIGHT YEARS FROM NOW.
INCRED-IBLE...
TMP
...EVERY-WHERE I GO, AMATEURS.
WAIT!
STOP! DON'T YOU IGNORE ME!!
WHOOM

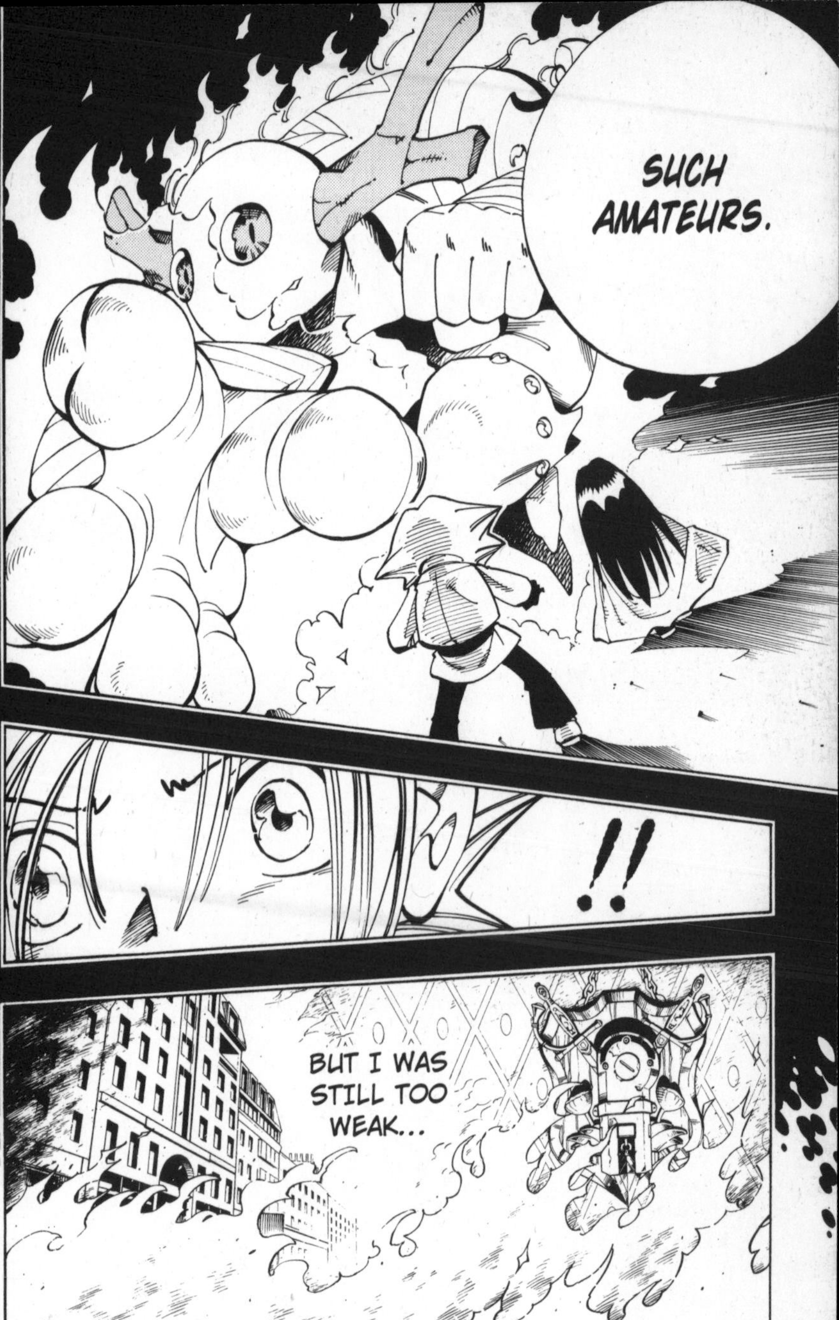
SUCH AMATEURS.
!!
BUT I WAS STILL TOO WEAK...

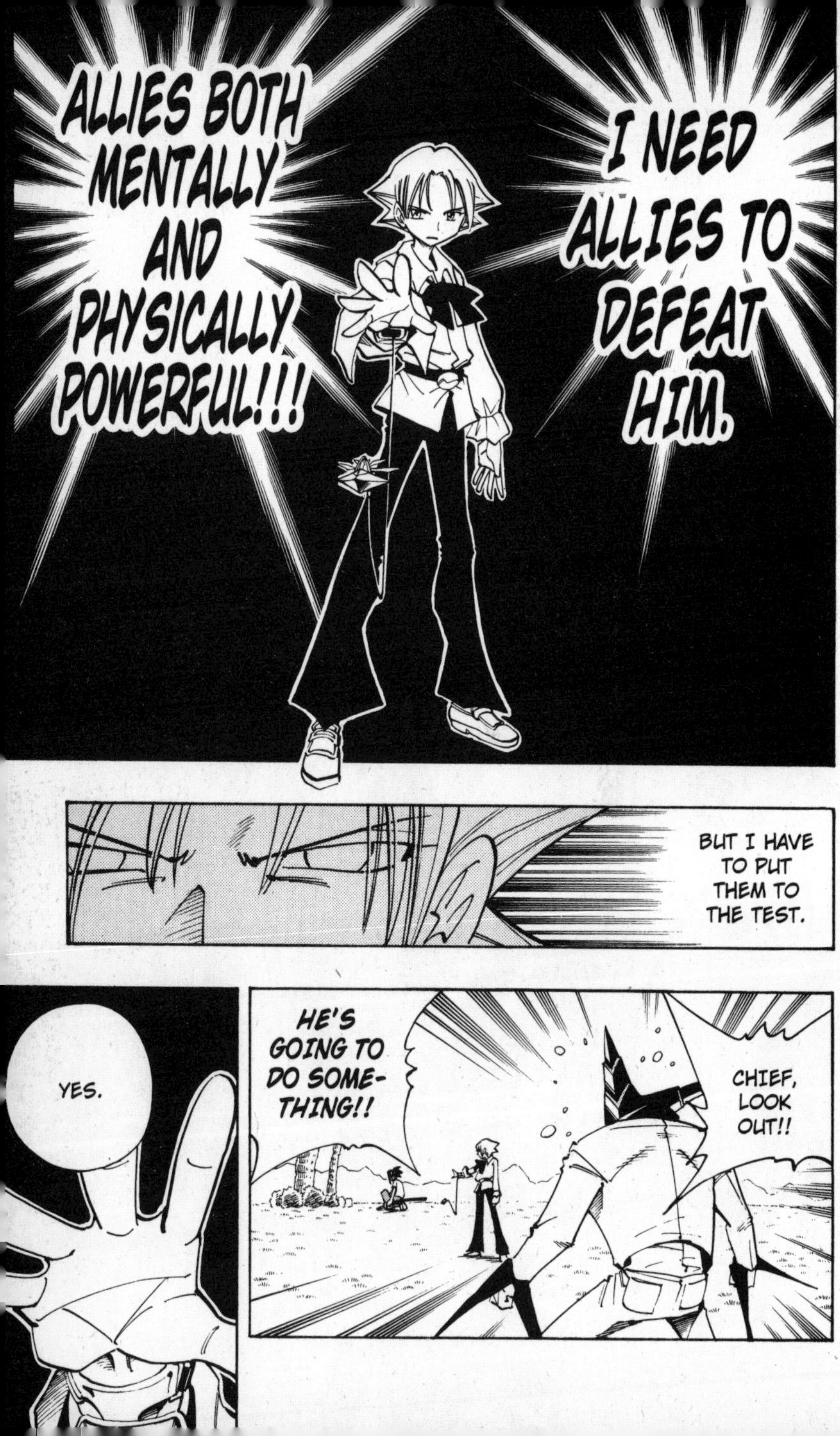
I NEED ALLIES TO DEFEAT HIM.
ALLIES BOTH MENTALLY AND PHYSICALLY POWERFUL!!!
BUT I HAVE TO PUT THEM TO THE TEST.
CHIEF, LOOK OUT!!
HE'S GOING TO DO SOME-THING!!
YES.

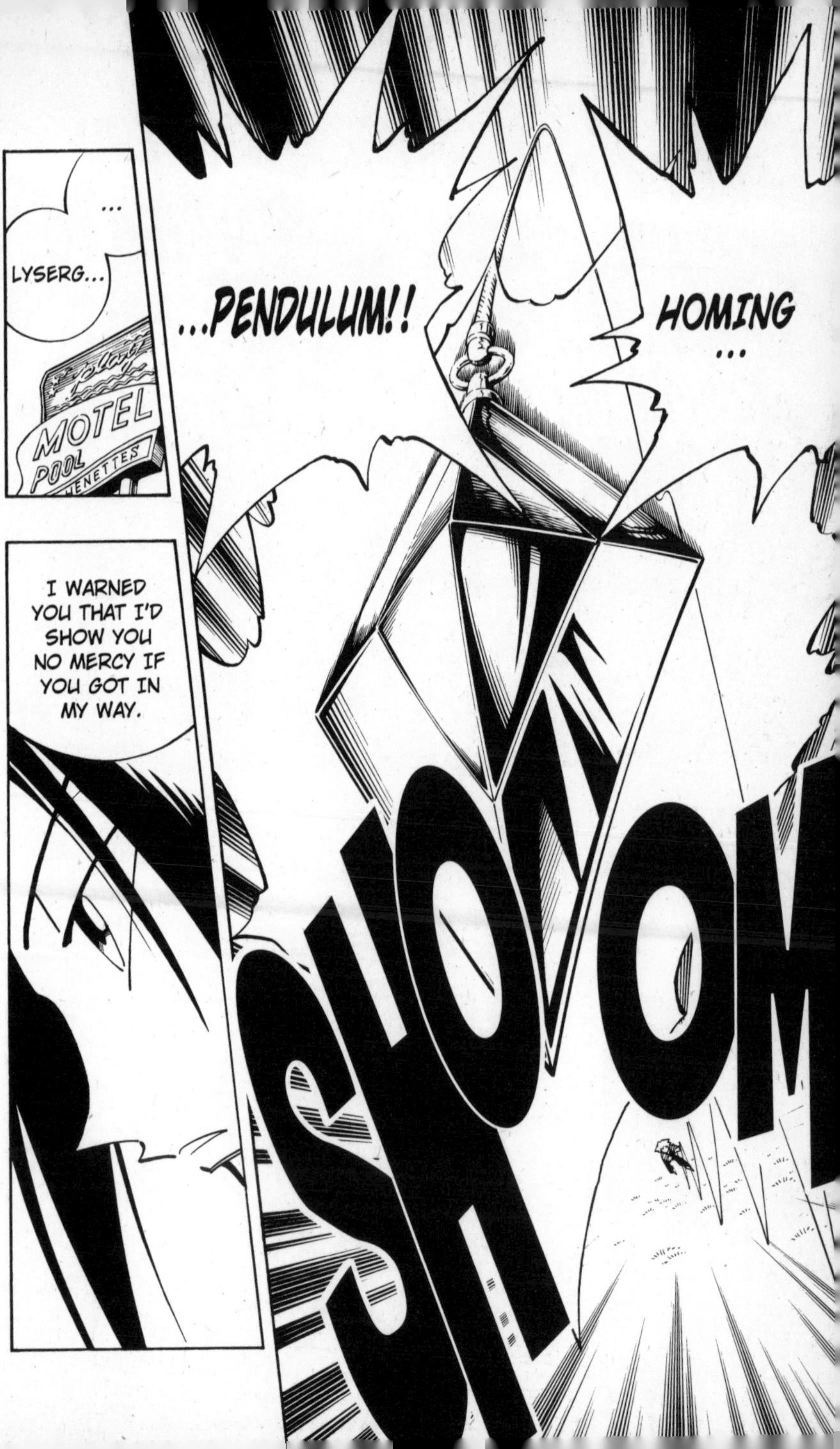
HOMING ...
...PENDULUM!!
SHOOOM
...
LYSERG...
MOTEL
POOL
I WARNED YOU THAT I'D SHOW YOU NO MERCY IF YOU GOT IN MY WAY.

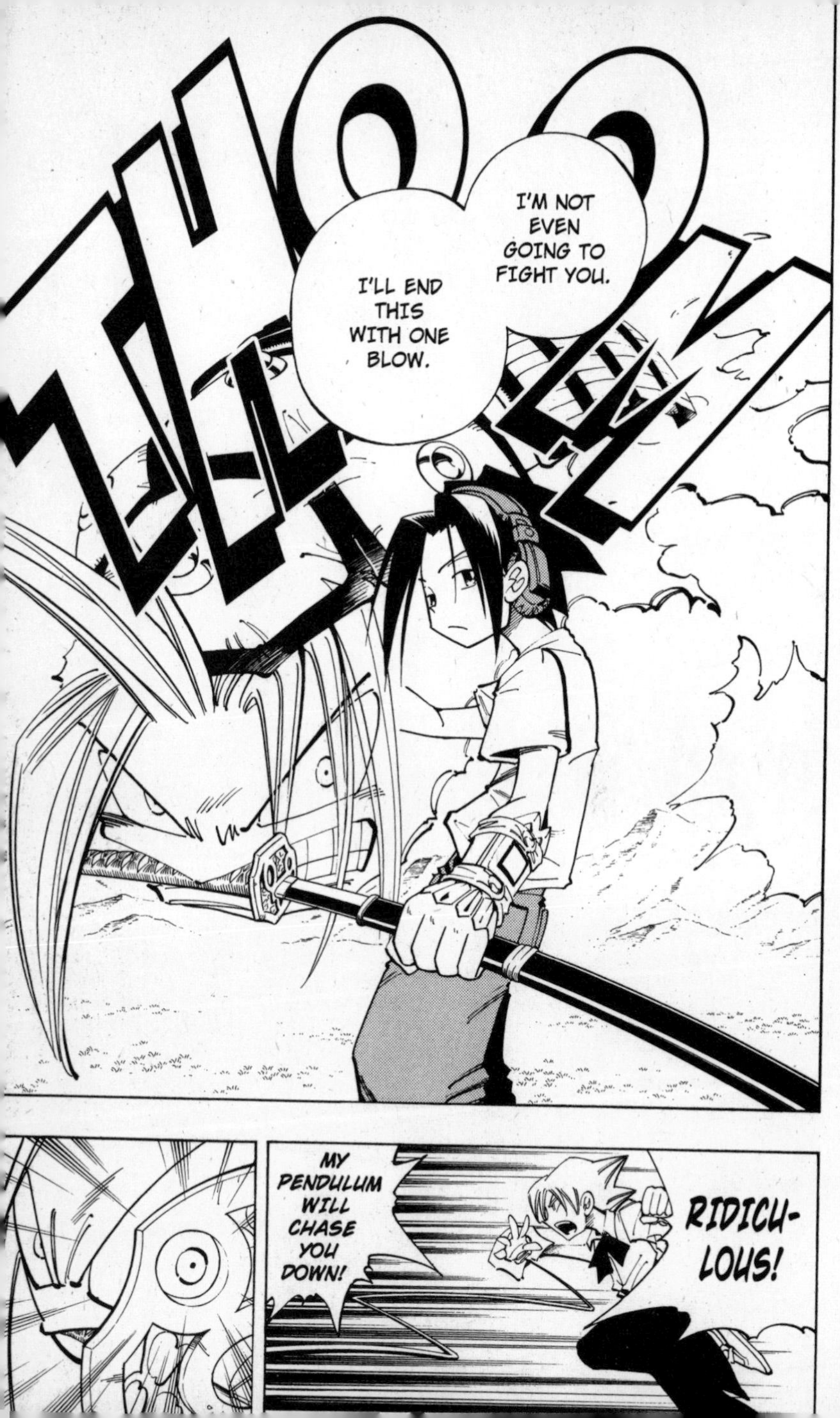
I'M NOT EVEN GOING TO FIGHT YOU.
I'LL END THIS WITH ONE BLOW.
RIDICU-LOUS!
MY PENDULUM WILL CHASE YOU DOWN!

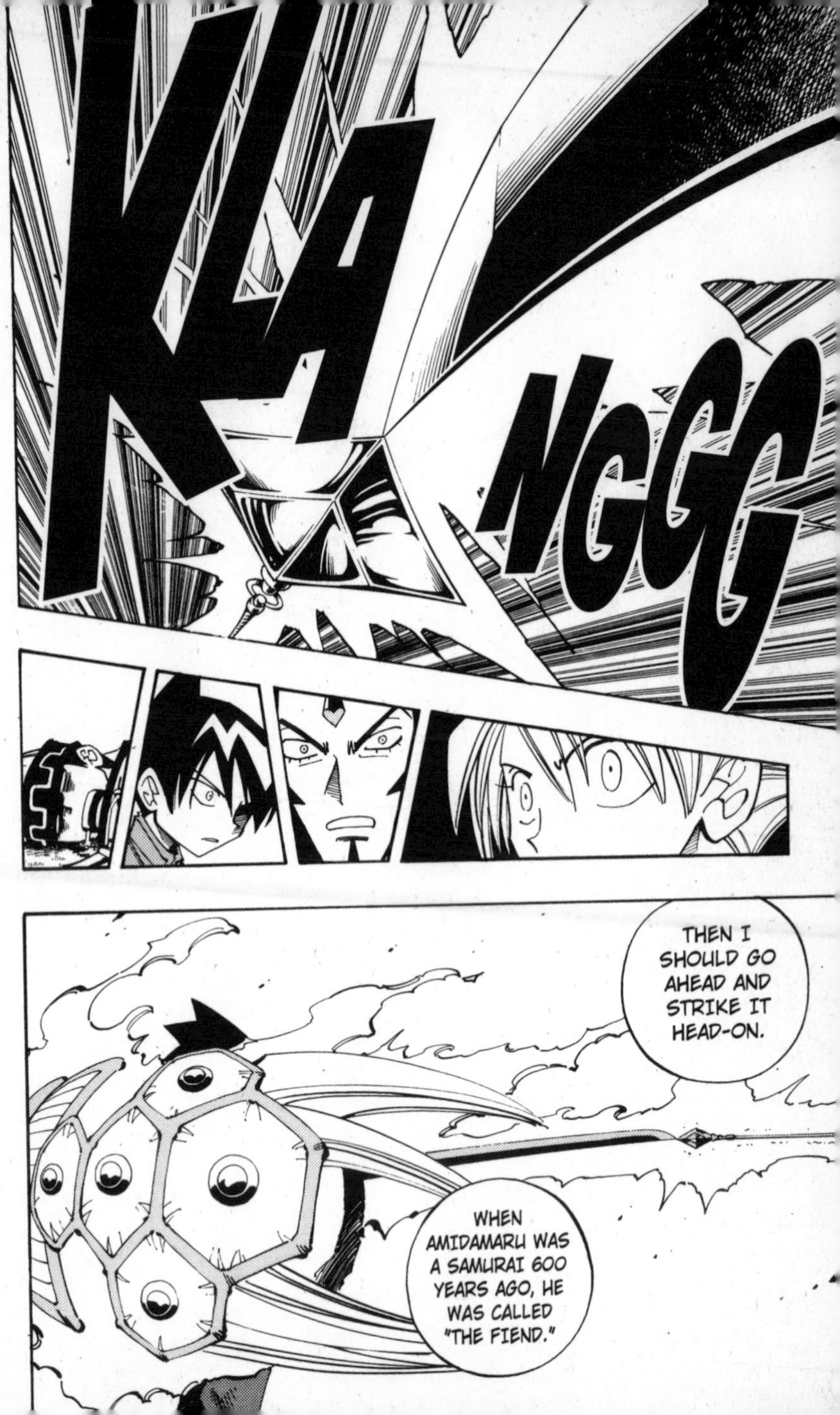
KA
NGG
THEN I SHOULD GO AHEAD AND STRIKE IT HEAD-ON.
WHEN AMIDAMARU WAS A SAMURAI 600 YEARS AGO, HE WAS CALLED "THE FIEND."

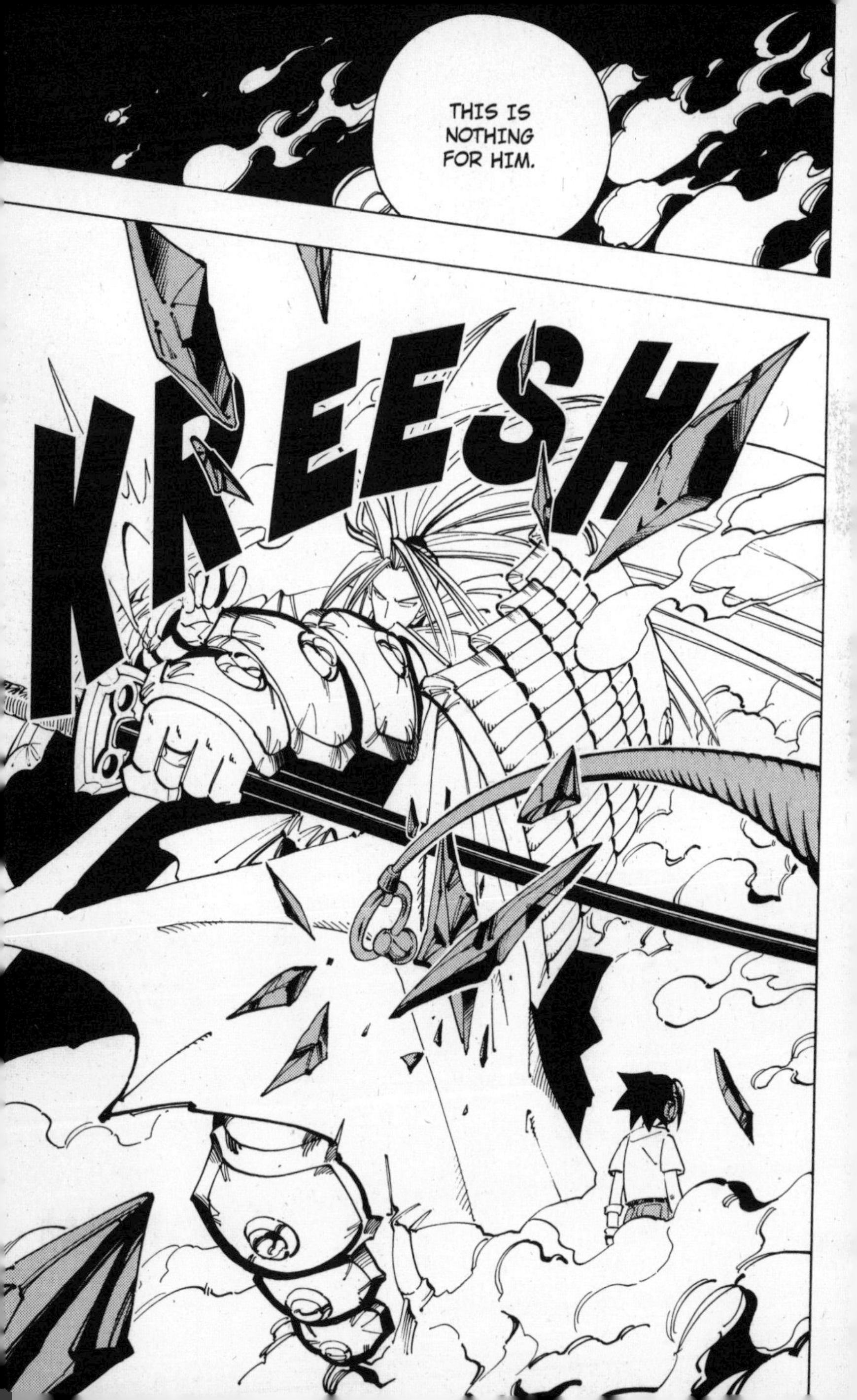
THIS IS NOTHING FOR HIM.
KREESH

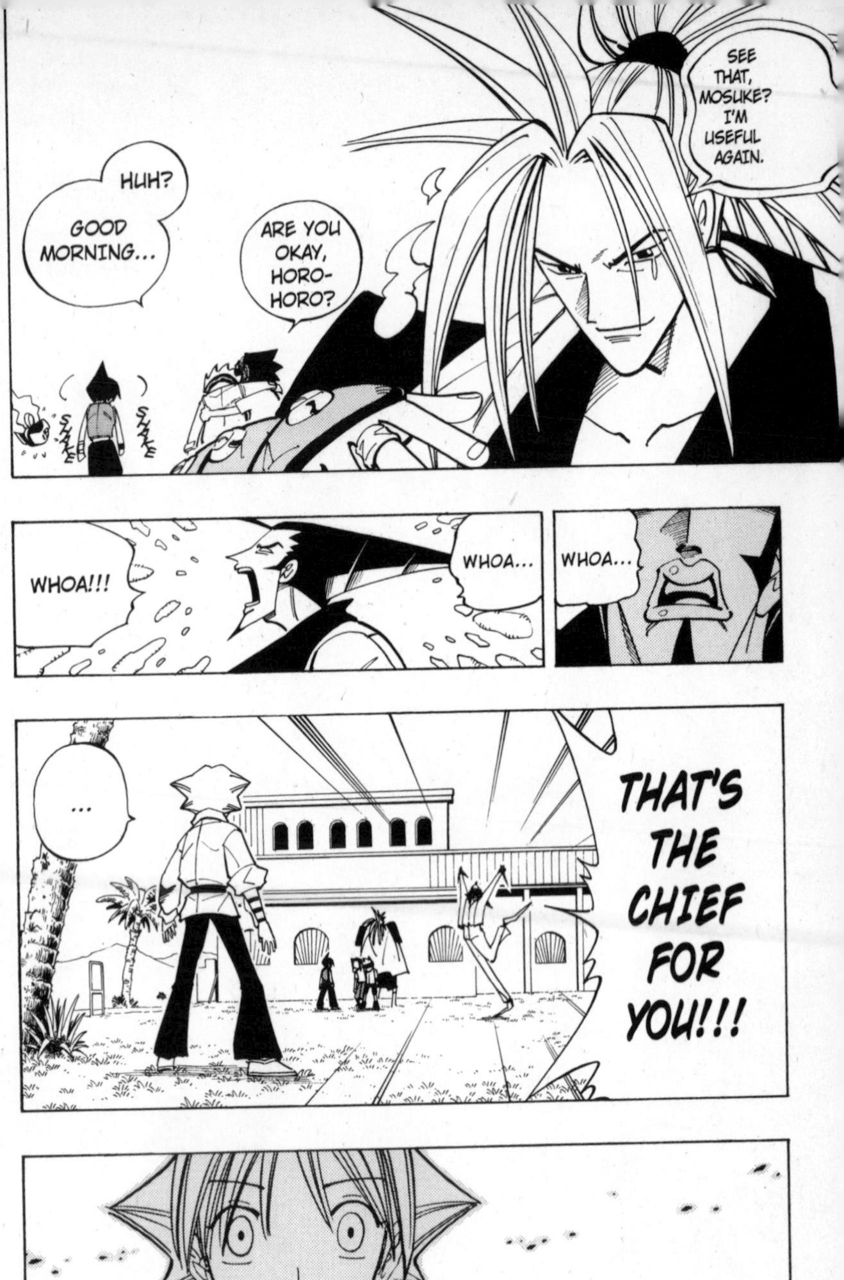
SEE THAT, MOSUKE? I'M USEFUL AGAIN.
ARE YOU OKAY, HORO-HORO?
HUH?
GOOD MORNING...
SHAKE
SHAKE
WHOA...
WHOA...
WHOA!!!
THAT'S THE CHIEF FOR YOU!!!
...

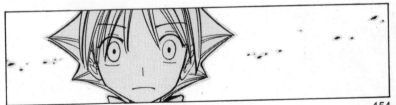

Shaman King™

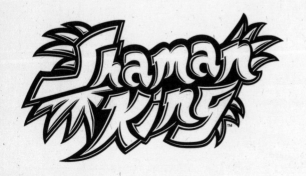

SHAMAN KING CHARACTER FILE No.46

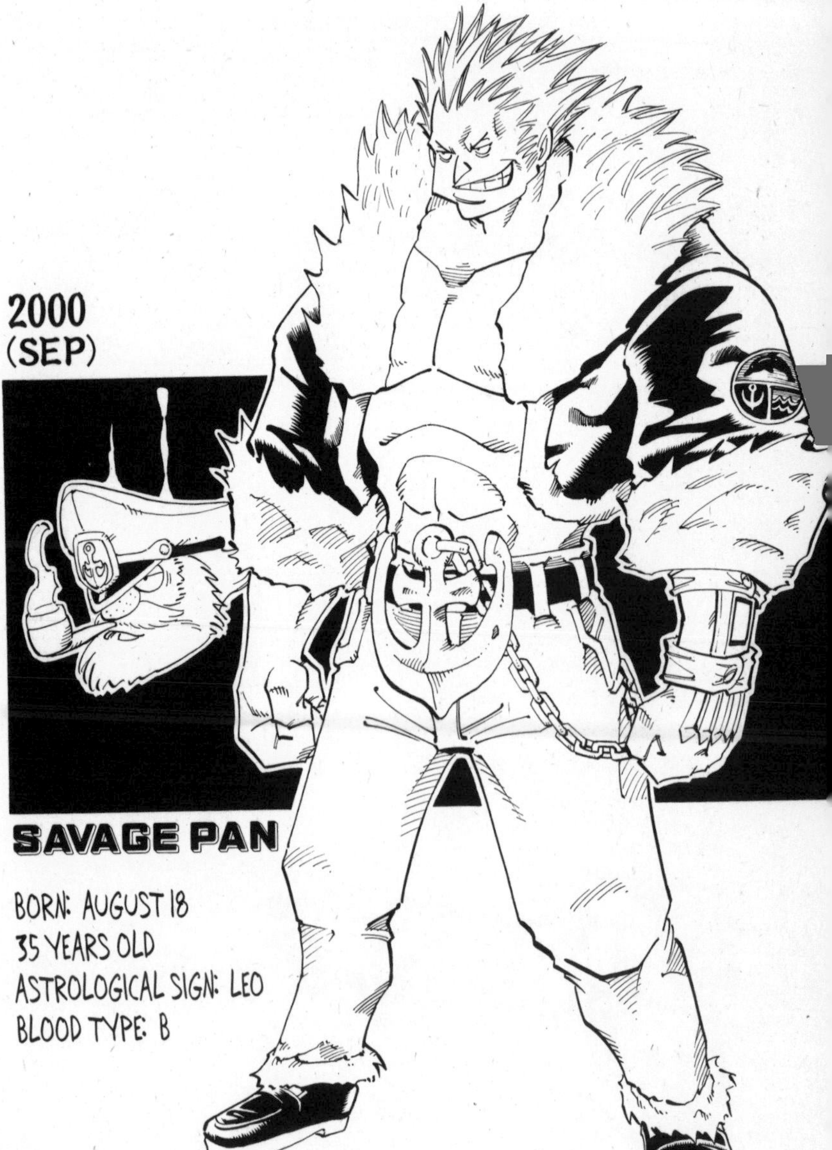

2000
(SEP)

SAVAGE PAN

BORN: AUGUST 18
35 YEARS OLD
ASTROLOGICAL SIGN: LEO
BLOOD TYPE: B

Reincarnation 88: Memories of Big Ben

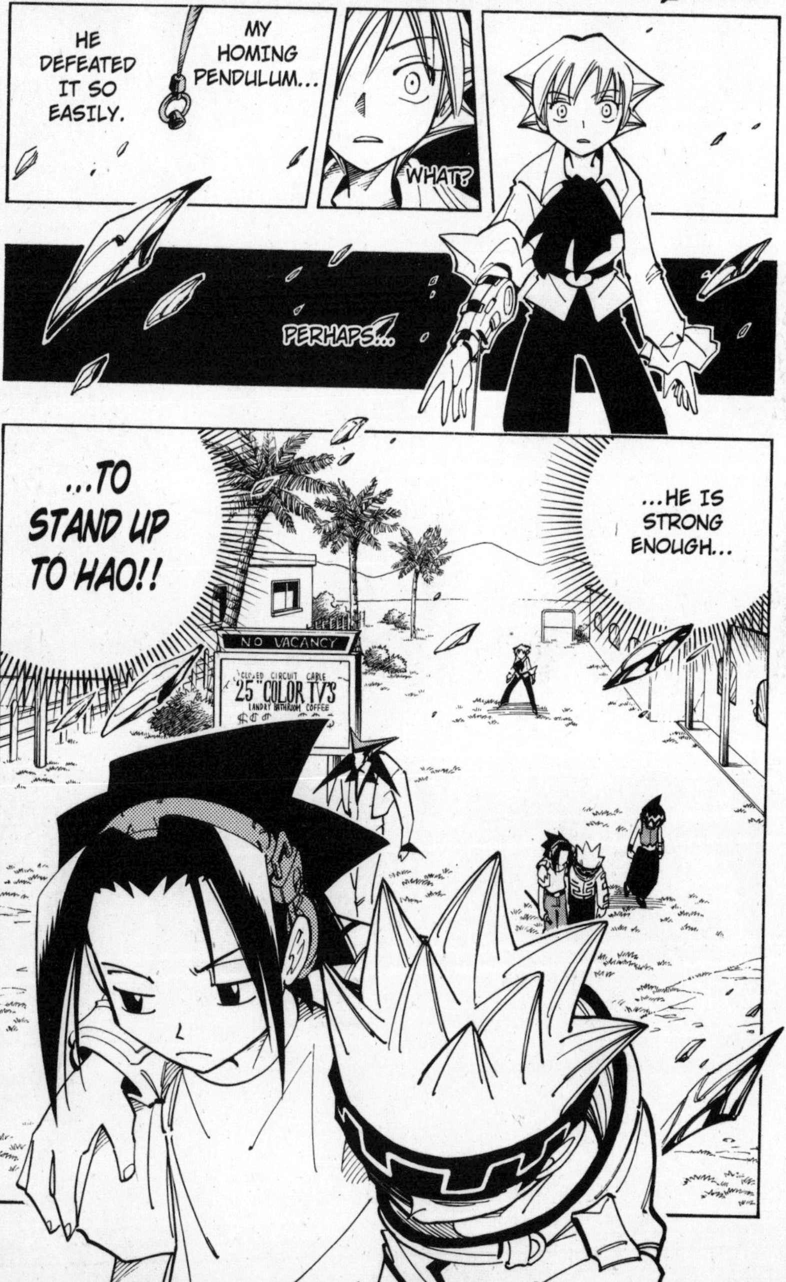
MY HOMING PENDULUM...
WHAT?
HE DEFEATED IT SO EASILY.
PERHAPS...
...HE IS STRONG ENOUGH...
NO VACANCY
CLOSED CIRCUIT CABLE
25" COLOR TV'S
LANDRY BATHROOM COFFEE
...TO STAND UP TO HAO!!

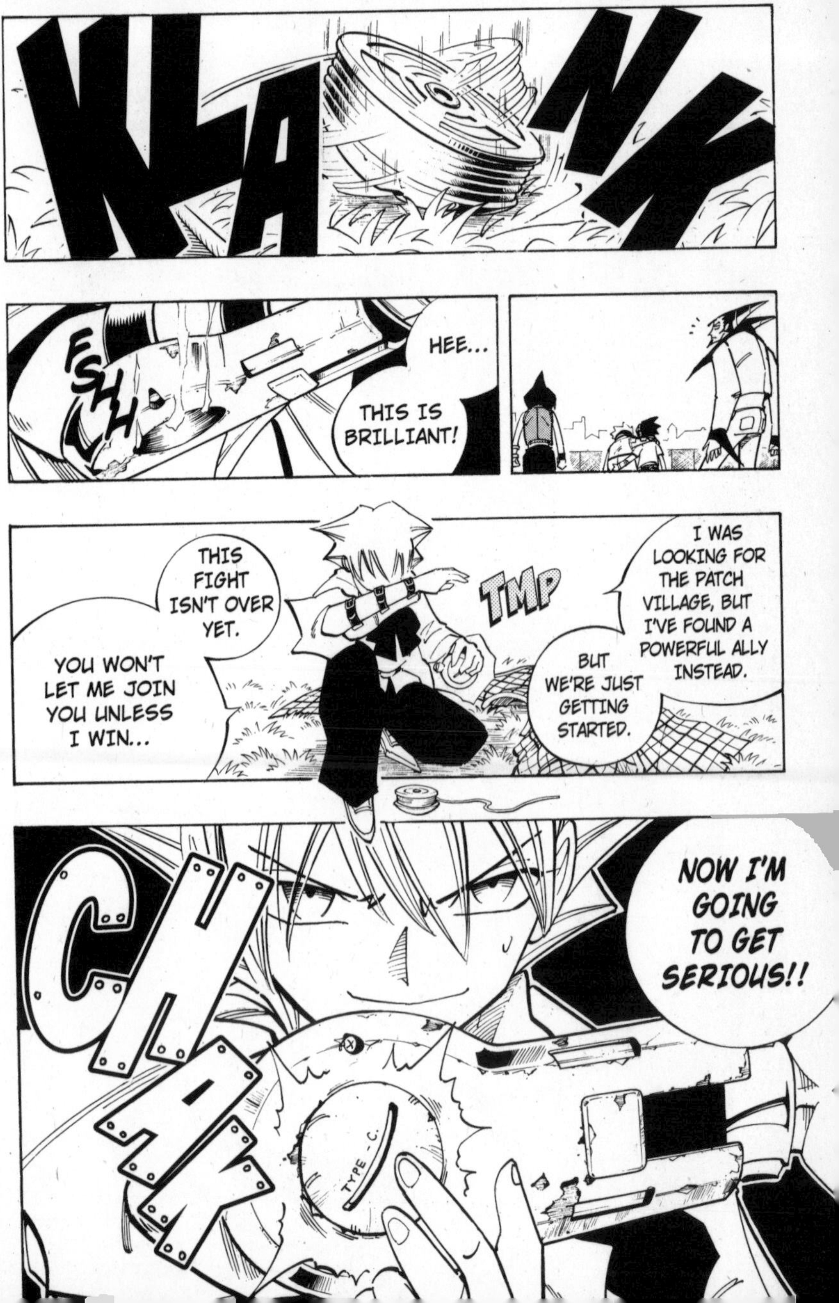
WHANK
HEE...
THIS IS BRILLIANT!
FSHH
I WAS LOOKING FOR THE PATCH VILLAGE, BUT I'VE FOUND A POWERFUL ALLY INSTEAD.
BUT WE'RE JUST GETTING STARTED.
TMP
THIS FIGHT ISN'T OVER YET.
YOU WON'T LET ME JOIN YOU UNLESS I WIN...
NOW I'M GOING TO GET SERIOUS!!
CHAK
TYPE -C.

Reincarnation 88: Memories of Big Ben

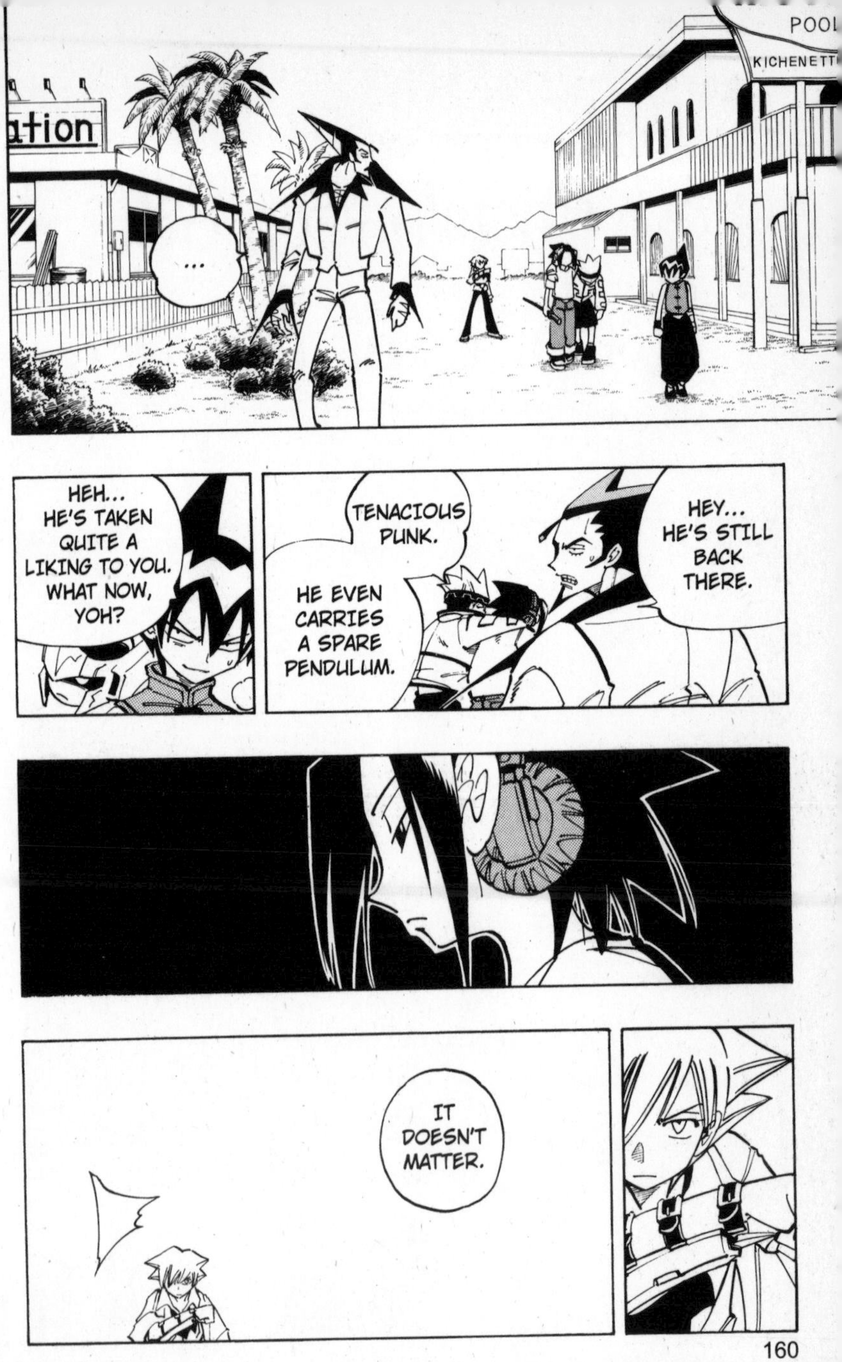
POOL
KICHENETT
ation
...
HEY... HE'S STILL BACK THERE.
TENACIOUS PUNK.
HE EVEN CARRIES A SPARE PENDULUM.
HEH... HE'S TAKEN QUITE A LIKING TO YOU. WHAT NOW, YOH?
IT DOESN'T MATTER.

READ THIS WAY

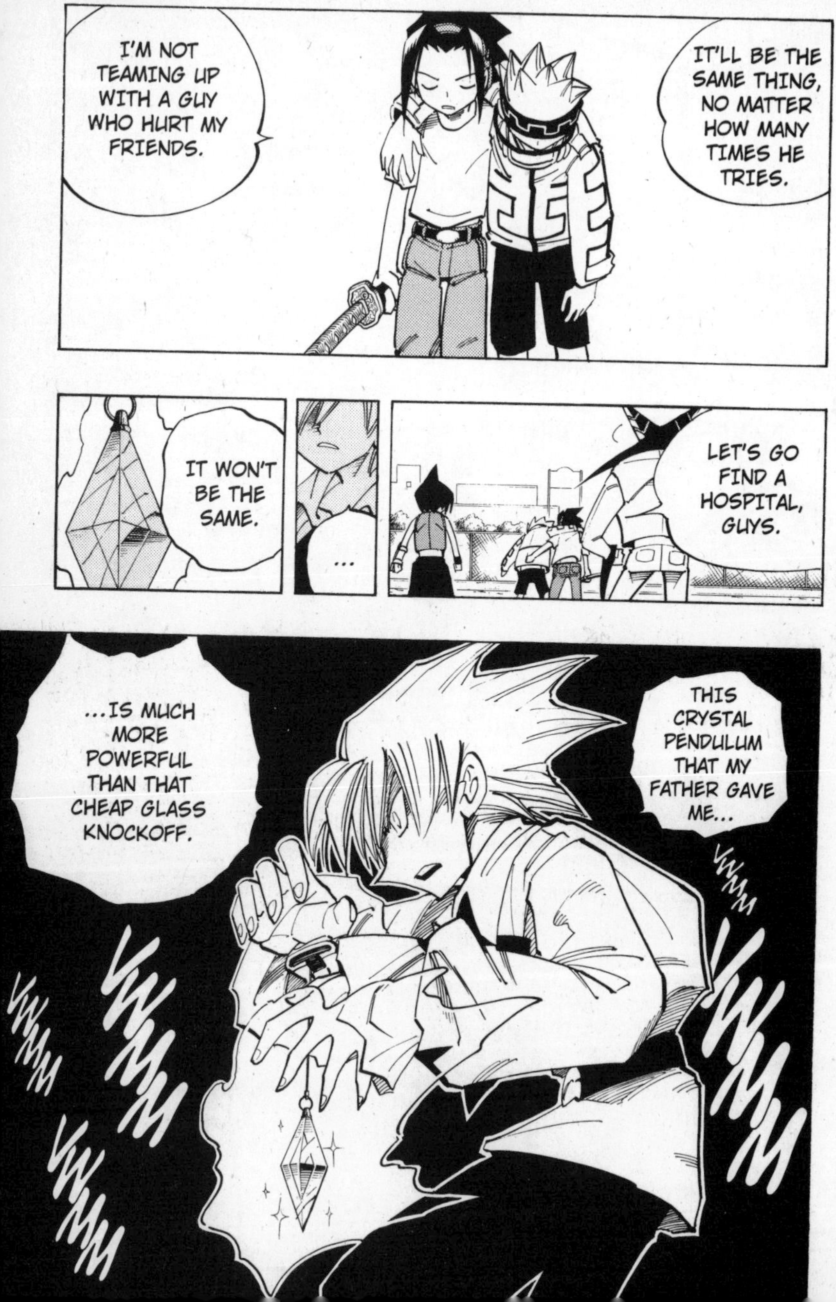
IT'LL BE THE SAME THING, NO MATTER HOW MANY TIMES HE TRIES.
I'M NOT TEAMING UP WITH A GUY WHO HURT MY FRIENDS.
LET'S GO FIND A HOSPITAL, GUYS.
...
IT WON'T BE THE SAME.
THIS CRYSTAL PENDULUM THAT MY FATHER GAVE ME...
...IS MUCH MORE POWERFUL THAN THAT CHEAP GLASS KNOCKOFF.
VWMM
VWMM
VWMM
VWMM
VWMM

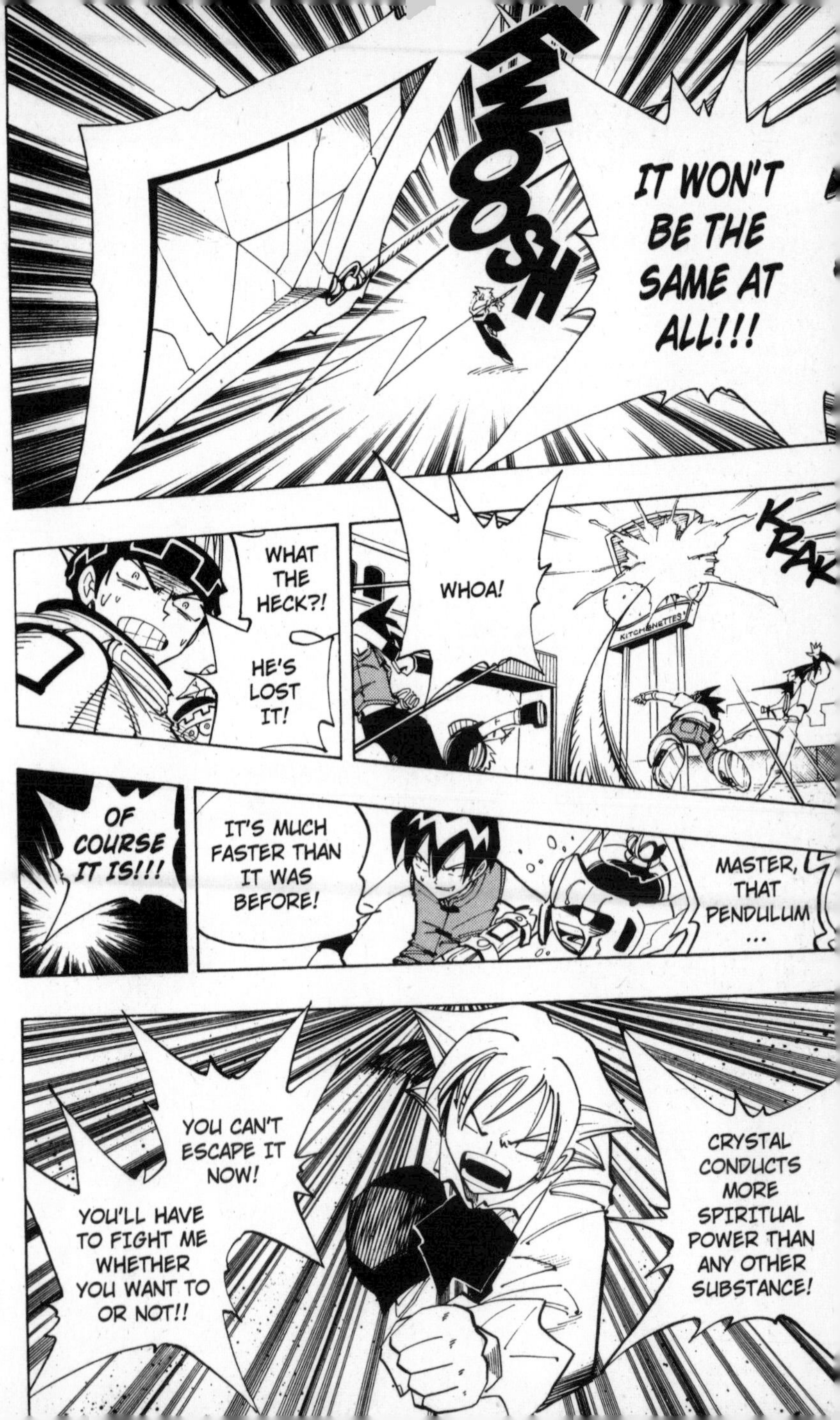
WHOOSH
IT WON'T BE THE SAME AT ALL!!!
KRAK
WHOA!
WHAT THE HECK?!
HE'S LOST IT!
MASTER, THAT PENDULUM...
IT'S MUCH FASTER THAN IT WAS BEFORE!
OF COURSE IT IS!!!
CRYSTAL CONDUCTS MORE SPIRITUAL POWER THAN ANY OTHER SUBSTANCE!
YOU CAN'T ESCAPE IT NOW!
YOU'LL HAVE TO FIGHT ME WHETHER YOU WANT TO OR NOT!!

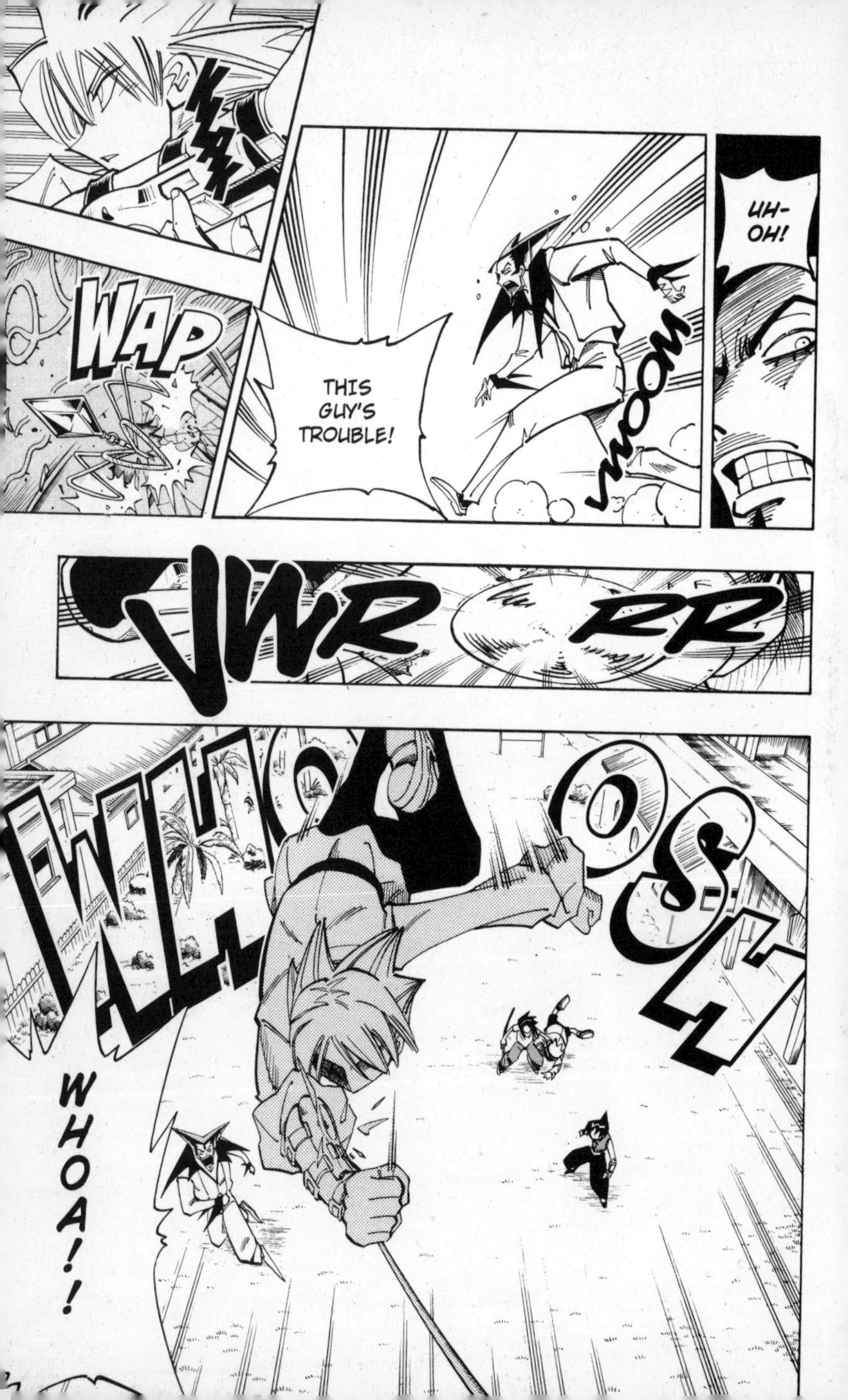
UH-OH!
THIS GUY'S TROUBLE!
WHOOM
KLAK
WAP
VWRRR
WHOOSH
WHOA!!

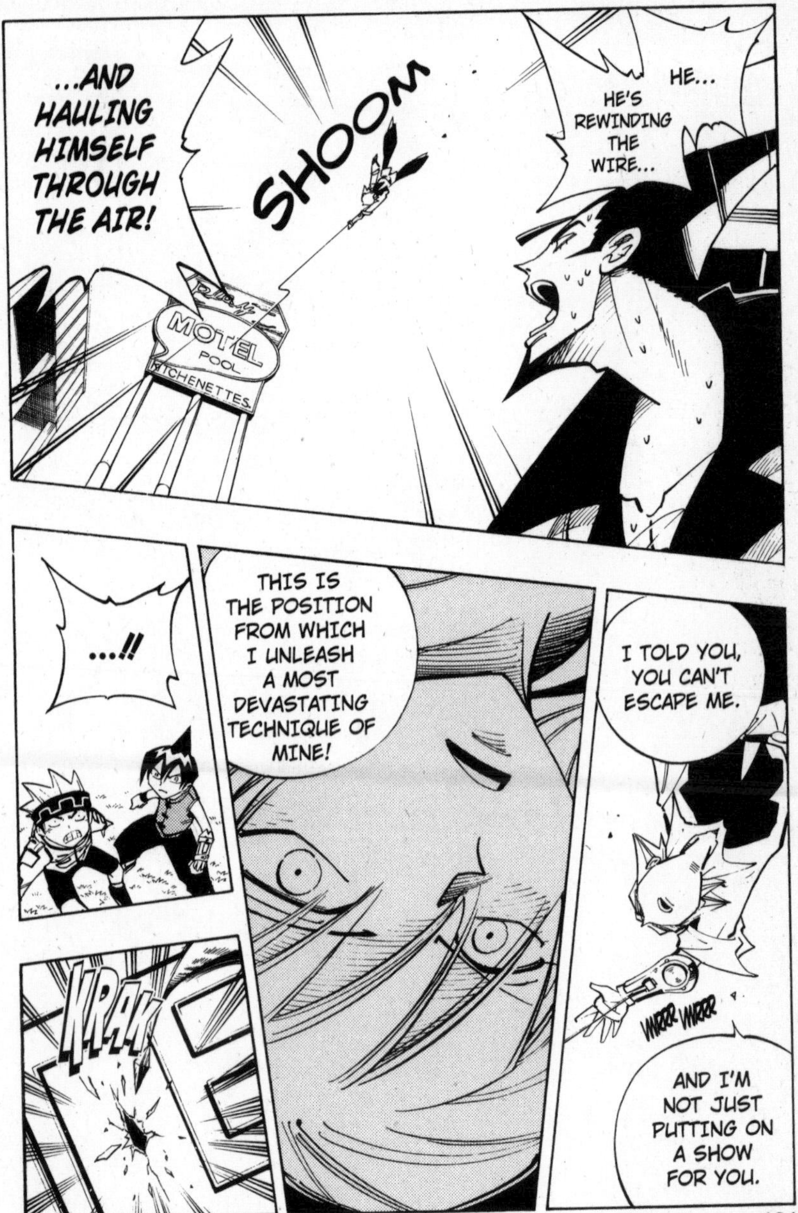
HE...
HE'S REWINDING THE WIRE...
SHOOM
MOTEL
POOL
...AND HAULING HIMSELF THROUGH THE AIR!
I TOLD YOU, YOU CAN'T ESCAPE ME.
WRRR WRRR
AND I'M NOT JUST PUTTING ON A SHOW FOR YOU.
THIS IS THE POSITION FROM WHICH I UNLEASH A MOST DEVASTATING TECHNIQUE OF MINE!
...!!
KRAK

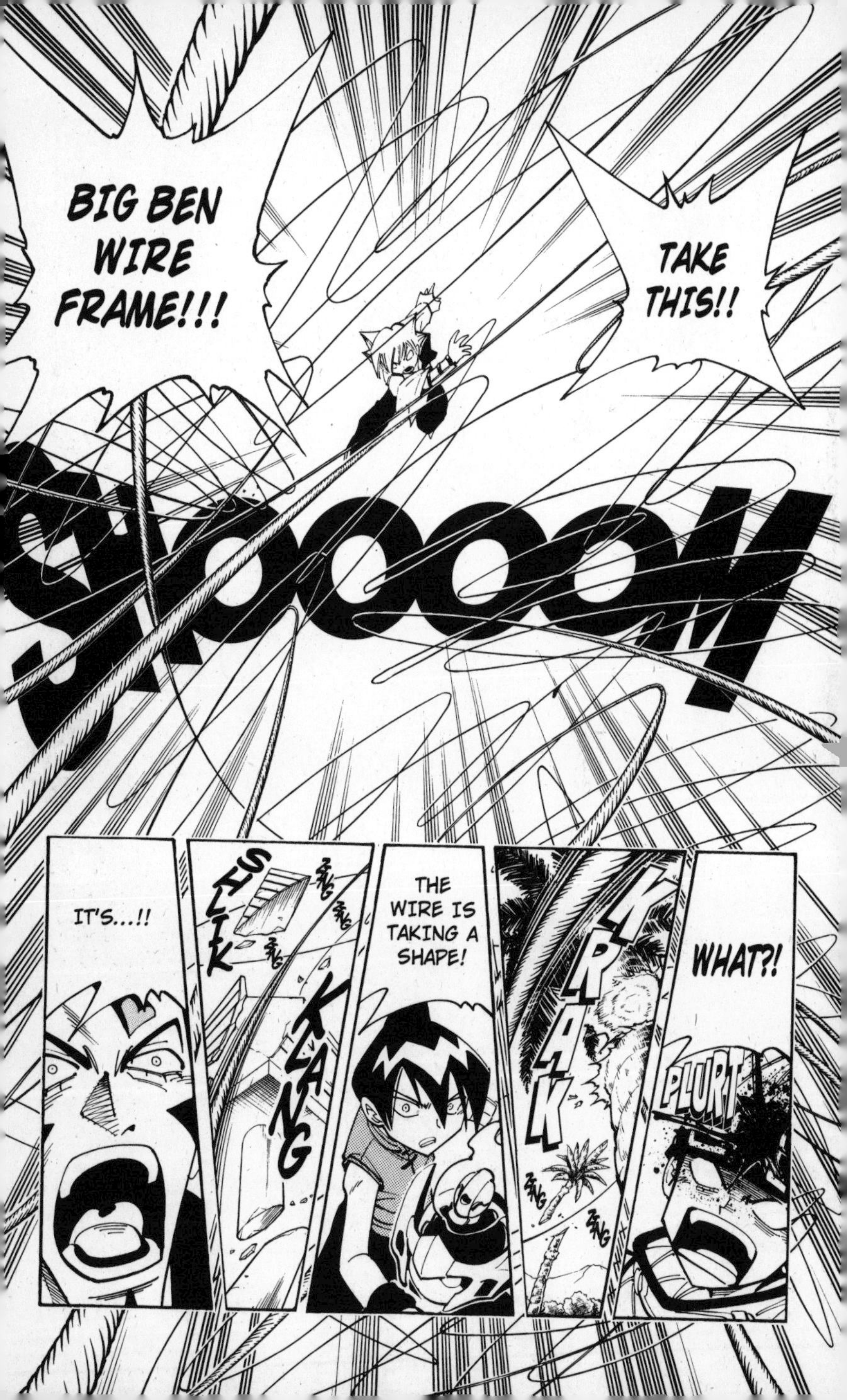
TAKE THIS!!
BIG BEN WIRE FRAME!!!
SHOOOM
WHAT?!
PLURT
KRAK
THE WIRE IS TAKING A SHAPE!
SHLIK
KLANG
IT'S...!!

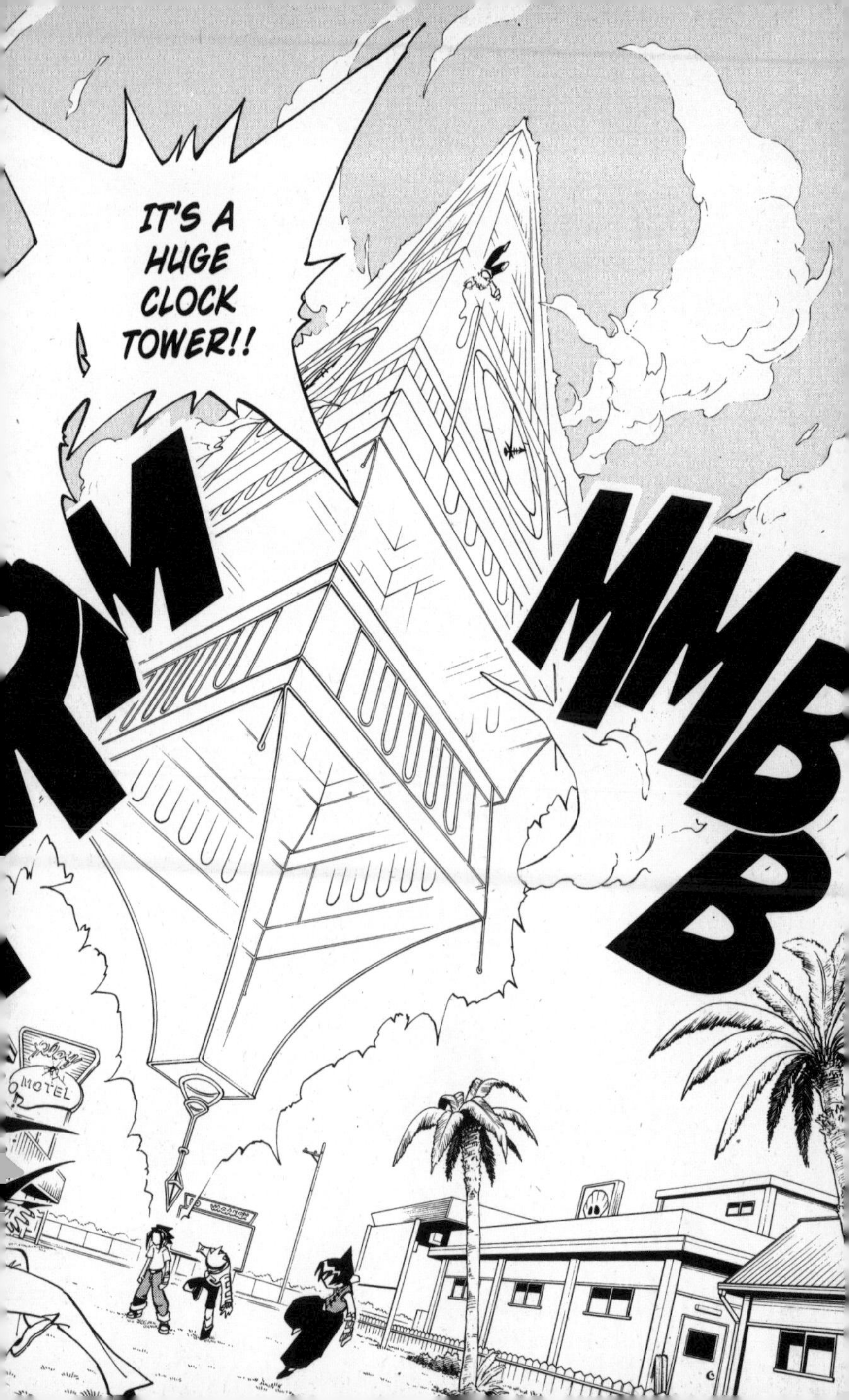
IT'S A HUGE CLOCK TOWER!!
RM
MMBB
MOTEL

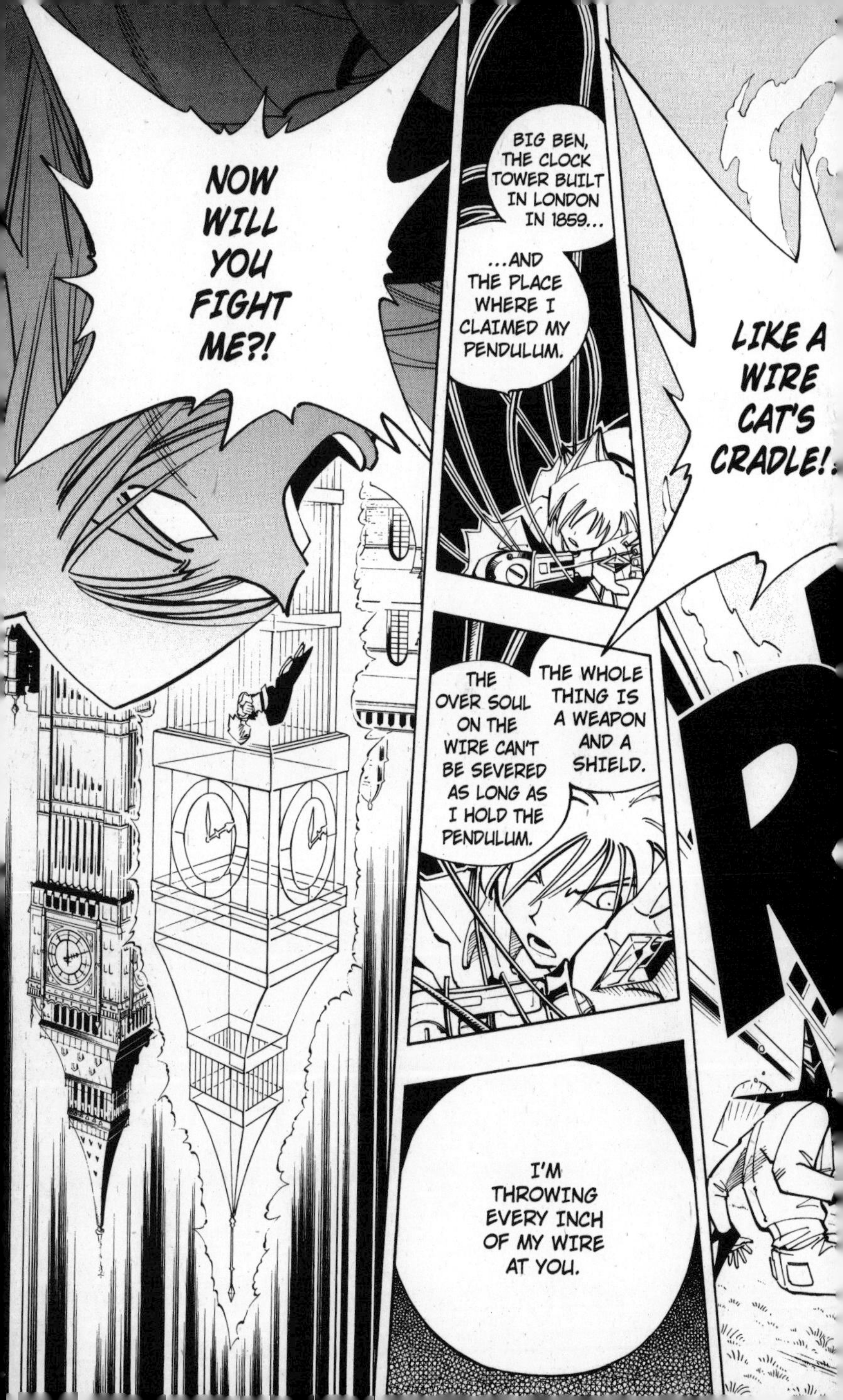
LIKE A WIRE CAT'S CRADLE!
BIG BEN, THE CLOCK TOWER BUILT IN LONDON IN 1859...
...AND THE PLACE WHERE I CLAIMED MY PENDULUM.
THE WHOLE THING IS A WEAPON AND A SHIELD.
THE OVER SOUL ON THE WIRE CAN'T BE SEVERED AS LONG AS I HOLD THE PENDULUM.
I'M THROWING EVERY INCH OF MY WIRE AT YOU.
NOW WILL YOU FIGHT ME?!

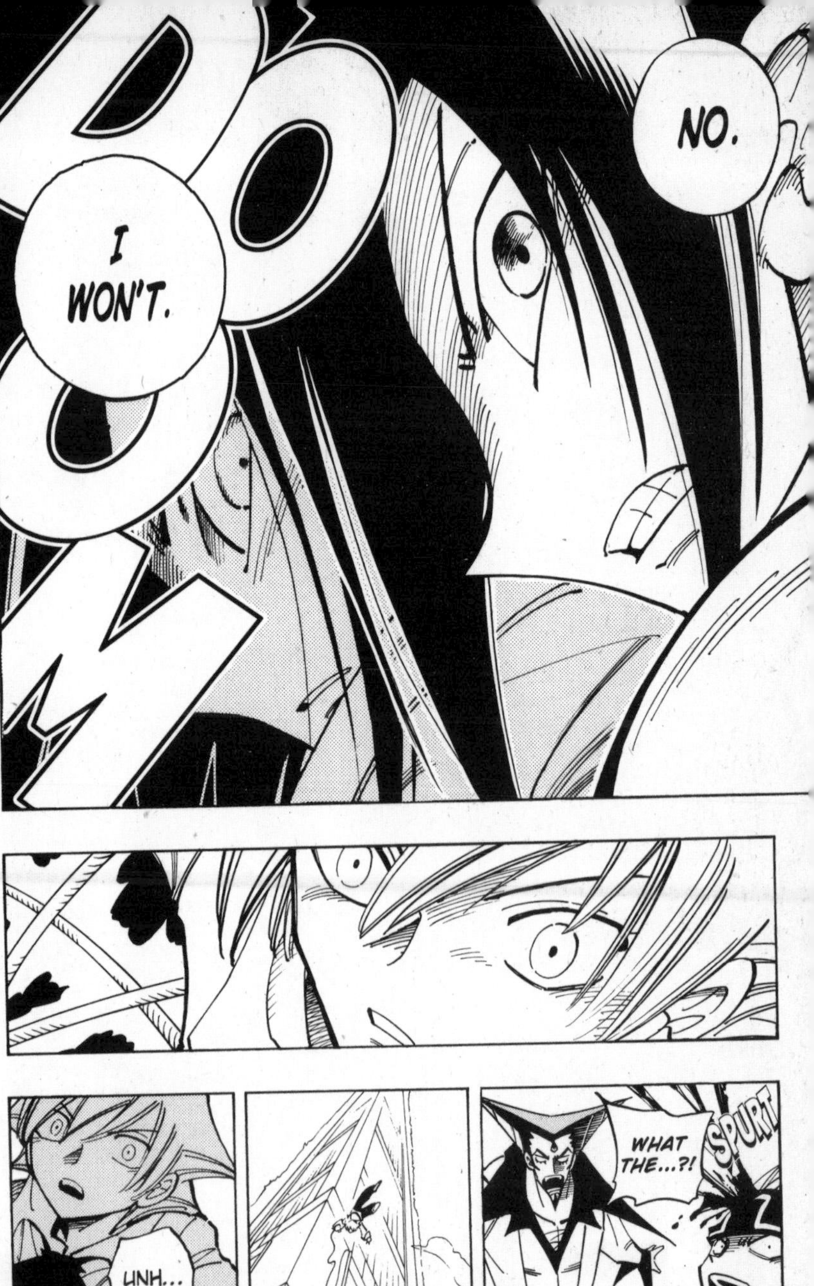
NO.
I WON'T.
DOOM
SPURT
WHAT THE...?!
UNH...

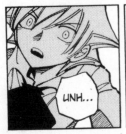

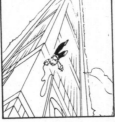

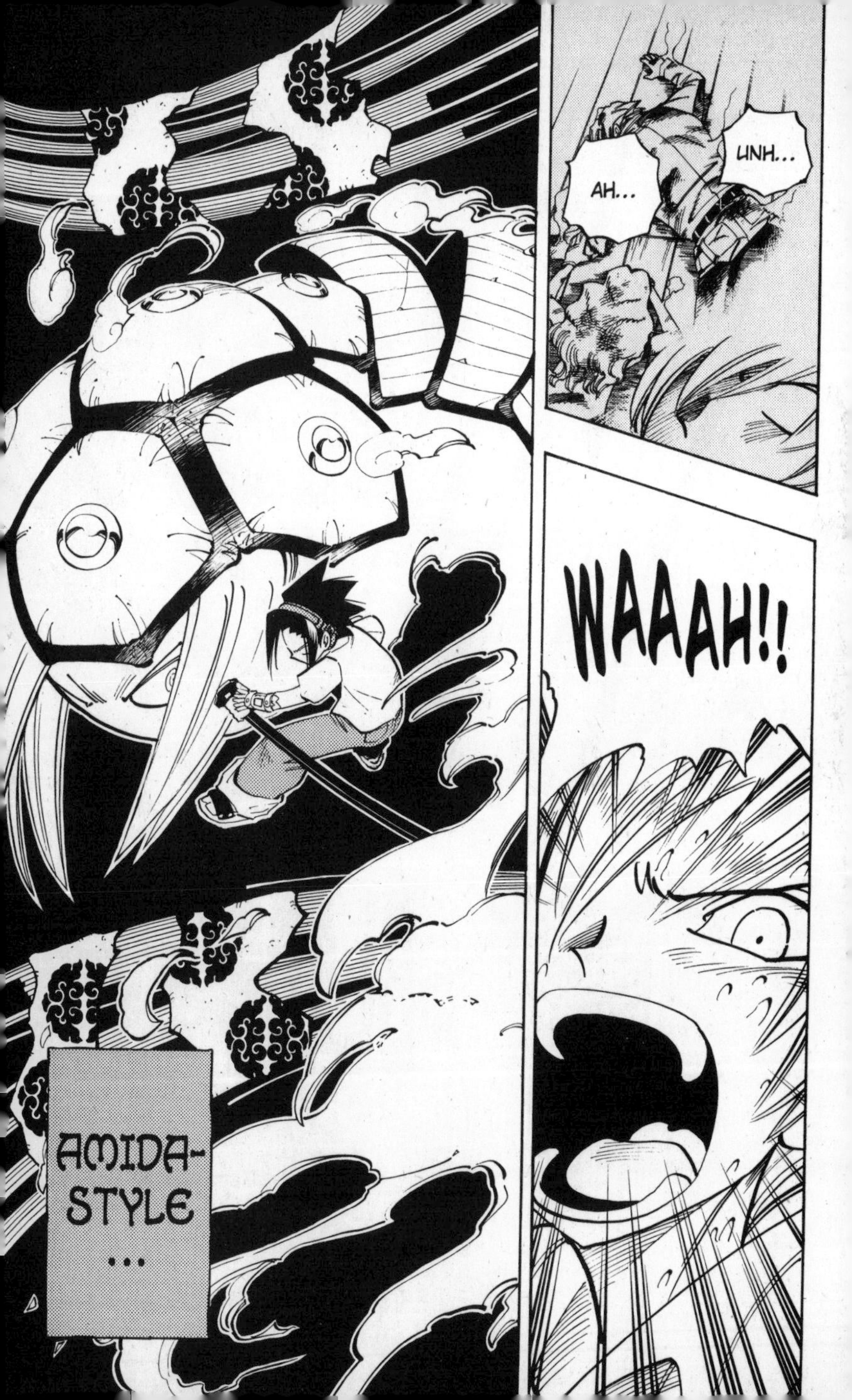
UNH...
AH...
WAAAH!!
AMIDA-STYLE
...

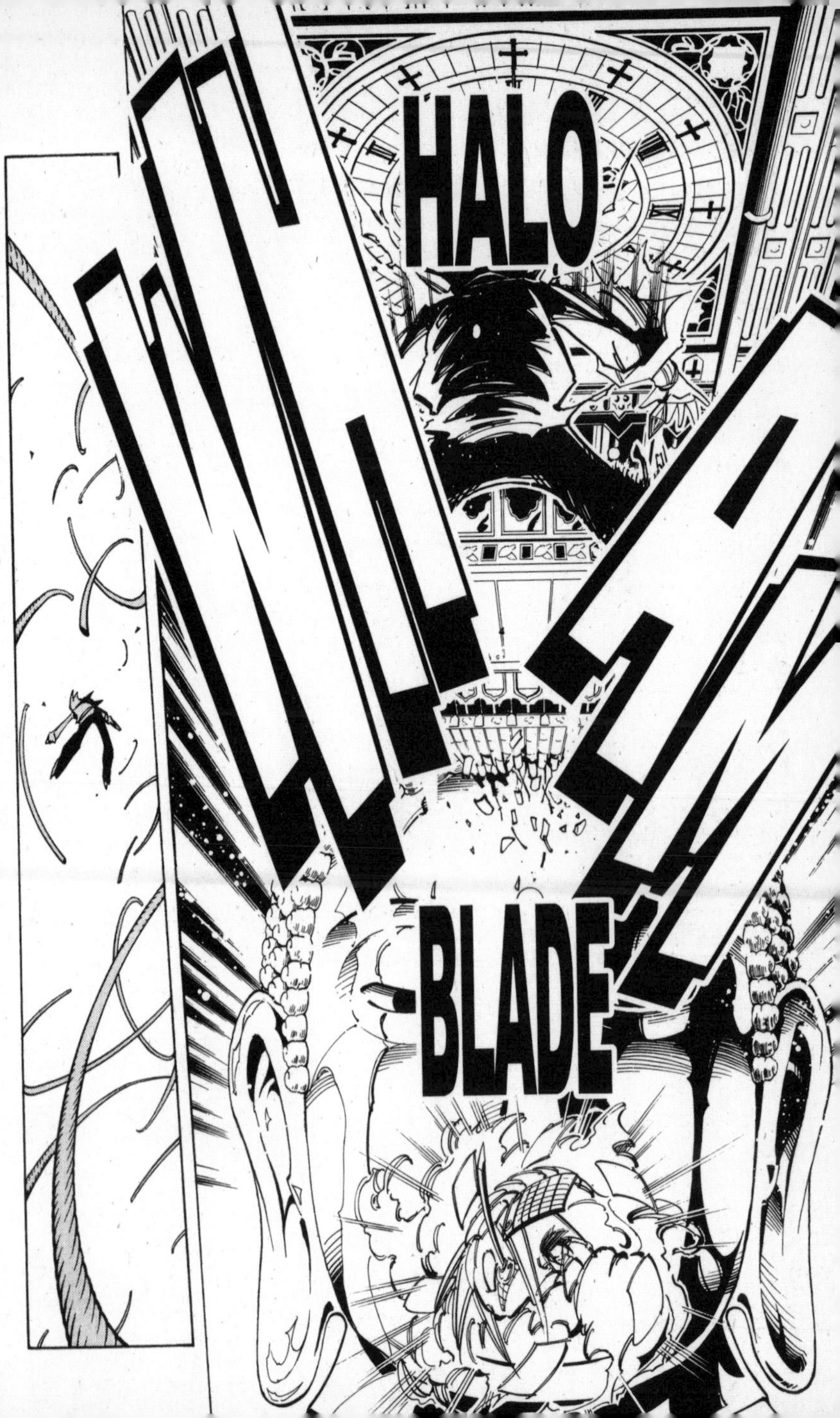
HALO
BLADE

READ THIS WAY

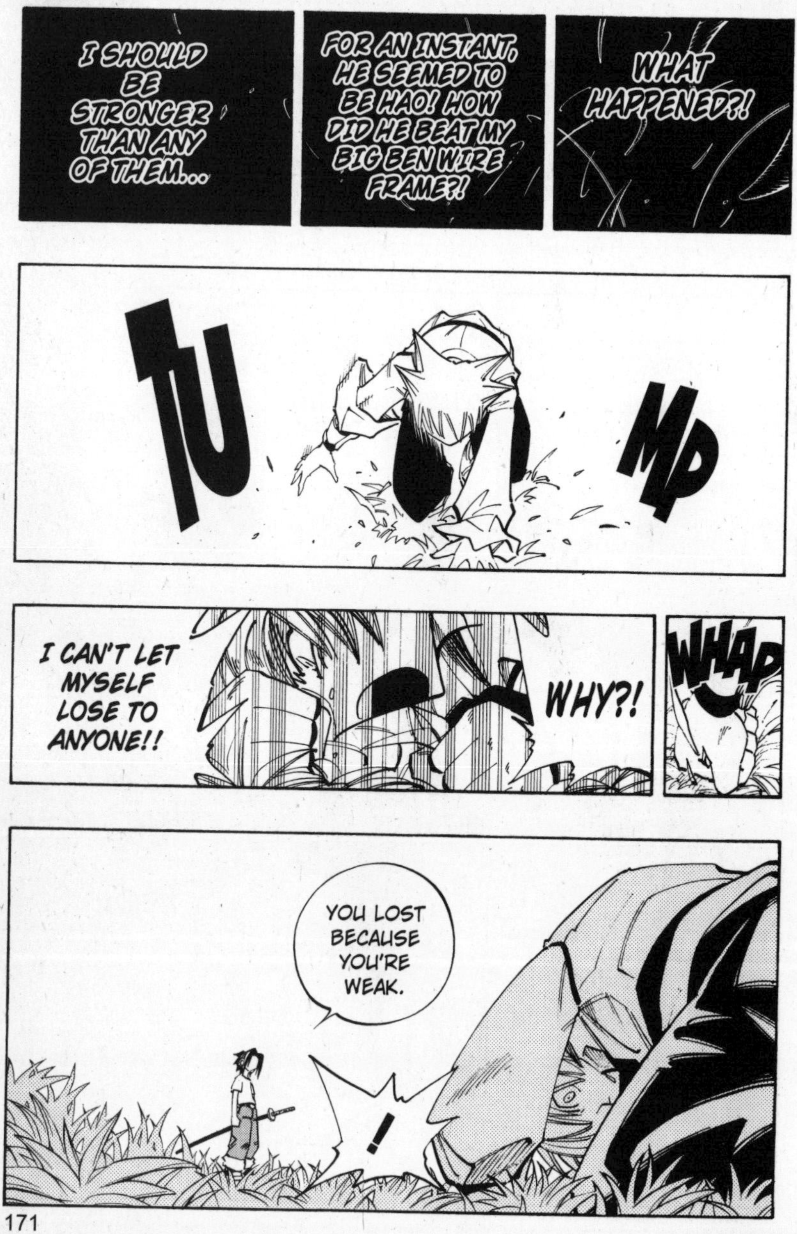

WHAT HAPPENED?!
FOR AN INSTANT, HE SEEMED TO BE HAO! HOW DID HE BEAT MY BIG BEN WIRE FRAME?!
I SHOULD BE STRONGER THAN ANY OF THEM...
TU MP
WHAP
WHY?!
I CAN'T LET MYSELF LOSE TO ANYONE!!
YOU LOST BECAUSE YOU'RE WEAK.
!

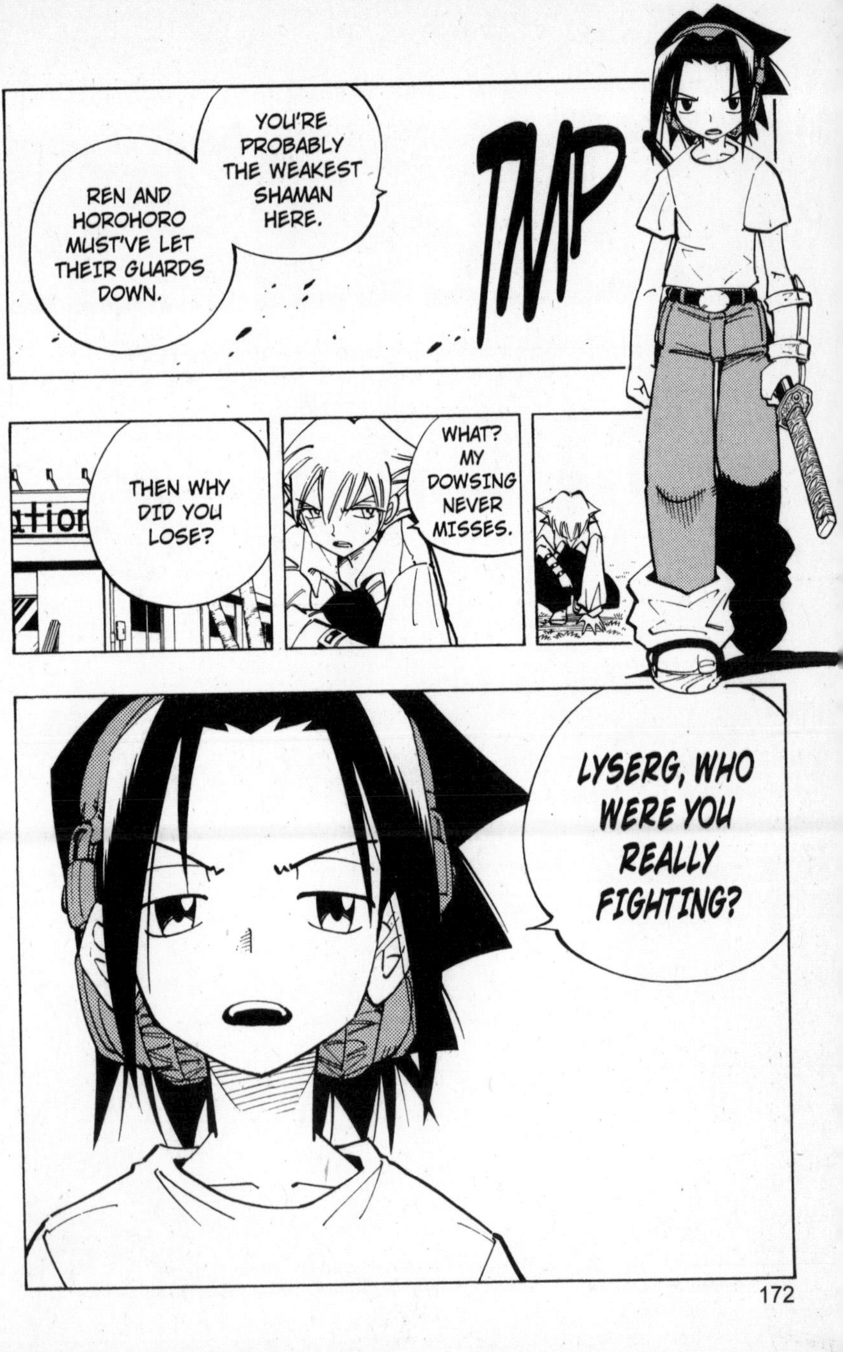
TMP
YOU'RE PROBABLY THE WEAKEST SHAMAN HERE.
REN AND HOROHORO MUST'VE LET THEIR GUARDS DOWN.
WHAT? MY DOWSING NEVER MISSES.
THEN WHY DID YOU LOSE?
LYSERG, WHO WERE YOU REALLY FIGHTING?

READ THIS WAY

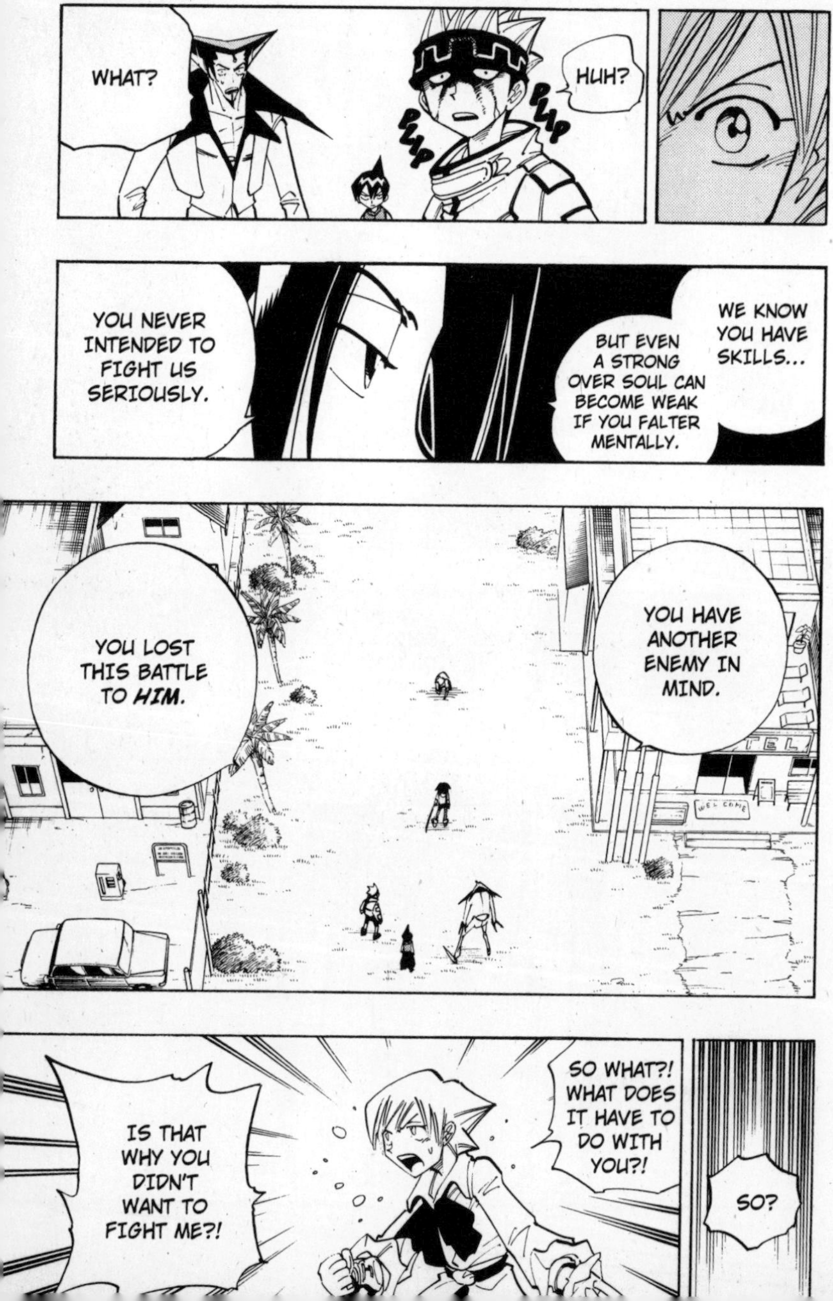
HUH?
PLIP PLIP
WHAT?
WE KNOW YOU HAVE SKILLS...
BUT EVEN A STRONG OVER SOUL CAN BECOME WEAK IF YOU FALTER MENTALLY.
YOU NEVER INTENDED TO FIGHT US SERIOUSLY.
YOU HAVE ANOTHER ENEMY IN MIND.
YOU LOST THIS BATTLE TO *HIM*.
SO?
SO WHAT?! WHAT DOES IT HAVE TO DO WITH YOU?!
IS THAT WHY YOU DIDN'T WANT TO FIGHT ME?!

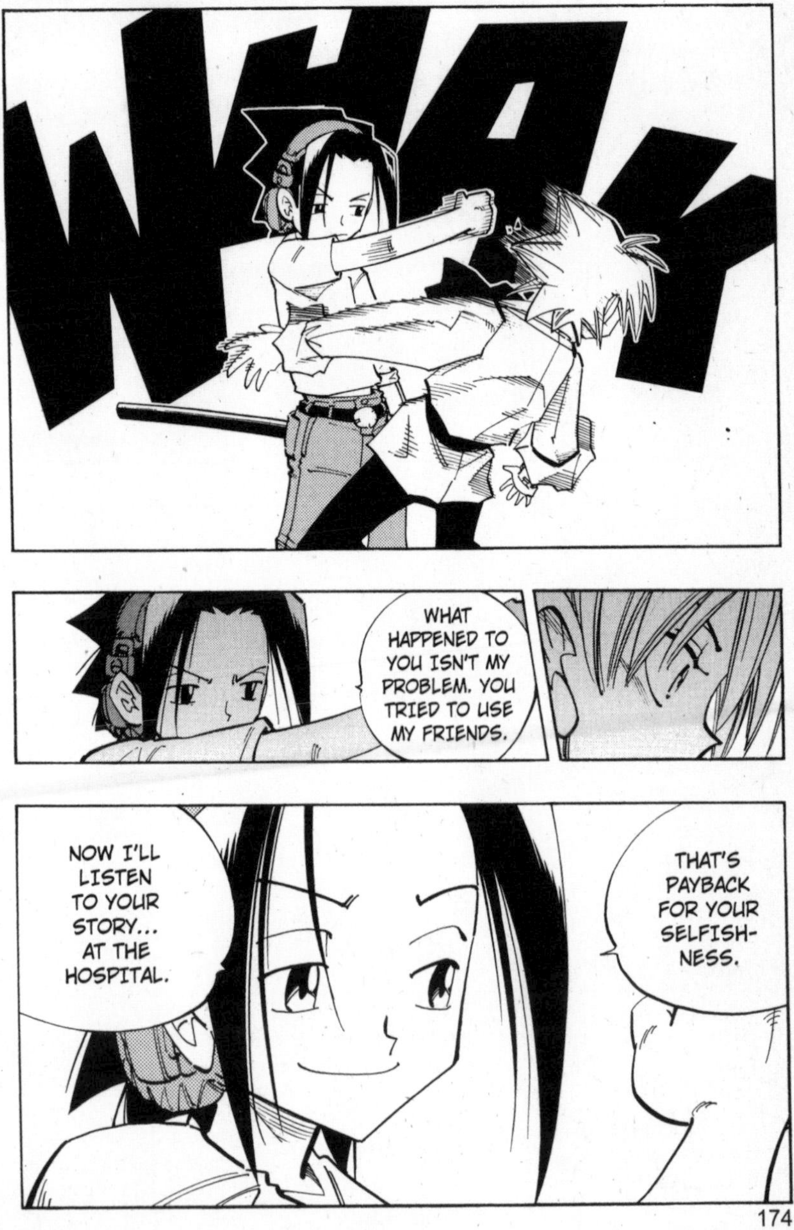
WHAK
WHAT HAPPENED TO YOU ISN'T MY PROBLEM. YOU TRIED TO USE MY FRIENDS.
THAT'S PAYBACK FOR YOUR SELFISH-NESS.
NOW I'LL LISTEN TO YOUR STORY... AT THE HOSPITAL.

Shaman King™

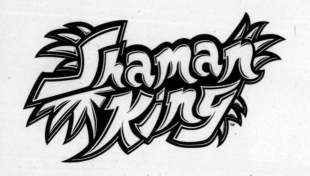

SHAMAN
KING
10

BREAD

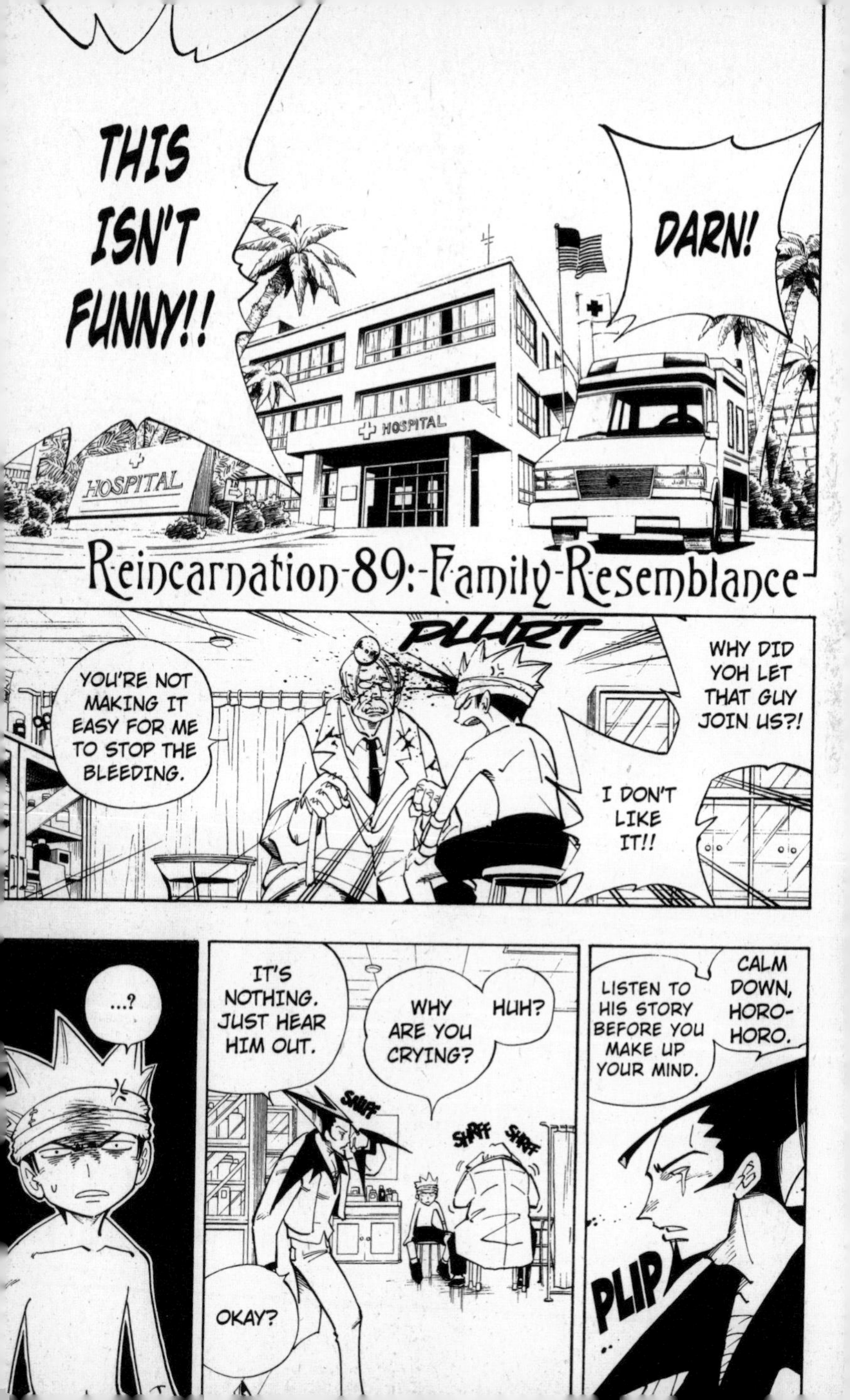
DARN!
THIS ISN'T FUNNY!!
HOSPITAL
HOSPITAL
Reincarnation 89: Family Resemblance
WHY DID YOH LET THAT GUY JOIN US?!
I DON'T LIKE IT!!
PLURT
YOU'RE NOT MAKING IT EASY FOR ME TO STOP THE BLEEDING.
CALM DOWN, HORO-HORO.
LISTEN TO HIS STORY BEFORE YOU MAKE UP YOUR MIND.
PLIP
HUH?
WHY ARE YOU CRYING?
IT'S NOTHING. JUST HEAR HIM OUT.
SNIFF
SHRFF
SHRFF
OKAY?
...?

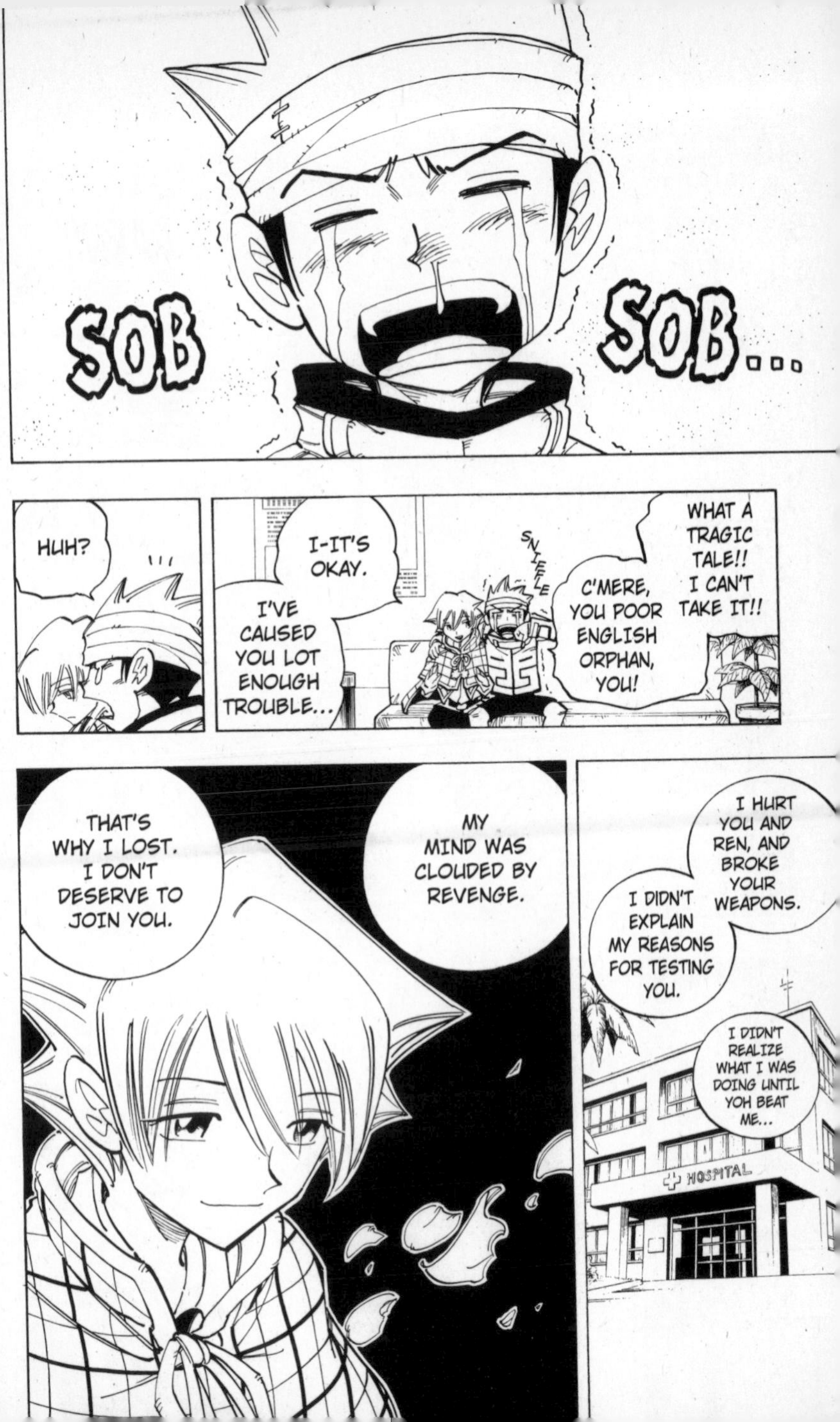
SOB
SOB...
WHAT A TRAGIC TALE!! I CAN'T TAKE IT!!
C'MERE, YOU POOR ENGLISH ORPHAN, YOU!
SNIFFLE
I-IT'S OKAY.
I'VE CAUSED YOU LOT ENOUGH TROUBLE...
HUH?
I HURT YOU AND REN, AND BROKE YOUR WEAPONS.
I DIDN'T EXPLAIN MY REASONS FOR TESTING YOU.
I DIDN'T REALIZE WHAT I WAS DOING UNTIL YOH BEAT ME...
HOSPITAL
MY MIND WAS CLOUDED BY REVENGE.
THAT'S WHY I LOST. I DON'T DESERVE TO JOIN YOU.

Reincarnation 89: Family Resemblance

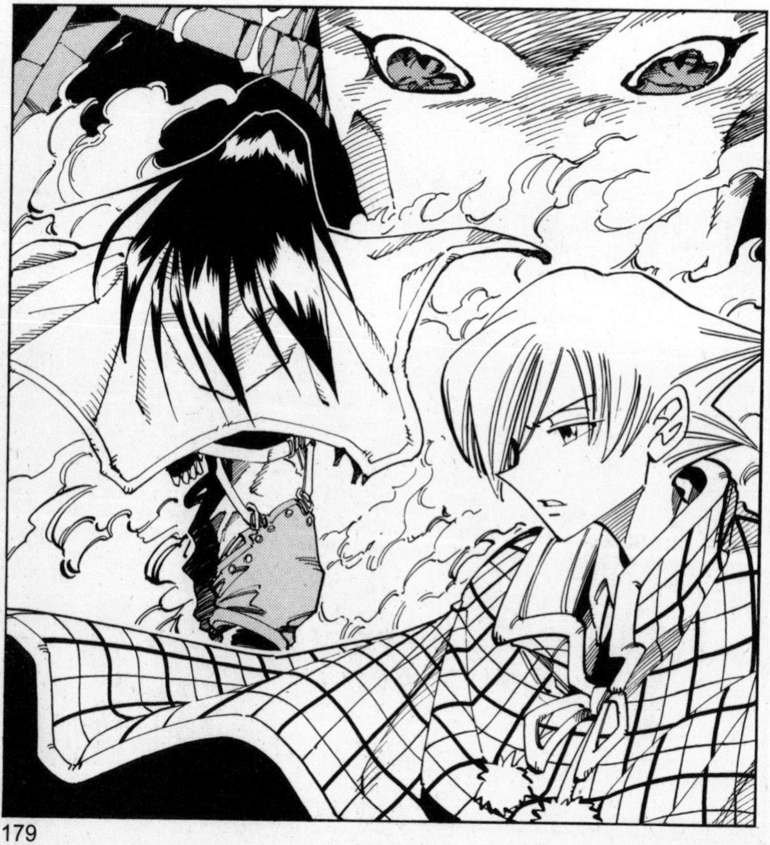

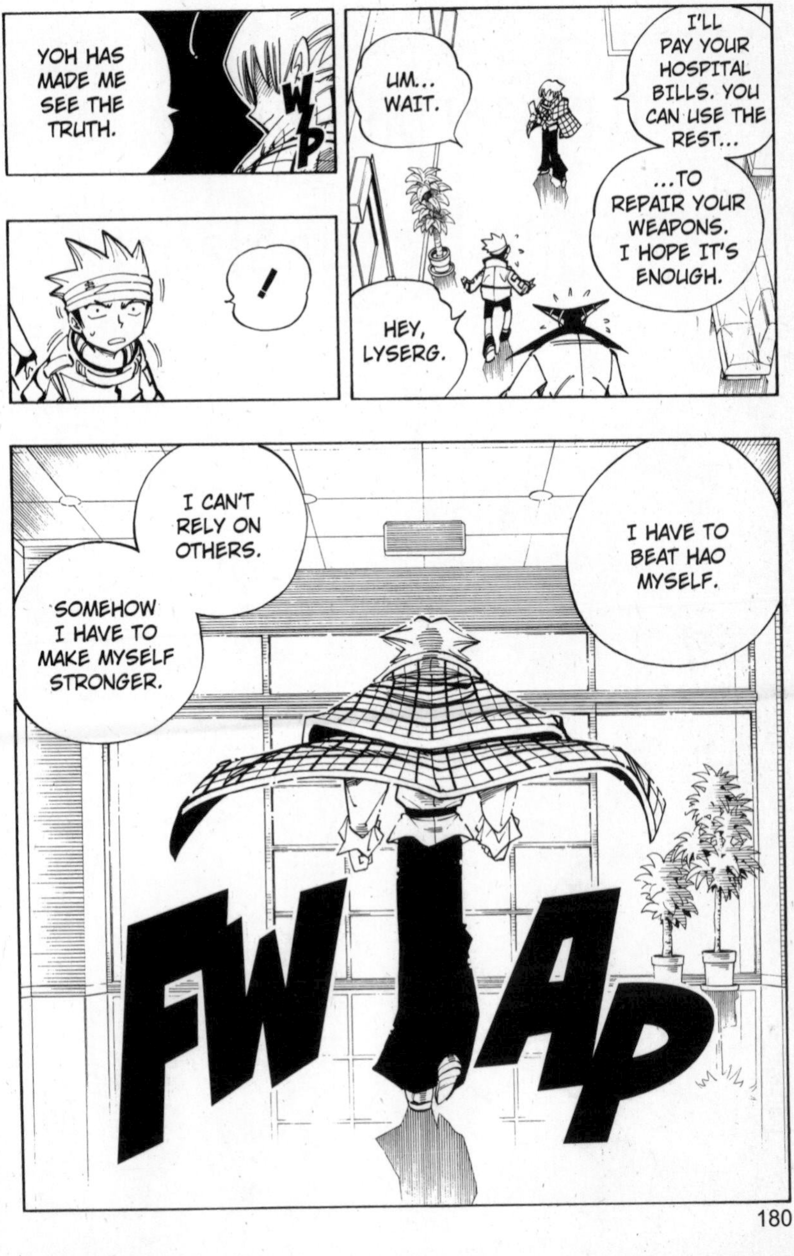
I'LL PAY YOUR HOSPITAL BILLS. YOU CAN USE THE REST...
...TO REPAIR YOUR WEAPONS. I HOPE IT'S ENOUGH.
UM... WAIT.
HEY, LYSERG.
YOH HAS MADE ME SEE THE TRUTH.
WP
!
I HAVE TO BEAT HAO MYSELF.
I CAN'T RELY ON OTHERS.
SOMEHOW I HAVE TO MAKE MYSELF STRONGER.
FWAP

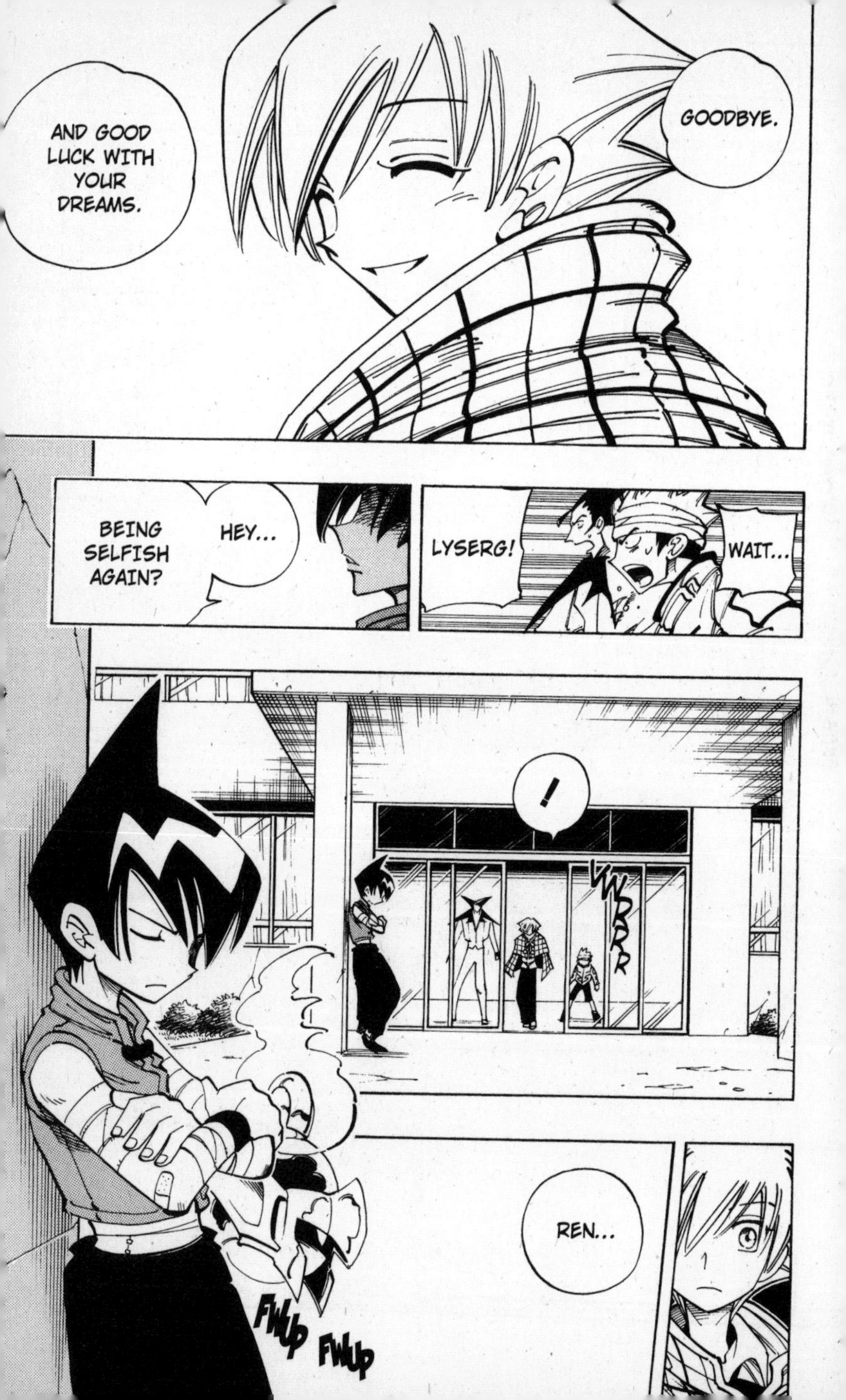

GOODBYE.
AND GOOD LUCK WITH YOUR DREAMS.
WAIT...
LYSERG!
HEY...
BEING SELFISH AGAIN?
!
WRRR
REN...
FWUP FWUP

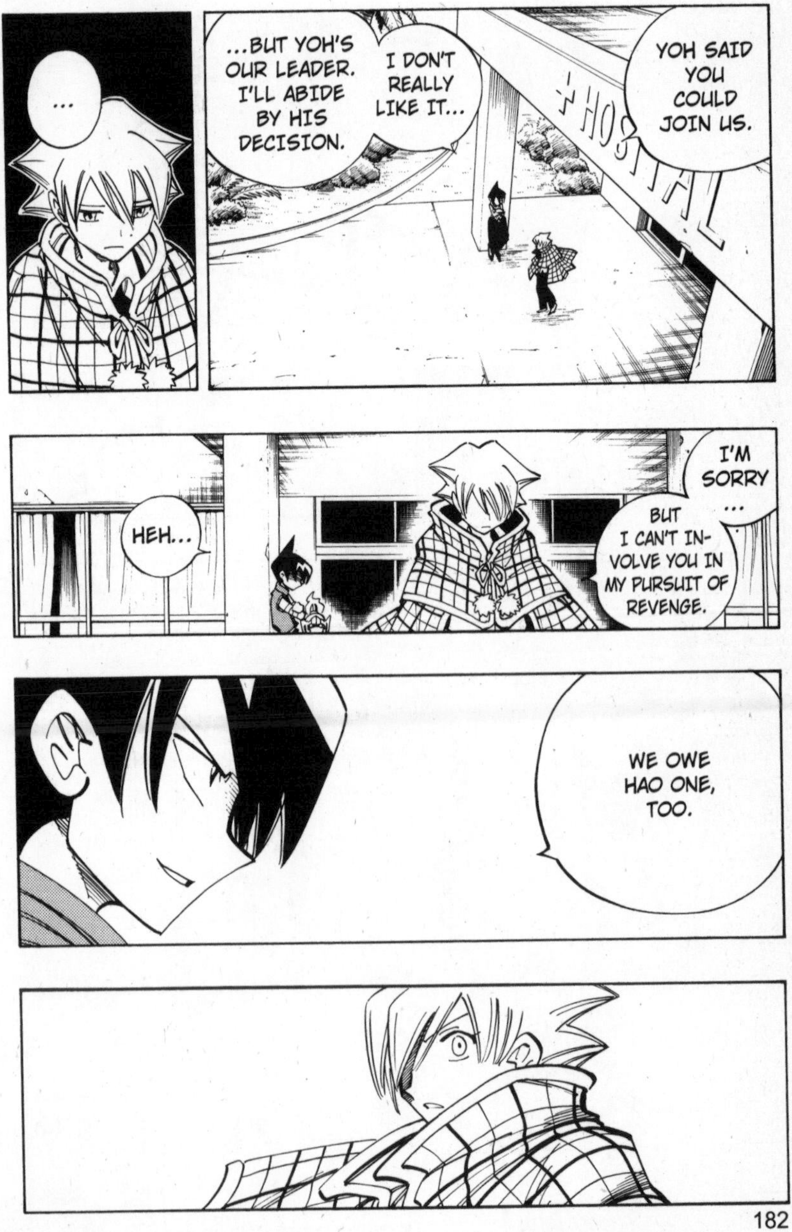
YOH SAID YOU COULD JOIN US.
I DON'T REALLY LIKE IT...
...BUT YOH'S OUR LEADER. I'LL ABIDE BY HIS DECISION.
...
I'M SORRY...
BUT I CAN'T IN-VOLVE YOU IN MY PURSUIT OF REVENGE.
HEH...
WE OWE HAO ONE, TOO.

READ THIS WAY

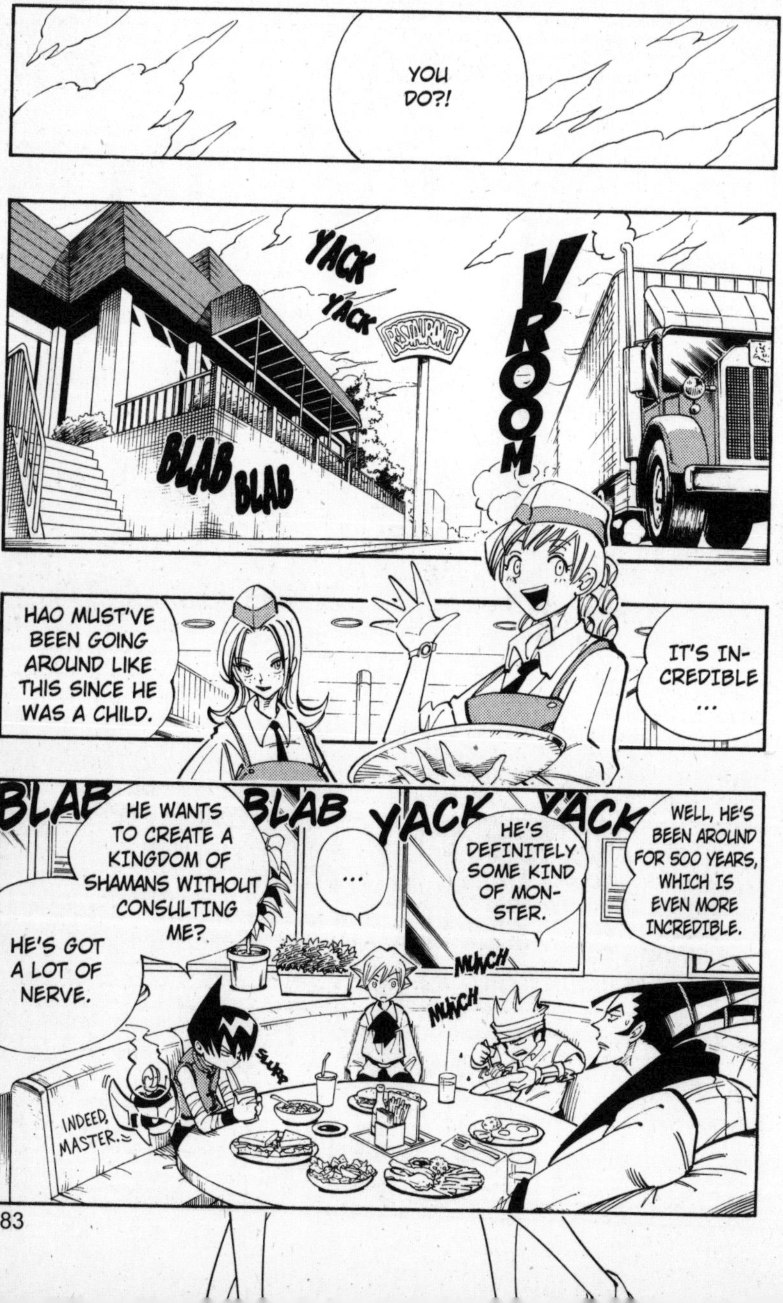
YOU DO?!
VROOM
YACK
YACK
BLAB
BLAB
IT'S IN-CREDIBLE ...
HAO MUST'VE BEEN GOING AROUND LIKE THIS SINCE HE WAS A CHILD.
YACK
WELL, HE'S BEEN AROUND FOR 500 YEARS, WHICH IS EVEN MORE INCREDIBLE.
YACK
HE'S DEFINITELY SOME KIND OF MON-STER.
BLAB
...
HE WANTS TO CREATE A KINGDOM OF SHAMANS WITHOUT CONSULTING ME?
BLAB
HE'S GOT A LOT OF NERVE.
MUNCH
MUNCH
SLURP
INDEED, MASTER.

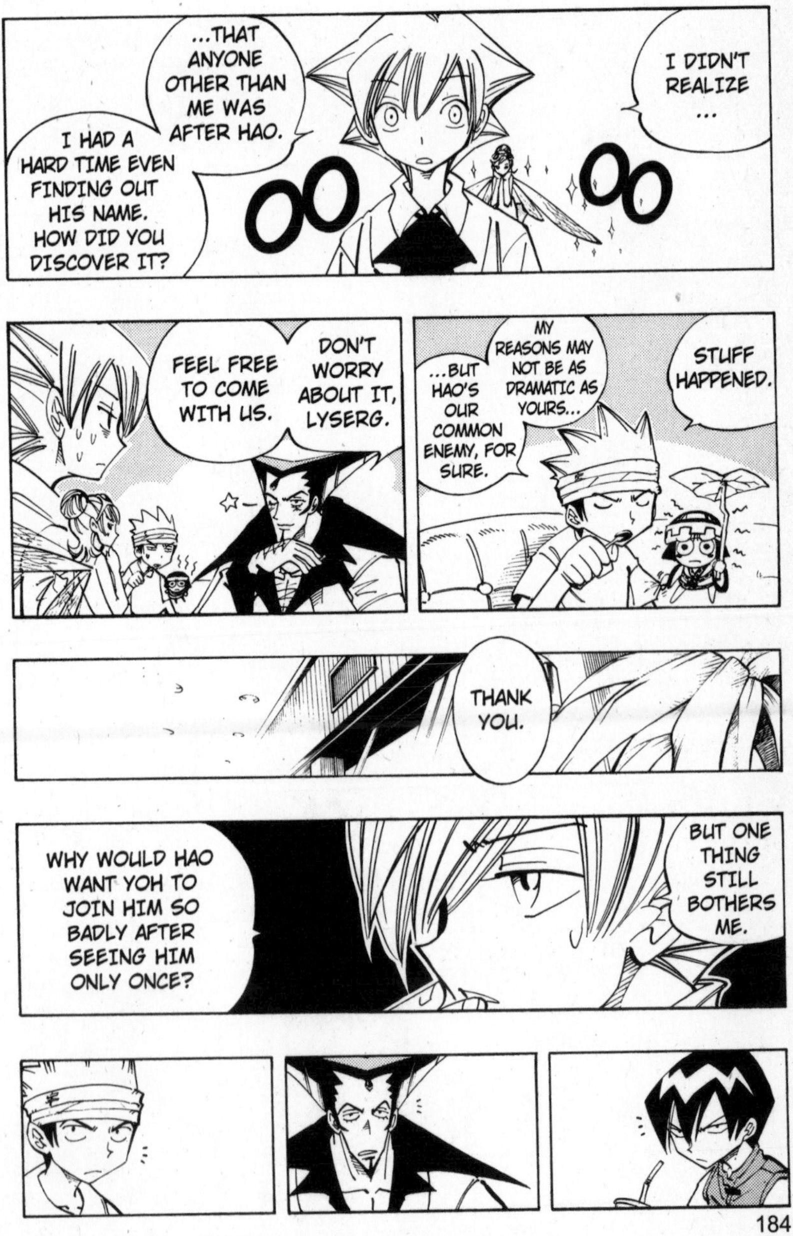
I DIDN'T REALIZE ...
...THAT ANYONE OTHER THAN ME WAS AFTER HAO.
I HAD A HARD TIME EVEN FINDING OUT HIS NAME. HOW DID YOU DISCOVER IT?
STUFF HAPPENED.
MY REASONS MAY NOT BE AS DRAMATIC AS YOURS...
...BUT HAO'S OUR COMMON ENEMY, FOR SURE.
DON'T WORRY ABOUT IT, LYSERG.
FEEL FREE TO COME WITH US.
THANK YOU.
BUT ONE THING STILL BOTHERS ME.
WHY WOULD HAO WANT YOH TO JOIN HIM SO BADLY AFTER SEEING HIM ONLY ONCE?

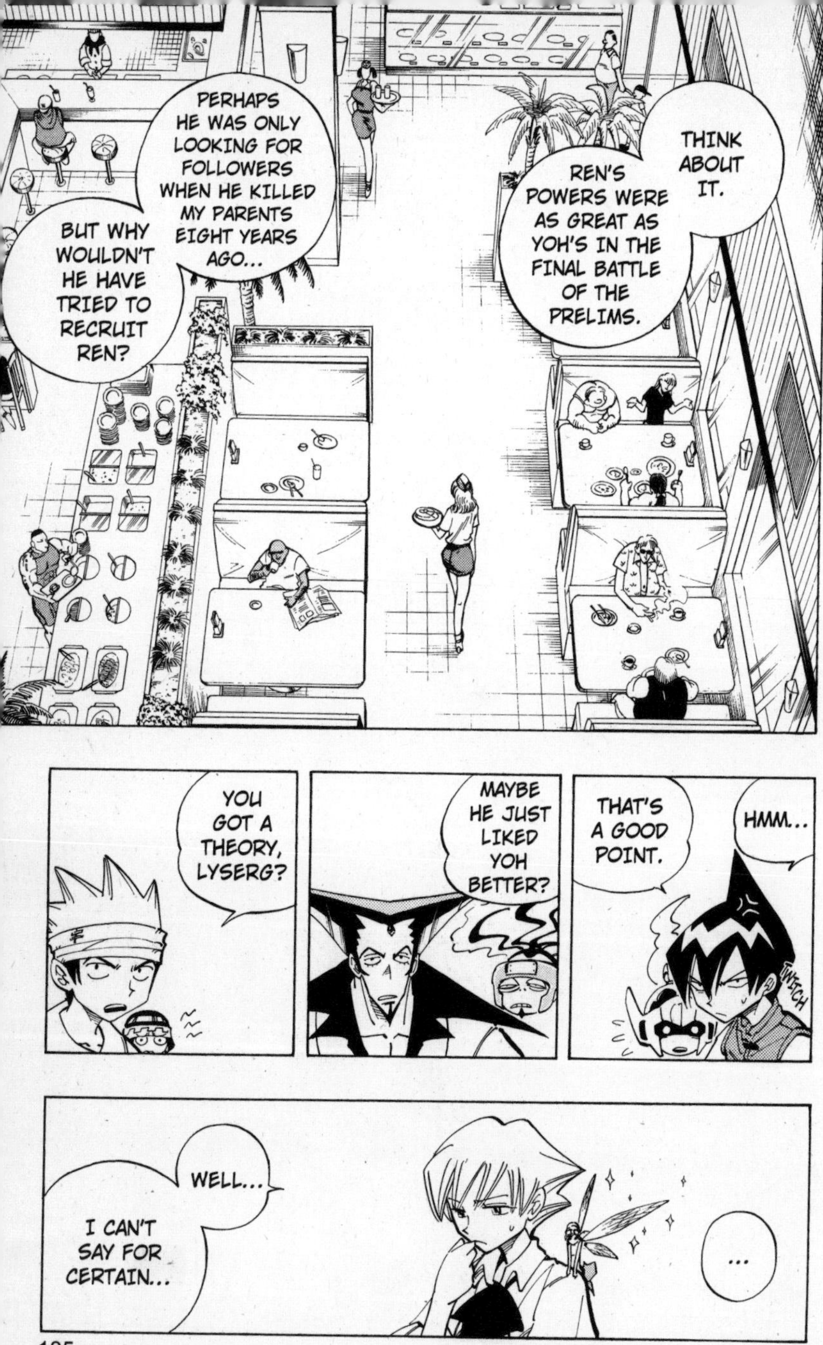
THINK ABOUT IT.
REN'S POWERS WERE AS GREAT AS YOH'S IN THE FINAL BATTLE OF THE PRELIMS.
PERHAPS HE WAS ONLY LOOKING FOR FOLLOWERS WHEN HE KILLED MY PARENTS EIGHT YEARS AGO...
BUT WHY WOULDN'T HE HAVE TRIED TO RECRUIT REN?
HMM...
THAT'S A GOOD POINT.
TWITCH
MAYBE HE JUST LIKED YOH BETTER?
YOU GOT A THEORY, LYSERG?
...
WELL...
I CAN'T SAY FOR CERTAIN...

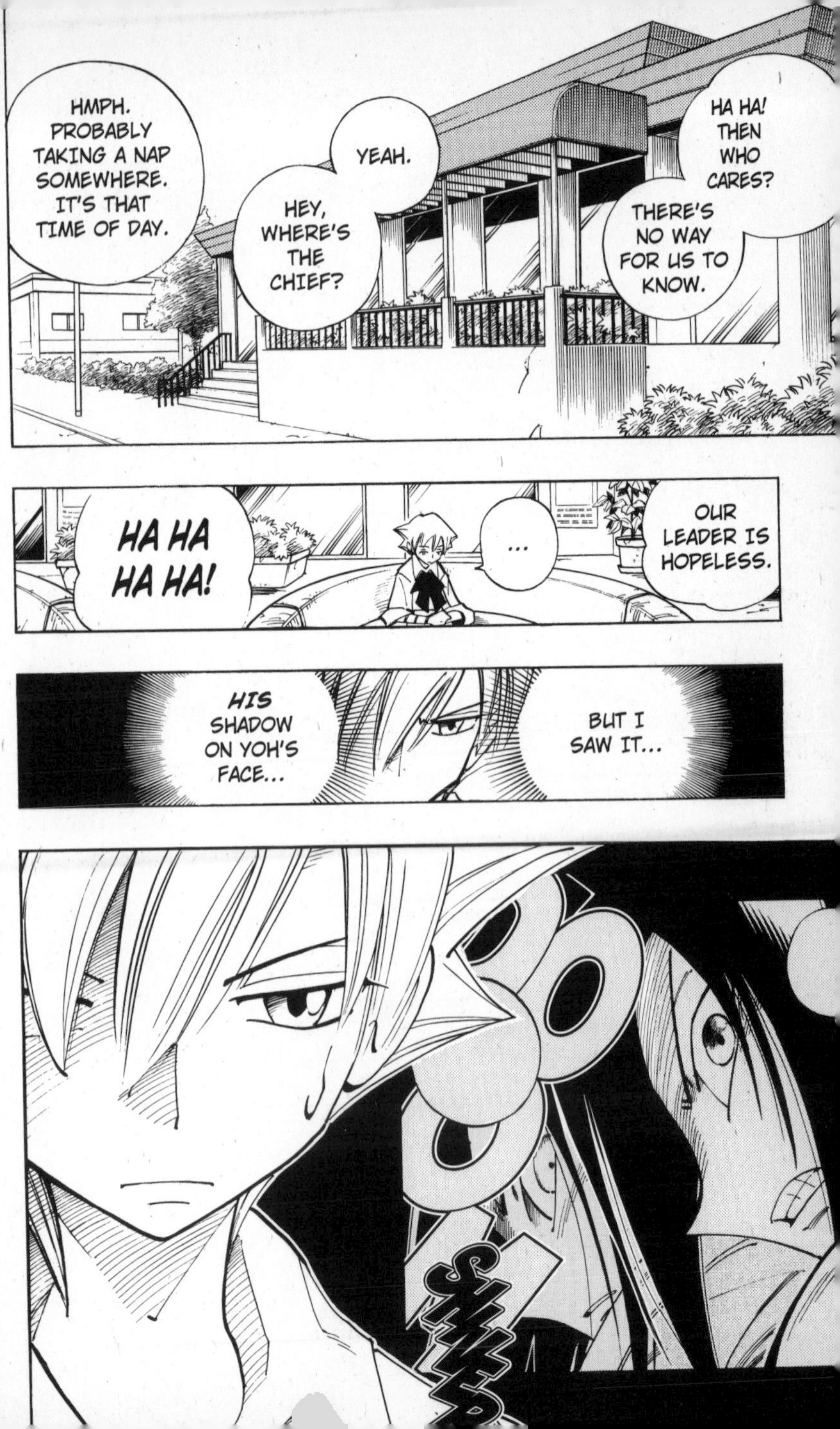
HA HA! THEN WHO CARES?
THERE'S NO WAY FOR US TO KNOW.
YEAH.
HEY, WHERE'S THE CHIEF?
HMPH. PROBABLY TAKING A NAP SOMEWHERE. IT'S THAT TIME OF DAY.
OUR LEADER IS HOPELESS.
...
HA HA HA HA!
BUT I SAW IT...
HIS SHADOW ON YOH'S FACE...

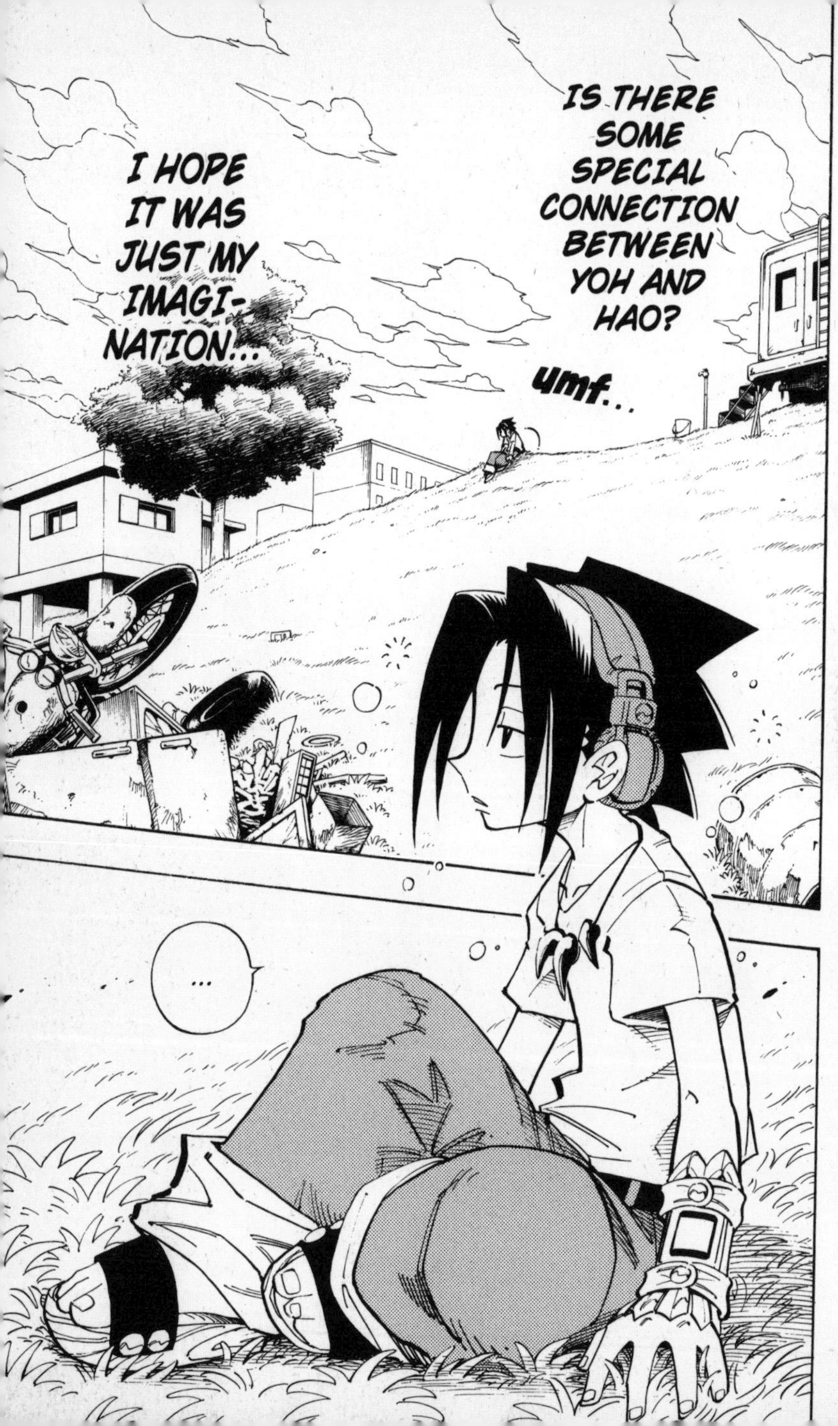
IS THERE SOME SPECIAL CONNECTION BETWEEN YOH AND HAO?
umf...
I HOPE IT WAS JUST MY IMAGI-NATION...
...

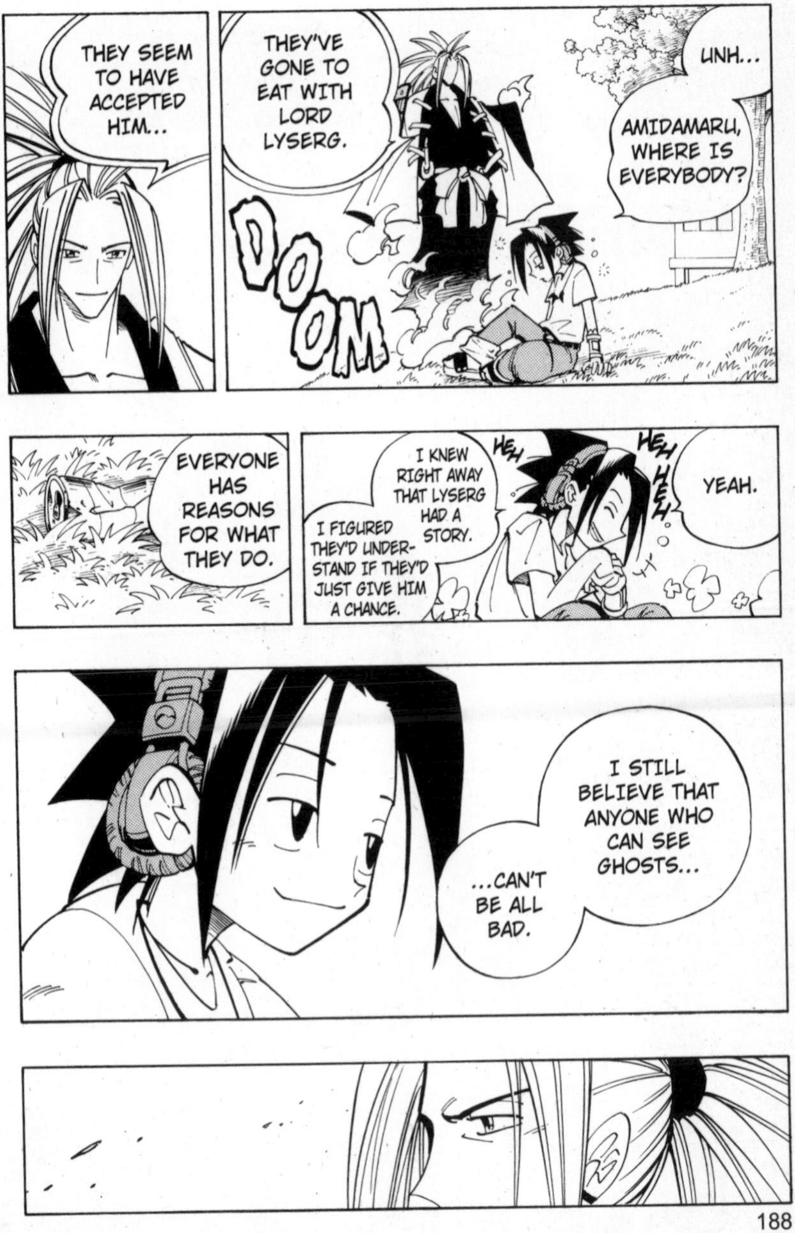
UNH...
AMIDAMARU, WHERE IS EVERYBODY?
THEY'VE GONE TO EAT WITH LORD LYSERG.
DOOM
THEY SEEM TO HAVE ACCEPTED HIM...
YEAH.
HEH HEH HEH
I KNEW RIGHT AWAY THAT LYSERG HAD A STORY.
I FIGURED THEY'D UNDERSTAND IF THEY'D JUST GIVE HIM A CHANCE.
EVERYONE HAS REASONS FOR WHAT THEY DO.
I STILL BELIEVE THAT ANYONE WHO CAN SEE GHOSTS...
...CAN'T BE ALL BAD.

READ THIS WAY

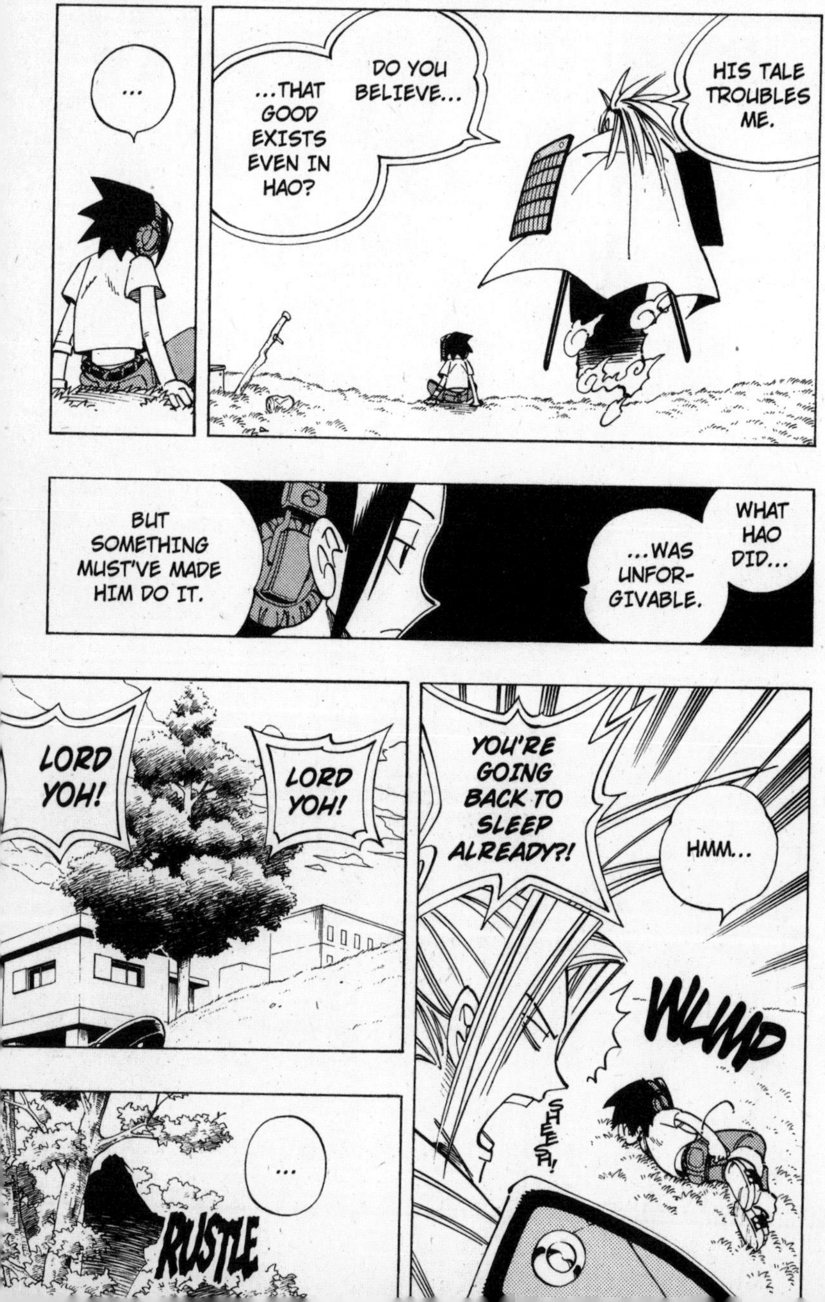

HIS TALE TROUBLES ME.
DO YOU BELIEVE...
...THAT GOOD EXISTS EVEN IN HAO?
...
WHAT HAO DID...
...WAS UNFORGIVABLE.
BUT SOMETHING MUST'VE MADE HIM DO IT.
HMM...
YOU'RE GOING BACK TO SLEEP ALREADY?!
WUMP
SHEESH!
LORD YOH!
LORD YOH!
...
RUSTLE

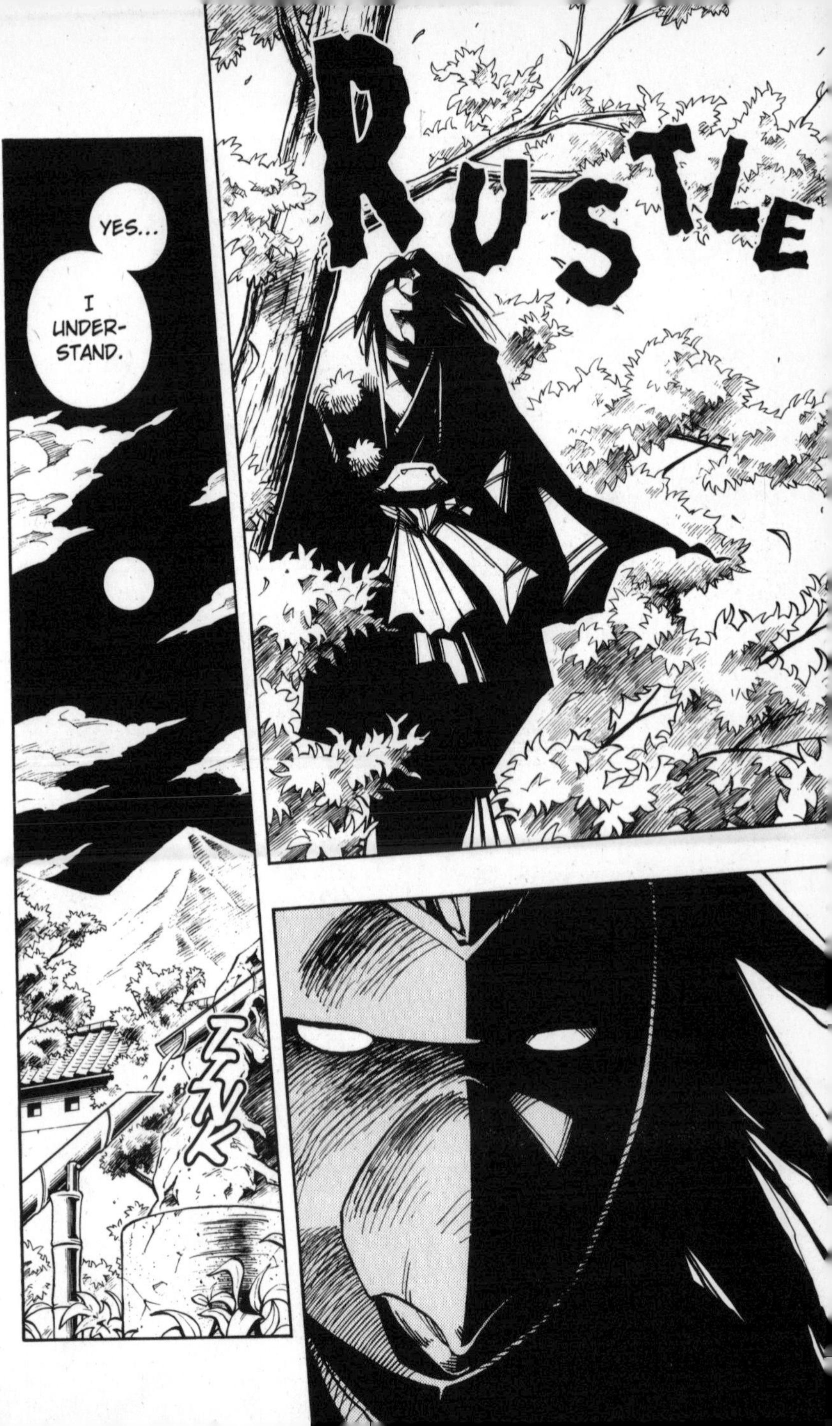
RUSTLE
YES...
I UNDER-STAND.
TINK

READ THIS WAY

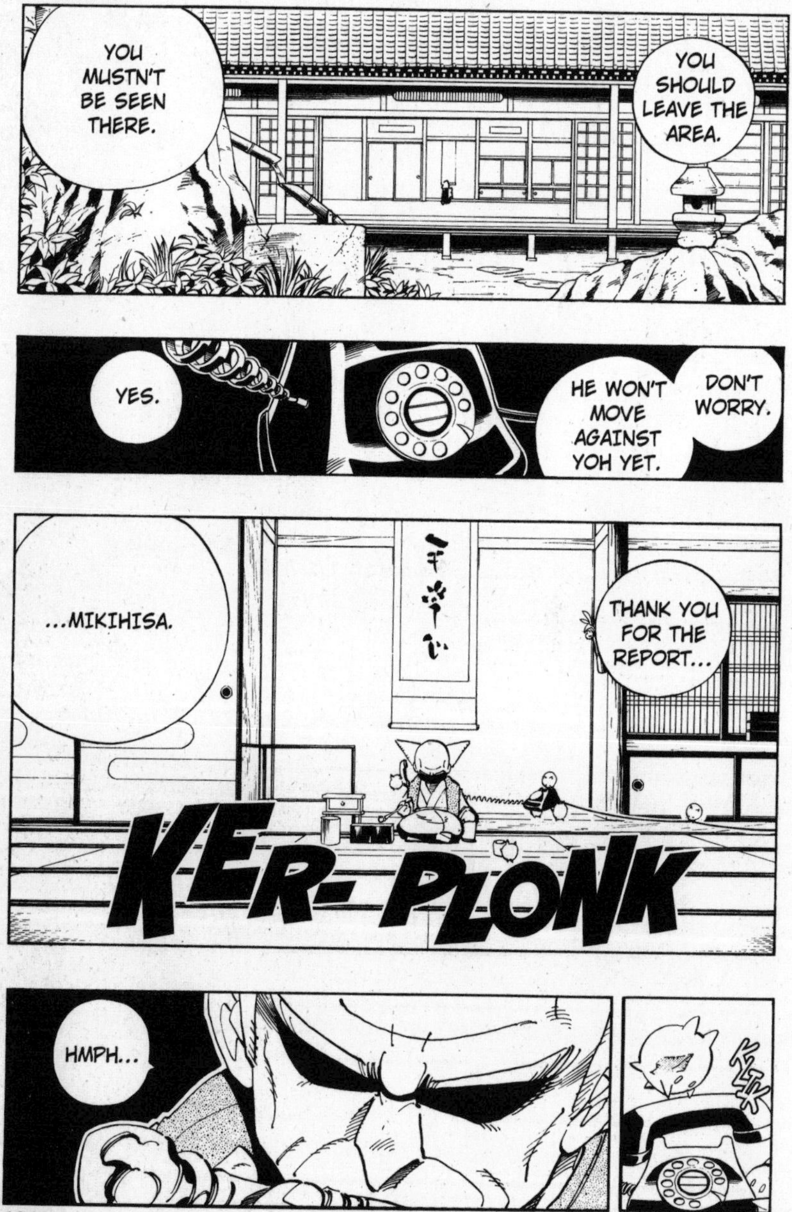
YOU SHOULD LEAVE THE AREA.
YOU MUSTN'T BE SEEN THERE.
DON'T WORRY.
HE WON'T MOVE AGAINST YOH YET.
YES.
THANK YOU FOR THE REPORT...
...MIKIHISA.
KER-PLONK
KLIK
HMPH...

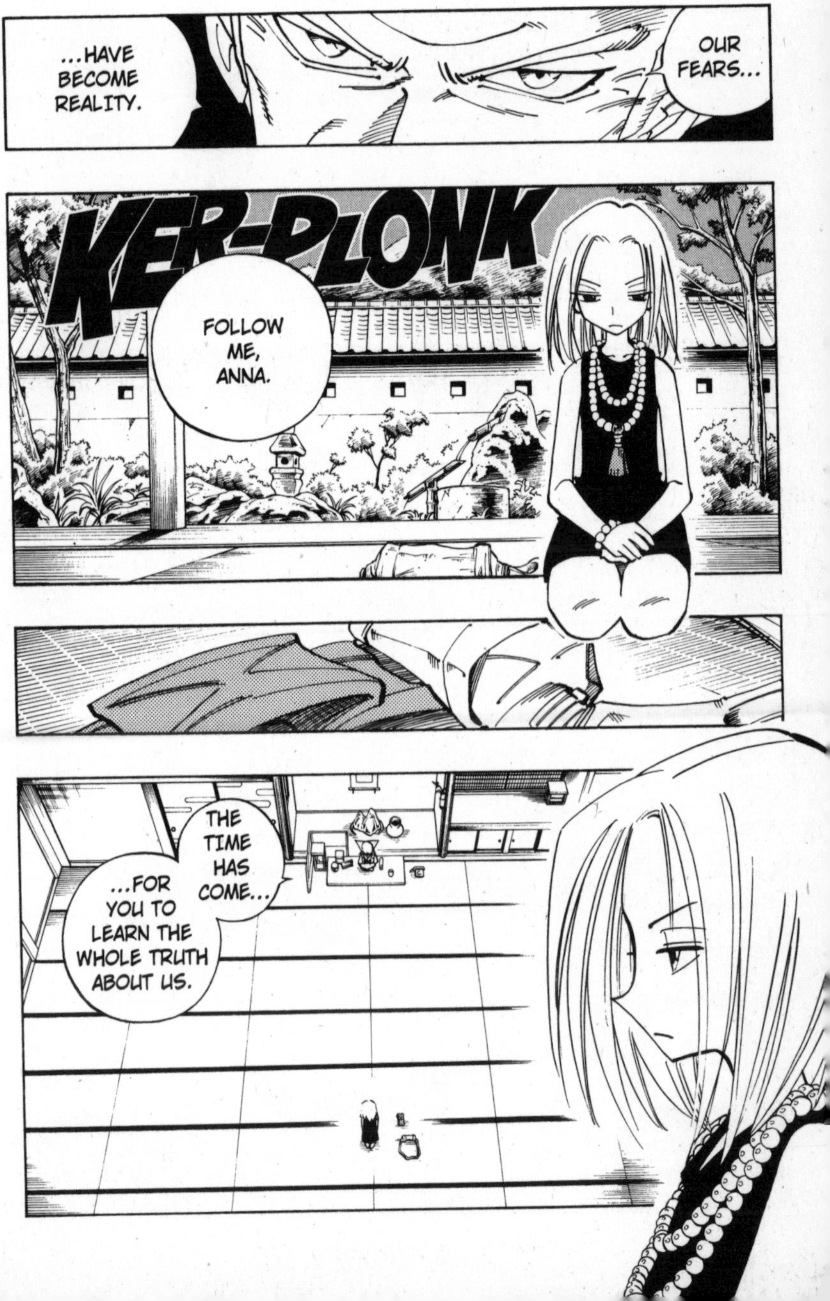
OUR FEARS...
...HAVE BECOME REALITY.
KER-PLONK
FOLLOW ME, ANNA.
THE TIME HAS COME...
...FOR YOU TO LEARN THE WHOLE TRUTH ABOUT US.

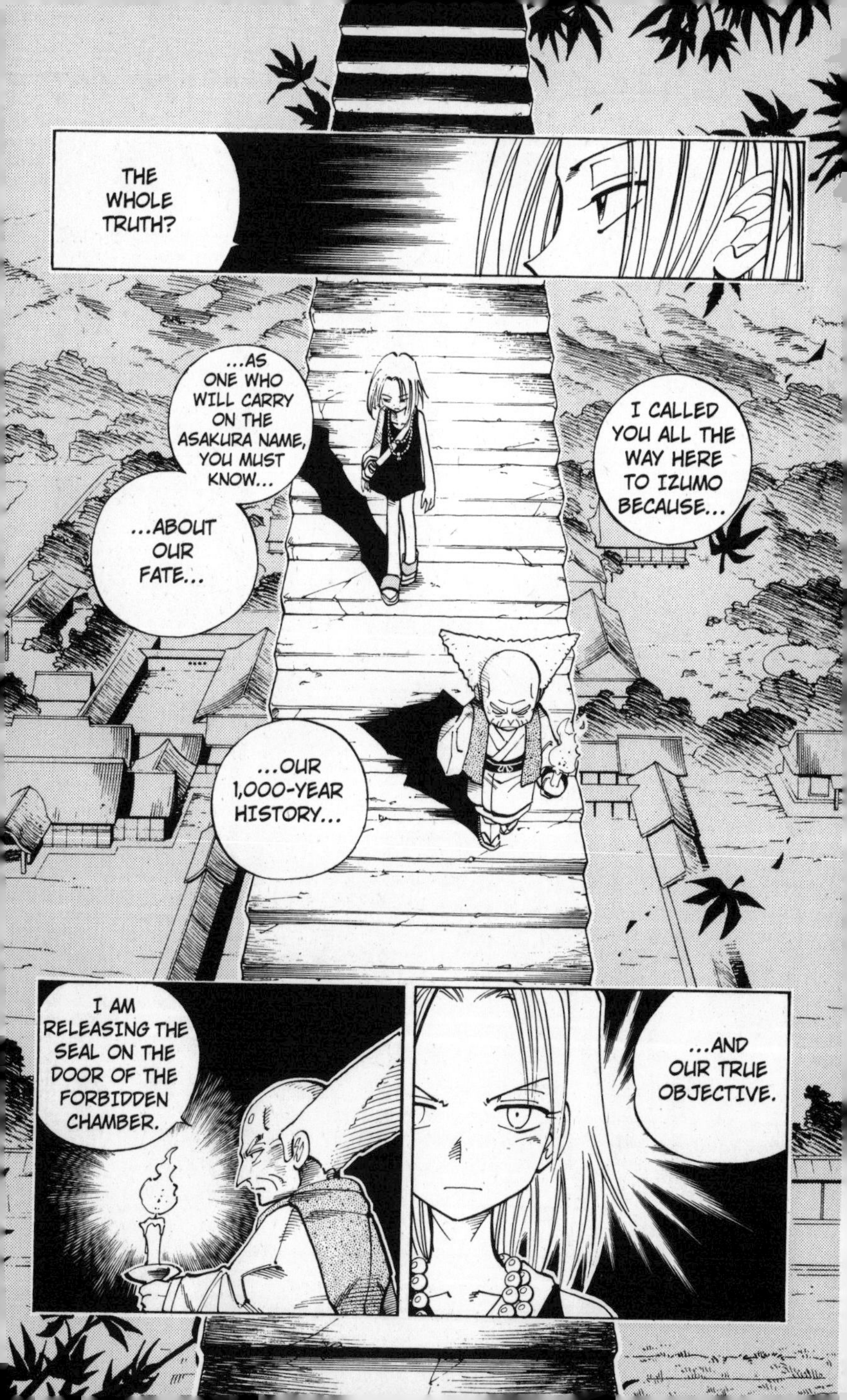
THE WHOLE TRUTH?
I CALLED YOU ALL THE WAY HERE TO IZUMO BECAUSE...
...AS ONE WHO WILL CARRY ON THE ASAKURA NAME, YOU MUST KNOW...
...ABOUT OUR FATE...
...OUR 1,000-YEAR HISTORY...
...AND OUR TRUE OBJECTIVE.
I AM RELEASING THE SEAL ON THE DOOR OF THE FORBIDDEN CHAMBER.

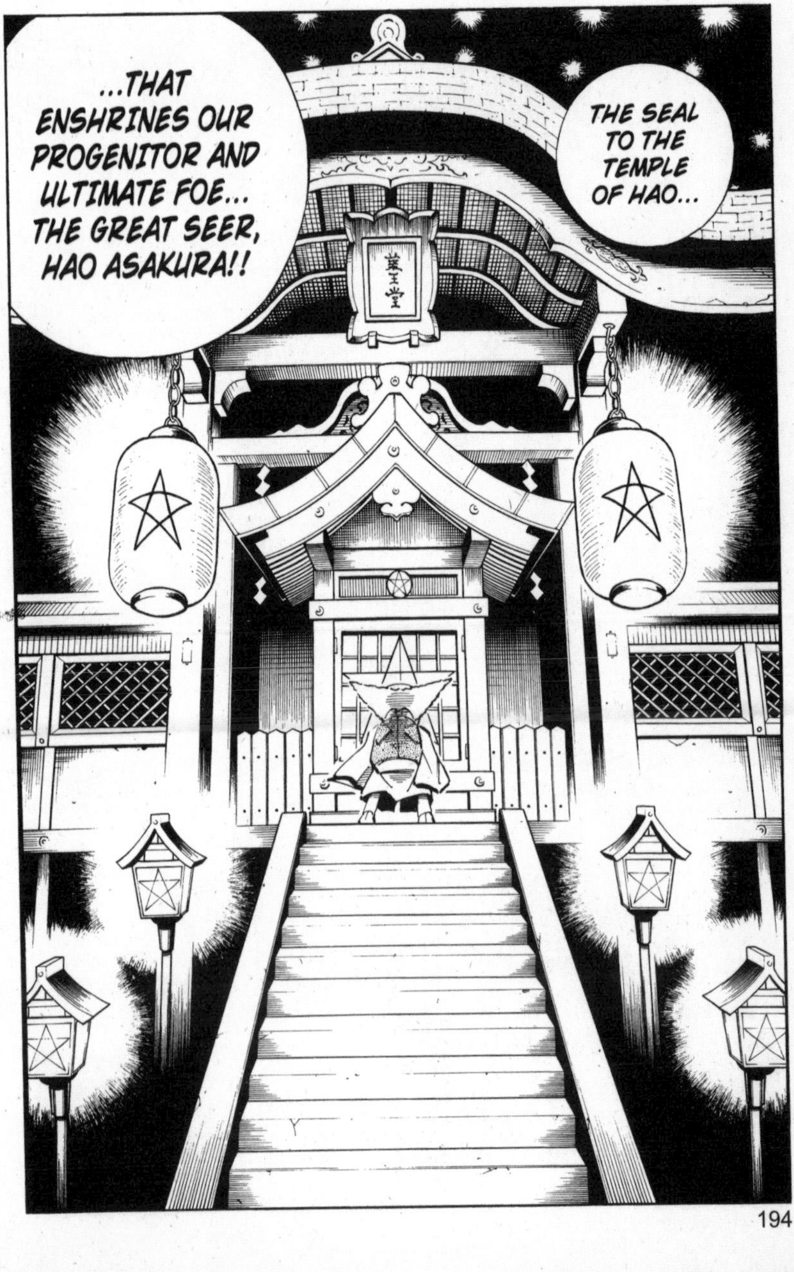
THE SEAL TO THE TEMPLE OF HAO...
...THAT ENSHRINES OUR PROGENITOR AND ULTIMATE FOE... THE GREAT SEER, HAO ASAKURA!!

Shaman King™

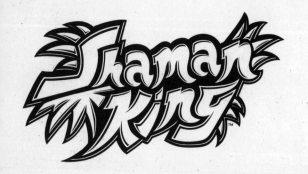

FUNBARI STORIES

FOUR-LEAF CLOVER

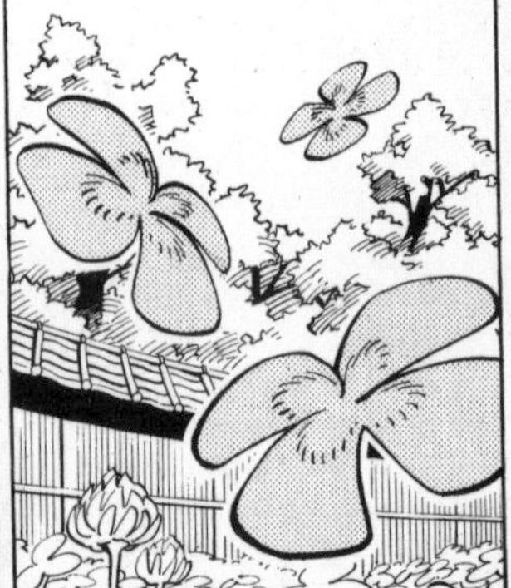

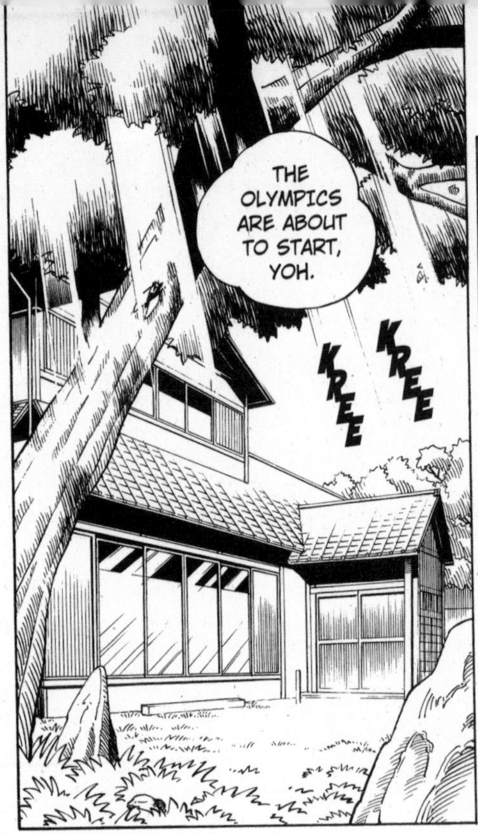
THE OLYMPICS ARE ABOUT TO START, YOH.
KREE
KREE

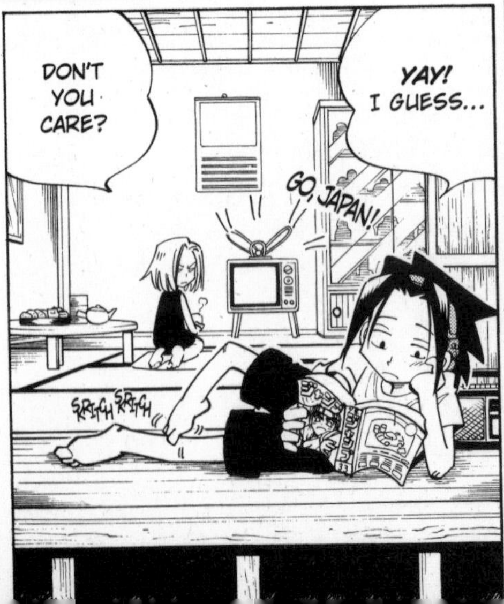
YAY! I GUESS...
DON'T YOU CARE?
GO, JAPAN!
SRICH SRICH

READ THIS WAY

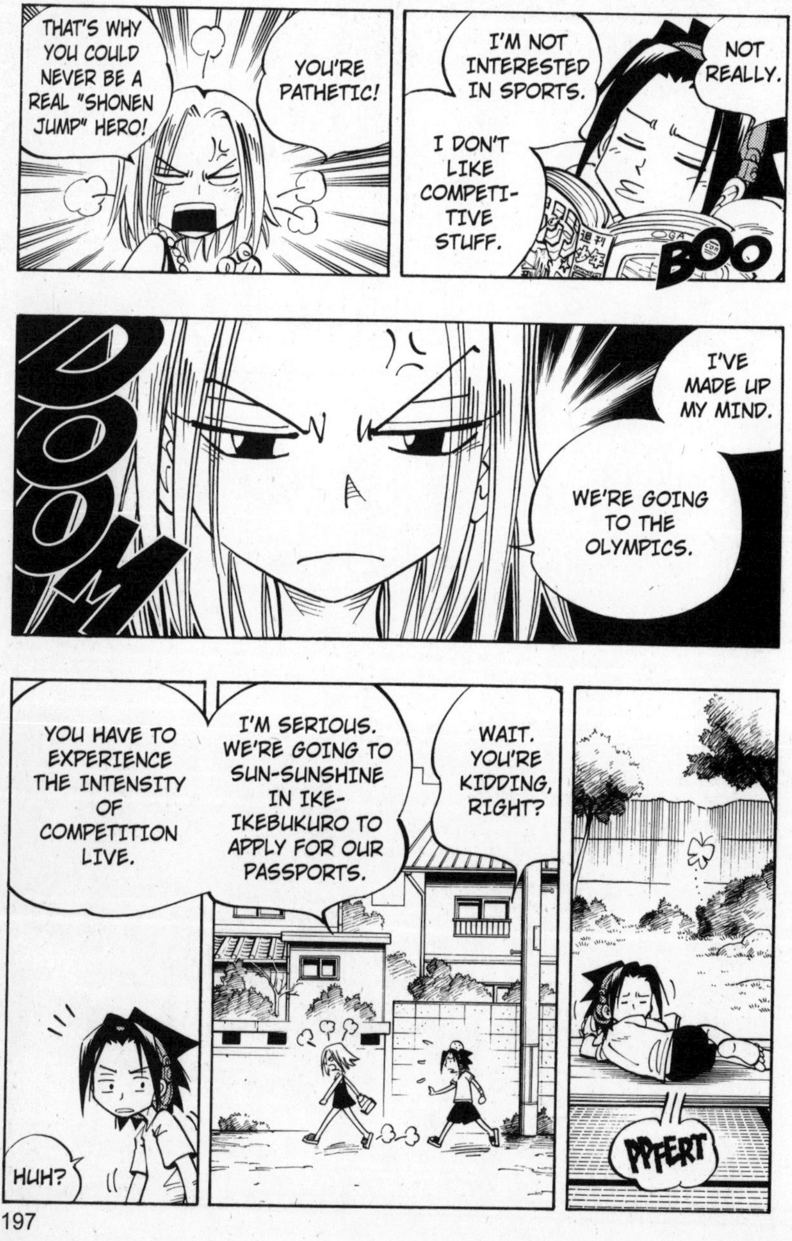
NOT REALLY.
I'M NOT INTERESTED IN SPORTS.
I DON'T LIKE COMPETI-TIVE STUFF.
BOO
YOU'RE PATHETIC!
THAT'S WHY YOU COULD NEVER BE A REAL "SHONEN JUMP" HERO!
I'VE MADE UP MY MIND.
WE'RE GOING TO THE OLYMPICS.
DOOM
PPFERT
WAIT. YOU'RE KIDDING, RIGHT?
I'M SERIOUS. WE'RE GOING TO SUN-SUNSHINE IN IKE-IKEBUKURO TO APPLY FOR OUR PASSPORTS.
YOU HAVE TO EXPERIENCE THE INTENSITY OF COMPETITION LIVE.
HUH?

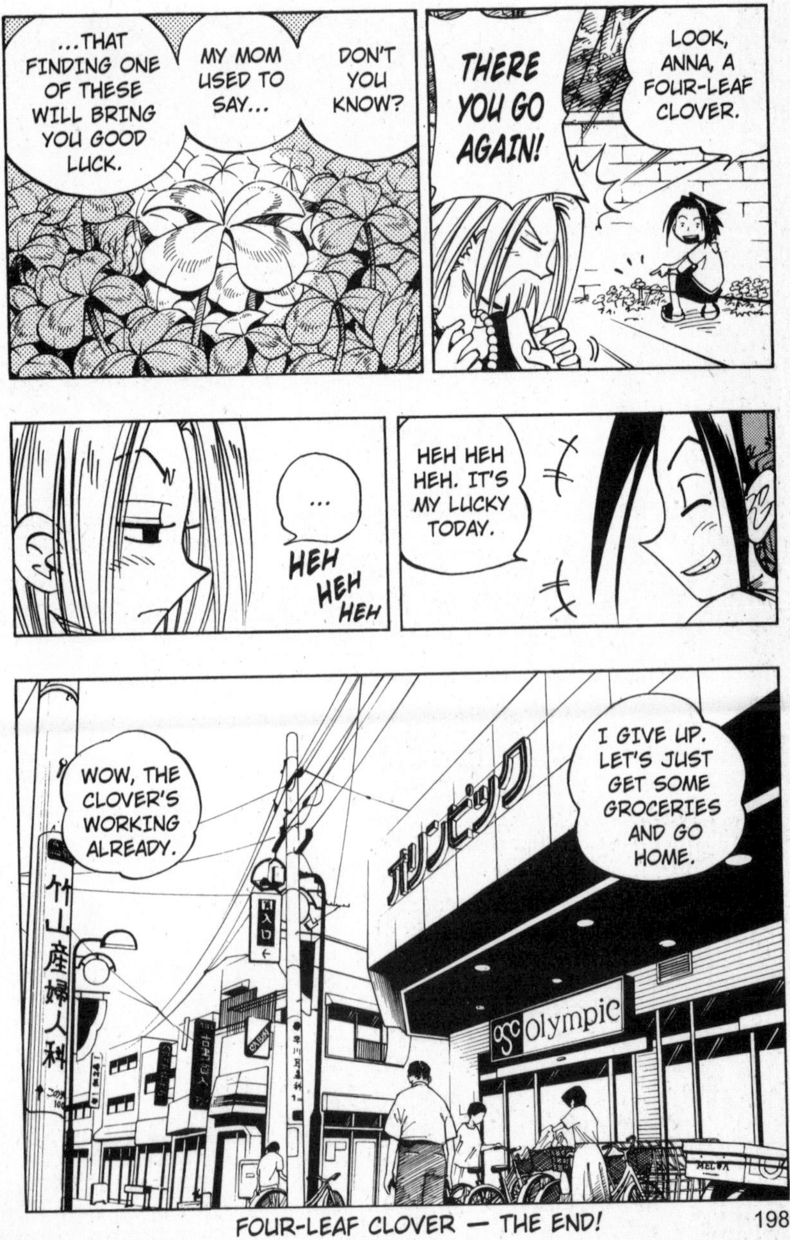
LOOK, ANNA, A FOUR-LEAF CLOVER.
THERE YOU GO AGAIN!
DON'T YOU KNOW?
MY MOM USED TO SAY...
...THAT FINDING ONE OF THESE WILL BRING YOU GOOD LUCK.
HEH HEH HEH. IT'S MY LUCKY TODAY.
...
HEH HEH HEH
I GIVE UP. LET'S JUST GET SOME GROCERIES AND GO HOME.
WOW, THE CLOVER'S WORKING ALREADY.
オリンピック
Olympic
竹山産婦人科
入口

FOUR-LEAF CLOVER — THE END!

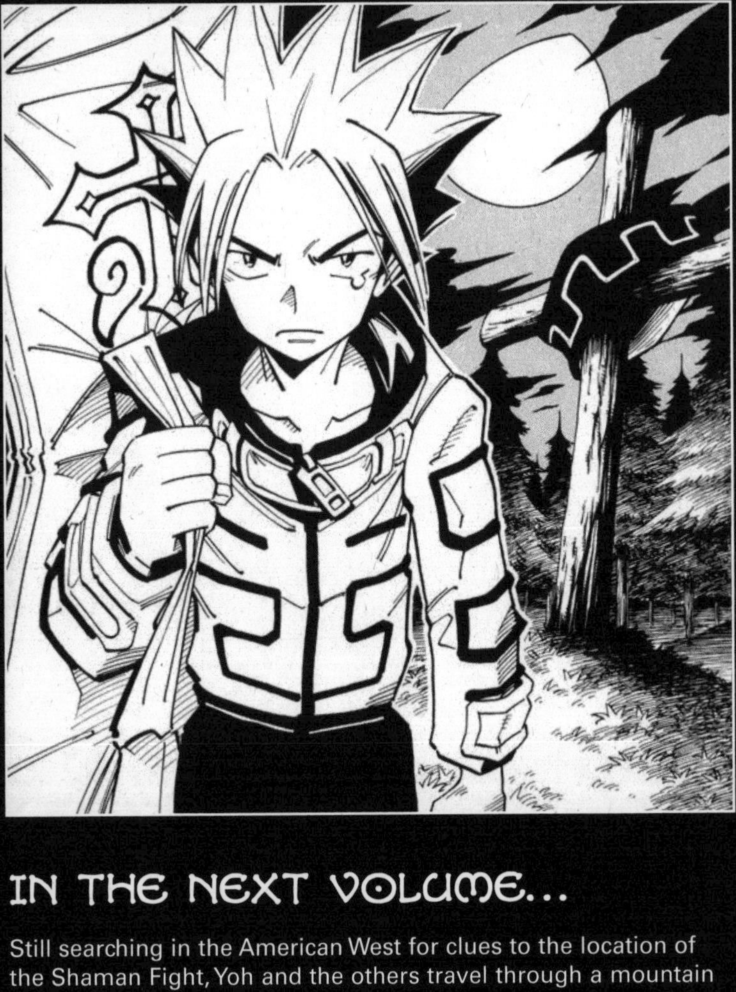

IN THE NEXT VOLUME...

Still searching in the American West for clues to the location of the Shaman Fight, Yoh and the others travel through a mountain range toward the site of the old Patch village. Horohoro suffers a setback when Kororo runs away, leaving him in the lurch! And the crew may be in over their heads when they face Hao's evil minions...but help is on the way!

AVAILABLE NOW!

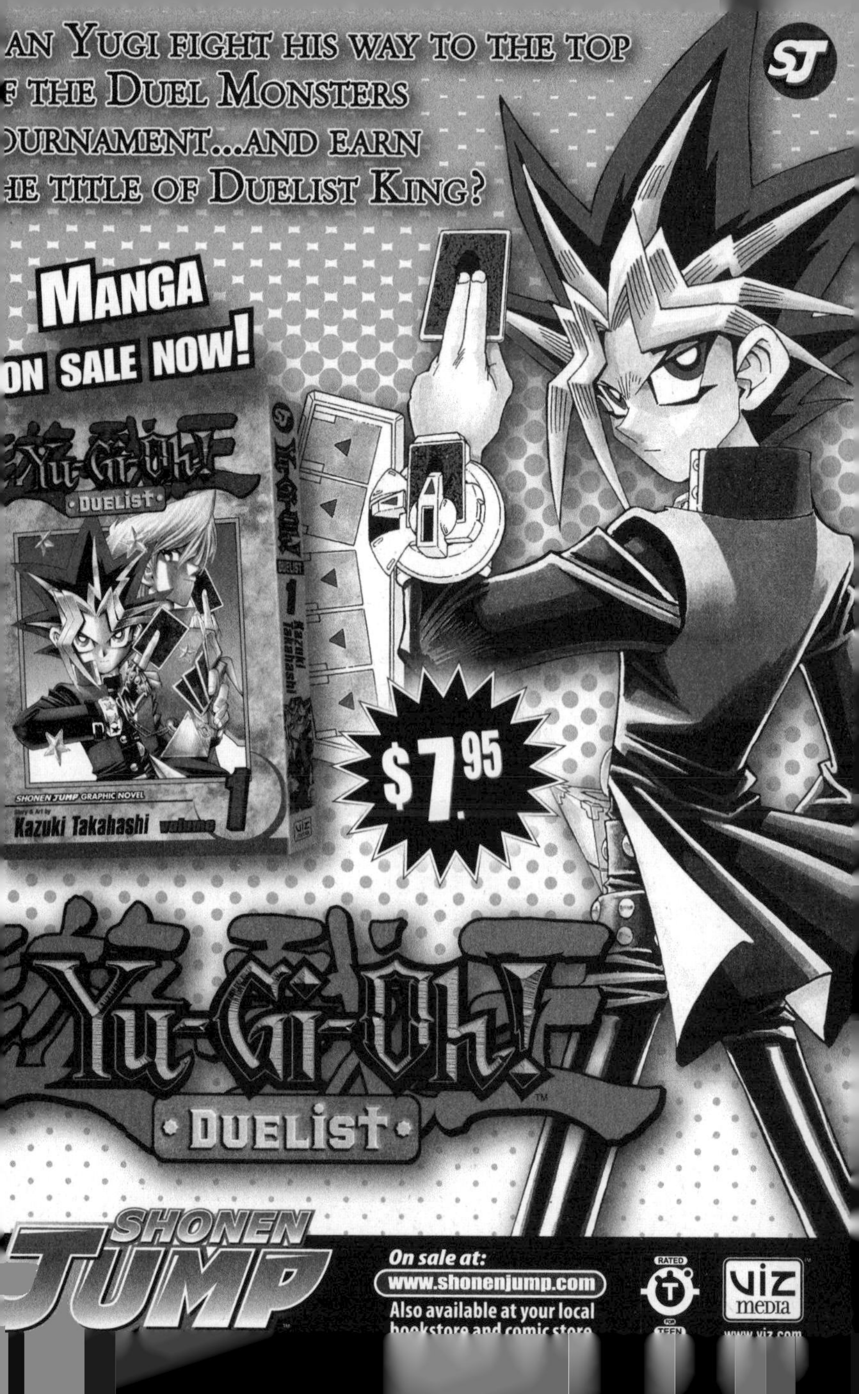

AN YUGI FIGHT HIS WAY TO THE TOP
F THE DUEL MONSTERS
OURNAMENT...AND EARN
HE TITLE OF DUELIST KING?
SJ
MANGA
ON SALE NOW!
Yu-Gi-Oh!
DUELIST
SHONEN JUMP GRAPHIC NOVEL
Kazuki Takahashi
volume 1
$7.95
Yu-Gi-Oh! DUELIST
SHONEN JUMP
On sale at:
www.shonenjump.com
Also available at your local
RATED T
viz media

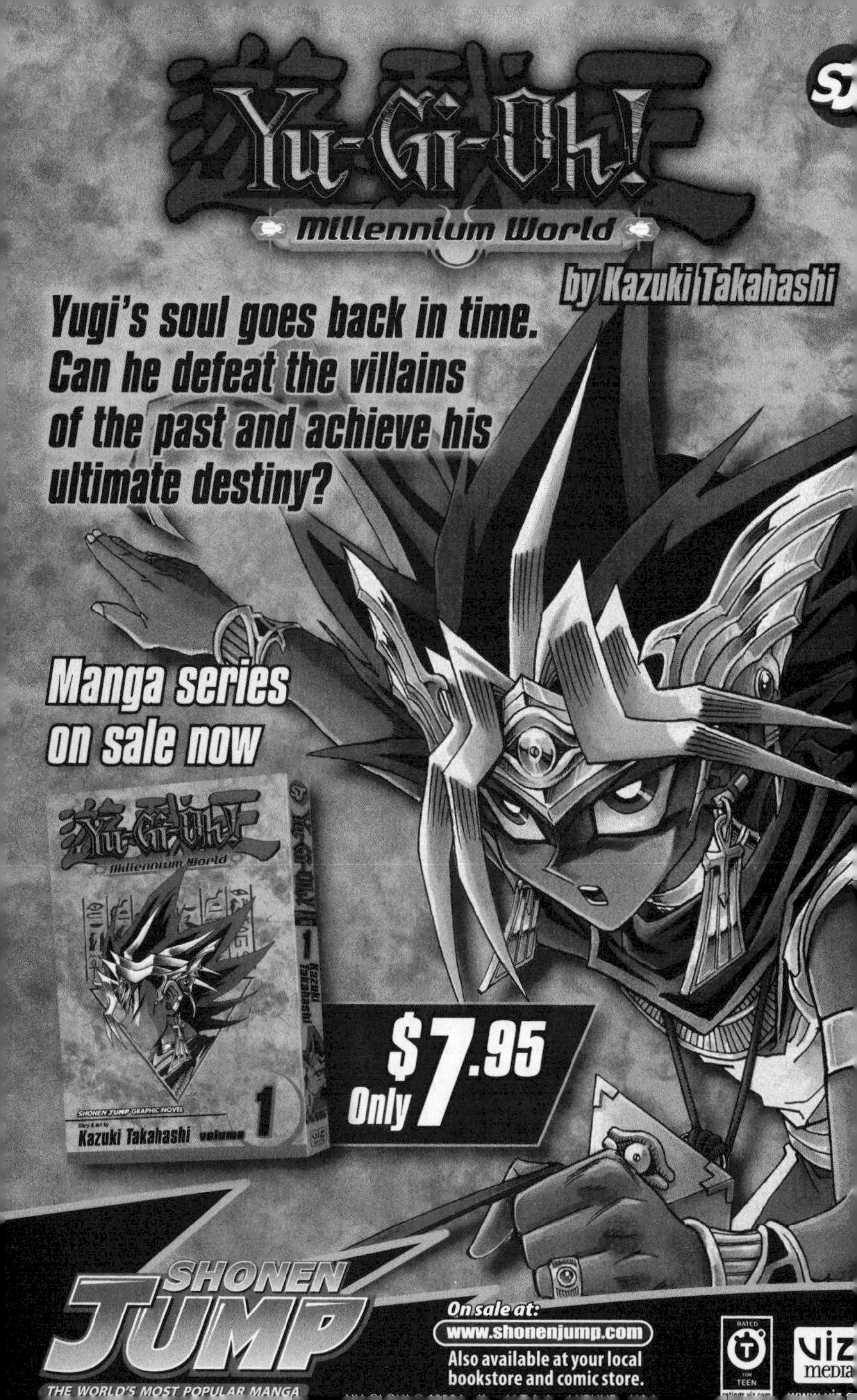
Yu-Gi-Oh!
Millennium World
by Kazuki Takahashi
Yugi's soul goes back in time. Can he defeat the villains of the past and achieve his ultimate destiny?
Manga series on sale now
Yu-Gi-Oh! Millennium World
SHONEN JUMP GRAPHIC NOVEL
Kazuki Takahashi volume 1
Only $7.95
SHONEN JUMP
THE WORLD'S MOST POPULAR MANGA
On sale at:
www.shonenjump.com
Also available at your local bookstore and comic store.
RATED T FOR TEEN
viz media

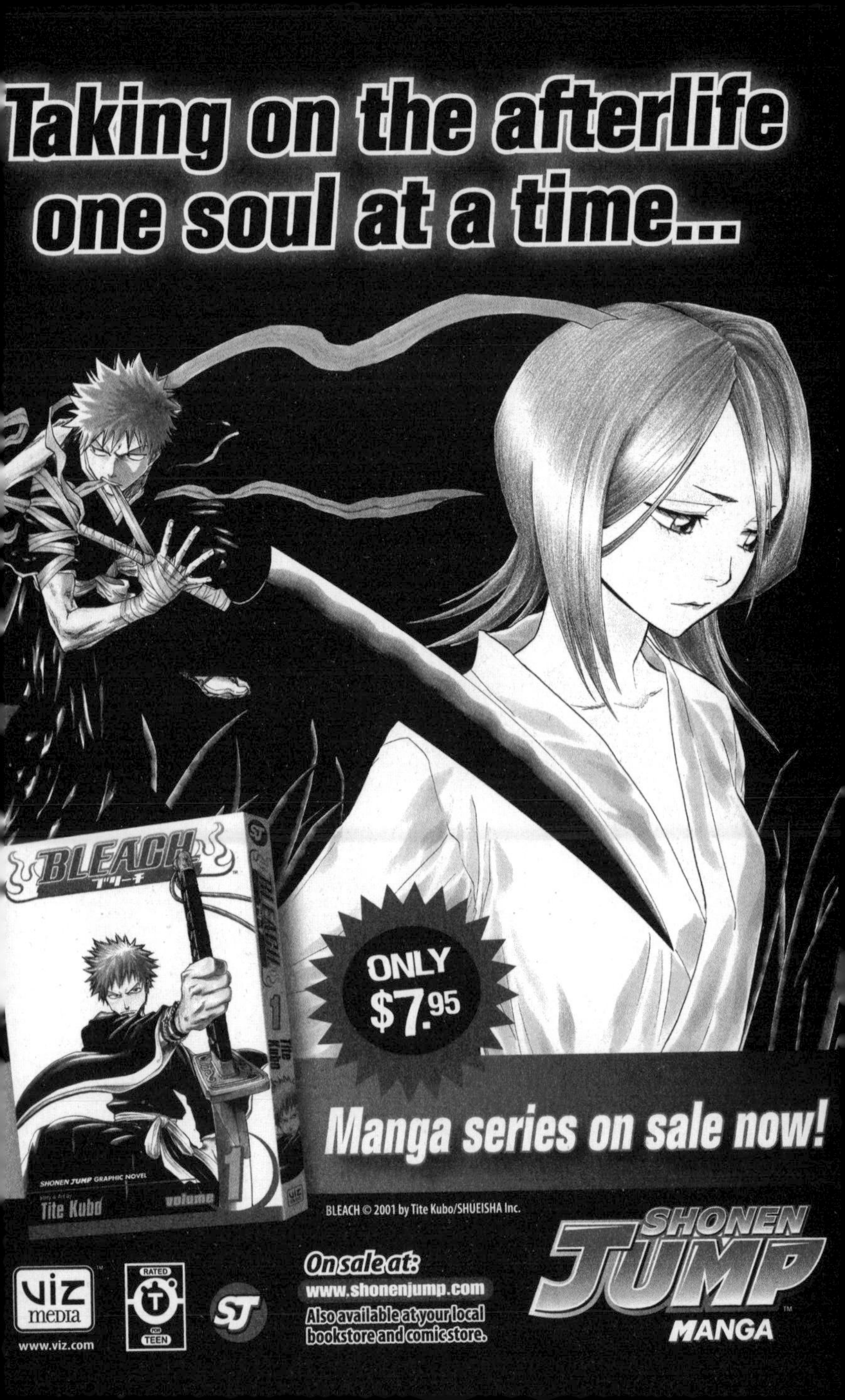
Taking on the afterlife one soul at a time...
BLEACH
ブリーチ
SHONEN JUMP GRAPHIC NOVEL
Tite Kubo
volume 1
ONLY $7.95
Manga series on sale now!
BLEACH © 2001 by Tite Kubo/SHUEISHA Inc.
SHONEN JUMP MANGA
On sale at:
www.shonenjump.com
Also available at your local bookstore and comic store.
viz media
www.viz.com
RATED T FOR TEEN
SJ

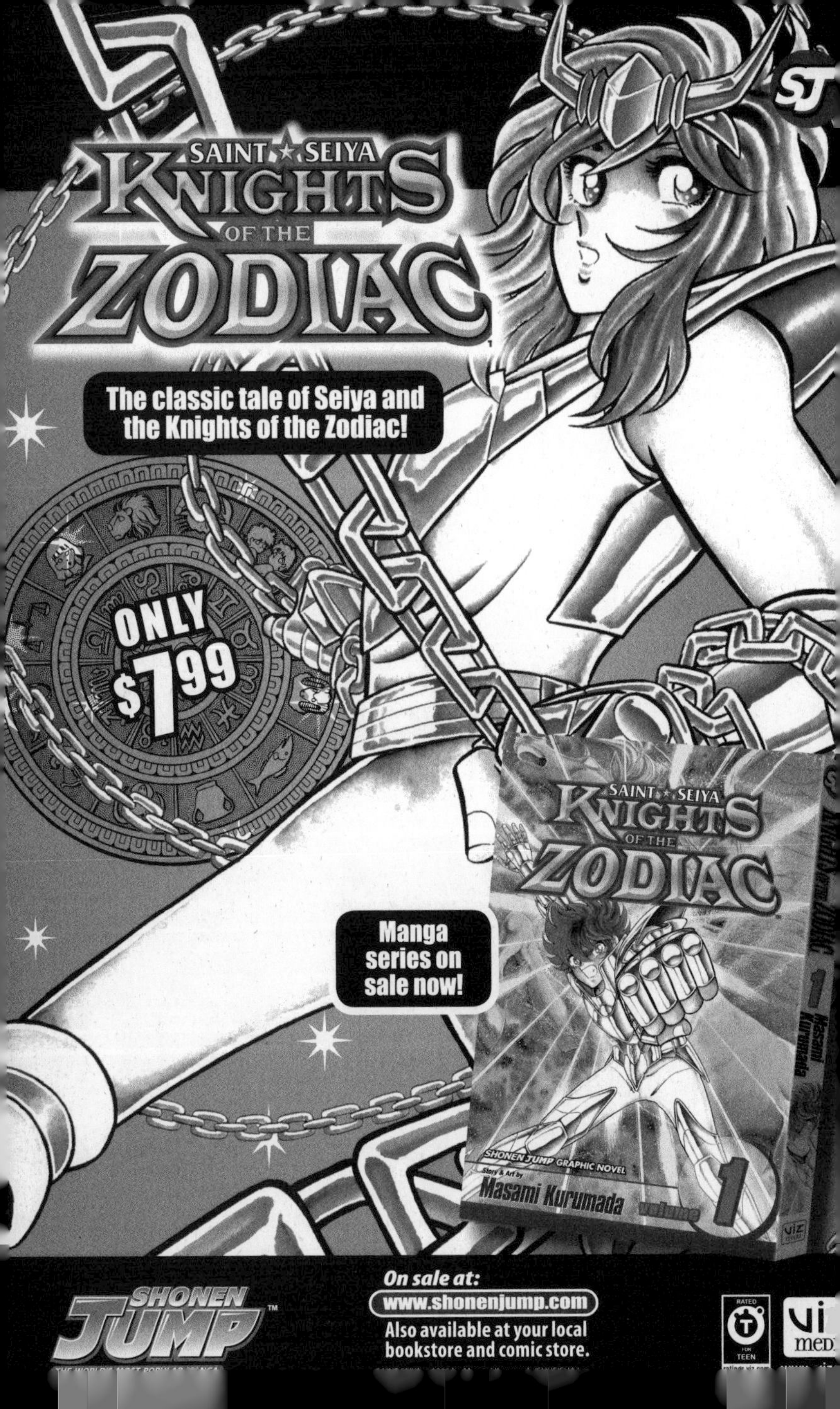
SJ
SAINT SEIYA
KNIGHTS OF THE ZODIAC
The classic tale of Seiya and the Knights of the Zodiac!
ONLY $7.99
Manga series on sale now!
SAINT SEIYA
KNIGHTS OF THE ZODIAC
SHONEN JUMP GRAPHIC NOVEL
Story & Art by
Masami Kurumada
volume 1
SHONEN JUMP
On sale at:
www.shonenjump.com
Also available at your local bookstore and comic store.
RATED T FOR TEEN

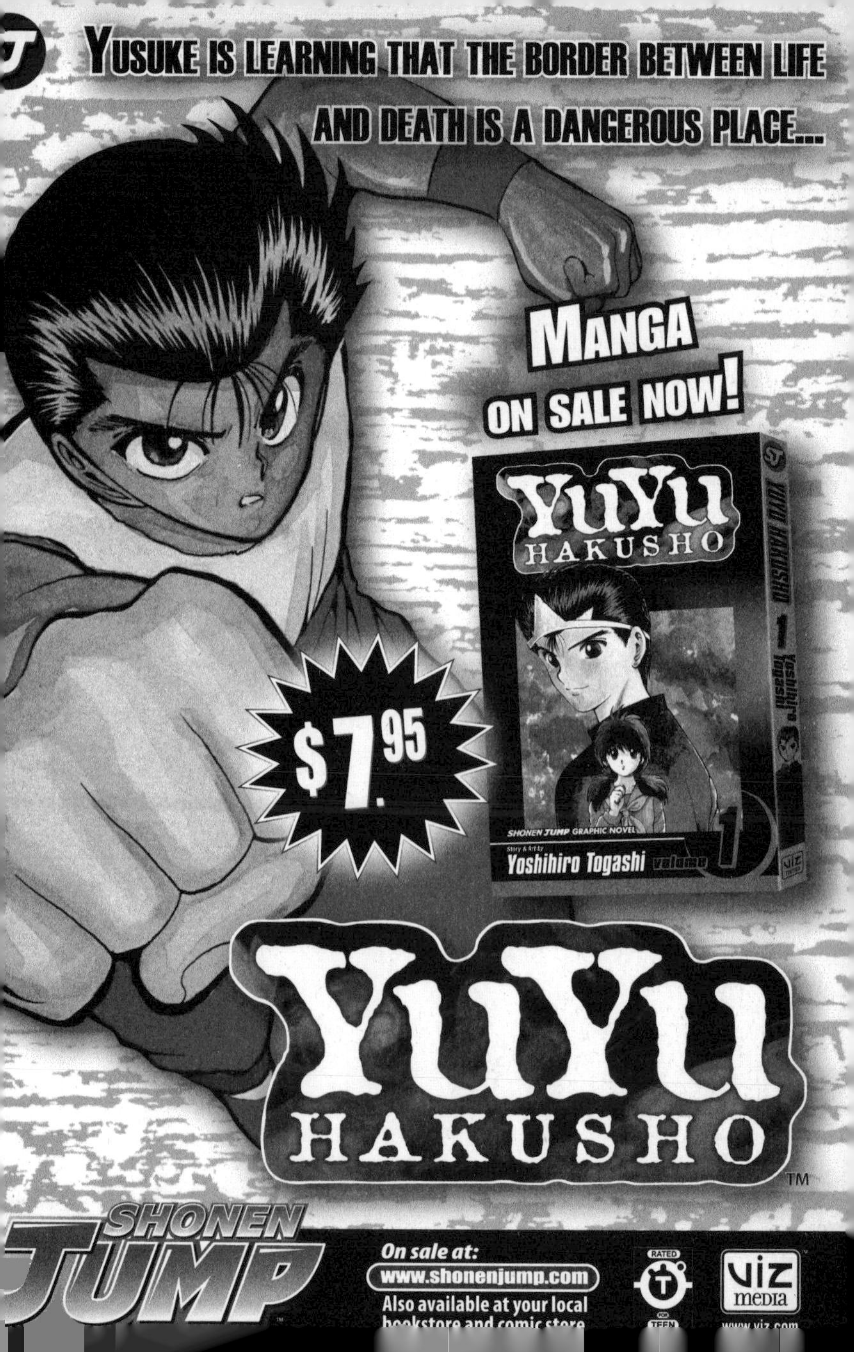

YUSUKE IS LEARNING THAT THE BORDER BETWEEN LIFE AND DEATH IS A DANGEROUS PLACE...
MANGA ON SALE NOW!
$7.95
YUYU HAKUSHO
SHONEN JUMP GRAPHIC NOVEL
Story & Art by Yoshihiro Togashi
volume 1
YUYU HAKUSHO™
SHONEN JUMP
On sale at:
www.shonenjump.com
Also available at your local bookstore and comic store
RATED T TEEN
VIZ media
www.viz.com

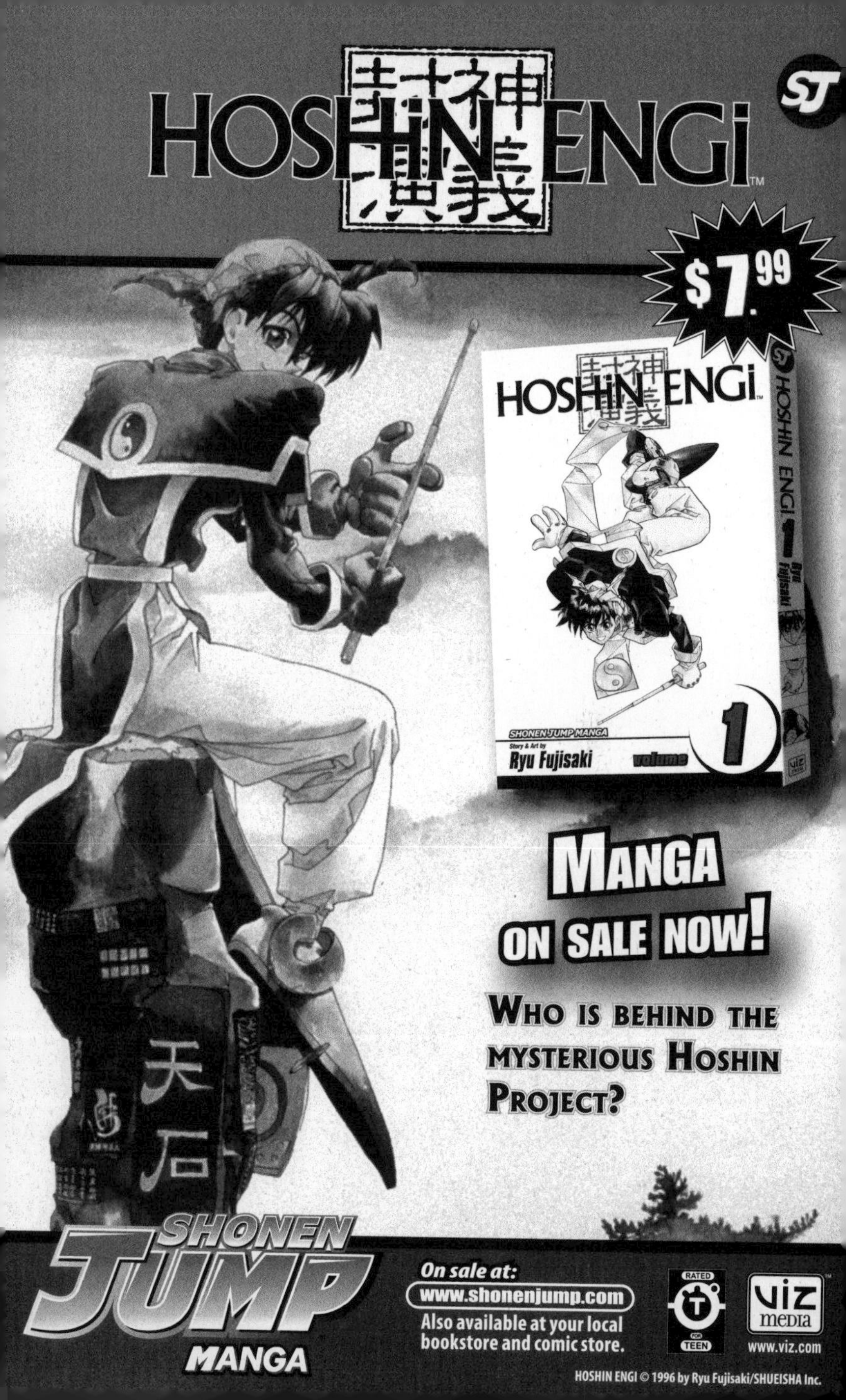

HOSHIN ENGI™
封神演義
SJ
$7.99
HOSHIN ENGI
SHONEN JUMP MANGA
Story & Art by
Ryu Fujisaki
volume 1
MANGA
ON SALE NOW!
WHO IS BEHIND THE MYSTERIOUS HOSHIN PROJECT?
SHONEN JUMP MANGA
On sale at:
www.shonenjump.com
Also available at your local bookstore and comic store.
RATED T FOR TEEN
VIZ media
www.viz.com
HOSHIN ENGI © 1996 by Ryu Fujisaki/SHUEISHA Inc.